Learning to Read
The Great Debate

LEARNING TO READ
The Great Debate

THIRD EDITION

JEANNE S. CHALL

GRADUATE SCHOOL OF EDUCATION
HARVARD UNIVERSITY

Harcourt Brace College Publishers
Fort Worth Philadelphia San Diego New York Orlando Austin San Antonio
Toronto Montreal London Sydney Tokyo

Publisher	TED BUCHHOLZ
Editor in Chief	CHRISTOPHER P. KLEIN
Senior Acquisitions Editor	JO-ANNE WEAVER
Project Editor	LAURA HANNA
Production Manager	LOIS WEST
Art Director	SUE HART

Address for editorial correspondence: Harcourt Brace College Publishers, 301 Commerce Street, Suite 3700, Fort Worth, Texas 76102.
Address for orders: Harcourt Brace & Company, 6277 Sea Harbor Drive, Orlando, Florida, 32887. 1-800-782-4479, or 1-800-433-0001 (in Florida).

Library of Congress Catalog Card Number: 95-79648

ISBN: 0-15-503080-9

Printed in the United States of America

5 6 7 8 9 0 1 2 3 4 039 9 8 7 6 5 4 3 2 1

A NOTE ON REFERENCES

IN THIS book, when a reference to a book, an article, a research report, or other material is not complete (i.e., only the author's name and the title or date of publication are given), the reader who wants full bibliographical information should turn to the Bibliography, Part 1, where these sources are listed under the author's name.

All published programs (instructional materials for children, sometimes with accompanying materials for teachers) mentioned are listed in the Bibliography, Part 2, under the author's name. When a program has two or more authors, it is listed under the name of the first author.

Throughout this book, I refer to some widely used or widely discussed reading programs by their titles or the names most familiar to publishers, teachers, school administrators, and researchers. Part 3 of the Bibliography lists these programs alphabetically by title or popular name, and provides complete reference data. It also contains some up-to-date information supplied in answer to a questionnaire that I sent to the publishers of these programs.

To the memory of my mother

INTRODUCTION TO THE THIRD EDITION

THIS IS THE THIRD edition of *Learning to Read: The Great Debate.* The first edition was published in 1967; the second in 1983, which was essentially an updated edition. This third edition contains a further update of research and practice in beginning reading to 1993 and also includes the text of the original and the earlier update.

The first two editions are kept intact to present a historical picture of *The Great Debate.* When it was first published in 1967, the debate on beginning reading was exceptionally heated. By 1983, when the first update was published, the debate had eased up somewhat. By the early 1990s, the debate had heated up again. Because of the long-term concern with beginning reading, I thought it would be instructive to researchers, teachers, administrators, and educational publishers to view the debate at successive historical periods—from 1910 to 1965, as reported in the first edition; from 1965 to 1983, the second edition; and 1983 to 1993, the third edition.

An update, rather than a revision, seemed appropriate because the book had become a standard work in reading research and practice. The first book was an educational best-seller and was declared a classic in the 1980s.*

*The *Great Debate* was updated several times prior to the updated edition of 1983 in *Instructor* (Chall, 1974), in a *Phi Delta Kappan* Fastback (Chall, 1979), and in a research volume on early reading edited by Resnick and Weaver (see Chall, 1979).

Between the 1983 and the present edition, several updates were published: in *Phi Delta Kappan* (Chall, 1989a), in a position paper written at the request of the U.S. Secretary of Education (Chall, 1989b), in a book published by the Orton Dyslexia Society (Chall, 1991), and in an article in *The Teachers College Record* (Chall, 1992).

The Original (Chall, 1967) and the First Update (Chall, 1983a)

Learning to Read: The Great Debate (1967) was a report of a three-year research study, sponsored by the Carnegie Corporation of New York, which sought to understand why there had been such consistent controversy in the United States on teaching beginners to read. The research consisted of a synthesis of the relevant research evidence from 1910 to 1965; an analysis of the most widely used reading textbooks (basal readers) and their accompanying teachers manuals, published in the late 1950s and early 1960s; interviews of authors and editors of various beginning reading programs on their views of beginning reading instruction; and visits to hundreds of classrooms in the United States, England, and Scotland.

Based on these analyses, I found that beginning readers learn better when their instruction emphasizes learning the alphabetic code, one that places first importance at the beginning on learning the relationship between letters and their sounds (that is, learning the alphabetic principle). They learn less well when taught by a meaning-emphasis, that is, one that emphasizes, at the very beginning, how to understand what is read.

It should be noted that in reading, *both* meaning and the use of the alphabetic principle are essential. To read, one needs to be able to use *both* the alphabetic principle and the meaning of words. What distinguished the more effective beginning reading instruction was its early emphasis on learning the code. Instruction that focused, at the beginning, on meaning tended to produce less favorable results.

Thus, it is the acquisition of the alphabetic code, the alphabetic principle, in the early grades that leads to quicker acquisition of reading skills than an emphasis on responding to the text meaning. The research also suggested that a code-emphasis was particularly beneficial for children at risk—children from low-SES families, children with suspected learning disabilities, children with below-average intelligence, and children for whom English is a second language.

The effects of the *Great Debate* were almost immediate. In spite of some early negative reviews, the major reading textbooks (basal readers) adopted its recommendations. After publication of *The Great Debate,* most basal readers contained a stronger and earlier emphasis on teaching the alphabetic code (Popp, 1975). Textbooks on the teaching of reading also put a heavier emphasis on the importance of teaching the alphabetic principle in early grades (Chall, 1983a).

For the second edition of *The Great Debate* (1983), my analysis of the research evidence from 1967 to 1983 found an even stronger advantage of a code-emphasis over a meaning-emphasis.

As will be reported next, the research evidence and the theory of the third period, 1983 to 1993, continued to give strong support to a code-emphasis for beginning reading. However, in spite of the strong evidence on the advantages of a code-emphasis as compared to a meaning-emphasis, practice and rhetoric moved in the direction of a meaning-emphasis. The meaning-emphasis approaches of the third period—whole language and literature-based reading instruction—have only recently begun to seek evidence to support the effectiveness of their approaches. (See the compilation of research on whole language by Diane Stephens, 1991.) There have been some attempts in the 1990s to call for a greater concern for the learning of the alphabetic principle. But on the whole, there has been a negative stance on code-emphasis and on the research that has supported it by those who associate themselves with whole language. (See Marie Carbo [1988], and Chall's response [1989a].)

In the present update, I review the research evidence and the major theories published from 1983 to 1993 on the major issue of the *Great Debate:* code-emphasis versus meaning-emphasis. After reviewing the evidence, I will try to explain why practice went in a direction opposite from the evidence.

Evidence from 1983 to 1993

BASIC RESEARCH

The research evidence presented here comes from cognitive psychology, psycholinguistics, developmental psychology, neurology, and the study of reading and learning disabilities.

Cognitive psychologists have been particularly interested in the relationship between word recognition and reading comprehension—an issue that has been central in the debate on beginning reading for more than a century. Overall, their studies have led to the conclusion that recognition and decoding, or facility with the alphabetic principle, is a necessary step in the acquisition of reading comprehension and other higher-level reading processes, the agreed-upon objectives of reading instruction. Therefore, any program that results in better word recognition and decoding at the early stages of learning to read—and especially with students at risk—provides an advantage to students, and this advantage is bound to pay off over time (Perfetti, 1985; LaBerge and Samuels, 1976; Stanovich, 1986 and 1991; Freebody & Byrne, 1988). With regard to the influence of word recognition and decoding on reading comprehension, Perfetti (1985) writes, "Evidence suggests that . . . word-processing efficiency leads to better comprehension, rather than merely being a by-product of comprehension" (p. 231).

Keith Stanovich (1986), who has conducted numerous studies on how reading is acquired among general and clinical populations, notes how inadequate word recognition can lead to inadequate reading comprehension:

> Slow, capacity-draining word recognition processes require cognitive resources that should be allocated to higher-level processes of text integration and comprehension. Thus, reading for meaning is hindered, unrewarding experiences multiply, and practice is avoided or merely tolerated without real cognitive involvement.
>
> (Stanovich, 1986, p. 364)

Research on eye movements has also found that reading is a "letter-mediated" rather than a "whole-word-mediated" process (Just and Carpenter, 1987).

Research on development from prereading to real reading also confirms the importance of learning letter-sound clues. Ehri (1987) concludes that the learning of letter-sound clues is important because they are required for storing words and accessing words from memory.

Nicholson (1992) found that poor readers use context to help with their reading, whereas good readers, who are skilled at decoding, do not need to do so, thus supporting early findings that learning to read involves learning how to decipher.

Freebody and Byrne (1988) found that more than 80 percent of the reading comprehension of second and third graders was accounted for by phonemic awareness and decoding strategies. They also found the relationship between decoding and comprehension changed with the age and grade of the readers.* That is, whole-word readers (termed Chinese readers) did better than the phonetic readers (termed Phoenician readers) in comprehension in the second grade. However, in the third grade, the Phoenician readers significantly outperformed the Chinese readers.

> The authors suggest that a whole word method (meaning emphasis) may serve a student adequately up to about second grade. But failure to acquire and use efficient decoding skills will begin to take a toll on reading comprehension by grade 3. In contrast, Phoenicians may be hindered in comprehension by performance in the early years, but begin to improve comparatively as they progress through school.*
>
> (Freebody & Byrne, 1988, p. 441)

PHONEMIC AWARENESS

From about the early 1980s, there has been an increasing number of studies on phonemic awareness—the ability to detect rhymes, alliteration, to segment and blend sounds in spoken words—in relation to learning to read (Bradley and Bryant, 1983, and Lundberg, 1987). Stanovich (1987) reported that "phonological awareness measures administered in kindergarten or earlier are superior to IQ tests as predictors of future reading achievement" (p. 11).

Sensitivity to the sounds of words is generally acknowledged to be causal with reading as well as correlational. Segmenting and blending phonemes (separating the sounds in words and putting them together again) are considered to be essential to early reading development. Moreover, when students are trained to develop an awareness of phonemes, their reading achievement improves.

Some researchers have treated phonemic awareness as a separate concept from phonics and decoding. Yet phonemic awareness is highly related to the

*Compare with Chall (1983a and 1983b)

ability to learn phonics. In fact, in the 1920s and 1930s, it was studied as phonic readiness, and the phonic readiness research came to essentially the same conclusions as the current phonemic awareness studies.

Phonic readiness and such specific aspects of it as detecting rhymes, hearing specific sounds in words, blending separate sounds to form words, segmenting the sounds in words, and so forth, were found to predict the ability to learn phonics and to learn to read (see Monroe, 1932, and Chall, Roswell, and Blumenthal, 1963). An extensive review of the phonemic awareness literature can be found in Linda Rath (1993).

Current research continues to find the importance of phonemic awareness in beginning and later reading. Juel (1988) found that first graders who had difficulty with phonemic awareness—such as blending sounds into words, segmenting words into sounds, and manipulating initial and final consonants—remained in the bottom fourth in their class in reading four years later.

Phonemic awareness has also been taught successfully and has been found to benefit reading on standardized tests (see Lundberg, Frost, and Peterson, 1988).

The strong effects of phonemic awareness on reading achievement prompted Stanovich to propose that lack of phonemic awareness may account for most problems in reading. Children low in phonemic awareness, he notes, have difficulty grasping the beginning concepts in word identification. Because of poor word identification, they read less, read less challenging texts, and fall further and further behind (Stanovich, 1986; see similar findings by Chall, Roswell, and Blumenthal, 1963).

Classroom Comparisons of Meaning versus Code-Emphasis Approaches (1983 to 1993)

The classroom comparisons from 1983–1993, as did the earlier comparisons of 1910–1965 and 1965–1983, found an advantage in achievement for children exposed to code-emphasis approaches. Thus Evans and Carr (1985) found that "traditional" teacher-directed instruction, using basal readers with phonics practice and applications in reading connected text had higher achievement than those taught by an individualized, language-experience approach. The teacher-directed phonics classrooms scored higher on year-end tests of reading achievement, including comprehension. Moreover, the language-experience classrooms did not achieve higher scores in oral language measures, although they engaged in more oral language activities.

A meta-analysis comparing basal reader approaches with more open approaches, such as language experience and whole language, found advantages by level of development. Children in kindergarten seemed to benefit more from whole language/language experience. For first graders, although whole language and language experience tended to produce similar effects as the basal approaches, those programs that had stronger instruction in phonics tended to score higher (Stahl and Miller, 1989). Basing their theoretical explanation on Chall's *Stages of Reading Development* (1983b), Stahl and Miller noted that it was important in kindergarten to concentrate on the functions of written language while it was important in first grade to concentrate on the connection between letters and sounds in spoken words (see also Nicholson, 1992; Stanovich, 1987; Williams, 1985; Adams, 1990).

Studies of Reading Disabilities. Students "at risk" for reading failure have long been thought to be deficient in phonological processing. Dyslexic students are often unaware of and have specific difficulty in mapping written symbols onto speech. Thus, deficits of phonological processing do, indeed, seem to underlie many of the difficulties of poor readers, writers, and spellers (see Adams, 1990; Williams, 1979; and Stanovich, 1986). These findings are similar to those reported in the first two editions of *The Great Debate,* Chall, 1967 and 1983a.

Research Syntheses. Several research syntheses related to beginning reading were published from 1983 to 1993. The first of these was *Becoming a Nation of Readers* (Anderson, Hiebert, Scott, and Wilkinson, 1985). It was produced by the Commission on Reading—10 scholars and teachers with long experience and expertise in reading and related disciplines appointed by the National Academy of Education (NAE) and sponsored jointly by the NAE and the National Institute of Education. Its conclusion on meaning-emphasis versus code-emphasis was that classroom research showed, on average, that children who are taught phonics get off to a better start in learning to read than children who are not taught phonics (Anderson, Hiebert, Scott, and Wilkinson, 1985).

Miriam Balmuth (1982, 1992) in *Roots of Phonics,* presents a fascinating history of English phonics and of its effective uses over hundreds of years in reading, writing, and spelling instruction in different parts of the world. More recently, Dina Feitelson (1988) in her *Facts and Fads in Beginning Reading* presents a cross-national analysis of the uses of phonics in teaching beginning reading.

Both the Balmuth and Feitelson syntheses concluded that for alphabetic languages, learning the relation between spoken and written words is an essential aspect of learning to read. Further, beginning reading achievement depends strongly on learning sound-symbol relations.

A more recent synthesis of the research on beginning reading is that by Marilyn Adams, who wrote that studies of the relative effectiveness of different approaches to teaching beginning reading collectively suggest, "with impressive consistency," that systematic instruction of letter-to-sound correspondences resulted in higher achievement in both word recognition and spelling—at least in the early grades, and particularly for slower and disadvantaged students (Adams, 1990; see also Chall, 1967 and 1983a).

Adams notes further that in spite of the differences found in the various studies, there seems to be something about instruction in phonics that has "general, substantive, and lasting value."

Calfee and Drum (1986) and Beck and Juel (1992) concluded from their syntheses that programs including early and systematic phonics had benefits over those that did not.

Beck and Juel (1992) further note the importance of decoding skill in the development of reading. They note that early attainment of decoding skills accurately predicts later skill in reading comprehension, and that there is "strong and persuasive evidence" that slow starters rarely become strong readers. Further, early proficiency in learning the code leads to early facility in reading, vocabulary growth, and knowing how texts are written.

Stanovich (1986) has placed decoding within broader, "Matthew Effects," in which the "rich get richer" (that is, the children who learn early to decode continue to improve in reading) and the "poor get poorer" (that is, children who do not learn to decode early become increasingly distanced from the "rich" in reading ability).

Whole Language. In the late 1970s, a new term appeared in the literature on reading—whole language. During 1982 to 1992, it became increasingly popular in the U.S., Canada, Australia, and New Zealand. Although there seems to be no general consensus on how it is best characterized, it seems to have a better fit with meaning-emphasis than with code-emphasis approaches. Overall, whole language focuses on language and meaning from the start, viewing decoding as a byproduct of reading for meaning. Generally, the position of whole language proponents has been that decoding does not need to be taught directly. Instead, it should be taught incidentally and only as needed.

Whole language also views learning to read as natural as learning to speak. There is an emphasis on literature although most meaning-emphasis programs also use literature. Another, more philosophical, aspect is the empowering of teachers to teach what they view as best.

RESEARCH ON WHOLE LANGUAGE

Diane Stephens (1991) collected 38 research studies on whole language and noted that "Whole language and research on whole language are both clearly in their beginning stages. The label was virtually unknown twenty years ago. Thirty-one of the thirty-eight studies cited here have been conducted since 1985; only one was published before 1980" (p. viii).

Her book on whole language research contains annotations of studies, including those in dissertation abstracts, and papers presented at national conferences. These 38 references make fascinating reading since they contain interesting descriptions and comments by those involved in the various projects. But one does not find the kind of data that have come to be expected in educational research—data that make it possible to conclude that one approach produces higher achievement than the other. Instead, one finds that more children in the first grade of a whole language class consider themselves good readers than do children in a traditional class. In another study one learns that more children in whole language rather than in traditional classes report that reading is a meaning-making process. In still another study, whole language at-risk minority children in first and second grades performed as well or better than their traditional matches on a standardized achievement test.

It should be noted that the definition of whole language seems to vary from study to study. Indeed, some do not seem to be particularly "whole language-like." Instead, they resemble an empathic, humane approach to teaching reading that has been favored by reading teachers for nearly 100 years.

Another cause for concern is that most of the studies reviewed by Stephens were of kindergarten and first-grade children (26 out of the 38)—the two grades in which higher achievement in meaning-emphasis approaches have been found by others. But this higher achievement tends to be reversed in the second grade and higher. (See Stahl and Miller, 1989; Freebody and Byrne, 1988; Chall, 1967.)

Only ten of the 38 were comparative studies, that is, comparing the results of matched whole language and traditional classes. The remaining 28 were case studies.

PHONICS AND ADULT LITERACY

A longtime educational concern, also a recent one, is the question of how best to teach adults with limited reading ability. Do the findings from the research on children hold for adults?

In a study of phonic knowledge and skills of adult illiterates, Read and Ruyter (1985) found that those adults who did not progress beyond a fourth-grade reading level lacked phonemic knowledge—how to segment or blend parts of words (see also Chall, *Stages of Reading Development,* 1983b, and Chall, 1992).

Thus it would appear that adult beginners, as most other beginners, have instructional needs in phonics and decoding.

The Research Evidence on Meaning versus Code-Emphasis Approaches, 1983–1993

Overall, research of the past decade supports the earlier research and theory. The evidence of the last 10 years from the classroom, clinic, and laboratory points to greater achievement when a beginning code-emphasis is used as it did in the two preceding periods—1910–1967 and 1967–1983. Furthermore, research findings from both the earlier and later periods are supported by a growing body of theory from cognitive psychology, linguistics, psycholinguistics, human development, learning disabilities, and study of the reading process. Indeed, the evidence for a beginning code-emphasis as compared to a beginning meaning-emphasis is stronger in each of the successive periods I studied.

DIRECT VERSUS INCIDENTAL PHONICS

The 1983 update, in addition, provided some evidence, also, for the greater benefit of systematic, explicit teaching of phonics as compared to implicit, indirect phonics (Chall, 1983a). Becker and Gersten (1981) found that Distar-trained (a direct approach) children retained their superiority in word recognition and comprehension up to sixth grade. They found also that the children who were exposed to direct instruction had lower dropout rates and fewer incarcerations (Gerston and Keating, 1987). Stahl, Osborn, and Pearson (1992), however, found recently that while direct phonics was more effective than less direct phonics, the essential factor in decoding and early reading acquisition was the teacher's provision of opportunities to read decodable words.

Similar findings were reported by Juel and Roper-Schneider (1985). They found that students who were given a direct phonics program had significantly greater achievement in both decoding and comprehension when the material they read contained high percentages of words containing patterns they were taught to decode.

Further evidence for the greater effectiveness of systematic, direct phonics versus incidental, informal phonics comes from a recent study of Reading Recovery. Two equivalent groups followed the regular Reading Recovery program with the exception of word analysis. One group was taught the usual Reading Recovery word analysis—an informal approach to the letter-sound correspondences; the other received systematic phonics instruction. The findings were that those who received the systematic phonics instruction did significantly better than those who were exposed to the incidental Reading Recovery approach to word analysis (Iverson & Tunmer, 1993).

CHILDREN "AT RISK"

Researchers of the past decade have been especially interested in optimal instructional programs for children at risk. Generally, the 1983–1993 research has found—as it did in the two earlier periods—that children "at risk" do better with a code-emphasis (Chall, 1967 and 1983a).

Adams (1990) confirms this, noting that while children with a rich literacy background may be able to figure out letter-sound relationships and learn to comprehend simple or even complex stories, children without such a background need more systematic approaches. Indeed, as I concluded in *The Great Debate* (1967) based on the 1910–1967 research, even those who have strong literacy backgrounds benefit from systematic phonics instruction. But the advantages are even greater for those without strong literacy experience provided by the home (see also Stahl, 1992).

THEORETICAL EVIDENCE

The 1983–1993 period has gained considerably in theoretical knowledge on beginning reading (see Perfetti, 1985; Williams, 1985).

More recently, Liberman and Liberman (1990) presented a comprehensive overview of whole-language versus code-emphasis approaches—together with research and theoretical bases for each, and their implications for reading instruction.

Their theoretical and empirical evidence contradicts the whole language position that learning to read and write are as natural and as effortless as learning to perceive and produce speech. They present contradictory evidence also on the whole language view that the relationship between spoken and written language need not be taught since the written language is transparent to a child who can speak.

On the other hand, they note that their theoretical and empirical evidence gives greater support to a code emphasis. Speech is managed "by a biological specialization" without explicit awareness of the sounds the alphabet represents. It is just this awareness that must be taught if the child is to grasp the alphabetic principle.

> There is evidence that preliterate children do not, in fact, have much of this awareness; that the amount they do have predicts their reading achievement; that the awareness can be taught; and that the relative difficulty of learning it that some children have may be a reflection of a weakness in the phonological component of their natural capacity for language.
>
> (Liberman and Liberman, 1990, p. 51)

Thus, Liberman and Liberman strongly confirm the first importance of the phonological aspects of language in reading and writing, in learning to read and write, and also in failure to learn to read—a view that is perhaps the oldest in the history of reading instruction, and in the study of reading failure.

Even stronger evidence for the primary importance of relating speech to writing comes from John de Francis (1989), a noted specialist in the Chinese language. In his book, *Visible Speech,* he shows that writing is based on a sound system and not on any other linguistic level. Even Chinese writing, he notes, is based largely on sound. Using writing systems of ancient and modern languages—such as Egyptian, Arabic, Japanese, Korean, Greek, and English—he stresses their basic identity as representatives of visible speech.

In a recent comprehensive review of factor analytic studies of verbal development, John Carroll (1993), reports the following regarding decoding and other language skills.

> There is evidence . . . that a general skill of word recognition and decoding can be defined factorially independent of some other skills in the language ability domain, and further, that this word recognition skill can be broken down into detailed processes . . . a reading decoding accuracy factor, and . . . a reading decoding speed factor, all independent of more general verbal comprehension, spelling, and reading speed factors.
>
> (Carroll, 1993, pp. 164–165)

Carroll (1990) also focused on the importance of adequate knowledge of phonics by teachers. Referring to an early large-scale study of reading achievement in the public schools of Newton, MA (Carroll and Austin, 1957), he noted several findings with implications for phonics instruction. First, reading achievement of third graders was "powerfully conditioned by the teaching effectiveness of their second-grade teacher." Also, the teacher's knowledge of phonics was an important factor in her ability to teach reading successfully. "For example, children in the third grade who had high scoring teachers (higher scores on a test of phonics) when they were in the first grade did significantly better than children who had low-scoring teachers in the first grade" (Carroll, 1990, p. 6).

He further noted that "the poor performance of some of the teachers may have been because of the kind of reading instruction the teachers themselves had had in their early school years—instruction that included little emphasis on phonics, or that did not help these teachers to develop good decoding skills" (p. 7).

Reading at Different Stages of Development

One of the issues in the meaning-emphasis/code-emphasis debate is whether or not reading goes through developmental changes from beginning to advanced stages. More specifically, does reading at the beginning require different knowledge and skills than it does later, as found by Buswell (1922)?

During the past decade, several studies have found that while a meaning-emphasis approach might be more beneficial for reading in kindergarten, a code-emphasis proved to be more effective later. (See, in this connection, Chall, 1967 and 1983a; Stahl and Miller, 1989; Freebody and Byrne, 1988.) Indeed, it was this developmental nature of reading that led to my finding an overall benefit of a code-emphasis even though some studies found that a meaning-emphasis produced better results in grade 1.

The past decade produced additional evidence on the developmental changes of reading. The validation data for the DAR, Diagnostic Assessments of Reading (Roswell and Chall, 1992), give further evidence for the developmental nature of the different components of reading. Thus, for students in grades 1 and 2, the correlations between word recognition and word meaning (presented orally) are generally low. In the early grades word recognition is the better predictor of other aspects of reading than word meaning. However, by the intermediate grades and higher word meaning becomes the better predictor of reading. Thus, the more potent factor in beginning reading achievement appears to be word recognition (and decoding), while in the intermediate grades and higher, the better predictors are word meaning and cognition.

The New Reading Debates

The reading debates of the past decade are quite similar to the earlier ones. As in the past, the current debates are concerned mainly with beginning reading. There seems to be an important difference, however. The professional literature of the past decade appears to be less reasoned than that in earlier periods. This is an ironic twist since the research and theoretical evidence on beginning reading today is much stronger than it was in the earlier periods. The debates of 1983 to 1993 tend also to use stronger language, and seem to be grounded more in ideology and emotion than on available scientific and theoretical evidence. The strong rhetoric and ideological base have led more than one journalist to call the current debates "reading wars."

This section treats the debates of the 1980s and early 1990s from the standpoint of science (the available scientific evidence for the proposed reforms); art (the practice); and ideology (the values and attitudes that seem to lie behind preferences).

I limit my analysis to the most heated of the new debates—whole language versus phonics. I am aware that other students of reading make different comparisons. For example, David Pearson views whole language in opposition to the use of basal readers (Pearson, 1989). Others place whole language on the side of reading whole books, particularly literature as opposed to short selections in basal reader texts; still others focus on the non-teaching of reading skills by whole language and that instead skills are to be inferred from reading connected texts. For others, whole language means empowering teachers to teach reading as they think best. For still others, it means integrating the teaching of reading with writing, speaking, and listening. For a growing number, it means a philosophy of education and of life, not merely a method of teaching reading.

It is, therefore, difficult to discuss whole language since its meaning may differ from person to person, and even includes, in some schools, teaching phonics and using basal readers as components of a whole language program.

There is a further problem in discussing whole language—the tendency of its proponents to claim originality for procedures that have been in use for hundreds of years. For example, many whole language proponents claim that their use of "authentic" literature is a unique and original feature of their program. Yet, authentic literature has been a part of reading instruction since Noah Webster's spelling book in the 1700s.

Whole language proponents tend to blame phonics instruction on the paucity of using literature in reading instruction. Yet, one should note that during the past two decades, the amount and quality of the literature included in reading textbooks were related to the amount of phonics taught. The more phonics, the heavier the literature in the book. This is possible because phonics leads to earlier and more advanced word recognition, which further makes possible the use of more advanced, quality literature. Further, the combined use of reading, writing, language, and speaking, claimed by many whole language enthusiasts as the discovery of whole language, has been the basis of remedial instruction since the early 1920s, when it was called a multisensory approach.

For my analysis, I will consider whole language in relation to early instruction in phonics. As will be seen, I think it is perhaps the essential distinction between whole language and traditional approaches to teaching reading.

The whole language/phonics debate will be discussed first by considering the reading research and theory of the past twenty years, the instructional practices during the same period, and the accompanying rhetoric. Second, I will consider the effects of whole language and phonics on reading achievement—whether one or the other has had greater benefits for reading achievement. And finally, I will consider whether either conception can help explain the trends in the reading scores on the national assessments.

As noted earlier, whole language can be classified as a meaning-emphasis approach. In the 1970s, it was called a psycholinguistic guessing game. From its beginnings it focused on meaning and language as the primary components of reading—whether beginning or more mature reading.

According to whole language theory, it is through reading for meaning and communication that the beginner acquires the ability to recognize and decode words, not by learning the association between spoken and written words and the association between letters and sounds. Reading is learned best, whole language proponents claim, when learned as language is learned—naturally and in context.

Whole language also de-emphasizes teaching, and particularly direct teaching. It has a strong preference for viewing reading as meaning-gathering right from the start. And it puts little emphasis on phonological aspects of reading—even for beginners and for those with reading and learning disabilities. To prevent problems in reading, whole language focuses on the reader's language and thought.

What about recognizing and decoding words? Do they have a place in defining reading? Indeed, doesn't literacy itself depend on acquiring knowledge about print and skill in its use, since even preliterate peoples have language and thought, but do not read? And for those with severe problems in learning to read—those with learning disabilities or dyslexia—why do they seem to do well with language and thought, but not with reading?

In answering such questions, the whole language response has been that learning how to recognize print comes naturally from being read to and from the reading of connected texts; that reading, and particularly phonics, do not need to be taught. Indeed, if taught, some claim, it may interfere with reading comprehension.

THE ROOTS OF WHOLE LANGUAGE

Whole language has deep roots in the past. It very much resembles whole word and sight methods that began in the 1920s and that favored, for the early grades, experience charts (that is, the child's own language production) for reading in place of reading textbooks. Then, too, the child was expected to infer sound-symbol relations; the teaching of letter-sound relations directly was not favored. Instead, early emphasis was placed on learning to recognize words "at sight and as wholes" and on "reading for meaning." Similar to whole language proponents today, the proponents of whole word approaches claimed that the best route to accurate word recognition was through reading words, sentences, and stories right from the start.

From about 1920 to the late 1960s, the central conception of beginning reading was that it depends primarily on language and cognition. From the late 1960s through the early 1980s, there was a return, for a brief time, to an earlier conception that instruction in decoding—learning the relation between letters and sounds—enhanced reading achievement. Indeed, the research and theory that support this conception have been confirmed and reconfirmed over an eighty-year period (see Chall, 1967 and 1983a).

Evidence on Phonological Factors in Reading

During the past twenty years, the extensive data on the importance of the phonological component in reading has grown quite strong. Basing their work on theories of psycholinguistics, cognitive development, child development, and learning disabilities, many researchers have reported on the centrality of phonology (phonemic awareness, phonics, decoding, word analysis, word attack, and so forth) in beginning reading. If it is not acquired early, word recognition and reading comprehension suffer. For most beginners, difficulty with reading usually stems from phonological problems, and if not treated, it leads also to lack of fluency.

The research on very young children of the past two decades has confirmed the earlier findings that phonological awareness of words (detecting rhymes, alliteration, segmentation and blending of spoken words) tends to be a more potent predictor of beginning reading than word meaning and intelligence. Those holding such positions tend to view reading as developmental, with beginning reading characteristically different from more mature reading. By way of contrast, whole language proponents have tended to view beginning and later reading as using essentially the same process.

Thus, the conception of beginning reading that gained acceptance in the late 1960s through the 1970s included phonological as well as cognitive and linguistic factors. The conception of beginning reading that gained acceptance in the 1980s—whole language—focused primarily on linguistic and cognitive factors.

CHANGES IN PRACTICE

How have these conceptions played themselves out in practice? Did reading instruction change? If so, did the changes in practice lead to improvement or to declines in reading achievement?

Let me state at the outset that it is extremely difficult to know how reading instruction is practiced in the United States during given periods of time and in given places. One can only approximate and infer. Although there are surveys of how well children achieve, we do not have surveys of how they are taught.

Therefore, we must rely on indices that reflect practice. For *Learning to Read: The Great Debate* (1967 and 1983a), I made judgments about the use of methods in classrooms by analyzing the major reading textbooks and their accompanying teacher's manuals. Others have since done the same.

Have the reading textbooks changed over the past twenty years? There is some evidence that they have. The most widely used basal readers of the 1970s, as compared with those of the early 1960s, taught phonics earlier and to a greater extent (Popp, 1975). They also used more extensive vocabularies grade for grade. The reading textbooks of the 1980s, on the other hand, taught less phonics than those of the 1970s, and they put a heavier emphasis on teaching reading comprehension and word meanings even in the first grade (Chall, 1991 and 1992). A recent analysis of first-grade readers by Hoffman et al. (1993) found significantly more words than in readers published in 1986–87, but the amount of instruction in phonics had further declined.

EFFECTS OF CHANGED PRACTICES ON READING ACHIEVEMENT

From 1971 to 1988 there were six national assessments of reading by the National Assessment of Educational Progress (NAEP). I use these NAEP findings for trends in reading achievement over the last twenty years and make inferences of the influences of the new reading conceptions on instructional practice and on student reading achievement.

From *The Reading Report Card of 1971–1984,* we learn that, from 1970 to 1980, there was a steady improvement in the reading comprehension of nine-year-olds. However, during the 1980s, the scores did not improve, and may have declined. Although nine-year-olds assessed in 1980 read significantly better than their counterparts in 1971, this progress was made during the 1970s, according to the NAEP report.

If we assume that practice followed the changing emphases as found in the basal readers, we may hypothesize that the reading improvements in the 1970s at age nine and the lack of improvement, and possible declines, in the 1980s stem from the change from a code-emphasis to a meaning-emphasis. The NAEP scores of nine-year-olds (fourth graders) increased during the 1970s when the children were exposed as first and second graders to the stronger code-emphasis programs of the 1970s. And they ceased to improve and possibly declined in the 1980s when the phonics component became weaker. Thus, although meaning-emphasis programs sought to improve reading comprehension by focusing on it from the first grade on, it would appear that this early meaning-emphasis may have led to a decrease, not an increase, in reading comprehension among nine-year-olds. In contrast, the reading comprehension scores of nine-year-olds during the 1970s, when they had experienced a stronger code-emphasis in the first and second grades (a greater emphasis on learning letter-sound relations and the alphabetic principle), increased.

Effects of beginning reading instruction on later reading achievement are also found in the NAEP data. Thus the higher reading scores in 1988 among seventeen-year-olds were explained by NAEP as due, at least in part, to the advantage gained from their higher fourth-grade reading scores in the 1970s. Here again we have evidence that an increase in reading comprehension in later grades came from higher scores in the fourth grade, which seemed to stem from beginning reading programs that put a greater emphasis on early learning of the alphabetic principle.

Overall, the methods and materials used, the instructional emphases, and the time of these emphases do seem to have an effect on students' reading achievement scores. Indeed, there is considerable evidence from the NAEP scores for the 1970s and 1980s that by grade 4 an early code-emphasis for beginning readers produces higher scores in reading comprehension than a meaning-emphasis. The NAEP data also show that programs that put a greater emphasis from the start on reading comprehension tend to produce lower reading comprehension scores among nine-year-olds and older.

These findings from NAEP generally confirm earlier research findings reported above that different instructional emphases are needed for different stages of reading development. Beginning reading may look like mature reading, but it is quite different. Beginning reading has much to do with phonology and letter and word perception. As reading develops, it has more to do with language and reasoning.

What does all this mean? First, it points to the importance of basing practice on sound theory and research, confirmed and reconfirmed over many years. The accumulated knowledge on reading suggests that different aspects of reading be emphasized at different stages of reading development, and that success at the beginning is essential since it influences not only early reading achievement but also reading at subsequent stages of development. It demonstrates that a beginning reading program that does not give children knowledge and skill in recognizing and decoding words will ultimately produce poor results.

The most recent National Assessment of Educational Progress, the *NAEP 1992 Reading Report Card for the Nation and the States* (Mullis, Campbell, and Farstrup, 1993), included data on classroom instructional practices that were related to students' reading achievement. Unfortunately, the data were collected only for the fourth grade. "Teachers of the fourth graders in the national and state assessments were asked to characterize their reading instruction by describing the amount of emphasis they placed on various approaches to teaching reading—literature-based reading, integration of reading and writing, whole language, and phonics" (p. 30).

The findings were that at grade 4, fewer classes used a phonics emphasis as compared to classes using literature-based, integrated reading and writing, and whole language programs. The classes that emphasized phonics in the fourth grade were also the lowest achievers. The interpretation of these findings was correct as reported by NAEP—the use of phonics in grade 4 suggests lower reading achievement. Phonics is usually taught in grades 1 and 2 and possibly 3. If used in grade 4, it usually means that the students are functioning below expectancy. To determine the effects of phonics, it would be necessary to estimate the extent of phonics instruction in grades prior to grade 4.

WHY PRACTICE DOES NOT FOLLOW RESEARCH

Why do we seem not to accept research findings from the past and instead ask the same questions again and again, getting essentially the same answers? Why, one may ask, do we not base our methods on the available research—especially when there is so much of it?

Why did practice from 1910 to 1960 move toward a meaning-emphasis approach when the evidence was more favorable to a code-emphasis? Why in the 1980s, when the evidence had become even stronger for a code-emphasis, did practice move more toward a meaning emphasis?

Stanovich (1987) suggests a reason—the strong negative attitude until recently toward word recognition. This negative attitude was so strong that those studying word recognition were often accused of denying that the goal of reading was comprehension.

Joanna Williams (1985) suggested that code-emphasis approaches tended to be overlooked because they were thought to be insufficiently focused in cognitive psychology. Still other explanations have been that meaning-emphasis approaches suited child-centered and progressive education (see Chall, 1967, 1983a).

Stahl (1992) attributes at least part of the controversy to misinterpretations. Meaning-emphasis proponents, he writes, have erroneously attributed to code-emphasis a concern only for phonics with no concern for the meaningful reading of texts. This is a misconception since most decoding programs, from Noah Webster on, have combined decoding with the reading of literature and other connected texts. And most meaning-emphasis programs are improved with the addition of systematic instruction in phonics. See, for example, Watson (1989), Meyer (1983), Stahl, Osborn, & Pearson (1992), Eldridge and Butterfield (1988).

Why are past findings seldom cited? Indeed, most recent empirical studies on the meaning versus code-emphasis controversy do not seem to acknowledge that their findings generally confirm earlier findings that go back to 1910. Instead, the findings are usually presented as new discoveries. This is particularly noticeable in the phonemic awareness literature where little or no reference is made to similar, earlier findings. Perhaps it is because the older studies used different terms which are currently not in favor, such as phonic readiness. Yet the studies that go back to the 1920s and 1930s also found rhyming, alliteration, sound segmentation, and auditory blending to be highly related to beginning reading achievement.

The recent findings that phonics correlates higher with reading achievement in the early grades than in the later grades also seem to make no reference to studies that reported similar findings in the past.

One wonders why the research on beginning reading has not benefited from one of the strongest features of scientific investigation—the use of cumulative evidence in confirming or disconfirming new findings.

Perhaps researchers of beginning reading do not cite the classic studies of the past because they wish to disassociate themselves from the older research that is often not accepted and even maligned. To acknowledge that their new research came to essentially the same conclusions as the old may be opening themselves to the same criticism and rejection. Would this also help explain the proliferation of new labels for old ones—for example, emergent literacy replacing reading readiness, phonemic awareness replacing phonic readiness; decoding replacing phonics; reading strategies replacing reading skills; word reading replacing word recognition, etc.

It is rare in the literature to find a statement such as the following.

> The major conclusions of the program comparison studies are based on masses of data, gathered through formal experimental procedures, and scrutinized through relatively sophisticated statistical techniques. Yet they are—point for point—virtually identical to those at which Jeanne Chall had arrived on the basis of her classroom observations and interpretive review of the literature.
>
> (Adams, 1990, p. 59)

There are still other factors that seem to be related to the return, again and again, to meaning-emphasis approaches for beginning reading when the research evidence is greater for a code-emphasis. Since the early 1920s, there has been a preference for meaning-emphasis approaches. These methods were adopted during the great educational reforms of the early 1900s, stemming from the early childhood education movement, progressive education, and the child-centered curriculum. Although meaning-emphasis methods can be traced back even earlier, it is during the 1920s that they gained widespread use and took on, as they do today, all of the qualities and values of love, care, and concern for children. These reforms claimed that reading for understanding from the start was the best way to learn to read. They abhorred rote learning. Concern with print and phonological aspects of reading were seen then, as they are by many now, as pulling the reader away from understanding toward rote learning, and therefore to be avoided.

The view in the 1920s was that concentrating on reading interesting stories (with little or no teaching of the forms and sounds of letters) will result in better reading comprehension. It was further held that this procedure will result in a lifetime love of reading, while learning with phonics, which was viewed as dull and dreary, would discourage the development of lifelong reading.

Although the research of the last eighty years has refuted these claims, they persist. Indeed, there seems to be no evidence on the greater love of reading from a given method of learning to read.

Why do the meaning-emphasis approaches to beginning reading return again and again? Why, when they are relinquished for a time, do they return as new discoveries under new labels? Why are they so persistent? I propose that they are persistent because they are deep in our American culture and therefore difficult to change. These conceptions promise a quick and easy solution to learning to read—reading without tears, reading full of joy. They are the magic bullet that is offered as a solution to the serious reading problems of our time and times past. Further, concern with phonological aspects of reading requires more knowledge, effort, and work of teachers and children. The meaning-emphasis approaches have always promised more joy, more fun, and less work for the child—and for the teacher.

A one-stage theory of reading seems more attractive to Americans than a sequential, developmental theory. Since the meaning-emphasis theories claim that reading is the same at the beginning and at the end, teachers need to know less for a meaning-emphasis than a code-emphasis which assumes a developmental view of reading.

Whole language, in particular, seems to say that a good heart goes a long way, and that a desire to learn to read is the strongest factor in learning. Its major concern is that the child be motivated to want to learn to read and that the higher cognitive processes be used in reading right from the start. It flees from the idea that there may be "basics" to be learned first.

These views are being debated in other subjects as well. In math, the current thrust is toward concept learning and away from computation. In history, the concern is for teaching broad ideas, not facts. Although the National Assessments indicate that our children have grave deficiencies in the most basic learnings, the current focus is away from teaching these and toward teaching concepts and higher mental processes. Thus, as for reading, the preferred emphasis today in most areas of the curriculum is on the higher mental processes from the start.

I propose that it is these particular views of the child, of the teacher, and of learning—views that have been with us for about a century—that make us accept or reject a particular conception of reading and its research findings. These views attract many teachers to whole language. It is a romantic view of learning. It is imbued with love and hope. But, sadly, research has shown it to be less effective than a developmental view, and least effective for those who tend to be at risk for learning to read—disadvantaged, minority children, and those at risk for learning disability.

Since the 1920s, the prevailing ideology of reading has been one that views children as self-motivated and joyous. This view holds that they learn to read as naturally as they learn to speak, if only we "surround them with books," and we encourage them to use their language and cognition. The teaching of skills and tools, especially those related to print, is to be avoided since it distracts the learner from the naturalness of the process and the acquisition of meaning.

Very little is said about the children who have difficulty learning to read with this emphasis. Faced with higher incidence of failure, proponents of this approach answer that poor reading stems from weakness in language and inappropriate instruction—instruction that focuses on teaching the skills and tools.

The values and ideology I have briefly depicted can be found to underlie most reading programs from the 1920s to the late 1960s. From time to time there is a greater acceptance of the need for teaching skills and tools—when it is realized that many children are falling behind. Historically, however, these periods seem to be short-lived. Such a period existed during the 1970s, but by the 1980s the thrust was again toward the more romantic, charismatic, and global methods—methods seen as natural and joyful.

Lately, there have been some increased signs of discontent with whole language and other meaning-emphasis approaches for beginning reading. The lower scores found when using these methods have resulted in a greater interest in teaching phonics. Newspapers have been reporting the complaints by parents, teachers and principals for about five years. There have also been heated controversies in England on the teaching of reading and they have gone back to phonics instruction. Still other signs of a coming change are found in the 1992 NAEP reading results (Mullis, Campbell, and Farstrup, 1993), which show declining scores. Another sign of a change to come is the increasing number of phonics programs published for use at home and in schools.

A Concluding Note

The research findings and theories on beginning reading during the last eighty years have grown ever stronger, with the newer research tending to confirm and refine the earlier research. Yet, the use of research and theory for improving practice has not been as consistent. While the research continues to produce findings in the same direction, practice seems to move back and forth. More often than not, it moves in a direction which is not supported by the research and theory.

It would seem that the time has come to give more serious attention to why practice has been so little influenced by existing research.

The Great Debate

BIBLIOGRAPHY

Adams, M. J. 1990. *Beginning to read: Thinking and learning about print.* Cambridge, MA: MIT Press.

Anderson, R. C., Hiebert, E. H., Scott, J. A., & Wilkinson, I. A. G. 1985. *Becoming a nation of readers: The report of the Commission on Reading.* Champaign, IL: The Center for the Study of Reading and The National Academy of Education.

Balmuth, M. 1982. *Roots of Phonics.* New York: McGraw-Hill; 2nd ed. 1992. Baltimore: York Press.

Beck, I., & Juel, C. 1992. The role of decoding in learning to read. In *What research has to say about reading instruction,* (2nd ed.), S. J. Samuels & A. E. Farstrup (Eds.), pp. 101–123. Newark, DE: International Reading Association.

Becker, W. C., & Gersten, B. 1981. A follow-up of Follow-Through: The later effects of the direct instruction model on children in fifth and sixth grades. Paper presented at the conference of the Society for Research on Child Development. Boston, MA. April, 1981. (ERIC Document Reproduction Service ED 202601.)

Bradley, L., & Bryant, P. E. 1983. Categorizing sounds and learning to read—a causal connection. *Nature, 301,* 419–421.

Buswell, G. T. 1922. *Fundamental reading habits: A study of their development,* Supplemental Educational Monographs, no. 21. Chicago: The University of Chicago Press.

Calfee, R., & Drum, P. 1986. Research on teaching reading. In M. Wittrock (Ed.), *Handbook of research on teaching,* (pp. 804–849). New York: Macmillan.

Carbo, M. 1988. Debunking the great phonics myth. *Phi Delta Kappan, 70,* 226–240.

Carroll, J. B. 1990. Thoughts on reading and phonics. Paper presented at the meeting of the National Conference on Research in English, Atlanta, GA, May 9, 1990.

Carroll, J. B. 1993. *Human cognitive abilities: A survey of factor-analytic studies.* Cambridge, England: Cambridge University Press.

Carroll, J. B., & Austin, M. C. 1957. *Underachievement in reading: A study of its extent and causes in the public schools of Newton, Mass.* Cambridge, MA: Laboratory for Research in Instruction, Harvard Graduate School of Education, Harvard University.

Chall, J. S. 1967. *Learning to read: The great debate.* New York: McGraw-Hill.

Chall, J. S. 1974. Reading seems to be improving. *Instructor, 83*(6).

Chall, J. S. 1977. *Reading 1967–1977: A decade of change and promise.* Bloomington, IN: Phi Delta Kappa.

Chall, J. S. 1979. The great debate: Ten years later, with a modest proposal for reading stages. In L. B. Resnick & P. A. Weaver (Eds.), *Theory and practice of early reading,* (pp. 29–35). Hillsdale, NJ: Lawrence Erlbaum Associates.

Chall, J. S. 1983a. *Learning to read: The great debate,* updated edition. New York: McGraw-Hill.

Chall, J. S. 1983b. *Stages of reading development.* New York: McGraw-Hill.

Chall, J. S. 1989a. Learning to read: The great debate, 20 years later—A response to 'Debunking the phonics myth.' *Phi Delta Kappan, 70*(7), 521–538.

Chall, J. S. 1989b. The role of phonics in the teaching of reading: A position paper prepared for the Secretary of Education.

Chall, J. S. 1991. American reading instruction: Science, art and ideology. In R. Bolen (Ed.), *All language and the creation of literacy,* (pp. 20–26). Baltimore, MD: The Orton Dyslexia Society.

Chall, J. S. 1992. The new reading debates: Evidence from science, art and ideology. *Teachers College Record, 94*(2), 315–328.

Chall, J. S., Roswell, F., & Blumenthal, S. H. 1963. Auditory blending ability: A factor in success in beginning reading. *The Reading Teacher, 17,* 113–118.

de Francis, J. 1989. *Visible speech: The diverse overview of writing systems.* Honolulu, HI: University of Hawaii Press.

Ehri, L. C. 1987. Learning to read and spell words. *Journal of Reading Behavior, 19,* 5–30.

Eldridge, J. L., & Butterfield, D. 1988. Alternatives to traditional reading instruction. *Reading Teacher, 48,* 32–37.

Evans, M. A., & Carr, T. M. 1985. Cognitive abilities, conditions of learning, and the early development of reading. *Reading Research Quarterly, 20,* 327–350.

Feitelson, D. 1988. *Facts and fads in beginning reading.* Norwood, NJ: Ablex.

Freebody, P., & Byrne, B. 1988. Word-reading strategies in elementary school children: Relations to comprehension, reading time, and phonemic awareness. *Reading Research Quarterly, 23,* 441–453.

Gersten, R., & Keating, T. 1987. Long-term benefits from direct instruction. *Educational Leadership, 54,* 28–31.

Hoffman, J. V., McCarthey, S., Abbott, J., Christian, C., Corman, L., Curry, C., Dressman, M., Elliot, B., Matherne, D., & Stahl, D. 1993. March. *Basal reader systems: An analysis of recent developments and trends at the first-grade level.* Austin, TX: University of Texas.

Iverson, S., & Tunmer, Wm. E. (1993). Phonological processing skills and the Reading Recovery program. *Journal of Educational Psychology, 85,* 112–126.

Juel, C. 1988. Learning to read and write: A longitudinal study of fifty-four children from first through fourth grades. *Journal of Educational Psychology, 80,* 437–447.

Juel, C., & Roper-Schneider, D. 1985. The influence of basal readers on first grade reading. *Reading Research Quarterly, 20,* 134–152.

Just, M. A., & Carpenter, P. A. 1987. *The psychology of reading and language comprehension.* Boston, MA: Allyn and Bacon.

LaBerge, D., & Samuels, S. J. 1976. Toward a theory of automatic information processing in reading. In H. Singer & R. B. Ruddell (Eds.), *Theoretical models and processes of reading.* Newark, DE: International Reading Association.

Liberman, I. Y., & Liberman, A. M. 1990. Whole language vs. code emphasis: Underlying assumptions and their implications for reading instruction. *Annals of Dyslexia, 40,* 51–77.

Lundberg, I. 1987. Phonological awareness facilitates reading and spelling acquisition. In *Intimacy with language: A forgotten basic in teacher education.* Baltimore, MD: Orton Dyslexia Society.

Lundberg, I., Frost, J., & Peterson, O. P. 1988. Effects of an extensive program for stimulating phonological awareness in preschool children. *Reading Research Quarterly, 23,* 263–284.

Meyer, L. A. 1983. Increased student achievement in reading: One district's strategies. *Reading in Rural Education, 1,* 47–51.

Monroe, M. 1932. *Children who cannot read.* Chicago: University of Chicago Press.

Mullis, I. V. S., Campbell, J. R., & Farstrup, A. E. 1993. *NAEP 1992 Reading Report Card for the Nation and the States.* Washington, DC: National Center for Educational Statistics, U.S. Department of Education.

National Assessment of Educational Progress. 1985. *Reading Report Card of 1971–1984. Progress Towards Excellence in Our Schools: Trends in Reading over four National Assessments.* ETS Report (Report, No. 15-R-01). Princeton, NJ: Educational Testing Service.

Nicholson, T. 1992. Historical and current perspectives on reading. In C. J. Gordon, G. D. Lahercano, & W. R. McEacharn (Eds.)., *Elementary reading: Process and practice,* pp. 84–94. Needham, MA: Ginn Press.

Pearson, D. 1989. Reading the whole language movement. *Elementary School Journal, 90,* 232–241.

Perfetti, C. A. 1985. *Reading ability.* New York: Oxford University Press.

Popp, H. 1975. Current practices in the teaching of beginning reading. In J. B. Carroll & J. S. Chall (Eds.), *Toward a literate society.* New York: McGraw-Hill.

Rath, L. 1993. A review of research on phonemic awareness. Unpublished manuscript. Cambridge, MA. Harvard Graduate School of Education.

Read, C., & Ruyter, L. 1985. Reading and spelling skills in adults of low literacy. *Remedial and special education, 6*(6), 43–52.

Roswell, F. G., & Chall, J. S. 1992. *Diagnostic Assessments of Reading and Trial Teaching Strategies (DARTTS).* Chicago: Riverside Publishing Company.
Stahl, S. A. 1992. *The state of the art of reading instruction in the USA* (IIEP Research Report No. 97), Paris: International Institute for Educational Planning.
Stahl, S. A., & Miller, P. D. 1989. Whole language and language experience approaches for beginning reading: A quantitative research synthesis. *Review of Educational Research, 59,* 87–116.
Stahl, S. A., Osborn, J., & Pearson, P. D. 1992. *The effects of beginning reading instruction: Six teachers in six classrooms.* Unpublished paper. University of Illinois at Urbana-Champaign.
Stanovich, K. E. 1986. Matthew effects in reading: Some consequences of individual differences in the acquisition of literacy. *Reading Research Quarterly, 21,* 360–407.
Stanovich, K. E. 1987. Introduction. *Merrill-Palmer Quarterly, 33.*
Stanovich, K. E. 1991. Word recognition: changing perceptions. In R. Barr, M. L. Kamil, P. Mosenthal, & P. D. Pearson (Eds.), *Handbook of reading research,* volume 2, pp. 418–452. New York: Longman.
Stephens, D. 1991. *Research on whole language: Support for a new curriculum.* Katonah, NY: Richard C. Owens.
Tunmer, W. E., & Nesdale, A. R. 1985. Phonemic segmentation skill and beginning reading. *Journal of Educational Psychology, 77*(4), 417–427.
Watson, D. J. 1989. Defining and describing whole language. *Elementary School Journal, 90,* 129–142.
Williams, J. 1985. The case for explicit decoding instruction. In Osborn, J., Wilson, P. T., & Anderson, R. C. (Eds.), *Reading education: Foundations for a literate America,* (pp. 205–214). Lexington, MA: Lexington Books.
Williams, J. 1979. The ABD's of reading: A program for the learning disabled. In L. B. Resnick, L. B. & Weaver, P. A., (Eds.), *Theory and practice of early reading,* (pp. 179–196). Hillsdale, NJ: Erlbaum.

PREFACE TO THE UPDATED EDITION

THE INTRODUCTION that follows contains an update of the relevant research and changes in practice during the 15 years since the publication of *Learning to Read: The Great Debate*.

The research update covers a considerable number of studies and experiments on beginning reading methods conducted in the laboratory, the classroom, and the clinic from 1967 to 1982. Also included are recent theories and models of the reading process that are relevant to the issues of *The Great Debate*.

Changes in practice are traced in basal reading textbooks, in standardized reading tests, and in professional textbooks for teachers. Changes in the nature of the debate are traced through the professional literature, correspondence and discussions, and through the proceedings of textbook adoption committees.

It is hoped that this update will be useful to those making decisions about beginning reading methods—teachers, school administrators, reading specialists, writers, editors and publishers of basal readers and other instructional materials, textbook adoption committees, school boards, and parents. It is hoped, too, that the update of the relevant research on beginning reading methods will help researchers design even more useful studies. I have, therefore, reported much of detail of the studies to help both researchers and those who make practical decisions about reading methods to make their own reasoned judgments on the issues.

Finally, I hope the update adds to an understanding of the debate—which although it has changed over the years, seems also to have remained the same.

On that last note, I should like to call to the reader's attention a recent study, *The Reading Group: An Experimental Investigation of a Labyrinth*, by Richard C. Anderson and associates of the Center for the Study of Reading, University of Illinois. It was received after the present manuscript was completed. I report it because of its theoretical relevance to the issues in *The Great Debate*, and because its conclusions may appear, to some, to be contrary to that reported here.

The Anderson et al. experiments were conducted on children in the third grade—children who, Anderson makes clear, are beyond the concerns on whether systematic, direct instruction in phonics should be a component of a beginning reading program." Instead, it is concerned with "The controversy . . . about whether, once phonetic principles are under control, children will turn their main attention to meaning . . . ." (p. 72)

Their major finding was that at the third grade, an experimental meaning emphasis was more effective than an experimental word identification emphasis. This finding, it would appear, does not counteract the studies reported in *The Great Debate*. As Anderson emphasized, he studied grade 3, when phonics was well under control. The research reviewed here and in the earlier edition was concerned with beginning reading—at grade 1 or 2—and for older students functioning at beginning levels. Indeed, the benefits of a meaning emphasis at about grade 3 has been reported by several researches, and fits a developmental view of the reading process. Anderson's additional finding that the poor readers in the 3rd grade did less well with the meaning emphasis than the good readers is in further agreement with the studies synthesized here. See in this connection *Stages of Reading Development* (Chall, McGraw-Hill, 1983) for a fuller treatment of the relation between instructional emphasis and reading development.

I am most appreciative of the help I received from Steven Stahl on the analysis of the research and from Suzanne Wade on the analysis of the professional method's textbooks. Their careful work made my analyses easier, and their good company made the task a pleasant one.

Special thanks are extended to Mrs. Kathy Diehl who sent me information on various aspects of the debate. I should also like to thank her many associates—too many to name here—for writing to me at her request, about their views on the debate.

I am grateful to James Squire who provided valuable information for this study and who has, over the years, given us his aid and sympathetic support.

To Ann Cura and Joan Dolamore who patiently typed and retyped the manuscript, I extend my warmest thanks.

Many have helped me, but the responsibility for this update is solely my own. I believe a special point needs to be made on this, for the issues considered here and the current findings although they may have changed, seem to be as controversial as they were in 1967 and earlier.

Jeanne S. Chall
Cambridge, Massachusetts
January, 1983

PREFACE

THIS BOOK presents the findings of a study conducted under a grant from the Carnegie Corporation of New York. The major work of the study was completed during the years 1962 to 1965 while I was at the City College of the City University of New York. A two-volume mimeographed report was presented to the Carnegie Corporation in September, 1965 and was also distributed to a limited number of readers for their criticisms and suggestions. In 1966 the original report was rewritten to its present form at Harvard University to permit a wider distribution of the findings.

A considerable amount of research on issues relevant to this study has been underway since 1965. Some of this new research, especially the USOE first-grade reading studies completed in 1966, is mentioned briefly throughout the text. The reports of the second- and third-grade continuations of some of these first-grade studies, scheduled for completion in 1967 and 1968 respectively, are not yet available. I wish to call the reader's attention to the existence of these and other studies, particularly since some of them may present a point of view somewhat different from the one taken here.

I am indebted to many people for their assistance—to the Carnegie Corporation for the grant which supported the study and the writing of the present book; to the City College and particularly to Harold H. Abelson, then Dean of the School of Education, for releasing me from part of my teaching duties during 1962–1964; to the Harvard Graduate School of Education, and especially to Dean Theodore R. Sizer, for cooperation in the completion of this book.

I wish to acknowledge with warm appreciation the assistance of my research staff who spent long and difficult hours analyzing the research and the various reading programs. They brought to this work the kind of dedication and commitment that made of our study a great adventure. Adele Kramer worked with me on all aspects of the study, but was especially concerned with the analysis of the experimental and correlational studies. Mildred Bloomfield, with the assistance of Lillian Shafran, worked on the analysis of the reading programs. Miriam Balmuth assisted in the analysis of the classroom experiments, and Marion Klein assisted in the analysis of the clinical studies. Elizabeth Nardine, Lucy Carroll, Joseph J. Tremont, and Frances Ricker helped in the final stages of the revision.

I also wish to thank the many authors and publishers who made copies of their reading programs available to us for analysis.

A special note of thanks is extended to the many authors and proponents who consented to a two-hour interview, but who must go unnamed here. Others who cannot be identified, but who contributed immeasurably to my understanding of the issues and problems in reading instruction, were the several hundred superintendents, principals, reading consultants, and teachers throughout the United States, England and Scotland who welcomed me into their schools and classrooms and talked freely of their views on the teaching of reading.

I am grateful to John Downing for arranging most of my school visits in England and Scotland and for his aid in observing the ITA experiment in England. Those in England and Scotland who helped me understand the problems of teaching reading not only in their own country but in the United States as well are M. D. Vernon, Joyce Morris, D. H. Stott, Sir James Pitman, D. E. M. Gardner, W. B. Inglis, J. C. Daniels, and Hunter Diack.

I am indebted to many people for their reactions to the early formulations of the study. Especially helpful were John B. Carroll, Arthur I. Gates, Albert J. Harris and Allan Barton and David Wilder who were directing a parallel study at Columbia University on the sociology of reading research. I also benefited from the comments and criticisms of the two-volume report by Edgar Dale, Arthur I. Gates, Helen M. Robinson, Charles C. Fries, Harold H. Abelson, Omar K. Moore, Nancy Larrick, Marion A. Anderson, Gladys Natchez, Helen Popp, and Joel Weinberg. While I know that the present book is the better for their criticisms of the earlier report, I am mindful too that I could not follow through on all of their suggestions.

To Margo Viscusi of the Carnegie Corporation, my thanks for her gracious and skillful assistance in converting a weighty technical report into a book; and to Florence Roswell for the continuous dialogue on education, life and reading that we have carried on for nearly twenty years.

Although I am keenly aware of and grateful for the assistance of many people, I am equally aware that the responsibility for the statements and views expressed in the present volume is solely my own.

Jeanne S. Chall
Cambridge, Mass.
March, 1967

CONTENTS

Learning to Read
The Great Debate

INTRODUCTION

The Crisis in Beginning Reading

WHAT IS THE BEST way to teach a young child to read? No two people, it seems, agree on an answer.

For over a decade almost every basic issue in beginning reading instruction—how to begin, when to begin, what instructional materials to use, how to organize classes for instruction—has been debated with intense heat and considerable rancor. Laymen and self-styled reading specialists have confidently provided answers in a stream of popular books and magazine and newspaper articles. Most of these answers have been rejected with equal confidence by teachers, administrators, and reading specialists in the professional educational literature. Each side has claimed that it knows how to give our children "the best" in reading instruction. And in the United States, where dedication to the best is tantamount to belief in democracy, the debate has often taken on political proportions.

Controversies over beginning reading instruction are not new. Previous generations have witnessed similar debates during periods when theories and practices were undergoing change. But this time there is a difference: The body of knowledge and practices now being attacked is the first to claim validity on scientific grounds. (Indeed, reading has been the most researched of the school subjects; for each study in arithmetic, there are probably three studies in reading.)

Another feature sets off the current debate from previous ones—the prevalence of "outsiders." The first forceful criticism and most of the current reforms have come not from professional educators of children but from interested laymen, popular writers, and college English teachers. More recently linguistic scholars, sociologists, and psychologists have entered the fray.

By now the debate has lost much of its bitterness, and each side is willing to concede points to the other. Nevertheless, the controversy has left parents, teachers, school administrators, and book publishers confused about which methods and materials are most effective.

What many people do not realize is that in spite of the general confusion, practices have been changing at an increasing pace. Many schools have adopted newly published reading programs that incorporate the very features originally rejected when first proposed by the critics. There has also been a swing toward an earlier start in reading instruction, whereas just a few years ago most educators were convinced that the later the child began learning, the better.

Are these changes justified by existing evidence or by the results of current experimentation? If so, what justified the original opposition? Perhaps the present changes are being made because we realize that the problem has not been solved satisfactorily and want to try something new—anything new—even if it is basically a return to the old. But many of the practices now being challenged were themselves adopted with great hope and promise, only to prove disappointing later on. Is it not possible that the current reforms, if not fully understood, may suffer the same fate?

Such questions have troubled me for a number of years. They needed answering not only for myself as a researcher and teacher of teachers of reading, but also for all those concerned with reading. These include parents, teachers at all levels (even university professors decry the inadequacy of their students' reading, writing, and spelling skills and tend to attribute it to their early instruction), authors of reading programs, publishers, and employers, who complain bitterly about the illiteracy of their employees. At a time when literacy is recognized as the key factor in the attack on poverty, how to give children the right start is more than an academic question.

In this book I shall attempt to bring together the relevant facts in the debate, facts uncovered during the course of a study conducted from 1962 to 1965. I believed then, as I do now, that it is particularly during a time of change and flux that we need to stop and take a look at where we have come from, where we are, and where we are going. Perhaps such a look can help avoid some of the errors of the past and engender greater sophistication in theory, research, and practice in beginning reading.

This book is addressed to a wide audience. For my fellow researchers and reading specialists, I have tried not only to answer questions that plague us all, but also to raise questions that require further thought and study. For authors, editors, and publishers of reading materials, I have attempted to provide evidence useful for making decisions on new reading programs. I have also included material for teachers and administrators who are faced with daily decisions on methods and materials, for their teachers in schools and colleges of education, and for parents who know only too well that reading is the most important skill their children learn in school and that all other education depends on it.

HOW THE STUDY CAME ABOUT

Despite thousands of research studies and scholarly discussions on reading since the turn of the century, it has been difficult for researchers to state with any degree of confidence that one particular method or approach[1] to beginning reading is really better than another. From time to time there has appeared to be a consensus on *how* and *when* to begin and *what* to emphasize at the beginning stages of reading instruction. Then a period of disagreement and confusion sets in.

Such a period began in 1955 in the United States with the publication of Rudolf Flesch's *Why Johnny Can't Read.*[2] This book took the nation by storm. It stayed on the best-seller lists for over thirty weeks and was serialized in countless newspapers. Although the general press reacted favorably to it, reviewers in educational periodicals almost unanimously rejected it (Riedler, 1962).

Flesch challenged—strongly, clearly, and polemically—the prevailing views on beginning reading instruction, which emphasized teaching children by a sight method. He advocated a return to a phonic approach (early teaching of correspondences between letters and sounds) as the best—no, the *only*—method to use in beginning instruction. He found

[1] Throughout this book *method* and *approach* are used synonymously. These terms refer to the particular sequencing, focusing, and pacing of a given set of stimuli to which the learner responds in certain ways in order to achieve a given objective or set of objectives. What constitutes method is itself an issue in the debate. In Chap. 1 I describe the prevailing as well as innovative methods in broad terms. Appendix A, in which twenty two beginning reading programs currently in use are analyzed and compared in terms of a variety of linguistic and psychological distinctions, contains a more detailed discussion of method.

[2] See "A Note on References" at the beginning of this book for a guide to using the bibliography for reference information.

support for this view in his interpretation of the existing reading research, particularly the research comparing sight and phonic methods. (Oddly enough, this same body of research formed the basis for the prevailing methods, and proponents of *those* methods used it to defend themselves.)

Several years later, the conclusion reached in other popularly written books—Sibyl Terman and Charles C. Walcutt's *Reading: Chaos and Cure* (1958) and Walcutt's *Tomorrow's Illiterates* (1961)—perhaps with less anger but with equal force and certainty, was essentially the same: that the prevailing approach to beginning reading, with its stress on sight reading, was incorrect.

England saw the beginnings of a similar controversy in 1956 with the publication of the first experimental report of J. C. Daniels and Hunter Diack. These authors concluded that their newly devised approach, which they called the "phonic-word method," produced better results than the prevailing mixed methods (sight, then phonics) then in use in England.

In the United States the dissatisfaction continued to spread. While the public was becoming more and more concerned about how children were being taught to read, various experts were proposing and developing a wide variety of solutions. The most important of these are described in Chapter 1.

In the fall of 1959, when the debate was at its most bitter point, the National Conference on Research in English[3] called together a special committee on research in reading for a three-day conference at Syracuse University. The purpose of the meeting was to map out programs of needed research. Participants generally agreed that the problem of beginning reading, although acknowledged to be a difficult one, desperately needed more attention from researchers. They felt that the research then available provided evidence so vague, contradictory, and incomplete as to encourage conflicting interpretations. No serious researcher could state with any degree of certainty, on the basis of such evidence, that either one or another approach to beginning reading was indeed the best or the worst.

A subcommittee of the larger one (composed of Ralph Staiger, now executive secretary of the International Reading Association; James Soffietti, linguist at Syracuse University; and myself) believed

The members of the NCRE Committee on needed research held in Syracuse were Russell G. Stauffer, Chairman; Guy L. Bond, Jeanne Chall, Theodore Clymer, Donald D. Durrell, William D. Sheldon, James Soffietti, and Ralph Staiger.

The Syracuse meeting, as well as another held the following year in Chicago, was initiated and brought into reality by William D. Sheldon.

that the problem was not insurmountable. We thought that large-scale cooperative experimentation undertaken with proper, clearly defined controls could provide better evidence on whether some approaches were indeed more effective than others for specific outcomes in reading, for particular kinds of children, with particular kinds of teachers, and in particular kinds of school situations.[4] To guide such experimentation we identified a series of variables that influence research on success in beginning reading.

I believed that the same guide could and should be used as a basis for a critical analysis of the research already in existence. This, in essence, is what I proposed to the Carnegie Corporation in 1961, and under a grant from the corporation I began such a study in 1962.

THE STUDY

The study, then, was to be concerned primarily with a critical analysis of existing research comparing different approaches to beginning reading. Such a critical analysis, I thought, would salvage whatever we already knew and would also help point up specific gaps in our knowledge. Since research should ideally be cumulative, I hoped that a detailed critical analysis and synthesis of the findings would help future experimenters design more crucial, meaningful studies.

My major concern was with studies investigating method—the *how* of beginning reading instruction. Although the *when* was also being challenged, with most critics calling for an earlier start (the most recent proposal suggesting eighteen months),[5] I studied this issue only in relation to method, for *when* to start is intimately related to *how*.

In analyzing the experimental comparisons I sought not only to find whatever kernels of truth were contained in these studies, but also to determine *why* it has been so difficult to arrive at any consistent conclusions from them. Why, for example, did Flesch and Terman and Walcutt conclude that a strong phonic emphasis was the best beginning approach? Why did other researchers and the authors of most basal readers[6] conclude from essentially the same body of evidence that the best way to start was with whole words (e.g., with a sight method), introducing phonics later and more slowly?

For further evidence on the issue of *how*, I sought to pull together the correlational studies of reading achievement, with particular emphasis on the beginning stage. What, for example, is known about the relationship between knowledge of the alphabet and phonics for achievement in

[4] Comparative studies along these lines for first-grade reading have been conducted recently under grants from the U.S. Office of Education. Some are continuing for another year or two. The results of the USOE studies are discussed in Chap. 4.
[5] See Doman, *How to Teach Your Baby to Read.*
[6] See Chap. 7 for a definition and description of basal readers.

the beginning stages of reading and for later progress in reading? What is known about the influence of general intelligence and language skill on success in learning to read?

Another area that I wished to investigate was the relationship between the extent and the kinds of reading failures children experience and the methods used in initially instructing these children. Would an analysis of some of the classic studies of retarded readers provide any evidence that certain beginning reading methods produce more reading failures than others? Indeed, many critics believe this to be the case.

A second aspect of the study was concerned with rigorously describing the different methods or approaches to beginning reading. It is difficult to discuss a method, and particularly to study its effectiveness, if we lack a clear definition of what that method includes or excludes. Often considerable time, energy, and money are spent in experimenting with a "new" method, when a careful analysis of that new method would show that it is quite similar in one or more significant essentials to a method widely used in the past, fairly well researched, and since discarded.

A third aspect of the study involved interviewing leading proponents of the various methods and observing these methods in schools suggested by them. The interviews were designed so that each proponent would explicitly state how he viewed the reading process, his own approach, and that of others. By observing classrooms I hoped to see whether I could distinguish the different approaches by such characteristics as the kind of motivation used. Frankly, I wanted to see for myself whether some approaches were as dull for the children as their critics said or as fascinating as their proponents claimed. I also wished to find out why a given school chose a given method—whether certain kinds of schools tended to prefer certain methods. Visits to schools would also permit me to talk informally with administrators and teachers about the methods they were using. In the classroom I hoped to discover whether other, unrelated factors contributed to the results claimed for a particular method—for example, the superior efforts of outstanding teachers.

Finally, the readers, workbooks, and teachers' guidebooks (instructional manuals) of the two reading series most widely used in the United States during the late 1950s and early 1960s were analyzed. This analysis was made because much of the criticism was based on erroneous knowledge of existing practices. Thus, though Flesch stated flatly that no phonics was taught in 1955, a mere perusal of the pupils' workbooks and teachers' guidebooks of these series shows that phonics was indeed a definite part of the reading programs.

For an insight into historical shifts in method a limited content analysis was made of earlier editions (1920, 1930, and 1940) of the most widely used basal series. The first-grade reading program of a newer basal-reading series (coauthored by one of the most vocal critics of prevailing methods) was also analyzed.

REFLECTIONS ON THE STUDY

What I learned, with the aid of a small staff, is presented in the succeeding chapters. What the book may not convey, however, are the joys and frustrations, the doubts and the certainties we felt while sifting through the mass of evidence.

The task was not an easy one. The joys were great, but the frustrations were even greater. The overriding impression was one of strong emotional involvement on the part of authors, reading specialists, teachers, administrators, and, unfortunately, even researchers. Their language was often more characteristic of religion and politics than of science and learning.

Visits to classrooms in particular impressed me with the ideological nature of the controversy. In general, I found emotion where reason should prevail. There appeared to be such a need to defend what one was doing—whether it was following the prevailing method or trying one of the newer ones—that it was difficult for each to perceive in what respects his method was similar to another and in what respects it was different. Each could see only the one special feature that was added or changed and usually failed to notice that much of the old was incorporated in the new and much of the new was inherent in the old.[7] Those adopting one of the newer methods were also, as a group, unaware of, or quite hostile to, other new methods that differed from their own in only minor respects.

I was personally buffeted by persuasive arguments and testimonials for or against a given method. It took time, distance, and much agonizing to arrive at the interpretations presented here. Since neither the issues nor the evidence was clear-cut, I describe, wherever possible, the process of reasoning I went through to arrive at my interpretations. Although this

[7] A recent article in *Look* (June 18, 1966, p. 39) quotes Maurice W. Sullivan as saying: "Every reading primer before his own programs . . . presented written English to the child in a hopelessly confusing way. . . ." This statement is valid only if one ignores Noah Webster's *American Spelling Book* (1790), used by millions of American children; the primers of Webster's predecessors; and those of his innumerable imitators. The statement is not even valid for today. See Chap. 1 and especially Appendix A for descriptions of other programs, published before Sullivan's, that follow similar principles.

lengthens the book, it will, I hope, shorten the reader's path to conclusions of his own in dealing with questions surrounded with confusion and controversy.

PLAN OF THE BOOK

This book is divided into five sections. The first introduces the debate in reading instruction: the various methods proposed for teaching beginning reading and the basic questions at issue. Here I also report on interviews with leading proponents of these methods, allowing them to declare their positions on the issues in their own words.

The second section is the heart of the Carnegie study. In it I present my analysis of the existing research on beginning reading and give my conclusions on this research.

Section 3 presents the results of a detailed study of basal-reading series in widespread use as well as reports on my interviews with the authors and editors of these series. Here I also make some suggestions for changes in the basal series.

Section 4 explores the implications of a basic finding of this study: that research results are only one of several factors that influence the practice of beginning reading instruction. In this section I discuss the larger world in which how children are taught to read is determined: the world of classrooms, publishing houses, schools of education, parents' meetings. I describe my visits to classrooms and my discussions with teachers and administrators and suggest some present and future trends in these influences on beginning reading instruction.

Section 5 contains the overall conclusions I have reached as a result of this study and my recommendations on how more children can be taught to become better readers in the future.

The bibliography at the end of the book lists published studies, books, and articles on beginning reading and published reading programs now available. It also contains a glossary of familiar names for widely used or widely discussed reading programs with complete bibliographical information for each, including publishers' data on planned revisions and new editions.

Appendix A contains a scheme for classifying beginning reading programs according to several important variables. This I used to classify twenty-two reading programs. It is also offered as a tool, which can be further expanded and refined, for analyzing other present and future programs. Finally, Appendix B contains the schedules used in the study.

1

WHAT THE DEBATE IS ALL ABOUT

WHAT is the debate over beginning reading all about? What are the various ways of teaching children how to read that parents, teachers, educators, and critics praise or blame so vehemently? What are the major issues in the controversy?

In this and the next chapter I describe the approaches to beginning reading that are important today—because they are in widespread use, because they influence programs in widespread use, or because they are expected to have an impact on how children are taught to read in the future. I also identify the issues in the debate and how the proponents of the various approaches feel about them.

In Chapter 1 the approaches have been divided into those representing what I call the conventional wisdom and those that challenge this bloc of beliefs. The challengers form no particular unified body; they do not even agree on what aspect of the conventional wisdom to criticize. They do, however, feel that some change is necessary.

ONE

The Conventional Wisdom and Its Challengers

OUR AGE IS NOT the first to produce "new" approaches to beginning reading instruction. A review by Charles C. Fries (1962) of courses of study, manuals, and journal articles published between 1570 and 1900 uncovers a succession of "discoveries" and "rediscoveries"—alphabet reforms, word methods, sentence methods, experience methods, phonic methods—each with its claim to be the "new," "natural," "true," "logical" way to begin. By ignoring the dates of publication, we can easily believe we are reading current reports.

From about 1930 on, however, we find a consensus of sorts about beginning reading methods. Although minority views during this period, as in the past, were expressed and followed in practice, most textbooks for teachers and published reading programs for children agreed on the following principles:

1. The process of reading should be defined broadly to include as major goals, *right from the start,* not only word recognition,[1] but also comprehension and interpretation,[2] appreciation, and application of what is read to the study of personal and social problems.

[1] Identifying the printed word, i.e., "knowing what it says."
[2] Understanding what the words say.

2. The child should start with "meaningful reading"[3] of whole words, sentences, and stories as closely geared to his own experiences and interests as possible. Silent reading should be stressed from the beginning.

3. After the child recognizes "at sight"[4] about fifty words (some authors called for more, some less), he should begin to study, through analyzing words "learned as wholes," the relationship between the sounds in spoken words (phonemes)[5] and the letters representing them (graphemes),[6] i.e., *phonics.*[7] However, *even before* instruction in phonics is begun, *and after,* the child should be encouraged to identify new words by picture and meaning clues.[8] Structural analysis[9] should begin about the same time as phonics and should be continued longer. (*Word perception*[10] is the term commonly used to describe the different ways of identifying new words,

[3] Implying both word recognition and comprehension.

[4] Identifying printed words immediately, without analysis of parts, e.g., without spelling or "sounding out."

[5] "A *phoneme* is a minimum structural unit in the sound system of a language. A phoneme as such does not have any meaning but since differences between phonemes distinguish one morpheme [or meaningful linguistic unit] from another, a difference between phonemes often signals a difference in meaning. For example, the difference between /b/ and /f/ distinguishes 'bat' from 'fat.'" (Sledd, 1959, p. 237)

[6] "Just as phonemes are the minimal sound units in a language, *graphemes* are the minimal visual symbolic units in a writing system. . . . graphemes (alphabetic letters, digits, punctuation marks, and the like) may appear in variant forms (upper and lower case, different type faces, different hand-written shapes, and so on)." (Carroll, 1964, p. 340)

[7] "*Phonics* is the study of the speech equivalents of printed symbols and their use in pronouncing printed and written words. . . ." (Albert J. Harris, 1962, p. 61.) Fries (1962) points out that in much of the writing on methods of teaching beginning reading the words *phonetic* and *phonetics* are used erroneously (i.e., "overlap in their use and meanings") for the words *phonic* and *phonics.* However, ". . . for all those who deal with *linguistics* as *the scientific study of language, phonetics* is concerned with such matters as the nature of the sounds of language, their differences, the articulatory movements by which the differences are produced, the vibrations that account for their acoustic effect. *Phonetics as a science is not concerned with the ways these sounds are conventionally spelled,* nor with the process of reading." (p. 139) In this book I have therefore tried not to use *phonetic* or *phonetics* when it is clear that *phonic* or *phonics* is meant. However, in quoting others, this usage could not be avoided. Indeed, most of the teachers' manuals in the most widely used basal reading series call their instructional program in phonics "phonetic analysis." See also William S. Gray's *On Their Own in Reading,* where *phonetic analysis* is used to refer to *phonics.*

[8] *Picture clues* are hints for identifying printed words suggested by the pictures on the page; they allow the child to make an intelligent guess about the word from the illustration. Meaning (or context) clues are clues for identifying printed words suggested by the surrounding words; the child makes an intelligent guess about the word from what other words indicate would "make sense."

[9] "Structural analysis means dividing a word visually into meaning parts which can be recognized or attacked as subunits. This includes dividing words into prefixes, roots, and suffixes, and separating compound words into their components (schoolroom)." (Albert J. Harris, 1962, p. 88)

[10] See Gray (1948 and 1960) for a fuller delineation of word perception.

phonics being *only one* of these ways. In fact, in many published programs the child is encouraged to use phonics only when the other ways fail.)

4. Instruction in phonics and other means of identifying words should be spread over the six years of elementary school. Usually, instruction in phonics is started slowly in grade 1, gathering momentum in grades 2 and 3.

5. Drill or practice in phonics "in isolation" (i.e., apart from the reading of sentences or stories) should be avoided; instead, phonics should be "integrated" with the "meaningful" connected reading. In addition, the child should not isolate sounds and blend them to form words. Instead, he should identify unknown words through a process of visual analysis and substitution.[11]

6. The words in the pupils' readers for grades 1, 2, and 3 should be repeated often. They should be carefully controlled on a meaning-frequency principle; i.e., they should be the words that appear most frequently in general reading matter and that are within the child's listening and speaking vocabulary.

7. The child should have a slow and easy start in the first grade. All children should go through a readiness or preparatory period, and those judged not ready for formal reading instruction should have a longer one.

8. Children should be instructed in small groups (usually three in a class) selected on the basis of their achievement in reading.

These eight principles, based partly on the interpretation of research findings, partly on theory, partly on the combined experience of classroom teachers, and partly on faith and belief, came to constitute the conventional wisdom of beginning reading instruction. From about 1930 to the early 1960s, these principles were incorporated in the most widely used basal-reading series and teachers' guides;[12] they have been taught by college teachers to future teachers of reading; and they have been followed by most classroom teachers (Austin and Morrison, 1961 and 1963; Barton and Wilder, 1964).

Since the middle 1950s, however, one after another of these principles has been vehemently challenged, largely as a result of the popular success of Flesch's *Why Johnny Can't Read.* Out of these challenges have come new reading programs, some resembling rather closely the older programs long ago discarded in favor of the "modern" programs of the 1930s. As in the past, most current innovators claim that theirs is the "new," "natural," "true," "logical," or "most scientific" way to begin.

[11] See Gray (1948 and 1960).
[12] See Chap. 8, in which I analyze two of these reading series.

I shall briefly describe some of the new programs in what I believe is the chronological order of their impact as challengers to the established order. A more detailed analysis is presented in Appendix A.

PHONIC INNOVATIONS: PARTIAL READING PROGRAMS

Even before *Why Johnny Can't Read* appeared, some school systems were using concentrated supplemental phonics programs—*Reading with Phonics* (Julie Hay and Charles E. Wingo), *Phonetic Keys to Reading* (Theodore L. Harris et al.), *Phonovisual Method* (Lucille D. Schoolfield and Josephine B. Timberlake). Since 1955, however, many more phonics programs have been published, only a few of which are mentioned here: Sister Mary Caroline's *Breaking the Sound Barrier*, Romalda B. Spalding and Walter T. Spalding's *The Writing Road to Reading*, and Caleb Gattegno's *Words in Color.*

Any general statement about phonics programs will be true about some and false about others. As a group, however, most of these supplemental programs share certain characteristics that differentiate them from the phonics component of conventional basal reading programs: They teach phonics more directly, they teach it earlier, and they cover more ground.

Some are frankly "synthetic" in that they teach the child the letters representing certain sounds that are then blended to form words. Some combine phonics with writing and spelling, while others teach phonics through little stories to be "read for meaning" that resemble the stories in conventional basal readers. Some insist that the child acquire a considerable amount of phonics knowledge before he begins reading words, sentences, and stories. Others suggest combining phonics instruction with the reading of stories from conventional basal readers and library books. Still others follow the conventional pattern of teaching phonics only after the child has mastered a sight vocabulary (words learned and recognized as wholes). Additional variations, perhaps minor, are that some start with the short vowels, others with the long vowels, and still others with consonants. Probably more important is the number of phonic elements and rules to be learned: some give the child a heavier "phonic load" than others.

Most significantly, however, none of these separate phonics systems claims to teach the child all that he needs in beginning reading. All are designed for use with existing published materials—particularly the conventional basal readers—which are to supply the needed practice in sight and meaningful reading.

The authors and proponents of these separate phonics programs

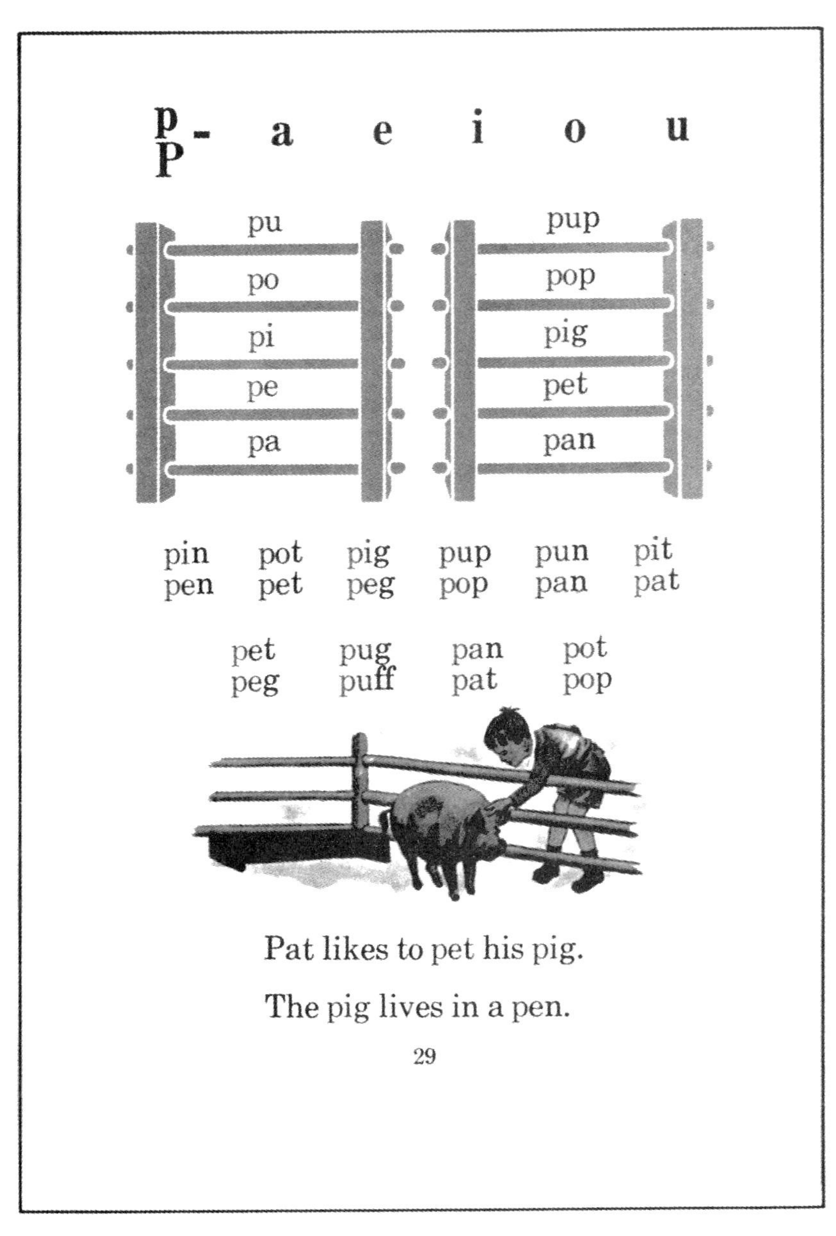

P- p- a e i o u

pu pup
po pop
pi pig
pe pet
pa pan

pin	pot	pig	pup	pun	pit
pen	pet	peg	pop	pan	pat

pet	pug	pan	pot
peg	puff	pat	pop

Pat likes to pet his pig.

The pig lives in a pen.

29

Page 29 from Julie Hay and Charles E. Wingo, Reading with Phonics, *J. B. Lippincott Co., Chicago, 1954.*

In the child's edition the first two letters of words beginning with *p* are printed in red; the others are in black. The illustration is in color.

Jim

Look, Tag, look.
See Jim.
See Jim go.
Go, Jim, go.
Go, go, go.

74

We work with words.
no he by she

Sound the words.
Jim go

Sight word
look

Page 74 from Tag *(An Audio-Readiness Book and Pre-Primer) of* Phonetic Keys to Reading, *The Economy Co., Oklahoma City, 1952.*

Color wash on the illustrations and on the bottom.

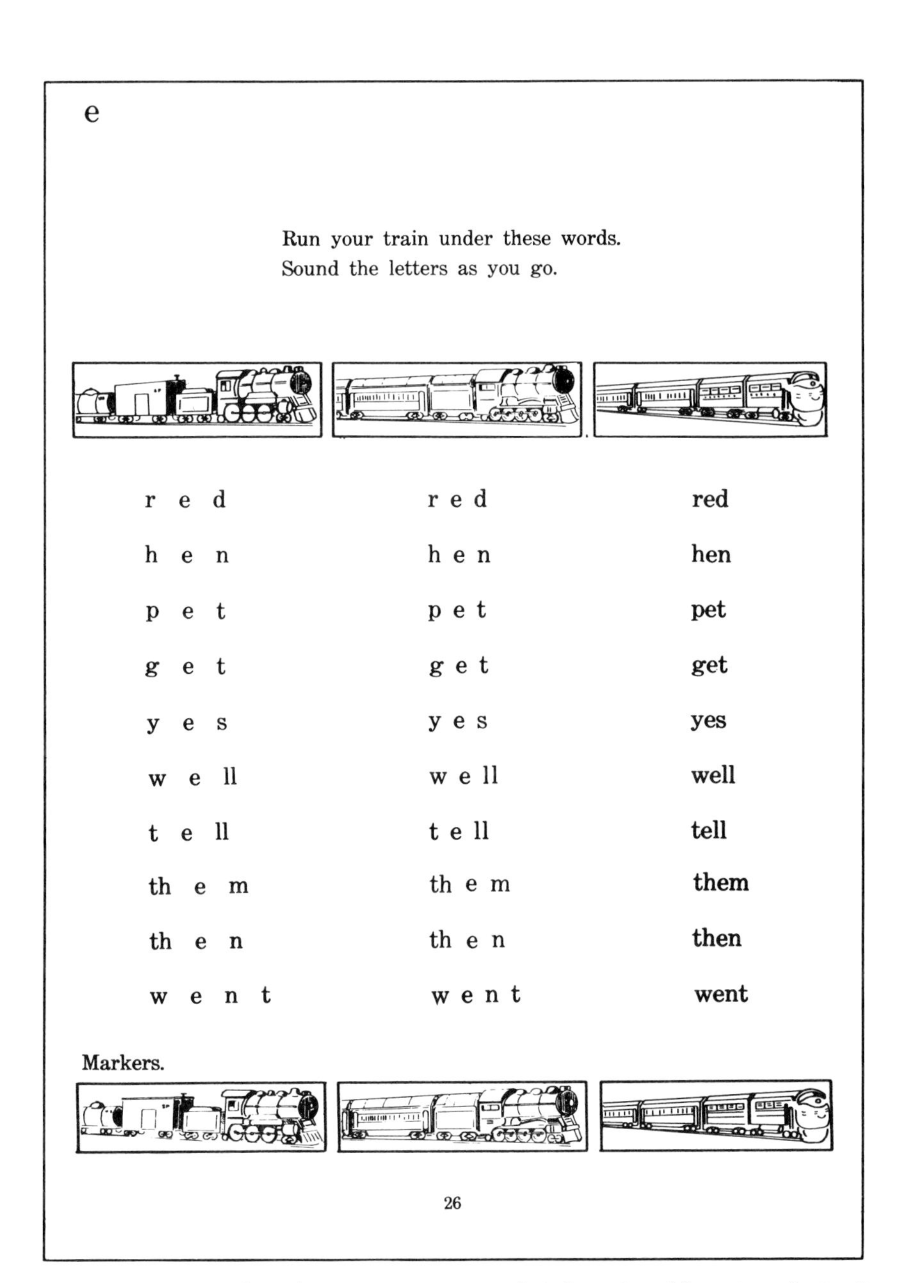

e

Run your train under these words.
Sound the letters as you go.

r e d — r e d — red

h e n — h e n — hen

p e t — p e t — pet

g e t — g e t — get

y e s — y e s — yes

w e ll — w e ll — well

t e ll — t e ll — tell

th e m — th e m — them

th e n — th e n — then

w e n t — w e n t — went

Markers.

26

Page 26 from Ruth Bolen Montgomery and Selma Coughlan, Sound, Spell, Read, The Phonovisual Vowel Book, *A Practice Book to Be Used with the Phonovisual Vowel Chart, Phonovisual Products, Inc., P.O. Box 5625, Washington, D.C., 1955.*

Original also in black and white.

The vowel says:

ă	*as in*	**at**
ĕ	*as in*	**end**
ĭ	*as in*	**it**
ŏ	*as in*	**on**
ŭ	*as in*	**up (put)**
y	**=**	**i**
w	**=**	**u**

Unless:

USE THE RULE ...

THEN

USE YOUR HEAD!

1. Mrs. E is knocking (not talking) at the back door.
2. It is part of a diphthong or a digraph.
3. It is a murmuring vowel.
4. It is at the *end* of a short word or an accented syllable.
5. It is an exception.

36

Page 36 from Sister Mary Caroline, I.H.M., Breaking the Sound Barrier, *Copyright © The Macmillan Company, 1960. Reprinted with permission of The Macmillan Company.*

The arrow, underlining, *RULE,* and *HEAD* are in red; the remainder in black.

the backs of the phonogram cards. When no figure is written above, it signifies that the first sound is the one used in the word. (Numbers are not needed above the phonograms c and g because simple rules tell which sound to use.)

The single vowels are on the phonogram cards 20, and 22 to 27.

The five kinds of silent final e have a special way of being numbered. On all seven pages of the notebook and also in the Ayres list in Chapter VI, all these silent final e's are identified by the numbers 2, 3, 4 or 5 written below them. If the e belongs to the first kind of silent e, no number is put under it.

The other pages of the Child's Notebook are presented in the same manner as described above.

Notes to Teachers about Page One

This page presents the twenty-one single-letter consonants, the six single-letter vowels, and the five kinds of silent final e's.

This is a spelling notebook. In it words when written alone are divided into syllables so that the relationship between the sounds and the symbols can be readily seen.

Each consonant has but a single sound except c, g and s. The Rules 2 and 3 below make it unnecessary to number the second sounds of c and g. Only s when it says "z" needs a 2 placed above it when learning to pronounce and write words.

I avoid using the terms "name" of a letter, "the long vowel" or "short vowel." Instead I use the sound itself because the other words are only names for sounds and are thus less direct.

The children must learn and understand and always apply the following seven rules.

Rule 1. q is always written with two letters qu when we say the sound "kw." The u is not considered a vowel here.

Rule 2. When c by itself has a sound, it always says "s" if followed by e, i or y (cent, city, cyclone); otherwise its sound is "k" (cat, cyclone, music).

Pages 98 and 99 from Romalda B. Spalding with Walter T. Spalding, The Writing Road to Reading: *A Modern Method of Phonics for Teaching Children to Read, Whiteside, Inc., New York, 1962. Reprinted by permission of M. Barrows and Company, Inc. Copyright © 1957, 1962 by Romalda Bishop Spalding.*

99

A model of Page One of the Child's Notebook.

Con so nants

b c d f g h j k l m n p qu r s t v w x y z

c before e, i or y says c, and

if g is before e, i or y it may say g

Vow els

a	at	na vy	want
e	end	me	
i	In di an	si lent	
y	ba by	my	
o	odd	o pen	do
u	up	mu sic	put

Silent final e:
- time
- have, blue
- chance, charge
- lit tle
- are (no job e)

generally accept most of the conventional wisdom—a broad definition of beginning reading, vocabulary control based on a meaning-frequency principle, and a slow, easy start (although some suggest beginning instruction in kindergarten). Their major disagreement with the conventional basal-reader programs is with their phonics component. In essence, they maintain that the phonics taught in the conventional basal-reader programs is "too little and too late."

PHONIC INNOVATIONS: COMPLETE READING PROGRAMS

A recently developed program based on an earlier and heavier phonic emphasis has been published by Lippincott—the *Lippincott Basic Reading Program.* This is a complete reading program containing preprimers,[13] primers,[14] readers for each grade, workbooks, and teachers' guides. This series is authored by a vocal critic of the prevailing view, Charles C. Walcutt (coauthor with Glenn McCracken). Walcutt advocated more extensive use of phonics in his *Reading: Chaos and Cure* and *Tomorrow's Illiterates.*

The series starts the young learner off on letters and sounds but in conjunction with early story and poem reading. In contrast to conventional basal series, however, the phonics program is more concentrated and moves faster.

In addition, the Lippincott Readers carry a significantly heavier vocabulary load than conventional series particularly in the first-, second-, and third-grade readers. The first-grade program, for instance, introduces over 2,000 words as compared to conventional series, which generally limit the number of words presented during the first year to about 350 different words. Thus, this new series has reversed the trend of decreasing vocabulary load,[15] grade for grade, that has been in progress since the beginnings of American reading instruction (Chall, 1958a).[16]

Another change the Lippincott series has made is in content. Stories tend to be based on fables, folk tales, and imaginary episodes rather than focusing on the day-to-day life of middle-class suburban families, which

[13] Little paper-covered books, usually more than one, which are the first of a long series. See Chaps. 7 and 8 for a fuller description.

[14] The first hardcover book of a basal series; it follows the preprimers and precedes the first reader.

[15] Vocabulary load is defined as the number of different words per 100 running words in a book.

[16] The 1962 edition of the leading basal-reading series (the Scott, Foresman Reading Series) has a heavier vocabulary load than the 1950 edition. However, it is still very light compared with the Lippincott Basic Reading Program.

for the past two decades has been the emphasis in most conventional basal-reading series.

Two older total reading programs, also incorporating a heavier and earlier phonic emphasis, are *The Carden Method,* published privately by the author, and *The Royal Road Readers,* coauthored by J. C. Daniels and Hunter Diack and published in England.

Though *The Carden Method* has been in existence for a long time, it has received new popularity since 1955. Mae Carden makes a special point about excluding pictures from her readers and emphasizes that hers is a total language program, stressing comprehension and literary appreciation as well as phonics.

The Royal Road Readers use a "phonic-word" method created by the authors as a way around the shortcomings of both the sight and the phonic approaches. The child who follows this program does not isolate and blend sounds, as he would do in synthetic phonics programs. Instead, he is expected to learn sound-letter relations from a beginning reading vocabulary that is controlled for spelling regularity, and he is taught what the letters "mean" through a process of visual analysis and substitution resembling quite closely the phonics instruction in conventional American basal series. Theoretically, controlling words for spelling regularity helps the child discover for himself the relationship between sounds and letters. Although Daniels and Diack do not call their approach "linguistic," in many ways it does resemble the linguistic innovations of Leonard Bloomfield, whose beginning reading program also controls vocabulary for spelling regularity.

LINGUISTIC INNOVATIONS

Linguistics is the scientific study of the nature of language. In recent years this field of inquiry has had a considerable impact on beginning reading methods.

As early as 1942, the late Leonard Bloomfield, a distinguished linguistic scholar, published two articles in *Elementary English* (a major American professional journal) criticizing the then prevailing approach to beginning reading. He questioned the initial emphasis on "meaning" and called, instead, for making learning of the "code" or "the alphabetic habit" the first step. Since the child comes to school with a considerable command of spoken language, he reasoned, reading instruction should begin by teaching him the printed equivalents for his oral vocabulary. And since English spelling is irregular, he added, this is best accomplished by teaching first those words that are spelled regularly.

t T

Tom	Ted	tan	Tim	tin	ten
tot	it	set	at	sit	sat
nut	met	net	not	mat	rat
to					

14

Pages 14 and 15 from Glenn McCracken and Charles C. Walcutt, Basic Reading, *Pre-Primer, J. B. Lippincott Co., Philadelphia, 1963.*

The illustrations are in color.

Run, rat, run,
Run, run, run.
  Run to a red sun
  Run to a red sun
Run, run, run.

—Adele H. Seronde

15

Jane made a cake.
Jane gave the cake to Joe.
Joe ate the cake.

14

Page 14 from Mae Carden, Carden Reading Method, *Grade 1, Book 1, Mae Carden, Inc., 1967.*

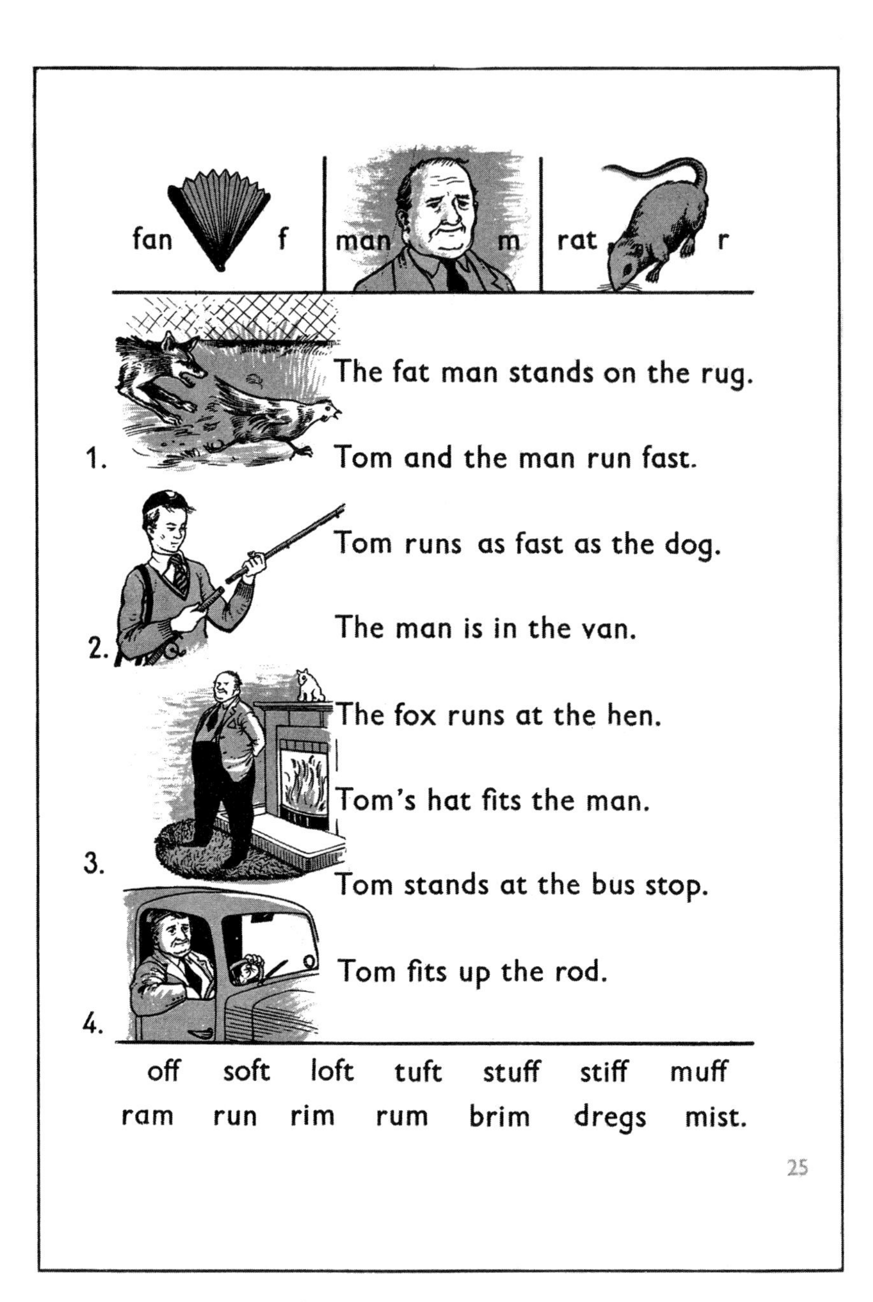

fan f | man m | rat r

1. The fat man stands on the rug.

Tom and the man run fast.

2. Tom runs as fast as the dog.

The man is in the van.

3. The fox runs at the hen.

Tom's hat fits the man.

Tom stands at the bus stop.

4. Tom fits up the rod.

off soft loft tuft stuff stiff muff

ram run rim rum brim dregs mist.

25

Page 25 from J. C. Daniels and Hunter Diack, The Royal Road Readers, *Book One, Part 1, Chatto & Windus Ltd., London, 1962.*

In the child's edition, some color wash on the illustrations.

Bloomfield's articles were ignored for a number of years. Ironically, it was Flesch who revived them in 1955 to support his call for a return to phonics, although Bloomfield had expressly stated that he was just as opposed to a "phonic" as he was to a "sight" method. Nevertheless, only after the Flesch book appeared were the Bloomfield teaching materials (coauthored by Clarence Barnhart) published, although they had been used experimentally in some schools since the 1930s. More recently, a classroom edition and accompanying teacher's manual have been published.

It is important to realize that Bloomfield's major disagreement with the conventional wisdom was a theoretical one involving the definition of beginning reading. The first task, he insisted, is learning the code, or the alphabetic principle. Meaning, considered so important by authors of conventional programs, comes naturally as the code is broken, Bloomfield argued, since the words in the first readers are already part of the child's listening and speaking vocabulary.

How do we teach the child the code? Not, as do the conventional basal-reading programs, by teaching first such high-frequency words as *look, come, go, to* (the *o*'s in these words representing four different sounds). Instead, he insisted, we should begin with words that are spelled regularly, from which the child can *discover for himself* the relationship between the sounds and the letters, e.g., *Nan, Dan, fan, man.* To facilitate this process, we should introduce only one letter for one sound; it is not until this correspondence is mastered that another should be learned. Oral reading should be stressed over silent at the beginning, and the use of context and picture clues should be discouraged. The Bloomfield system contains no illustrations.

Bloomfield was even more strongly opposed to sounding and blending than the authors of the conventional basal-reading programs. Like the proponents of the conventional wisdom, he insisted that words always be read as wholes. Unlike these proponents, however, he urged that the letters be mastered (identified by name) before word reading is started. When a new word is taught or when a child fails to recognize a word, Bloomfield said, he should spell it (say the letters), not sound it.

More recently, Charles C. Fries has presented in his *Linguistics and Reading* an account of modern linguistic knowledge and his suggestions for a "linguistically sound approach" to the teaching of reading, especially in the beginning stages.

Fries, like Bloomfield before him, takes issue with the broad definition of reading accepted by those within the prevailing view. He divides the reading process into three stages: The first is the "transfer" or beginning stage, in which "... the process of learning to read in one's

37

A rap. A gap.

Dad had a map.
Pat had a bat.
Tad had a tan cap.
Nan had a tan hat.

Nan had a fat cat.
A fat cat ran at a bad rat.

Can Dad nap?
Dad can nap.
Can Pat fan Dad?
Pat can.

Lesson 37, page 45 from Leonard Bloomfield and Clarence L. Barnhart, Let's Read, *Part 1 (Experimental Edition), C. L. Barnhart, Inc., P.O. Box 359, Bronxville, N.Y., 1963.*

native language is the *process of transfer* from the auditory signs for language signals, which the child has already learned, to the new visual signs for the same signals." (p. 120) The second is the "productive" stage, in which the responses to the visual patterns become unconscious. The third is the "imaginative" stage, ". . . when the reading process itself is so automatic that the reading is used equally with or even more than live language in the acquiring and developing of experience—when reading stimulates the vivid imaginative realization of vicarious experience." (p. 208)

Like Bloomfield, Fries is opposed to sounding and blending. Instead, he recommends that during the transfer stage the child practice on words grouped according to contrasting spelling patterns—e.g., *can, cane, rat, rate*—the most common and consistent patterns being presented first. In this way the child can discover for himself the relationship between sounds and letters.

A beginning reading program written by Fries in collaboration with Agnes Fries, Rosemary Wilson, and Mildred Rudolf, available for experimental use since 1963, has recently been published by Charles E. Merrill Books, Inc.

There are other reading programs in print that claim to be based on linguistic principles. *The Linguistic Science Readers,* coauthored by Clara G. Stratemeyer and Henry Lee Smith, Jr., also control vocabulary on spelling regularity. In addition, they introduce another feature, one based not on linguistics but on the authors' conception of what interests children. Unlike the Bloomfield and Fries programs, the Stratemeyer-Smith readers have color illustrations and a story line. Also, the main characters are animals rather than the conventional basal-reader brother-sister-baby threesome with their pets and their friends.

The *Basic Reading Series,* coauthored by Donald Rasmussen and Lynn Goldberg, is quite similar to Bloomfield's program but contains illustrations and introduces "exceptions" (high-frequency, irregularly spelled words such as *the*) earlier.

Robert and Virginia Allen have developed a linguistic approach for teaching reading to preschool and primary-grade children (*Read Along with Me*) that, unlike the Bloomfield and Fries programs, teaches phonics and encourages sounding and blending. In fact, the publisher's announcement states that it may be used ". . . as a means of relating phonics more closely to reading, and as a remedial tool for those children who have been unable—or reluctant—to respond to more conventional methods of teaching reading."

Another linguistic program that selects words on a spelling-regularity principle and teaches the sound values of the letters is *Sounds and Let-*

The Cat on the Van

Dan is on the van.

Nat is on the van.

The pan is on the van.

The cat can bat the pan.

Dan can pat the cat.

The man ran the van.

36

Page 36 from Charles C. Fries, Agnes C. Fries, Rosemary G. Wilson and Mildred K. Rudolph, Reader 1 *of the* Merrill Linguistic Readers, *Charles E. Merrill Books, Inc., Columbus, Ohio. Copyright 1966.*

+ and −

1. Can a pot hit a jet? + −

2. Can a pet get into a pit? + −

3. Can Dot cut a nut? + −

4. Can a hut rot in a pot? + −

5. Can a man get into a jet? + −

6. Can a dot bet in a pot? + −

7. Can a nut jig in a net? + −

8. Can a net rip? + −

11

Page 11 reprinted from SRA Basic Reading Series Workbook for Level B *by Donald E. Rasmussen and Lenina Goldberg. © 1964, 1965, Donald E. Rasmussen and Lenina Goldberg. Used by permission of the publisher, Science Research Associates, Inc., Chicago.*

ters by Frances Adkins Hall. *The Structural Reading Series* by Catherine Stern also incorporates the above features, but in addition uses color as a cue and teaches writing and spelling at the same time.

A different kind of linguistic approach has been suggested by Carl Lefevre in his book *Linguistics and the Teaching of Reading.* Lefevre has not yet developed a reading program. But if he does, it will probably be closer to the older "sentence" and "experience" methods (as well as the current conventional basal-reader approach) than to the linguistic approaches cited above. Lefevre is concerned more with syntactical aspects of the language (sentence structure and grammar) and less with the relationship between sounds and letters.

Another beginning reading program that may be classified as representing a linguistic approach is the *Language through Picture Series,* or *First Steps in Reading English Series,* coauthored by Christine M. Gibson and Ivor A. Richards. This program controls both letters and sentence patterns. The letter control is primarily visual. Unlike the Bloomfield program, there is no attempt to control the first words either on spelling regularity or on a one-sound-to-one-letter principle—e.g., *this* and *his* are among the first words taught. Like Bloomfield and Fries, Gibson and Richards do not teach the sound-letter relationships directly. Their major concern is with control of syntax or sentence patterns.

We can see from these brief descriptions that there is no *one* "linguistic method." Since linguistic scholars interpret the relevance of linguistic discoveries for beginning reading instruction differently, the reading programs they develop are bound to differ.

At the same time, most of the current linguistic innovators in beginning reading agree on at least one point. They tend to question the broad definition of beginning reading, with its primary stress on "mature reading from the start," a definition long accepted by most reading specialists and incorporated into conventional reading programs. Instead, perhaps with the exception of Lefevre and Gibson and Richards, they propose that "decoding" be the primary emphasis at the beginning, to be followed later by the broader goals of interpretation, appreciation, and application.[17]

In many respects the linguistic innovations resemble the phonic innovations, although many linguistic scholars oppose the phonic innovations as much as they do the conventional programs. More recently, however, as can be seen from *Sounds and Letters,* the Allen Reading Materials, *The Structural Reading Series,* and the *Programmed Reading Series* (discussed below), there appears to be a rapprochement between

[17] See footnote 3 in Appendix A for C. C. Fries's reaction to this classification.

8. b a g   c a b
   r a g   t a b
   t a g

Nan can tag Dan.

Can Dan tag Sam?

Dan has a tan bag.

Nan had rags in a rag bag.

Nan's rag bag has a tab.

Dad has a tan cab.

A fat man had Dad's cab.

Sam can tap Dan's tan bat.

Page 8 from Frances Adkins Hall, Sounds and Letters, A., Nan and Dan Reader, *Linguistica, Box 619, Ithaca, N.Y., 1964.*

Page 33 from Catherine Stern et al., We Read and Write, *Book C (1–2 level) of* Structural Reading Series, *L. W. Singer Co., Inc., New York, 1963.*

The illustrations are in color. The consonants in the upper section are printed in blue; the vowels in red. The remaining letters are in black.

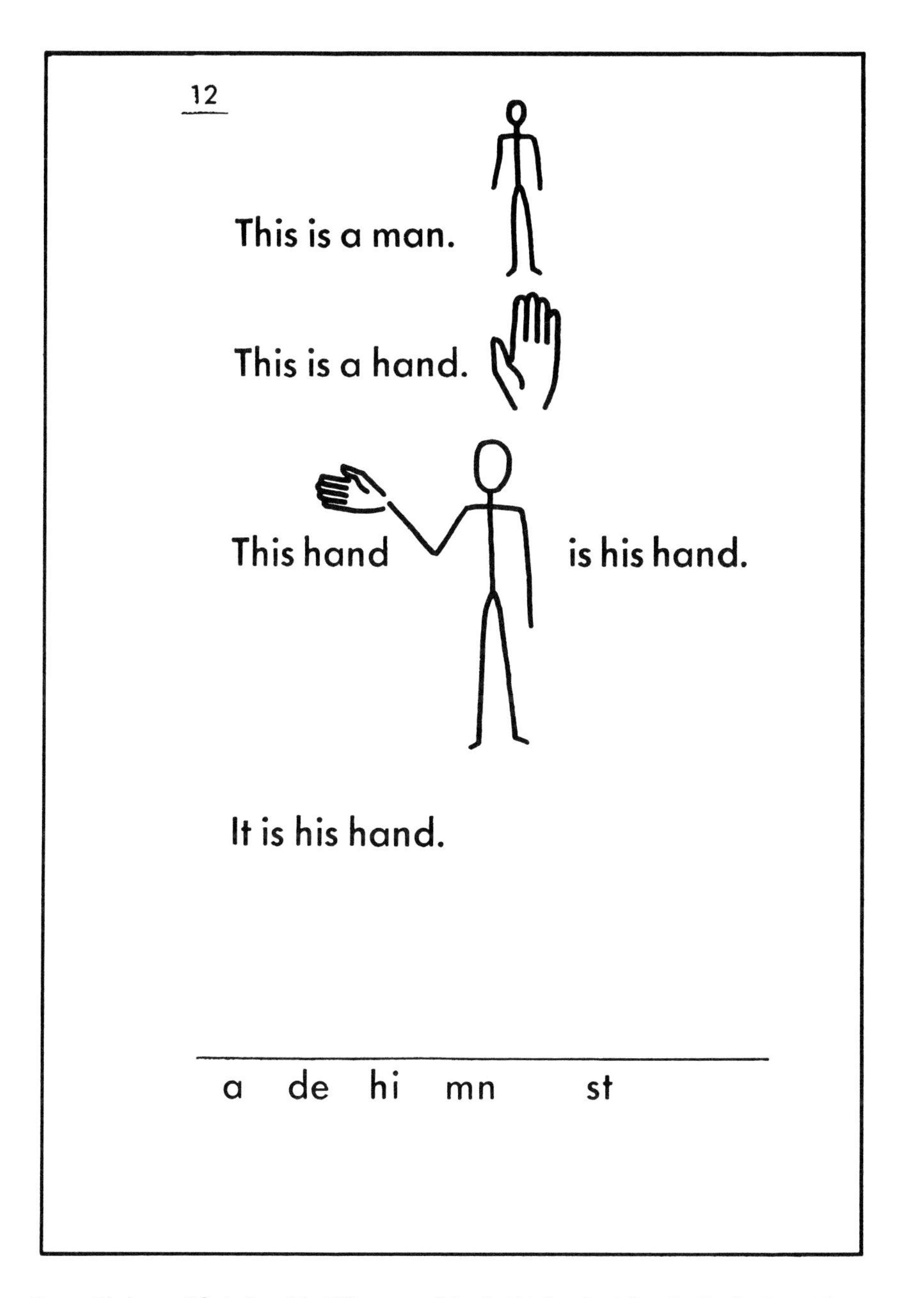

Page 12 from Christine M. Gibson and I. A. Richards, This Is Book One: First Steps in Reading English, *part of* The Language Through Picture Series, *Washington Square Press, Inc., New York, 1959.*

the two. In fact, *Sounds and Letters*, the Allen Reading Materials, *The Carden Method*, the Lippincott Basic Reading Program, and *The Royal Road Readers* may be classified as either phonic or linguistic (see Appendix A for finer distinctions).

ITA AND SIMILAR REFORMS

The Initial Teaching Alphabet (ITA), devised by Sir James Pitman, is another innovation that sprang from dissatisfaction with conventional approaches to acquiring the code. However, while Bloomfield and Fries accept English spelling as it is, introducing it to the child *as if* it were regular and then gradually revealing "the awful truth," Pitman changes the alphabet itself, augmenting it to forty-four characters to make it correspond more closely to the sounds in our language. In addition, ITA uses only lowercase letters; capital letters are simply a larger type size of the lowercase form.

The Initial Teaching Alphabet is to be used only in the beginning stage in reading. After the child can read in ITA with some fluency, he transfers to "traditional orthography," our conventional alphabet and spelling. If this procedure appears rather farfetched, consider that children and adults who are literate in one language that uses the roman alphabet can, if they learn to speak another language, usually learn to read the second language quite readily.[18]

It is important to note that those who originally devised and experimented with ITA in England did not propose a change in method. The only change proposed was in the medium—the print. ITA, they thought, would prove more beneficial than the traditional alphabet and spelling, whether the emphasis was on a sight or a phonic method. The reading scheme (basal series) used by the ITA experimental groups in the English experiment is the most popular in England. This series incorporates the principles on which conventional American basal-reading programs are based.

The American experience with ITA is somewhat different. In the demonstration currently under way in Bethlehem, Pennsylvania, a series

[18] Indeed, the École Française, a bilingual private school in New York City, teaches American children to read French first, then English. That is, the fundamentals of the reading process (decoding) are taught to kindergarten and first-grade children in the French language, which is spelled more regularly than English. In the second grade, the children learn to read English. According to the headmistress, most children need little instruction in English reading. Some "errors" I observed during oral reading of English in a second-grade class involved pronunciation of an English word with a French accent. This was usually corrected by the child from the general sense of what he read.

by Albert J. Mazurkiewicz and Harold J. Tanyzer (*Early-to-Read: i/t/a Program*) is being used for the experimental groups.[19] This series innovates in method as well as in medium by putting greater stress on early learning of the alphabet and phonics. It also calls for the children to do more writing, and it has a heavier vocabulary load. Thus, should the American ITA demonstration achieve better results than conventional American basal-reader programs, we must still ask whether ITA or the changes in method account for the difference.

ITA is not the only modified alphabet or spelling scheme offered as a reform for beginning reading instruction. The history of alphabetic and spelling reforms can be traced back to 1644, when Richard Hodges, a schoolmaster of Southwark, England, offered a diacritical marking system to the public (Downing, 1964b). Hodges's system was followed by numerous others, two of which received rather wide experimental trial in the United States during the nineteenth century—Leigh's transition alphabet and the Phonotype of A. J. Ellis and Benn and Isaac Pitman. Proponents of these systems claimed that they saved from one to two years' time in teaching children how to read.

Among current competitors of ITA is John R. Malone's Single-sound UNIFON, a consistent auxiliary orthography for teaching English and other European languages. For English, UNIFON uses forty characters; all are uppercase letters, designed to take up similar space in a rectangle for ease in coding by "optical reading machines" (Malone, 1963). Other systems include the Simplified Spelling Society's system of respelling with no additional characters (Dewey, 1960) and Edward Fry's Diacritical Marking System (1963).

MOORE'S RESPONSIVE ENVIRONMENT

Omar K. Moore has made the popular press in recent years with dramatic stories of two-, three- and four-year-olds learning to read using automated and manual typewriters. I cannot here go into the theoretical aspects of Moore's work, which are considerable, except to say that his major purpose is not to demonstrate what has been known for a long time—that young children can and do learn to read—but to develop a theory of problem solving and social interaction.[20]

[19] This series was also used in cooperative first-grade studies sponsored by the USOE that compared ITA with other approaches (see Chap. 4).
[20] See, for example, Moore, *Autotelic Responsive Environments and Exceptional Children* and "Early Reading and Writing," a film report by Moore and Alan Ross Anderson. The first source contains references to selected writings by Moore and others on the theoretical aspects of his work.

Page 1 from Albert J. Mazurkiewicz and Harold J. Tanyzer, Early-to-Read i/t/a Program, *Revised Book 2, i/t/a Publications, Inc., New York, 1966.*

Some color wash in the child's edition.

In the methods and materials he uses, Moore departs significantly from conventional approaches. He starts the child on learning the letters (and some heuristic sound values for some of the letters; e.g., *M* is *mm*) and then proceeds to words and sentences. A new child is first introduced to the Moore laboratory by a child guide who has already been through the program. He is then left in the laboratory with an automated typewriter. In exploring the instrument he strikes a key, and the automated typewriter calls out the name of the letter or symbol struck. This goes on until the child learns the names of the letters and punctuation symbols. Then he is taken through a series of steps in which a letter or symbol (perhaps a number) is presented to him on a screen similar to television either by automated equipment or by a teacher (called a "booth assistant"), and he reproduces it on the electric typewriter.

Several children I watched at this particular stage were copying words like *dad, lad, fad, sad,* following the Bloomfield spelling-regularity and one-sound-to-one-letter principles. However, Moore does not stick to any set program.[21] He uses conventional basal readers (which contain irregularly spelled words right from the start), general storybooks, and various graded exercises. He has children *write* words and sentences, as well as *read* and *type* them. His program also contains a speaking, listening, and writing-from-dictation sequence.

Like Bloomfield, Moore separates the process of learning to read into stages, the first being the acquisition of the code, or the alphabetic principle. Later the stress is on interpretation, application, and appreciation. Also, sound-letter relations are not taught directly, although the child is given heuristic hints. Instead, the child "spells out" the words when he first learns them and as a means of recall and attack.

INDIVIDUALIZED READING

A different form of innovation, Individualized Reading (or IR), is concerned with patterns of classroom organization, pacing, motivation, and subject-matter content of reading materials. Essentially, proponents of Individualized Reading accept the conventional broad definition of beginning reading. They also accept a slow and easy start, with meaningful reading of words and sentences from the beginning, before word analysis is begun. Their major criticism of conventional basal-reader programs is that the content is "vacuous." They claim that, too often, chil-

[21] Moore's comment on the above statement was: "I have a set method for getting a program. The program comes from the child himself until he can be turned loose on almost any written material that interests him." (personal communication)

dren are taken through stories and exercises in "lock-step" groups, whether or not they are interested in the stories or need the exercises.

Instead, IR proponents propose that teachers use a large variety of reading matter—juveniles (fiction and nonfiction), magazines, newspapers, and readers—allowing each child to select his own reading materials (self-selection) and to proceed at his own pace (self-pacing). The theory is that if the child is left alone, he will select books that satisfy his vital interests and are of an appropriate level[22]—neither too easy nor too difficult (Veatch, 1959).

It is hard to describe Individualized Reading in any greater detail because such programs vary considerably. Some teachers make no use of basal readers but rely entirely on self-selection of trade books. These "purists" tend also to rely solely on independent pupil-teacher conferences (from two to ten minutes per day, depending on the size of the class) for instructing the children. Others make use of group instruction in "skills" from basal readers and workbooks. And still others, who say they follow an IR program, give daily basal-reading instruction in groups, also allowing the children some time to read self-selected trade books or other materials.

Thus, there is a labeling problem here, just as there was for the phonic and linguistic innovations. A program may be called a conventional basal-reader program or an Individualized Reading program, depending upon who names it. Like other innovations, Individualized Reading has been known and practiced before, often under a different label; in the 1920s, for example, it was known as "free reading."

THE LANGUAGE EXPERIENCE APPROACH

The Language Experience (or LE) approach[23] incorporates much of the basic philosophy of Individualized Reading. But it also shares one essential feature with the linguistic and phonic innovations—early acquisition of the code.

Like Individualized Reading, LE stresses the importance of each child's unique interests and needs. In this it seems to go Individualized Reading one better. It makes the first step in reading not self-selection of books written by others, but reading of the child's own writings. This, according to Language Experience proponents, veritably guarantees vital interest. The child's first stories are drawn from his own artistic produc-

[22] See Fleming (1966), in which this aspect of the theory is questioned by empirical findings among fifth-grade pupils.
[23] See San Diego County (1961) and Lee and Allen (1963).

tions and are recorded by his teacher. Later the child writes his own captions and stories, aided by some "formal" instruction in the writing and spelling of common words. While "editing" the child's stories, the teacher shows him the connection between sounds and letters. As with Individualized Reading, each child is encouraged to proceed at his own pace.

This approach, too, differs considerably from teacher to teacher. When I observed it in San Diego, I found some teachers supplementing the LE program with daily reading in groups from conventional basal readers, while others never used basal readers, relying only on child-written materials and trade books.

MONTESSORI

The current interest in the Montessori method is another example of the rediscovery of an old innovation. Dr. Maria Montessori's method enjoyed great but short-lived popularity in the United States from 1909 to 1917 (Hunt, 1964). The present interest in Montessori may be attributed to two basic features of her method—emphasis on early learning (from three to six years of age) and self-pacing of learning in a "prepared" or "structured" environment.

As far as I can determine, no special Montessori method has been developed for reading instruction in the United States. The following brief treatment of the Montessori method for beginning reading is derived from her own reports on teaching reading and writing to preschool retarded Italian children.

In teaching these children to read Italian (which is spelled more regularly than English), Montessori started by having them learn to identify, write, and sound the letters of the alphabet. Later, they learned to blend the sounds into words and then to combine the words into meaningful sentences.

The steps for mastering each of these aspects of reading and writing are described so beautifully in a recently published translation of her writings (1964) that it would be an injustice to try to summarize them here. In *The Montessori Method,* she describes not only her method, but herself—an intelligent, perceptive, loving physician-teacher, who saw in the most retarded and disadvantaged child the emerging man, deserving of his teacher's respect.

In many ways Moore's responsive environment resembles Montessori's method; indeed, he acknowledges his indebtedness to her. In both methods the young child practices individually carefully laid-out steps which he takes at his own pace. Both teach the alphabet first, although

Montessori taught the sound values of the letters directly, while Moore only gives hints.

Thus we see that the Montessori method falls within two major streams of current innovation: early mastery of the code and greater individualization.

PROGRAMMED LEARNING

Programmed learning as applied to reading instruction is also concerned with self-paced and self-directed learning. But the steps are laid out for the learner in a much more structured way. Each bit of learning is so organized that each successive step depends upon mastering the previous one, and the pupil gets immediate confirmation of his response.

Theoretically, any approach to beginning reading—sight, sentence, meaning, phonic, or linguistic—can be programmed. It is interesting to note, therefore, that the programmed beginning reading courses currently available—*The Basal Progressive Choice Reading Program* by Myron Woolman et al., *Programmed Reading* by Cynthia Dee Buchanan and Sullivan Associates, and Grolier's *First Steps in Reading for Meaning*—rely heavily on a phonic-linguistic approach. All three start the child on the letters and their sound values and control vocabulary on a spelling-regularity principle. However, although the Programmed Reading Series and the Woolman Program claim to be "linguistically based," they teach the relation between sounds and letters, have the child isolate sounds, and encourage blending. In content (subject matter) all three programs also differ from conventional materials; they contain discrete words and sentences with humorous illustrations but no definite "story line."

CONTENT CHANGES IN BASAL READERS

I should also mention some other innovations in basal readers, mostly in the area of content. The Writers' Committee of the Great Cities School Improvement Program of the Detroit Public Schools has developed what is probably the first basal-reading series with both Negro and white children and adults as the main characters.[24] The first three preprimers of the City Schools series contain about half the number of different words in the usual three preprimers of conventional basal series. In general, the authors seem to accept all other aspects of the prevailing view: a slow,

[24] Since publication of this program in 1962, several of the major publishers have come out with new editions of their standard basal-reading programs in which the characters are multiracial.

PICK AND PRINT

PRINT	PICK LIST
(28)	
1. TOM'S MOM HAS A GLASS ________.	JOB
2. TOT HAD ________ AND BUNS.	JUMP
	JOG
3. SAM JUST GOT A ________.	JUG
4. BOB ________ ON SCOT. SCOT GOT MAD.	JUMPS
5. MOM'S GLASS ________ GOT LOST.	JUST
6. SAD DAD HAS NOT GOT A ________.	
7. DAD'S CAB GOT PAST A ________.	JAM
8. JAN ________ GOT A HAT.	

IQB ☐

77

Page 77 reprinted from Reading in High Gear: The Accelerated Progressive Choice Reading Program, Learner's Workbook, *Cycle 1 by Myron Woolman. © 1966, 1964, Myron Woolman, The Institute of Educational Research, Inc. Used by permission of the publisher, Science Research Associates, Inc., Chicago.*

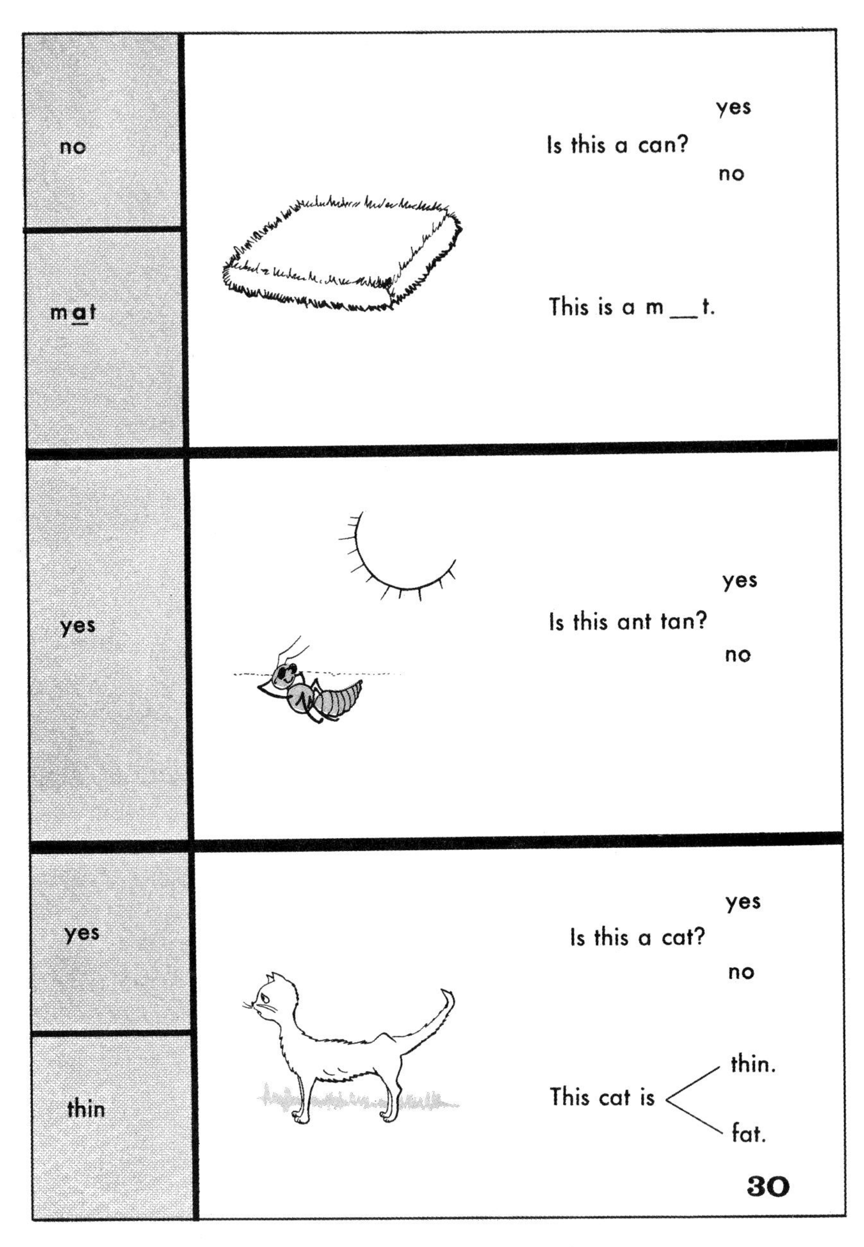

no

m<u>a</u>t

Is this a can?

yes

no

This is a m __ t.

yes

Is this ant tan?

yes

no

yes

thin

Is this a cat?

yes

no

This cat is thin. / fat.

30

Page 30 from Cynthia Dee Buchanan, Programmed Reading, Book 1. *Copyright © 1963 by Sullivan Associates. Webster Division, McGraw-Hill Book Company, St. Louis, 1963.*

Some color wash on illustrations in child's edition.

14

Look, look, Mother.

See Wiggles.

Wiggles can get the ball.

See Wiggles get the ball.

See Wiggles play ball.

Page 14 from Laugh with Larry, City Schools Reading Program. *Copyright © by The Board of Education of the City of Detroit. Used by permission of Follett Publishing Co., Chicago.*

Illustrations are in color in child's edition.

easy start; emphasis on meaning and appreciation from the beginning; introduction of sight words first; control of vocabulary for meaning frequency. Also, phonics and other word-analysis skills are introduced later and taught primarily through an analysis of known sight words.[25]

Two new series that are designed to be more realistic to urban children and to children of different ethnic and socioeconomic groups are *The Bank Street Readers,* developed by the Bank Street College of Education, and the *Chandler Language-Experience Readers,* edited by Lawrence W. Carillo.

The Bank Street Readers are innovative mainly in their emphasis on urban life. The Chandler Readers use photographs of children of multiethnic backgrounds and predominantly urban settings. The text, according to the authors, is translated from children's own speech.

SUMMARY OF RECENT INNOVATIONS

The programs discussed above admittedly represent only a sample of recently published materials. Still others are in the experimental stage or in manuscript form awaiting a favorable verdict from the editorial departments of educational publishers. The profusion of new programs indicates that we are indeed in a state of flux in beginning reading.

Generally, we can detect three major lines of innovation in the new programs:

1. Innovations to bring about earlier acquisition of the alphabetic principle
2. Innovations to bring about greater individualization of instruction
3. Innovations to bring about more vital, realistic, and imaginative content, or to underplay content altogether

Some of the new programs reflect only one of these trends, some two, and some all three. However, all continue to incorporate some of the aspects of conventional programs.

SIGNS OF THE FUTURE

Since this chapter was written, three beginning reading programs in the "research-and-development" stage have come to my attention. I mention them here because I believe they will have a significant impact in the

[25] In recent correspondence with the publisher (Follett Publishing Company), however, the senior editor of this series noted that "the primary reading method used is phonic. . . ." This is another example of the difficulties involved in studying beginning reading.

I play with my friends.
Do you play, too?

I look at TV.
Do you look, too?

After school,
What do you do?

30

Page 30 from Bank Street College of Education, Around the City, *Primer of the* Bank Street Readers. *Copyright © The Macmillan Company, 1965. Reprinted with permission of The Macmillan Company.*

Illustrations are in color in child's edition.

"Look! We are going down.

How I like to slide!"

10

Page 10 from Lawrence W. Carillo, ed., Slides, *the second of the six paperback readers in the* Chandler Language-Experience Readers, *Chandler Publishing Co., San Francisco, 1965.*

future—not only on practice, but also on the way in which beginning reading programs will be developed. Unlike the great majority of the new programs discussed above, all three have received substantial government or foundation support. Each is being developed and carefully tested by an interdisciplinary team of psychologists, linguists, and teachers. Thus, the development of each program should result in an instructional program that can be used in classrooms and should also add to our knowledge of the process of learning to read.

An experimental first-grade curriculum in reading is being developed at Cornell University by Harry Levin, director of Project Literacy,[26] and his associates. During the summer of 1965 a team of specialists formulated the guidelines for a program "based on recent theories of the nature of reading and theories of learning and motivation." The experimental program was tested in a first-grade class during the 1965–1966 school year; it was revised and extended in a summer workshop in 1966, and will be tested on other children during the coming years.[27]

Since September, 1965, Douglas Porter, Helen Popp, and their associates at Harvard University have been developing and testing "wide-range, flexible self-instructional reading programs" under a Ford Foundation grant. Their purpose is to develop "a set of self-instructional reading programs along with supporting validation data that specify the results to be expected from use of the programs on specified populations (child and adult)." Instructions for using the programs, along with diagnostic and criterion tests for guiding individual students, are also being developed.[28]

At Stanford University, Richard C. Atkinson, Duncan N. Hansen, and their associates have been developing a computer-assisted instructional program in beginning reading under a USOE grant.[29] These authors do not claim that theirs is a complete program that needs no teacher. Indeed, they assume that the child will receive regular classroom instruction and will spend only about fifteen minutes daily on the computer program. The computer has a visual as well as an audio unit. The child hears a word or letter or sentence through a set of earphones while the screen flashes the visual form, and he is given an instruction. If what he does is correct, the computer gives him the next step. If it is

[26] Project Literacy was organized at Cornell University on Feb. 1, 1964, under a developmental projects award from the Cooperative Research Branch of the USOE. This project represents one of the USOE's major commitments to basic research and curriculum development connected with both child and adult literacy. See *Project Literacy Reports,* Cornell University, Ithaca, N.Y.

[27] *Project Literacy* (1966).

[28] See Porter et al. (1965).

[29] Atkinson and Hansen (1966).

wrong, the computer tells him so and gives him other exercises designed to teach him the same thing.

Like the new programs described in the major portion of this chapter, these three incorporate several changes, although they also include many aspects of programs "within the conventional wisdom." Two characteristics that all three have in common and that distinguish them from conventional programs are their stress on early acquisition of the code and their emphasis on greater individualization of instruction. But what distinguishes them most is the way in which they are being developed. Even if their authors do not come up with better programs, they are bound to increase our general knowledge of how children learn to read.

TWO

Challenged and Challengers Speak Their Minds

TO ROUND OUT my picture of what the great debate is all about, I interviewed twenty-five proponents of different beginning reading approaches —mostly authors of published programs.[1] I wanted to clarify the assumptions and objectives not explicitly stated in their published programs. In addition, I wished to obtain their views on issues that are subject to vigorous debate.

To these ends, each proponent was asked to discuss the following questions:

How should reading be defined?

[1] The senior authors and one editor of three widely used conventional basal-reading series; nine phonics proponents, including six authors of published systematic-phonics programs and a board member of the Reading Reform Foundation; five proponents of modified alphabets and simplified spelling schemes, of whom two are inventors of modified alphabets for beginning instruction; four authors of linguistic-type programs; and two proponents of the Language Experience approach (one the author of a recent book on the method). I also interviewed Omar K. Moore, coinventor, with Richard Kobler, of the computerized typewriter, but solely responsible for the Responsive Environment methodology. For obvious reasons I do not name those interviewed with the exception of Moore, because of his unique position. The interviews took place during 1962 and 1963.

Is there any difference between beginning reading and later reading?

What motivates the beginner more strongly—his interest in the story or his desire to master the process or skill involved in reading?

Should the beginner read orally or silently?

Which should the teacher stress with beginners—skill and accuracy in word recognition or understanding of the meaning of the words read?

Should writing and spelling be coordinated with beginning reading instruction?

How good is the content typical of the basal readers currently in use?

Is vocabulary control necessary in beginning reading materials?

How important are illustrations in beginning reading instruction?

How should classes be organized for beginners?

Should parents help their children learn to read?

Why do some children fail to learn to read?

Are children reading less well today than fifty years ago?

DEFINITION OF READING

The basal-reader authors generally accepted the broad definition of reading outlined in the last chapter: perception (word recognition), comprehension and interpretation, appreciation, and application. Two put greatest emphasis on meaning and interpretation. One of these said:

> Reading is understanding printed language and reacting to it—reacting in the broad sense of understanding, both literal and interpretive. I would even settle for the simple word, *understanding.*
>
> In our readiness program, the major preparation is for understanding what is read. We place a lot of emphasis on spoken language patterns and on understanding concepts. Even the most common things are not known, like the size of a cow or a pig.
>
> In teaching reading, we teach the pupil that reading is not just saying words. Even in the first grade, we try to give the pupil an appreciation of the difference between the real and the fanciful.

Another basal-reader author answered:

> Reading is the meaningful interpretation of symbols—a process through which we understand. It is a process of communication between readers and writers, and a means to an end. It is not an end in itself.

A third author thought it possible to omit appreciation and application from the definition:

I don't have a definition of reading. But I agree pretty much with the one by Gray[2] that reading involves perception (recognition), plus understanding, plus appreciation and use. We need the last two, but whether to call these reading or not, I don't care. I am willing to let the linguists settle for the first two. The last two can be the accompaniment of reading.

The Language Experience proponents held views similar to those of the basal-reader authors, but put even greater emphasis on appreciation and use.

The phonics proponents offered a wide range of opinions on this question. Four accepted the basal-reader authors' definition of reading and four proposed a two-step definition—word recognition first, then meaning, appreciation, and use.

The linguistic proponents interviewed were the most consistent group. For them, reading was a matter of recognizing the words; meaning, appreciation, and application were part of language study. Omar K. Moore and the alphabet reformers agreed with this view.

BEGINNING READING AND LATER READING

When asked whether beginning reading differs from later reading, the basal-reader proponents said that the emphasis may be different at the beginning, but that generally all four aspects of reading are important at all stages. One author said:

Yes, beginning reading is different from later reading. Later reading is done for different purposes. Also, in later reading, the emphasis changes in terms of the different strands (word recognition, comprehension and interpretation, appreciation, and use). In grades 1 to 4 word perception is emphasized; in later stages, comprehension and interpretation are emphasized.[3]

According to a second basal-reader author, the difference is mainly in purpose:

The mature reader is dominated by his own purpose; the immature, by another's purpose. The child selects one book out of one, the mature reader selects one book out of many. The mature reader also uses his reading in some way. The immature reader does not. The immature reader also accepts what he reads.

A third basal-reader author stated the difference in this way:

The beginner is obviously having more difficulty with word recognition techniques, but it is a difference in degree, not kind. The first grader can be helped to do some

[2] See Gray (1948 and 1960).
[3] This does not tally with my analysis of conventional basal-reader programs (see Chap. 8).

interpretation, some critical reading, and some creative reading. But he is not often asked to. Instead, he is usually asked to find the color of the farmer's cow because the color is given in the book.

The Language Experience proponents were more convinced than were the basal-reader authors that beginning and later reading are the same. If there is any difference at all, they said, it is only in the number of concepts understood: "The mature reader has more concepts."[4]

Six of the nine phonics proponents also saw no essential difference between beginning and mature reading. Only two said that there was a definite difference.[5]

The linguistic proponents, the alphabet reformers, and Omar K. Moore said a definite distinction should be drawn between beginning and later reading. For them, beginning reading is a matter of learning to decode. Later, or mature, reading involves interpretation, application, and appreciation.

All those who said a change takes place, either in degree or in kind, generally agreed that it happens when the "mechanics," or the decoding aspects of reading, have been mastered. But they did not agree on the age or level at which this typically occurs.

The basal-reader proponents felt the change comes in grade 2 or 3 for most children and at grade 4 for others. By that time, the child has acquired the basic skills and can go on to use his reading. But even this point was questioned by one author: "Again, I don't think there is any real difference. Some people make the distinction between *learning to read* and *reading to learn*. There isn't any hard and fast one."

The linguistic group, the alphabet reformers, and Omar K. Moore believed the change from beginning to mature reading can come earlier—at the end of grade 1 for the average pupil and at the end of grade 2 for the slower one. By that time, the code is mastered, and reading becomes an "unconscious" process.

[4] We see here, and also in the responses of the basal-reader authors, a great concern with meaning—to the point even of believing that the beginner's major hurdle is a lack of "concepts." This may be true for difficult reading matter, but it is highly questionable for first-grade reading materials. See Chap. 8, pp. 313–316 for further discussion of this point.

[5] The views of this group are puzzling but can be understood in the context of the debate. Unlike the linguists, they have no theory of their own about the reading process. Instead, they seem to accept, often uncritically, many of the assumptions of the prevailing view. They wish only to make the basal approach work better, and they are particularly sensitive lest they be accused of overemphasizing the "mechanics" or decoding aspects of reading to the "detriment" of meaning, appreciation (joy and creativity), and application. In this connection, see footnote 3 in Appendix A for C. C. Fries's views.

READING READINESS

The basal-reader authors generally held to the prevailing view that formal reading instruction should begin, for most children, at age six (or in first grade). All these authors were concerned about the current push toward getting the child started earlier. One stated the consensus of the group as follows:

> The evidence is inconclusive regarding the value of introducing reading in kindergarten. There is no evidence that teaching children at five profits them generally.

At the same time, this author mentioned that he was involved in experimental tryouts of teaching reading in kindergarten. He explained that he was doing the work because of the tremendous public interest in introducing reading at this stage.

Another basal-reader author said:

> I would accept that you can teach reading to children at different ages. If you are careful about the materials, you can teach children to read at age three. Whether we should do it is something that I can't answer. There is no question that children are living in a world that has been affected by affluence. They travel, have books, watch TV. Children are now exposed to more verbal stimulation than they were in the past. This is true for most children but not for all. Some children who live in deprived urban environments have very limited language.

The basal-reader authors generally felt that "we can do it earlier, at age five, for most children. *But should we? Is it worth it?*"

The authors recognized that the "readiness books" (the prereading workbooks) of their series might be contributing to a slow start. One stated that teachers were spending too much time on these books, using *all three* when one would be sufficient for average and above-average children. The next revision of his series, he said, will suggest that teachers go through the readiness books (and the preprimers) quickly, unless there is a good reason not to.

The basal-reader authors also noted that kindergarten teachers' lack of preparation makes an earlier start difficult. Most kindergarten teachers have *not* been trained to teach reading.

Two-thirds of the phonics proponents, on the other hand, believed that most children can benefit from starting as early as at age five, and some even at age four. According to one, "the American notion about readiness is absurd. Montessori taught four-year-olds to read."

Another said:

> Reading readiness is vastly overemphasized. I would think that reading readiness is just like talking readiness. We don't investigate too closely whether a child is ready to talk or not. The parents usually encourage the child to talk. They inevitably succeed,

> although sometimes their child is slower than others. In fact, the less anxious the child is to learn to read, the more he should be encouraged to do so, since every child must learn. Most children in the upper social levels are encouraged at home, and it is actually the child in the lower social levels who suffers most from the prevailing notion on "readiness" which delays exposure to reading until he is "ready." Blaming such factors as "difficulty at home," "shyness," or "personal problems" as reasons for not being "ready" for reading is ridiculous. In fact, if the shy or troubled child is taught, it ameliorates his problems.[6]

Other phonics proponents advocated a slow beginning at age five, especially for those who will have trouble in learning to read.[7] Most phonics proponents assumed that a phonic approach is easier than a meaning-sight approach and that the child can therefore start earlier if he starts with phonics.

Three of the nine phonics proponents accepted the current concept of readiness and did not favor an earlier start. They agreed essentially with the basal-reader authors that children differ and that starting at age six was generally a good idea. It is interesting to note that these three are more intimately connected with elementary schools—as teachers or supervisors of reading—than the other six. They are also authors or proponents of phonics systems that resemble the basal-reader phonics programs. Also, they define reading as the basal-reader authors do, stressing comprehension, appreciation, and application right from the start.

The linguistic proponents, as a group, called for starting before age six—at five or even younger. They noted that the five-year-old has a good

[6] This statement contains much that can be substantiated and much that cannot from the existing evidence. True, there may have been too great a stress on testing readiness before the child is exposed to reading instruction, as well as an inordinate fear of the dire consequences resulting from such exposure. In this connection, see de Hirsch et al. (1966) for a recent, sensible, research-oriented view of reading readiness.

[7] Many teachers in England hold the same view. When told that American children start at age six or later, they commented that this was probably all right for the brighter ones, for "they will catch up easily." But for the slower ones, they believed starting earlier, at age five, as they do in England, is better. "It gives the slower ones the extra time to 'catch on.'" The recent longitudinal studies of Dolores Durkin on American children who learn to read before they enter school tend to confirm this view (Durkin, 1964). She found early readers were ahead of non-early readers through the elementary grades and that the advantage of an early start was inversely related to intelligence. Thus, the less able seemed to benefit even more from an early start. (See also *Children Who Read Early*, Teachers College Press, 1966.) Giving slower children an earlier start is, of course, opposed to the conventional American conception of "readiness." Since the 1930s, the conventional wisdom has been that the more able children benefit from starting earlier, while the less able do better if they start later. It is interesting to note that some of the head-start programs do not follow the conventional view in this respect. For them, the earlier the start (with children not deemed ready), the better! See, for example, Carl Bereiter and Siegfried Englemann, *Teaching Disadvantaged Children in Preschool*, Prentice–Hall, 1966.

command of the spoken language. Therefore, "readiness" training should stress learning the letters (in preparation for learning the relation between spoken and written language), rather than practicing oral language, as most of the reading-readiness programs now do.

The alphabet reformers felt that children would be able to start earlier by using a modified alphabet, since coping with the unpredictability of English spelling makes the task of learning to read more difficult.

Omar K. Moore expressed the most extreme view. He stated that starting at six is later than necessary. Furthermore, he said, many of the factors considered essential for success in beginning reading are really unessential. The best time to start, according to Moore, is at age two or three, when the child is still free to explore, when learning is a "game," and when he is not upset by success or failure. The most important readiness factors for Moore are the abilities to sit, speak, and listen to a natural language (he has developed other procedures for the deaf).

The Language Experience proponents tended to accept the conventional wisdom on readiness. Six is the beginning age for their program. However, in contrast to the prevailing view, they did not consider readiness tests or success with readiness workbooks a valid indication of actual readiness. Theirs was a more comprehensive view, expressed by one proponent as follows:

> There are wide individual differences among children, much more than we think. The less mature will make slower progress in reading. Therefore, it is wise to explore their maturity—muscular, mental, perceptual. We must differentiate instruction for these children, and pay more attention to activities that will build their maturity so that they may learn with less difficulty. I don't think we can identify readiness by a test, nor can we develop readiness with a little reading-readiness workbook that provides activities in visual and auditory perception. A good readiness program in kindergarten is an activity program—natural, incidental, work and play. Slower children need a longer kindergarten period, and not an emphasis on specific exercises. Kindergarten should be without reading and without specific perceptual training. We should educate the whole child.

Each proponent's view on readiness was closely related to his definition of reading and to his "method." Those with a complex definition of beginning reading tended to have a larger conception of readiness and to advocate a later start. Those who defined beginning reading in terms of learning to decode tended to favor an earlier start and had a more specific conception of readiness. For them, readiness training involved learning to identify and name the letters.

The alphabet reformers, although they generally did not favor early teaching, believed that simplification of the alphabet (in relation to the sounds of English) would make the task easier. Hence, reading instruction could be initiated earlier.

Another factor bearing on an early start was the pupil-to-teacher ratio. Omar K. Moore could be sure of the success of such an early start because his children were taught individually—one teacher (or machine) to one pupil.[8]

The Language Experience proponents, as well as the basal-reader proponents, on the other hand, placed great emphasis on mature reading right from the start. In their view, the child needs to be more mature intellectually, perceptually, emotionally, and socially to benefit from these methods. Furthermore, since the LE approach is less systematic than the basal-reader approach, it requires a greater degree of readiness for success.

One Scottish headmaster said:

> Oh, I know you in America start later than we do. But then you expect your beginner to do more difficult things. We expect our beginners to learn to know that c-a-t is "cat." For that, we find the age of five quite satisfactory.

MOTIVATION

The different groups of proponents were less consistent on the question of whether the child is motivated by his interest in the stories and pictures or by his desire to master the process or skill of learning to read. Generally, though, their opinions formed a continuum, with the Language Experience proponents and the basal-reader proponents toward the content end; the phonics proponents somewhere in the middle; and the linguists, alphabet reformers, and Omar K. Moore toward the mastery end.

All three basal-reader authors agreed that interest in content and mastery of skills are both important. It is not a matter, they said, of appealing to the child either through his interest in content *or* through his pleasure in mastering the process of learning to read; we must appeal to him on both counts. However, as they amplified their statements, they gave evidence of putting greater stress on content. For them, the child masters the process because he is interested in what he reads.

One author said:

> If the child is bored, he will give up. But if he is truly interested, he will master the skills. We want the child to master the skills, but not through fear of failure.[9]

At this point, the series editor described a recent visit to a first-grade class in which the children were using one of the supplemental systematic-phonics programs. He was shocked by the amount of scratching and masturbating that went on in the room during the phonics lesson!

[8] In this connection, see Holmes (1962).

[9] Note here that skill mastery is associated with difficulty and failure.

> Basically, I go along with our ex-editor who said that no child will work to improve his mind. He reads to find out what happens next. That is why we try to put the very best kind of story with the very best kind of ending in our series. Teachers don't know why our stories are good, but they are. We follow two basic formulas for plots—one where a situation develops and is resolved, and the other where the situation changes into a surprise ending where something completely unanticipated happens.

The author of another series said:

> Mastery is important for interest, but our approach is the other way around. We try to attain mastery through a motivated approach.

Another basal-reader author put it a bit differently:

> It is not an either/or thing. The two go together. For beginners, the motivational factor is not a very important one, except for a few children who come from such desolate homes and backgrounds that reading does not have much meaning for them. Most middle-class children come to school wanting to learn to read.[10] For them, the problem is almost immediately one of broadening their interests to include children's literature. I don't quite agree with Bloomfield's point that mastery is the major motivation to appeal to, and that it matters little what the child reads. I don't think a child has to read ten *vans*[11] to learn to read. We can use materials that are interesting to most of them. The family adventure stuff is saccharine, yes, but mostly to adults.

Although mastery was important to the Language Experience proponents, their keynote was "vital interest in content" on the part of the individual child. They put strong faith in the child's need to communicate and express himself, a need they regarded as the source of his desire to read and write. The acquisition of skills, they claimed, is incidental; the child will learn the skills because he must fulfill this need.

Most of the phonics proponents held that both interest in content and mastery of the skills are essential. The two cannot be separated, they said.

The linguists and the alphabet reformers were again closest in their views. They believed that both appeals are important. But no one in these two groups gave interest in content first priority.

Omar K. Moore's position on motivation varies considerably from that of all the others. He discourages any emotional reaction on the part of his teachers (or his computer) to the child's success or failure. The primary motivation, according to Moore, should spring from the child's natural curiosity and desire to learn to read. The child's reward comes

[10] This statement suggests a dilemma: Most basal series are written to appeal to the largest number of children (the middle class), but according to this author, these may be the children who need the story appeal least.

[11] See Chap. 1 and Appendix A for an analysis of the Bloomfield System.

from his own discoveries and achievements. There is no need to entice and "sugarcoat." The child *wants* to learn. In fact, he *needs* to learn as much as he needs to eat and sleep.

ORAL VERSUS SILENT READING

Whether oral or silent reading is preferable is generally not considered to be a controversial issue; but after reading the various criticisms (and the defenses) of prevailing methods, I sensed an underlying disagreement on the question. Should the beginner do more oral than silent reading? Should he *say* the words he learns, or should he respond to them implicitly? This question, as we shall see later, is closely related to another—whether the primary emphasis in beginning reading should be on *word recognition* or on *meaning*.

The opinions of the different proponents were divided much as they were on the readiness issue.

The basal-reader and Language Experience proponents stressed silent reading. The phonics proponents were divided. Most shared the views of the linguists, the alphabet reformers, and Omar K. Moore, all of whom preferred oral reading. However, all proponents agreed that silent reading is the more mature, the ultimate response.

One basal-reader author was quite certain that silent reading should be the predominant *beginning* response mode:

> Oral reading should not be done except for "prepared audience" purposes or diagnosis. Generally, I believe that the child should get away from oral reading as early as possible. He can do silent reading after he learns to read about sixty words. There is a chance for him to read with comprehension and meaning when he gets away from lip movements and word-by-word reading.

Another basal-reader author said:

> It depends on the purpose. If diagnostic, then oral reading should come first. If for interpretation and meaning, silent first. The goal is to get as soon as possible to silent reading and normal speech patterns in oral reading.

Only one of the three basal-reader authors admitted that he did not know exactly why silent reading should precede oral reading, although all basal-reader manuals recommend it:

> We may be wrong. This is where the new research may come in. We used to say that oral reading is harder, that the child is faced with problems of exact pronunciation, interpretation, and intonation. Teachers keep saying, "How did Joey really say it? Read it the way Joey said it. Read with expression!" This kind of thing really introduces more difficulties.
>
> The linguists say that it is much harder to do silent reading. That is an assumption that they are making. We may both be wrong.

The Language Experience proponents appeared to be less concerned than the others with the distinction between oral and silent reading. Basically, they believed that they had the reading-for-meaning problem solved. As one proponent put it:

> There is no differentiation between oral and silent reading in the primary grades under a Language Experience approach. If the child wants to read his story out loud, he does. If a given child continues to read orally, we are not afraid that he will always read orally and become a word caller,[12] because the content is meaningful. Therefore, it makes no difference whether his reading is oral or silent. Almost immediately, though, when the child has a mastery of the words, and begins to read books, he stops reading orally to himself, because he is alone and he realizes that he gets the story faster when he reads silently. It is an unconscious transfer as soon as he learns the skill, because everything is read for meaning. Language Experience approach children are after meaning all the time.
>
> Finger pointing and vocalizing will continue through second grade because words are not firmly mastered. We don't worry about that because it is a sign of immaturity, like learning to walk. It is not an indication of disability. It would become serious in the latter part of the third grade with an immature child who has not caught on to the reading "trick," and does not know the words.

The phonics proponents were not consistent. Again, six out of the nine said that oral reading is definitely the more essential form of practice at the beginning. The typical reason given was the following:

> Oral reading should come first until we are sure that the child can read accurately. Silent reading follows oral reading. If we emphasize silent reading too early, we can encourage the child to practice errors. We must be certain of accuracy in recognition first.

Three of the phonics proponents, the same three who adhered to the prevailing basal-reader view on readiness, agreed with the prevailing view on oral reading. While acknowledging that oral reading is important, they believed that silent reading should *precede* it. The reason given was that "oral reading is an art and children need the time to look over the words silently first, so that they can read smoothly."

The linguists, alphabet reformers, and Omar K. Moore definitely considered oral reading the major and primary response mode for the *beginner*. While they recognized that efficient silent reading is the ultimate goal of reading instruction, they insisted that the beginner should respond *orally* to the printed symbols. The following was a typical reply from the linguistic group:

> Silent before oral reading is ridiculous. Even if we think it is silent, it is really subvocal speech. Silent reading is a later development.

[12] Note here the questionable assumption that oral reading usually leads to "word calling" or "reading without meaning."

A typical reply from the alphabet reformers was:

> Oral reading is essential for feedback to visual symbols. If the child is to develop a phonetic sense, he must have enough oral practice for the phonetic relationships to become conscious. But with irregularities, it would only be a handicap.

Omar K. Moore said:

> Silent reading should be a later development, other things being equal. We want to hook up reading with speech. If the child reads orally, you know at least that he has gone over the word. If he reads silently, it is harder to test him. We can only quiz him on the content if he reads silently, and that is hard to do.

Here again, we see an alignment that reflects differences in the way the various groups define beginning reading. The basal-reader authors and some of the phonics proponents tend to view the child as a miniature adult who, from the beginning, must be encouraged to engage in mature reading; they therefore stress silent reading from the start. In fact, they assume that oral reading, which they seem to view as "platform" or "diagnostic" reading, is more difficult. The linguistic proponents, the alphabet reformers, most of the phonics proponents, and Omar K. Moore accept the linguistic definition of beginning reading, i.e., the transfer of the spoken word to its printed equivalent. Hence they stress oral reading at the start.[13]

WORD RECOGNITION VERSUS WORD COMPREHENSION AS THE FIRST OBJECTIVE

Two of the basal-reader authors felt that it is important, in fact necessary, to stress word meaning over skill and accuracy in recognizing words, arguing that as the child grasped the meaning of a word, he would also recognize it.

One expressed his view as follows:

> I don't think recognition of a word can be accomplished without knowing its meaning.[14] Therefore, the two must go hand in hand. The true understanding of a word is

[13] See Chap. 6 for the views of researchers investigating reading disability in backward readers who have not yet progressed beyond the early stages of learning to read.

[14] In this connection, I quote one of Harry Levin's anecdotes, his first approximation of a definition of the major component skills in reading:

"A man received a letter in a foreign language that he spoke fluently but could not read. He had a friend who could make the sounds indicated by the writing, but who understood nary a word. (This, incidentally, is not strange to those who have learned the ritual use of Hebrew or Latin.) The man who received the letter took it to his friend who said the words that gave joy to the recipient of the missive. Which one was reading? . . ."

"I suggest that, as a first approximation, reading may be broken into two broad sub-skills. The first is the skill of decoding the writing system to its associated language. English orthography is an impressive and complicated representation of the

important. Even a word like *father*—a man married to mother, with children—may not be understood. Having worked a lot with slum children, I know it is not always clear. Not even with a child of superior social class.

The other said:

Recognition is always in terms of meaning, not in terms of identification only. Our definition of perception is that it must have meaning, yet we recognize that identification is important. Certainly we don't go along with the philosophy of some authors that all words should be gotten from context. Even the first letter is not enough. We have to give the beginner a consonant framework. But always within a sentence, and where individual words are worked with, a combination of context and phonics.

The third basal-reader author—the one who questioned other aspects of the prevailing view—stated that word recognition can be separated from meaning:

Word recognition can be done separately. I think it is fine to teach the alphabet and word parts, as part of a game. How much emphasis should be given to each—recognition or meaning—depends on the child. If the child is disadvantaged, and limited in language, then more emphasis should be given to meaning. With upper-level, suburban children, the emphasis need not be on meaning. The teacher can go directly into skills. A good teacher varies her method to the needs of the pupils.

The Language Experience proponents were even firmer than the basal-reader proponents; they believed that recognition cannot possibly be separated from meaning. One Language Experience proponent stated their position as follows:

Recognition and understanding are completely one. The recognized word is always related to understanding. Understanding of the word always comes first, because the child has experienced it and has expressed it. There is no separate drill in this program on word recognition apart from meaning, except as words are extracted from a meaningful context. There is practice and repetition of words, but only after the initial experience with the same words in meaningful and larger units. The writing is indispensable to this. Writing and copying take the place of phonics drill.[15]

Among the phonics group, three out of nine were firmly convinced that the major emphasis at the beginning should be on recognizing words

sounds of the language. . . . In one form or another, the child must learn this code. Most importantly, teaching must be oriented to making access to the code completely automatic—to make the code transparent.

"The second rubric of component skills in reading concerns the use of the code—the written version of the language—for the many uses to which reading may be put. This category includes comprehension, reading for different levels of meaning, reading for pleasure, and so forth. By dividing the process of reading into these two very broad categories, I am not implying that one is more important than the other or that emphasizing one skill excludes the other. I am frankly at a loss to understand the furor that this essentially bland statement arouses. To say that reading is really comprehension is like saying that ice skating is really performing figure eights!" (Levin, 1966, pp. 139–140)

[15] Compare Grace Fernald's view on the same issue, as discussed in Chap. 6.

and learning the relationships of sounds and letters. Six of the nine, however, stated that meaning is just as essential as recognition and that both must be stressed at the beginning.[16]

The following are some excerpts from the replies of the phonics proponents:

> As soon as a word is sounded, it should be defined.
>
> Both recognition and meaning should be stressed right from the start. Separating them is a false dichotomy.
>
> Both are important. I see no reason for recognizing a word if its meaning is not known.[17]

The alphabet reformers were also divided on this point. One advocated stress on both recognition and meaning; two said that recognition should be given greater emphasis; and one said that the issue does not exist when reformed alphabets are used, since all things are made easier by modifying the alphabet. One did not respond.

Only the linguistic proponents and Omar K. Moore stated definitely that one should be stressed over the other. They agreed that essentially, the major task in beginning reading is learning to recognize words. The first grader, they felt, already knows the meanings of the words he reads; therefore, meaning is really *not* the instructional problem.[18]

USE OF WRITING AND SPELLING

We find a break in the usual alignment on the issue of whether writing (and spelling) should be taught along with reading. The linguistic pro-

[16] It is interesting to speculate why most of the phonics proponents were so close on this point to the basal-reader proponents. Perhaps the phonics proponents wished to placate their critics by minimizing their differences on this "crucial" aspect of the philosophy of the prevailing view. Or is it that, theoretically, they accept most of the assumptions of the prevailing approach? The fear of producing word callers, especially since systematic-phonics methods have been accused of doing just that, perhaps makes them insist that word meanings are as essential as word recognition right from the start.

[17] If children really followed this principle, they might never increase their vocabularies through reading. Carried to its logical conclusion, the statement implies that no child would attempt to sound a word and hence discover that he did not know its meaning. Only if a word does not sound familiar do we have any idea about whether the meaning is known to us.

[18] The *published* "linguistic" programs do, however, check the child's understanding of what he reads. Why? Is it that such programs can be accepted in schools only if they do not differ too much from existing programs? Or is it, perhaps, that preliminary trials have shown that too much emphasis on recognition results in loss of meaning? My guess is that by including reading for meaning these proponents are adjusting to existing theory and current classroom practices. The critics of the prevailing methods no doubt adopt some current ideas to get their programs accepted, while the defenders, in turn, incorporate some of the concepts of their critics in areas where they feel themselves to be vulnerable.

ponents were closest to the basal-reader proponents. They, too, believed that reading should precede writing.[19]

In principle, the basal-reader proponents accept the "integration of the language arts." In practice, however, only listening, speaking, and reading appear to be integrated in the published conventional basal-reader programs. The teachers' manuals accompanying the basal readers recommend little writing as part of learning to read.[20]

The phonics proponents were divided on this issue. Some recommended no writing; some recommended considerable writing and spelling as the children learn to read. Others advocated dictation and early writing of the letter-to-sound correspondences. Generally, though, the phonics proponents associated with schools tended to recommend that spelling and writing be taught later, in grade 2—a procedure followed in most schools.

The alphabet reformers were strong proponents of early writing as reinforcement for reading and for learning the sound-letter correspondences. They also stressed early "creative" writing. I think their views on writing probably reflect the influence of the system followed in the English infant schools, where all children write a great deal from the very beginning, at age five. Early writing is not, as I see it, an integral part of alphabet reform, but an import from the English infant schools. However, the greater regularity of spelling permitted by ITA may give the child an earlier confidence in spelling words he has not been taught.[21]

CONTENT OF BASAL READERS

All groups agreed that the content of basal readers can be improved. The authors of the basal readers, as would be expected, were generally the least critical. One offered these comments:

> The stories are interesting, humorous, universal in their appeal, and we are constantly trying to make them more appealing in terms of psychological reality—and as a pattern of the American way of life.
>
> The content is ideal for the purpose. The readers tie in with the known concepts of the children, especially at the early levels. As a skills program, the series are sensible. The preprimers have been emphasized too much. They are really a slight part of the total program. We could have more scientific materials, especially at the

[19] In actual practice, they teach spelling with reading, since words are spelled out by the teacher when they are first taught. However, the linguistic proponents generally do not have the children write even these words. See, for example, Fries et al. (1965), where only two references to children's writing and copying of words (pp. 69 and 81) appear in a manual of 107 pages.
[20] See Chap. 8 and Appendix A.
[21] See in this connection Chap. 4, p. 121, and Chap. 9, pp. 273–277.

> beginning. Basically, though, I consider the basal reader a carrier of skills and vocabulary and, therefore, the interest is not so much an issue.[22] However, the materials should be as interesting as possible. Therefore, we use pictures.

Another said:

> Our own books start with a story of a family—white, middle-class, suburban. By the primer, we include folktales and soon go into literature. The family is a device which may or may not be justified. The critics emphasize this, and you would think it is nothing but this throughout the primary grades. But we do introduce very early the heritage of children's literature. If I had my choice, I would start with folk tales and fairy tales. I tried to write a preprimer fairy tale but found it extremely difficult.

The alphabet reformers held views similar to those of the basal-reader authors. Although they felt the stories could be more interesting, they accepted the view that the content should be chosen, not only for its intrinsic value, but for its suitability to the teaching method.

The phonics group was highly critical of the basal-reader content, especially of what they termed the "watered-down" beginning books. This opinion fits in with their view that a faster start can be achieved with a phonic method.

Omar K. Moore felt that the existing beginning materials are either stupid, or dull, or clumsy—in fact, insipid. "The readers need more poetry, fables, and a greater intellectual challenge," he explained.

The linguistic proponents were the least critical of the content of basal readers; they recognized, of course, that their method also places a limitation on content, although of another kind. Since they select words for beginning reading materials on the basis of spelling regularity, they, too, cannot make their stories as interesting as they would like.

The Language Experience proponents were the most critical of the story content of the basal readers, stating that children found them dull and not "vital," especially at the preprimer, primer, and first-grade levels.

VOCABULARY CONTROL

All three basal-reader authors agreed that some kind of vocabulary control is needed. They did not feel, as their critics do, that the basals "over-control" words.

One author said:

> We need the control of vocabulary because we try to develop skills and don't wish to clog up the material with word difficulties. When I was learning Russian, I felt like a child learning from a preprimer.

[22] This contradicts somewhat this group's belief, reported above, that the child's interest in the stories is of greater importance in motivating him to learn to read than his desire to learn *how to read.*

> I am impatient with critics like Trace.[23] What they are doing is looking at reading in two ways: recalling their childhoods and looking at reading matter as adults. It is a problem for a child, as for an adult, unless he is a scholar, to continue reading when the books are loaded with concepts.[24] The average child won't do it.

Another basal-reader author believed that vocabulary control had been overemphasized in all beginning reading programs:

> There are other factors in difficulty—length of sentence, dependent clauses, unusual constructions, unusual sentence patterns. Our vocabulary, too, has been controlled on the basis of useful, high-frequency words but not on phonetic regularity. Although we try to select words that are generalizable phonetically, we can't seem to do this too well at the beginning of grade 1. We have to develop supplementary materials for that. This is a dilemma for all textbooks. High frequency is related to meaningfulness and to spelling irregularity.

The phonics proponents, as a group, saw the need for control but felt that words could be introduced at a faster pace than they are now in most of the basal readers. They seemed to accept the idea that control should be on the basis of frequency and "meaningfulness."

The linguists, on the other hand, called for a different kind of control—one based on spelling regularity.

The alphabet reformers were divided. Some recognized that vocabulary control is necessary at the beginning; others stated that the basal readers are now too repetitious and that a modified alphabet obviates the need for vocabulary control.

The Language Experience proponents were definitely opposed to the vocabulary control of the basal readers, stating that it was too rigid and made for dull stories: "If a word is known and interesting to a child, even if it is a 'difficult' word, he will learn and remember it."

Omar K. Moore said: "You have to start some place, and that is with the child's own vocabulary."

ILLUSTRATIONS

The basal-reader authors expressed opinions on the importance of illustrations that ranged from certainty that the pictures were fine to some real doubt about their worth; none, however, seriously questioned the need for pictures.

[23] See Trace, *What Ivan Knows That Johnny Doesn't.*

[24] Learning to speak and read a foreign language appears to be confused here with learning to read one's native language. Upon entering first grade the typical English-speaking child has about four thousand "concepts" (Lorge and Chall, 1963); he has probably been familiar with the concepts in the typical conventional basal reader for grades 1, 2, and 3 since the age of three. The hurdle for the first grader is to learn to recognize in print the concepts he already knows. This is no small feat. Therefore, all programs require some control in introducing words.

One author said:

> The pictures are necessary for setting the background and for developing attitudes. They show emotions and how the children feel.

Another said:

> There is no evidence that pictures are harmful. We have no evidence that there are too many. As far as I am concerned, I like a novel with pictures. From the point of view of children, if the illustrations are artistic, there is an appeal to them. In the preprimer, it is part of the method where there is a picture-word approach.
>
> In the first grade the pictures are a big part of the word-analysis program.[25] By the second grade, they are not as important. Even in the third grade, children find delight in the pictures as much as in the book. But there is no question that there may be a delimiting effect of pictures on concepts and creativity. Maybe we can have fewer pictures, but the competition keeps us from cutting down.

The third author had no strong feelings about pictures one way or the other:

> Probably the basals overdo the pictures. We have a variety of artists and try for realistic styles now. But we don't have too much evidence on the value of the pictures. Our use of pictures may be too fancy compared to the rest of the world. I don't know if the rest of the world is right about this.

The phonics proponents tended to feel that most beginning reading programs contain too many pictures. Most believed that pictures are helpful in motivating the child or for illustrating something unknown to him, but that they may draw his attention away from the words.

The linguists and Omar K. Moore essentially agreed on the question of illustrations. They felt that the pictures in most beginning books are too prominent and too colorful, that they serve no useful purpose, and that they are often distracting. However, they considered illustrations useful for picturing unknown objects.

The alphabet reformers were generally noncommital on this issue. But one noted that "illustrations are an important selling point for teachers. Teachers can't select readers on important criteria so they use irrelevancies, like illustrations."

The Language Experience proponents criticized the illustrations used in most beginning reading programs because, they said, they are not representative of our population. But one did remark, "You must have illustrations because of competition."

ORGANIZATION OF CLASSES

Reading can be taught to a whole class at a time, to several small groups within a class, or to each pupil individually.

[25] Compare with my findings in Chap. 8.

Questioning the proponents of various approaches about what kind of organization they favored uncovered differences of opinion within each group. Nevertheless, some trends could be distinguished.

The basal-reader proponents stated that all forms of organization have their place and should be used, as their manuals recommend. However, they tended to favor some form of within-class grouping as the major organizational pattern. Individual instruction and self-directed learning (as proposed by the Individualized Reading proponents) were also mentioned as important, especially as the children acquire greater skill. Whole-class teaching was favored least, although it, too, had its place, "especially for some activity like reading to the whole class, discussion, and later, for dictionary work."

Five of the phonics proponents preferred whole-class teaching, especially for phonics practice. The other four, like the basal-reader proponents, favored small, within-class groups organized according to ability. Individualized instruction was favored least by the phonics proponents.

The linguists and alphabet reformers advocated leaving classroom organization up to the teacher. They were confident that getting each child to read and move at his own pace would be relatively simple because their systems were so logical and would facilitate the task of learning to read.

The Language Experience proponents were, of course, in favor of complete individualization, arguing that "each child is an individual and has different interests." They did acknowledge the need for some group work, but opposed whole-class teaching.

Omar K. Moore also favored individual instruction, but for different reasons. For him, it was a matter of differences not in "vital" interests but in the opportunity that individual instruction affords the young learner to explore his environment; a large class, which requires didactic teaching, diminishes the child's desire to explore and learn on his own.

There appears to be some relationship between the proponents' views on method and their opinions on classroom organization. Since most of the systematic-phonics programs (although not all) depend on didactic teaching—with the teacher explaining and the children practicing the sound-letter relations—the majority of the phonics proponents favored whole-class teaching. However, note that nearly half favored the prevailing practice of breaking the class into small groups, even for phonics instruction. Those who advocated small-group instruction were either teachers or supervisors.

A more important factor in determining organizational preference, I believe, is the broader educational philosophy held by a given proponent. Those who tended toward a "progressive-education" philosophy generally opposed whole-class teaching in principle. They preferred either within-class groups or completely individualized instruction. Those who did not favor progressive education seemed to prefer whole-class teaching.

TEACHING BY PARENTS

The basal-reader authors agreed that some form of parental aid is good, but they were concerned lest the parents take over the professional role of the teacher. The following statement represents the views of all three authors:

> Parental aid is a good thing in general. Sociologically, more and more parents are college graduates and, therefore, can be enlisted to help their children. But the teacher has to make some of the professional choices, such as when the child is going to use phonics. She knows best. The role of the parent is supplementary. Parents can see to it that the child has many books to read. Parents can also read to and with the child. But certain professional decisions have to be made by the curriculum director and by committees of teachers. We should help support parents more, though.

One of the authors was quite opposed to direct teaching by parents. He criticized a current experiment in which parents are instructed (via TV classes and manuals) on how to prepare their preschool children for beginning reading by teaching them the letters and their sound values. He did note, however, that *his* father had taught *him* to read before he entered school. "But this was part of our culture," he said.

Generally, though, the basal-reader authors leave the decision about parental aid to the individual school. Their reading consultants speak at PTA meetings. But as senior authors, they do not follow a general policy of "pushing" parents into helping their children since "in some communities the parents themselves are illiterate."

The phonics group was divided on the issue of parental instruction, with only three favoring direct teaching by parents. Those who were directly involved in the elementary schools, either as teachers or supervisors, tended to believe, as did the basal-reader authors, that parents should "help," but not "teach," and that even the help should be guided by the child's teacher.

The linguistic group believed that parents *can, should,* and in fact *do* do much direct teaching.

The alphabet reformers in general said that parents should help only under guidance from the child's teacher. (This was predictable, since parents do not know the modified alphabets and would find it difficult to teach them to their children.)

The Language Experience proponents advocated only informal teaching by parents: "Parents should read to the child. If the child shows an interest, the parents can show him how to form letters, etc."

Only Omar K. Moore was definitely and emphatically opposed to all parental aid. As he put it, "I do my best to keep parents out of it—or more generally, 'significant others.' This is important to keep it autotelic, i.e., free of extrinsic rewards and punishments."

FAILURE IN READING

When I asked why some children fail to read, I received replies that reminded me of the fable of the blind men and the elephant.

The basal-reader authors gave long lists of combinations of causes involving the child himself, his family, our culture, and the school situation. Most often cited were overcrowded classes; poor instruction; unprepared teachers; sociological changes; lack of good reading materials; and emotional, psychological, and physical handicaps in the child. The only reference to methods came from one of the basal-reader authors, who stated that if the same method were used for all children, some might develop problems.

The phonics proponents invariably named "wrong method"—the prevailing one, of course—as the primary cause of reading failure. As a group, they were convinced that a "phonics-first" method would eliminate most reading failures. Most of the phonics proponents acknowledged that some children have personal handicaps that prevent them from learning, even with a phonic method. However, they believed that a stronger phonic emphasis can prevent many of these failures.

As a group, the linguistic proponents also believed that a change in the prevailing methods would reduce the number of reading failures—a change to a linguistic approach, that is.

The alphabet reformers, as would be expected, held that the irregularity of English spelling was responsible for reading failures. "Our language confuses the brighter child even more than the duller one," said one of the inventors of a modified alphabet. "A change in methods will not make any difference. Both the phonic and sight methods have failed in the past. What we need now is a more sensible alphabet."

READING TODAY AND FIFTY YEARS AGO

Are children reading less well today than they did fifty years ago? The basal-reader authors all said "no." In fact, they ventured, children may be reading better now. As evidence they cited greater use of library books, increased sales of all kinds of reading matter, and more widespread reading in general.

The Language Experience proponents agreed with the basal authors, stating that there is more library-book reading now than ever before.

Seven of the nine phonics proponents also answered "no." But they did note that because of social and cultural changes we all need to know more today, and hence we need to read better. Two phonics proponents (neither one directly connected with the schools) were convinced that children *are* reading less well now than they did fifty years ago. These two were so convinced that when asked for the evidence, they replied that the fact was obvious.

The linguists, as a group, said that they really did not know.

The alphabet reformers replied "definitely no," or "I haven't the slightest idea," or "we need to do better now."

Omar K. Moore noted that reliable evidence is difficult to obtain, although our standards today may be lower than those held fifty years ago "if we compare 'educated people' with 'educated people.'" But, he emphasized, this may be an outcome of larger social and cultural changes: a loss of respect for exactness and formality in all areas of modern living that may also be reflected in speech, spelling, and grammar.

The almost overwhelming agreement on the part of most proponents—both those favoring the current methods and those calling (indeed, screaming) for reforms—that reading standards have *not* suffered since the shift away from the phonic methods of the early 1900s struck me as rather odd. If this is true, what is the reason for the angry accusations in popular articles and books that have been critical of the prevailing view? Apparently many critics of the prevailing methods use such accusations as attention-getting devices, but few are willing to commit themselves to a face-to-face evaluation because of lack of evidence.

We now have some answers to the question, What is the great debate all about? It is about many facets of the process of teaching children how to read—some theoretical, some very concrete. What makes children interested in learning to read? When should they start? What material should we give them to read? Should they read it silently or orally? What, after all, is reading at the beginning—is it naming or sounding letters or is it comprehending and reacting to stories? And so on and on and on. Nevertheless, if we consider the approaches independently of historical patterns, we see them as falling roughly into two groups. Stated as simply as possible, the distinction between the two is this: One group (let us call it the "code-emphasis" group) believes that the initial stage in reading instruction should emphasize teaching children to master a code—the alphabetic code. The other (the "meaning-emphasis" group) believes that children should, and do, learn to read best when meaning is emphasized from the start.[1]

In terms of the debate, the many issues may be boiled down to one big question: Do children learn better with a beginning method that stresses meaning or with one that stresses learning the code?

This question, with its many ramifications, underlies the rest of this book.

[1] See the classification of twenty-two current reading programs in Appendix A for a detailed presentation of the bases for this division and a summary of the major differences between the two categories.

2

THE EVIDENCE: RESEARCH ON BEGINNING READING INSTRUCTION

DO children learn to read better with a beginning method that stresses reading for meaning or with one that concentrates on teaching them how to break the code? The research on this question is copious and varied.

Most of this research is experimental, and most of the experiments have taken place in classrooms, where it is extremely difficult to control all *relevant conditions, rather than in the laboratory.*

Laboratory experiments usually involve only one aspect of method, all other conditions being carefully controlled. For example, is it better to learn words or letter-sound correspondences first—"better" or "worse" being measured by the ease of learning new words? Such a question was asked by Bishop (1962), who answered it by analyzing the test results of word-taught, letter-taught, and nontaught (control) groups of subjects.[1] *Laboratory experiments are particularly valuable in that they permit the study of basic questions and in that more conditions can be controlled than in classroom experiments: Teachers invariably make adjustments in methods to suit their own style of teaching. Thus it is unfortunate that until quite recently there have been very few laboratory experiments dealing with the beginning reading process. More such experiments are being carried on today and will be in the future, particularly because of encouragement and support from the USOE's Project Literacy program.*

[1] See Chap. 4, pp. 115, 116, for a discussion of this experiment.

Classroom experiments—the typical kind of research carried on by students of beginning reading methods—usually take the form of comparison between Method A and Method B. Under this research design, several first-grade classes are taught by Method A (let us call them the experimental group) and several other first-grade classes are taught by Method B (let us call them the control group). After two years, all the children are given the same tests. If the group using Method A scores significantly[2] *higher on the tests (e.g., of oral reading and spelling, selected because they are considered good measures of what both methods are trying to accomplish), then it may be concluded that Method A is better than Method B*—but only *for oral reading and spelling, for the kinds of children tested, and for the end of grade 2.*

Will Method A continue to be better for the same children after five years? Will it be better after two years with children who are duller or brighter than those originally studied? A longer follow-up period (retesting at the end of fifth grade) is needed to answer the first question, and other classroom experiments with brighter and duller children are needed to answer the second. Furthermore, a classroom experiment cannot tell the investigator anything about outcomes he has not tested. Thus, he can say nothing about the greater "love of and lifetime use of reading" by the children taught under Method A as compared with Method B unless he retests or interviews the same children as adults—which, incidentally, no one has done.

Even the limited conclusions permitted by each classroom experiment are valid only *if we can reasonably assume that the experimental and control groups do not—before and during the experiment—differ in ways that may influence how they learn*

[2] This is usually thought of in terms of statistical significance. That is, the difference should be one that would not, as determined by standard statistical formulas, be found by chance alone.

to read or spell. Thus, it is essential for the researcher to determine and report that his experimental and control groups are about equal in terms of intelligence, socioeconomic status of parents, and other personal-cultural factors that may influence reading achievement. Also, the teaching should be of the same quality, the instructional time in reading should be equal, and so forth. In other words, it is incumbent upon the investigator to "equate" the two groups in anything that may in itself influence results for good or bad. If this cannot be done when the experimental and control groups are first formed, it should be done through the use of proper statistical procedures when the results are analyzed.

Classroom experimentation is further complicated by the need to define clearly each of the methods compared—how they differ and how they are similar. As we shall see later, lack of such definition has been one of the greatest stumbling blocks in the design of these experiments.

Another kind of research that is relevant to the problems of beginning reading methods is associational, or correlational, rather than experimental. In correlational research the essential questions asked are: What goes with what? And under what conditions? For beginning reading, such questions have been asked as: What is the relationship between a child's knowing the alphabet (naming the letters) in kindergarten and his reading achievement at the end of first grade? Do those children who knew more letters in kindergarten (all other conditions being equal) know how to read better at the end of grade 1? Or, what is the relationship between knowing the sound values of letters (scoring high on a phonics test) and reading comprehension (score on a standardized silent reading test) in the third grade? Do third graders who read better know more phonics?

If the researcher finds, for example, that phonic ability is highly correlated with reading ability—that is, if high scores on the phonics test accompany high scores on the reading test–he still does not know which is the cause and which the effect, or whether both are effects of a more fundamental cause. To determine which causes which, he must consider the findings of experimental research and, ultimately, formulate a theoretical position.

Still other research relevant to beginning reading has been carried on in the clinic in the form of case studies. The aim of clinical research is to determine why certain individuals perform as they do. Why, for example, do some children fail to learn to read? Or learn slowly and with great difficulty? How can they be helped to do better?

While clinical research can be extremely informative, one of its major pitfalls is that the findings may be limited to the particular cases studied.

The different kinds of research have generally been carried out by investigators from different disciplines. The laboratory experiments have, on the whole, been the province of the experimental psychologist. The classroom experiments and correlational studies have been conducted by educational psychologists and others interested in educational research (graduate students of education, administrators, classroom teachers). The clinical studies have been carried out by neurologists and psychiatrists as well as by psychologists.

Each group has tended to publish its findings in journals read by those of similar background and interest. Indeed, reading research may be said to have three cultures–the laboratory, the classroom, and the clinic. Seldom have the three groups' findings on similar questions been integrated.

Section 2 reports the research findings from these three cultures. Chapter 4 presents a synthesis and interpretation of the experimental research from the classroom and laboratory. Chapter 5 presents a synthesis of the findings from the correlational studies. And Chapter 6 takes up the evidence from several well-known clinical studies of children who have failed to learn to read. Chapter 3, the opening chapter, sets the scene with a discussion of the nature and state of the research in beginning reading.

Before we examine the intricacies of the research, I shall present here a brief summary of my findings. But I urge the reader to read all the chapters in this research section, for it is important to know not only what the researcher has found, but also how he found it—what he used as evidence and how he reasoned to arrive at his conclusions.

My analysis of the existing experimental comparisons of a meaning emphasis versus a code emphasis tends to support Bloomfield's definition that the first step in learning to read in one's native language is essentially learning a printed code for the speech we possess. It does not support the prevailing view that sees the beginning reader as a miniature adult who should, from the start, engage in mature reading. Early stress on code learning, these studies indicate, not only produces better word recognition and spelling, but also makes it easier for the child eventually to read with understanding —at least up to the beginning of the fourth grade, after which point there is practically no evidence.

Although the experimental studies confirmed the definition of beginning reading proposed by most linguists, our analysis neither proved nor disproved that their methods (or those of the alphabet reformers) were better than other code-emphasis methods, e.g., systematic phonics.

The experimental research provides no evidence that either a code or a meaning emphasis fosters greater love of reading or is more interesting to children. Nor does it tell us whether one commercially published code or meaning program is better than another. It does, however, show us that the two emphases produce different learning patterns.

There is some experimental evidence that children of below-average and average intelligence and children of lower socioeconomic background do better with an early code emphasis. Brighter children and those from middle and high socioeconomic backgrounds also gain from such an approach, but probably not as much. Intelligence, help at home, and greater facility with language probably allow these children to discover much of the code on their own, even if they follow a meaning program in school.

The correlational studies support the experimental finding that an initial code emphasis produces better readers and spellers. They show a significant relationship between ability to recognize letters and give the sounds they represent and reading achievement. Although knowledge of letters and their sound values does not assure success in reading, it does appear to be a necessary condition for success. In fact, it seems to be more essential for success in the early stages of reading than high intelligence and good oral language ability.

The clinical studies of pupils with reading problems indicate that both code and meaning approaches produce reading failures.

There is some evidence that an initial reading method emphasizing "word," "natural," or "speeded" reading produces more serious failures than one emphasizing the code. The remedial treatments described in these studies all concentrated on teaching the pupil to decode printed words, and they all reported success in helping the disabled reader eventually to read normally—*i.e., with speed, comprehension, and appreciation.*

In short, the clinical reports analyzed give us reason to believe that a stronger code emphasis would help prevent reading failure, although never eliminate it entirely: There is sufficient evidence to show that such failure stems also from the personal characteristics of the learner.

Very little of the research evidence tells us about differences in results with the two kinds of approaches at the end of fourth grade and beyond. We might hypothesize, however, that whether the code emphasis keeps its advantage in the intermediate or upper elementary grades and beyond depends on how reading is taught in these grades. If the reading programs do not put enough stress on language and vocabulary growth and provide sufficiently challenging reading materials, the early advantages may be dissipated.

THREE

Research on Beginning Reading—Science or Ideology?

ONE OF THE MOST important things, if not *the* most important thing, I learned from studying the existing research on beginning reading is that it says nothing consistently. It says too much about some things, too little about others. And if you select judiciously and avoid interpretations, you can make the research "prove" almost anything you want it to.

What I have learned, too, or at least hope to have learned, is humility. As a result of reading the research of others, interviewing leading proponents of different approaches, and talking informally with administrators and teachers, I have been struck by how easy it is to misinterpret research findings. The best of us can be led into making too hasty conclusions and overgeneralizing from limited evidence. Therefore all of us concerned with reading—laymen, teachers, experts in reading, critics of various approaches—should question whether we have been rigorous enough in our search for evidence.

Since we look to the researchers for our facts, however, we are bound to turn our gaze on them first, to ask, How good a job have you done?

RESEARCH RATIONAL OR EMOTIONAL?

The answer is disturbing. Taken as a whole, the research on beginning reading is shockingly inconclusive.

Why should this be the case? Educational researchers have, after all, devoted more time and effort to the study of reading than to any other school subject.

Despite the volume of research, we could hardly have expected the reading specialists to have produced better results than they did, according to a study by David Wilder (1966). They were never given the institutional support that scientists require if they are to produce definitive research. The schools of education where the researchers studied and worked were cut off from essential contacts with research activity in the basic sciences; these schools did not even offer full-time research positions until quite recently. Furthermore, reading research has never received financial support on the scale and over the period of time required to yield reliable answers to questions that needed answering. Instead of conducting much-needed high-quality research, therefore, the reading specialists turned to teaching courses, speaking at conferences, and giving workshops on reading. Or they engaged in clinical practice and remedial reading or wrote instructional materials for children.

Since research was largely a part-time interest of a minority of experts—indeed, only 1.6 percent of reading experts queried in 1963 by Barton and Wilder (1964) received half or more of their income from research bureaus or projects—it is not surprising that it exhibits serious failings.

The research in beginning reading has generally been inadequate in both depth and scope. The questions it has attempted to answer have usually not been answered well. Other important questions have not been asked at all.

Most studies of beginning reading, it seems, were undertaken *not* because they grew logically out of previously published studies that needed further refinement in order to build a unified theory about the reading process. Instead, it appears as if researchers usually wanted to buttress a strongly held view about a method or practice that was already in use or that was a reaction to one in use in a particular school system at a particular time. Thus, they attempted to answer such practical questions as: Which method is better? When is the best time to start? When the researcher obtained an answer, he seldom went beyond to investigate *what* in the method or practice produced better results and *why*. We can identify a series of practical questions of this type that have been researched over and over again, the most recent studies going very little beyond the earlier ones. In fact, some of the older classroom experiments, particularly those carried out by Gates, were more firmly grounded in a theory of the reading and learning process than the more recent ones.

The research in beginning reading has also been parochial. Like scientists in other fields, especially in the social sciences, these researchers have been influenced by the philosophical assumptions and social problems of their time, both in selecting problems and, more particularly, in drawing conclusions and making recommendations.[1] Such influence is inevitable, since no one can escape the time in which he lives. However, a researcher must be aware that the present will be tomorrow's past, just

[1] See, in this connection, Huey (1908), especially chap. XV, "The Views of Representative Educators concerning Early Reading." Even before any extensive empirical research was undertaken on the *when* and *how* of beginning reading instruction, Huey cited the views of "our foremost and soundest educators" who were "profoundly dissatisfied" with reading as it was then carried on. Among the things that displeased them were "premature reverence for books . . . and a neglect of own [sic] thinking which has atrophied the naïve originality of the children and made them slaves to 'what is written. . . .' "

Huey continues, "As child nature is being systematically studied the feeling grows that these golden years of childhood, like the Golden Age of our race, belong naturally to quite other subjects and performances than reading; and to quite other objects than books; and that reading is a 'Fetish of Primary Education' which only holds its place by the power of tradition and the stifling of questions concerning it. It is believed that much that is now strenuously struggled for and methodized over in these early years of primary reading will come of themselves with *growth,* and when the child's sense organs and nervous system are stronger; and that in the meantime he should be acquiring [his] own experiences and developing wants that will in time make reading a natural demand and a meaningful process, with form and book always secondary to [his] own thought."

Huey then quotes Dewey (New York Teachers' Monographs, November, 1898) and comments as follows: "Professor Dewey says that while there are exceptions, present physiological knowledge points to the age of about eight years as early enough for anything more than an incidental attention to visual and written language-form. . . . While the fetish of Greek is passing, there remains, he says (in "The Primary Education Fetish," *Forum,* vol. XXV) the fetish of English, that the first three years of school are to be given largely to reading and a little number work. This traditional place was given to reading in an early century, when the child had not the present environment of art gallery, music, and industrial development, but when reading was the main means of rising and was the only key to culture. Reading has maintained this traditional place in the face of changed social, industrial, and intellectual conditions which make the problem wholly different.

"Against using the period of six to eight years for learning to read and write, Professor Dewey accepts the opinion of physiologists that the sense organs and nervous system are not adapted to such confining work, that such work violates the principle of exercising the fundamental before the accessory, that the cramped positions leave their mark, that writing to ruled line forms is wrong, etc. Besides, he finds that a certain mental enfeeblement comes from too early an appeal to interest in the abstractions of reading." (pp. 301–305) Thus, a later start and a meaning emphasis seem to have been recommended as early as 1908, long before the 1920s and 1930s when the research findings were gathered.

as it was yesterday's future. He runs grave risks if he ignores what has gone before.

A sense of perspective has also been lacking, to an even greater extent than in the researchers themselves, in the interpreters and summarizers of research on beginning reading. They have tended to overgeneralize findings, especially those that fitted into prevailing educational views. They have paid only slight attention to studies that did not support these views. And they have tended to find all kinds of justification for their stands, even when faced with contradictory evidence.

Too often, the interpreters and summarizers have forgotten that no single research study can stand by itself, that each must be seen in the light of other relevant research on the reading and learning process. If we are to gain lasting benefits for theory and practice, the research must be interpreted periodically as new evidence comes to the fore, not only in reading but also in psychology, linguistics, medicine, sociology, and other disciplines. This, unfortunately, has not been done often enough in the field of reading in general and beginning reading in particular.

These are strong statements. Let me illustrate what I mean with a few examples.

We are still debating when is the best time to begin reading instruction. The study that has had the greatest impact on the prevailing theory and practice was one reported by Mabel Morphett and C. Washburne in 1931. From a comparison of the mental abilities and reading achievement of first graders in the Winnetka, Illinois, schools, Morphett and Washburne concluded that a mental age of six and one-half was probably the best age to start formal reading instruction.

Subsequent studies by Washburne and others appeared to confirm the conclusion that a start at this relatively late age produced better results. In fact, considering a mental age of six and one-half ideal for beginning became part of the conventional wisdom as expressed in most textbooks for teachers on the teaching of reading and most published reading programs in the United States. Even Fred J. Schonell, whose textbooks on the teaching of reading have probably been the most widely used in England, seemed to favor a mental age of six (1948), while all around him five-year-olds were learning to read in the English infant schools, and nannies in upper-class homes were teaching youngsters to read even before they entered these schools.

Did the research really "prove" that a child must reach a mental age of six or six and one-half before he can benefit from beginning reading instruction? Yes, if we ignore the study reported by Arthur Gates in 1937, only six years after the Morphett and Washburne study. Gates found in one of four classes he studied that children with mental ages as low as five could cope successfully with first-grade reading. Who was right?

If we examine both studies, we must conclude that both were intrinsically valid; yet both were relevant only for the particular situations studied. The Morphett-Washburne findings make sense when we realize that the children they studied were an intellectually superior group: The median mental age at the beginning of grade 1 was about seven. The standard of success (for their first graders) was quite high, and instruction was based mainly on independent silent reading. In such a situation, a child with a mental age below six, not quite ready to do most of the learning on his own and aware that he was less able than the other children, might well be judged a "failure" according to the stringent definition of reading success used by the investigators.

The classes Gates studied had a more normal IQ distribution in terms of the general population. Also, they used easier materials, and the children seem to have received more direct and differentiated instruction. Thus, a child with a lower mental age found himself in a better position to learn. Furthermore, Gates's criterion of success was less stringent.

AND THERE IS A TIME FOR RESEARCH . . .

What is of even greater interest, however, is that the Gates study received only minor attention in the summaries of research and in the textbooks on methods of teaching reading. Why? Probably because Gates's findings ran counter to the current mainstream of educational thought and practice. In the 1930s and 1940s the ideal school was a child-centered institution; its purpose was to provide activities that would encourage the child's inner growth and his emotional and social development. The more informal the program, the better. Educators put little faith in specific training, relying mostly on activities they felt would foster growth and maturation. In fact, they actually feared imposing training on the child lest it frustrate him and produce not only small or no gains in learning but also permanent dislike of the activity taught and permanent personality damage.

Now the climate of opinion has reversed. The first sputnik propelled the United States into a great push toward academic achievement. Then research by Dolores Durkin (1964) and others[2] indicated that younger

[2] See Fowler (1962) for a post-sputnik summary of pre- and post-sputnik research on early learning. Significantly, although much of the evidence on early learning has been in existence for a long time, it has really only been put to use after the first sputnik was launched.

children can and do learn to read and that an earlier start may be better than a later one.

We are less concerned at present with social and emotional development and more with academic achievement. The conventional wisdom appears to be changing from "the later the start, the better," to "the earlier the start, the better." This trend is also seen in the various head-start programs for culturally disadvantaged preschool children and in the current renaissance of the Montessori schools, some of which begin reading instruction at age four.

Which position is correct? Time—and the failures that this new set of assumptions may bring—might provide some answers. But it will not be easy to find out unless we follow the children in these new "experiments" over a long period of time. We will be debating this issue again and again unless we undertake—with the kind of financial support that has generally been lacking—long-term longitudinal studies designed to test out fully the effects of either an early or a late start.

It is interesting to ponder whether the studies of Durkin and others would have engaged the interest of investigators during the 1930s and 1940s. I venture to guess that had they carried out their studies then, their findings would have been largely ignored or would have gotten lost in the shuffle, and thus their research would have "said" nothing to us.

That this supposition is not unfounded is suggested by what happened to the writings of Bloomfield and other linguistic scientists on how to begin reading instruction. During the past several years one could hardly pick up an educational journal or attend a conference on reading without finding some discussion of linguistics and its potential contribution to beginning reading instruction. As reported in Chapter 1, beginning reading materials based on "linguistic principles" are coming off the presses at a fast and furious pace, and at least two major books on linguistics and reading have appeared since 1962—Fries (1962) and Lefevre (1964).

Is it that the linguists have only recently completed significant research that they are now making available to us? No. Their findings and recommendations have been known for a long time. As early as 1942 Bloomfield published his two articles in *Elementary English Review* criticizing the then prevailing beginning reading methods and materials, which relied on vocabulary selected primarily on a meaning-frequency basis, and recommending instead a vocabulary based on spelling regularity. Even earlier than that, in *Language* (1933), he made his basic recommendations on the application of linguistics to the teaching of reading and spelling. The Bloomfield teaching materials, which have only recently been published (1961 and 1963), were also written about that time.

Why were Bloomfield's recommendations and materials ignored for so long? The reason is probably to be found in the educational preference of the time. In 1942, when Bloomfield outlined his criticism of beginning reading instruction, most reading researchers and practitioners were convinced that a less formal approach to education in general, and to reading instruction in particular, was desirable. They were veering away from formal teaching. Bloomfield's recommendations and his instructional materials smacked too much of formality, of dull drill, and of the old-fashioned phonics from which they were trying to escape.

Over and over again, if we look back into the research on beginning reading, we find that almost every issue debated and experimented with today has been the subject of study and experimentation at some time in the past. The studies made by Donald Durrell and his students (1958) on the importance of knowing the alphabet (identifying letters by name) for beginning reading success were preceded by the studies of Frank Wilson and C. W. Flemming published in 1938 (see Chapter 5). Durrell came to essentially the same conclusions as Wilson and Flemming. But somehow these earlier works were "lost" and were seldom mentioned in summaries of research.

Even Pitman's ITA is not new in principle. Using modified alphabets as the first step in learning to read has been tried and researched in the past (Winch, 1925). Yet this research appears to have been lost from view during certain periods, only to be revived again at a later date, often under the guise of new discoveries and under new labels.

WHY DON'T WE LEARN FROM THE PAST?

There are many reasons why we don't. Probably the most important one is that most researchers have been concerned more with answering specific practical questions than with accumulating tested knowledge and developing theory. Indeed, most of the research in beginning reading has been the work of teachers and administrators who were interested—and rightly so—in answering practical, timely questions. They undertook one small study either as a doctoral or master's thesis or as "action research." Few of the really major figures in the field of reading instruction have done the major research.

The reading field has also suffered from a dearth of synthesizers and theorists—people who pull together the evidence from the hundreds and thousands of small studies and try to build theories. Of course, the task of synthesizing is always difficult. But it has proved particularly so in the area of beginning reading instruction. Even on the most basic issues of beginning reading—the very definition of beginning reading, what it is and what its goals should be—clarity and agreement have been rare, as I have shown in my overview of current innovations (Chapter 1) and in my analysis of the views of various proponents on issues in the current debate (Chapter 2). Much of the heat expended in the present debate stems from disagreement on the definition and goals of beginning reading and from the many related issues arising from this disagreement. Unfortunately, while researchers have implicitly agreed on the ultimate goals of reading instruction, no one has conducted experiments to test how effectively a method develops the qualities of mature reading implicit in these goals. Thus, a critic could always state that although a given method might result in the child's recognizing words or understanding a passage better than another method, it was not more effective in terms of attaining a goal of reading that he believed to be more important.

A good illustration of this is the study of the value of systematic phonics in early reading instruction reported by Donald Agnew in 1939. Agnew found that an early, relatively heavy, and consistent emphasis on phonics in grades 1 to 3—as compared with a later, lighter, and less consistent emphasis—resulted in significantly higher scores on tests of phonic ability, accuracy of oral reading, word pronunciation, eye-voice span, vocabulary, and some aspects of silent reading comprehension (ability to follow directions and recall details). However, a heavier phonic emphasis did not significantly improve accuracy and speed of silent reading or other aspects of silent reading comprehension (predicting outcomes and reading for general significance).

Agnew concluded from his findings:

> If the basic purpose in the teaching of primary reading is the establishment of skills measured in this study (namely: independence in word recognition, ability to work out the sounds of new words, efficiency in word pronunciation, accuracy in oral reading, certain abilities in silent reading, and the ability to recognize a large vocabulary of written words), the investigations would support a policy of large amounts of phonetic training.[3] *If, on the other hand, the purposes of teaching primary reading are concerned with "joy in reading," "social experience," "the pursuit of interests," etc., the investigations reported offer no data as to the usefulness of phonetic training.* (p. 47, emphasis mine)

Tracking down the different interpretations of Agnew's conclusions proved to be an interesting bit of detective work. Agnew's study, some writers reported, indicates that an early emphasis on phonics promotes attainment of some important goals of beginning reading. Others, however, said that although Agnew found early, heavy, and consistent phonics to be a significant advantage in terms of word recognition, it did not affect interest!

The point is that no method has ever been systematically tested in

[3] Phonics training.

terms of pupil interest. Yet over and over again, a particular method is said to be more interesting, to produce readers who are more interested in reading, and therefore to be preferable. As would be expected, the "more interesting" approach is often the one favored by the researcher himself.

Until there is some agreement on the major goals of beginning reading, it will always be possible to reject experimental findings by conveniently shifting goals. It is easy to say, "Yes, you found greater gains for some goals of reading, but not for those I think important."

Imprecise terminology is another cause of difficulty in synthesizing research findings. Throughout the experimental literature, methods are called *look-say, sight, word, phonic, alphabet, sentence, natural, organic, eclectic,* and now *linguistic.* Seldom are these labels fully defined, and what one author calls a *sight* method another may call a *combination sight and phonic* or an *eclectic* approach. What W. H. Winch (1925), for example, called *look-say* is closer to the Bloomfield-Barnhart (1963) *linguistic* approach of today. Even the same terms have undergone historical changes; a *word* method of 1920 seems quite different from a *word* method of 1960.

A third difficulty is that researchers in reading, like researchers in other scientific fields, have looked to acclaimed leaders in their field to set the framework for the design and interpretation of their investigations. It is difficult to understand why, in the face of a great deal of experimental evidence showing more favorable results for a code emphasis, so many researchers either have failed to acknowledge their own and others' findings or have suggested that a code emphasis fulfills minor objectives only. Yet phenomena of this type are quite common in the natural and physical sciences as well.[4]

[4] See Kuhn (1962) for a discussion of how resistance to "new scientific truth" has characterized the history of the natural and physical sciences. He writes: "In the past [this strong resistance] has most often been taken to indicate that scientists, being only human, cannot always admit their errors, even when confronted with strict proof. I would argue, rather, that in these matters neither proof nor error is at issue. The transfer of allegiance from paradigm to paradigm is a conversion experience that cannot be forced. Lifelong resistance, particularly from those whose productive careers have committed them to an older tradition of normal science, is not a violation of scientific standards but an index to the nature of scientific research itself. The source of resistance is the assurance that the older paradigm will ultimately solve all its problems, that nature can be shoved into the box the paradigm provides. Inevitably, at times of revolution, that assurance seems stubborn and pigheaded as indeed it sometimes becomes. But it is also something more. That same assurance is what makes normal or puzzle-solving science possible. And it is only through normal science that the professional community of scientists succeeds, first in exploiting the potential scope and precision of the older paradigm and, then, in isolating the difficulty through the study of which a new paradigm may emerge." (pp. 150–151)

Some light is thrown on this situation by the writings of the late William S. Gray, acknowledged leader of, and spokesman for, reading experts for four decades; major summarizer and interpreter of reading research; and author of America's leading basal-reader series, the Scott, Foresman & Company series.[5] In 1948, in *On Their Own in Reading,* a book dedicated to "all who guide children in their efforts to acquire independence in word attack in reading," Gray views with alarm the swing, since 1900, from one extreme ("an undue emphasis on learning the form and sound of separate words")[6] to its opposite ("guessing from context with little attention to the visual form of words").[7] At the same time, however, he dramatically poses the question: "Shall we, in response to public demand, reinstate the old mechanical phonic drills and content that inevitably result in dull, word-by-word reading?"

You can guess the answer. To Gray, and to other leaders in reading, phonics meant a return to "drill" and the "dull content" of the phonics readers of the early 1900s. Gray explains his objection as follows:

> In the very nature of things, reading material constructed on this artificial basis [words selected on phonic elements previously taught] was certain to lack continuity of thought. Indeed, pages of such primers and first readers may be read almost as effectively by beginning with the last sentence and reading to the top of the page as by reading in the usual way from top to bottom. (p. 19)

He reproduced a page from the Beacon primer, a phonic reader of 1912, to illustrate his points.

I reproduce the same page, together with a page from Gray's own primer, which selects words and content for "meaningfulness" and "continuity of thought," and I invite the reader to try both pages from bottom to top, as well as from top to bottom.

In my opinion, both are improved by being read from bottom to top. They have more punch! At the same time, I imagine we could debate at length which is the duller.[8]

What is essential, however, is that Gray assumed that an early emphasis on phonics (or decoding, in our terminology) led inevitably to

[5] Gray was coauthor, with William Elson, of the 1930 edition and senior author of the 1940 and 1950 editions.
[6] My code emphasis.
[7] My meaning emphasis.
[8] Actually, it is possible to write interesting readers with either kind of restriction. Dr. Seuss has done so, and so have many others who have followed his lead. See his *Hop on Pop,* a veritable phonic or linguistic reader that controls words on a common phonic-element or spelling-pattern principle, and *Green Eggs and Ham,* a book that contains only fifty high-frequency words common to primers and first-grade readers in the conventional basal-reading series. Both are published by Beginner Books, Random House.

Reproductions of:

Page 50 of the Beacon Primer, 1912 (a phonic reader) *	Page 41 of *The New Fun with Dick and Jane*, 1956 (a meaning reader) †
Black and white ink drawing of a horse	*Full-color illustration of Dick jumping over blocks with entire family looking on*
My name is Dick.	*Do What I Do*
I am a big horse.	"See me jump," said Dick
You may pat me.	"Oh, my! This is fun.
You may ride me.	Come and jump.
Will you ride on my back, Tom?	Come and do what I do.
I will not run fast.	Look, look!
I will not kick.	Who can jump?
I will not jump.	Who can do what I do?"
I will stand still.	
I like to have Tom ride on my back.	
I can run like the wind.	

* *From J. H. Fassett,* Beacon Primer, *Ginn and Company, Boston, 1912.*
† *From W. S. Gray et al.,* The New Fun with Dick and Jane, *Primer of* The New Basic Readers, *Scott, Foresman & Company, Chicago, 1956.*

dull content and that it also made for mechanical, "word-by-word" reading, which impedes comprehension and enjoyment. As an alternative, he gave his endorsement to the "meaning-first, word-analysis later" approach that was adopted by his own and most other basal-reading series. This endorsement had formidable effects. As A. Sterl Artley noted in his foreward to the 1948 edition, "[The] worth [of this approach] has been demonstrated in our schools so convincingly that today his philosophy, ideas, and procedures—even his nomenclature—are not only generally accepted but are being incorporated into most instructional materials."

I have painted a rather dismal picture here, and some perspective is in order. The confusions and difficulties that arise when generalizations are derived from existing research are not peculiar to the field of beginning reading. They characterize other fields in education as well.

Until quite recently researchers in reading have had to do their thinking and investigating on a shoestring. When we consider that most of the early research was done by professors, teachers, and administrators in their spare time and with the occasional help of a doctoral or a master's student, it is surprising that we know as much as we do.

The support that is now being made available for educational research by private foundations and government is reason to take a more optimistic view of the future.[9] Even more encouraging is the growing trend toward buttressing the research with a firmer theoretical basis from other disciplines, particularly psychology and linguistics.[10]

Finally, I certainly am not saying that the research has been valueless. If this were in any way the case, there would be no point in analyzing it at length, as I do in the remainder of this section.

[9] It will not all be clear sailing, however. More research may engender more confusion if it is not synthesized and put into a meaningful framework. Furthermore, while large research budgets may give us the wherewithal to uncover more facts, a sense of humor and simple honesty are needed if negative findings are to be reported from, say, a ½- or 1-million-dollar research project carried out over a five-year period, or even longer. Indeed, more research will require more people to read, sift through, and make sense out of the findings resulting from it. We will need, most of all, the few who have the imagination and insight to create the theories which may then be confirmed or denied by years of careful research.

[10] See, for example, the *Project Literacy* reports.

FOUR

Experimental Evidence on Approaches to Beginning Reading

WHEN I SET ABOUT examining the experimental research, I found myself facing some important problems: What research should be considered? How was it to be found? How should it be read and analyzed? How could the results of all these studies be synthesized into some valid findings and conclusions? And so forth.

These may appear to be naïve concerns, especially when one is dealing with a body of research that has been reviewed many times before. However, reviews of this same research had led to very different conclusions and recommendations. Clearly, the way in which to review it was a crucial point.

SELECTING AND ORGANIZING THE EXPERIMENTS

I selected the experimental studies from references in all the relevant sources known to me. I do not claim to have included all experimental studies on the big question of a code or meaning emphasis, but I believe that I sought out, with equal persistence, references cited by both the critics and the defenders of currently prevailing meaning-emphasis programs. The bibliography at the end of the book lists all the studies considered.

The studies chosen were then sorted according to the questions they seemed to be asking. I narrowed them down to four groups concentrated on the following four questions:

1. Which achieves better results—a look-say or a phonic method?

2. Which achieves better results—a method that teaches more phonics or one that teaches less?

3. What do experimental comparisons involving a linguistic approach tell us about the values of such an approach?

4. What do experimental comparisons involving the use of modified alphabets tell us about the benefits of these innovations?

I also asked a fifth question: Do the experimental studies indicate that the effectiveness of the various methods depends on characteristics of the individual child being taught—his mental ability and his socioeconomic background? In other words, is one method better or worse for the bright or the dull, for the rich or the poor?

EXTRACTING THE "TRUTH" FROM EACH STUDY

Since previous summaries based on practically the same body of experimental research had arrived at conflicting conclusions, I knew before starting that a major problem was how to read the research. Reading abstracts of the studies and their authors' conclusions would not suffice. Instead, I would have to look at each study carefully and to ask such questions as why it was made; how the author defined "reading"; what methods and materials were being compared; what the size, age, grade level, and other characteristics of the population studied were; how the author defined reading "success"; what care was taken to assure comparability of the groups studied; and so on. To this end my associates and I listed all the important conditions that could influence the outcome of a study, and we checked each study against the list (see Appendix B, Schedule I).

As I had suspected beforehand, practically none of the studies specified all these conditions. Most did not indicate how the experimental and control groups were selected, how much time was allotted to various aspects of reading, how the teachers were selected, whether the quality of the teaching was comparable in both groups, or even whether the teachers followed the methods under study.[1] Even more important, most studies did not specify clearly what a "method" involved, but instead merely assigned labels (e.g., "phonics"), expecting the reader to understand what was meant.

Many of the early studies did not use standard measures of outcomes or statistical tests of significance to determine whether the various results obtained could have been attributable to chance differences. At the same time, some of the first studies, with their small populations, "homemade" tests, and simple statistical techniques, had many strengths that the later, more statistically sophisticated ones lacked, and I included them for that reason. The studies of Buswell (1922), Gates (1927), Gates and Russell (1938), Winch (1925), and Valentine (1913), for example, were more thoroughly grounded in theory (whether of the learning or of the reading process), used more imaginative instruments to test the different components of reading, and were more analytic in presenting test results. Also, they tended to "look at the learners," describing in considerable detail how the children under study approached words, what errors they made, their attitudes toward reading, how their teachers reacted, etc.[2]

This kind of analysis is virtually nonexistent in the recent comparisons, which often present results only in terms of tests of significance on various subtests of standard instruments. Seldom do the investigators try to explain what in fact these various subtests are measuring.[3] Notable exceptions are the studies by MacKinnon (1959) and Daniels and Diack (1956 and 1960). The latter devised instruments to measure different outcomes, and MacKinnon did a very rare and worthwhile thing—he observed the day-to-day reading performance of children on different kinds of reading material, in addition to testing at the end of the experiment.

Although most studies were unsatisfactory in some respects, I assumed that all the authors were honest researchers searching for honest answers, and I looked for the grains of underlying truth to be found in

[1] Indeed, in one of the recent USOE first-grade studies referred to earlier and summarized briefly at the end of this chapter, we found that there was a considerable variation in the way the teachers followed a given method and in the results they achieved with it. We found little relationship between what they said they did and what they actually did during reading lessons. But what they actually did with the method made a difference in pupil achievement (Chall and Feldmann, 1966).

[2] See especially Gates (1928).

[3] See in this connection the most recent of these comparisons—the cooperative first-grade studies supported by the USOE and reported in *The Reading Teacher,* May, 1966.

each study. Had I considered only studies that fulfilled all necessary experimental conditions, I would have been left with just a handful—if that many.

In analyzing the studies I gave priority to the authors' findings rather than their conclusions, and for a very good reason: Many authors drew conclusions that seemed to go counter to their own findings. Every researcher runs the risk of generalizing his findings beyond his data. To counter this tendency, it is necessary to consider the author's conclusions in terms of both his findings and his assumptions. For example, Mosher and Newhall (1930) concluded that there is little advantage in a phonic over a look-say method, although results in eight out of the ten tests they gave the children favored phonics slightly. They justified their conclusion on the grounds that the two largest differences favored the look-say approach. Because Mosher's earlier study (1928) had also concluded that a look-say was better than a phonic method, although no comparison was made of the look-say experimental group with a control group taught by a phonic method, I felt that the investigators were perhaps too favorably disposed toward their own method and would tend to pull any "uncertainties" of their findings in the direction of their preference.

CLASSIFYING METHODS AND MATERIALS STUDIED

When a researcher says he is testing a phonic method, what does he mean?

As I have mentioned, few of the studies specified clearly what the methods being studied entailed. Often the labels and titles were misleading. Thus, Currier's study "Phonics and No Phonics" (1923) really compares varying amounts and kinds of phonics. Many investigators speak of *phonetics* (the scientific study of speech sounds) when they mean some form of *phonics.*

To account for this problem I set up my own classification system. I called a method "look-say" if the author stated that it taught no phonics at all and emphasized visual recognition of the whole word, "getting the thought," and reading whole sentences.

I classified as "systematic-phonics" programs those which taught phonics early and systematically—usually, but not always, before sight (whole) words. Such programs usually taught phonics separately from connected reading. The approach was often synthetic rather than analytic (i.e., the children were taught the separate letter-sound correspondences and were given practice in blending these sounds). Not all the programs classified as "systematic phonics" programs met all these criteria. However, they all put an *earlier, heavier,* and *more direct* emphasis on teaching the sound values of the letters than other programs with which they were compared.

I classified as "intrinsic-phonics" programs those which stressed sight or thought reading, introduced phonics later, and taught a more moderate amount of it—all *intrinsic* to meaningful reading, which was the supreme consideration. Children following these programs usually learned the sound values of letters through a process of analyzing known sight words. Other means of identifying words, e.g., context and picture clues, received greater stress than word analysis. Generally no separate period was set aside for phonics practice. There was some variation, however, on this last point and on the extent to which the phonics taught followed a preordered "system" or was based solely on the pupils' needs as determined by the teacher.

For linguistic and modified alphabet treatments I accepted the authors' classifications. However, as we shall see later, some programs that investigators labeled "linguistic" or "modified linguistic" can just as readily be classified as "systematic phonics."

The modified alphabet studies were easily classified.

Thus, we can place the systematic-phonics treatments at the far end of the code side of our code-meaning continuum; near them we can also place most of the linguistic approaches and the alphabet reforms. At the far end of the meaning side we can place the early look-say or "thought" methods that teach no phonics. Near them, though closer to the code side, we can place the intrinsic-phonics programs.

This classification is, of course, based on *emphasis*. All code programs, then as now, give practice in reading for meaning, and all meaning programs give practice in the code.

SYNTHESIZING FINDINGS

I noted above that different investigators used performance on different measures of reading success as a basis for concluding that one method was superior to another. Some used accuracy of oral reading; others, speed of reading or degree of comprehension. Some tested spelling; others spoke of "attitude toward reading." Still others tested a variety of outcomes.

I suspected that their conflicting findings were due, at least in part, to this diversity. Thus, to sharpen understanding of what "really occurred," I decided that results for the different measures should be tabulated separately. All aspects of reading do not necessarily improve at the same rate from year to year, and different methods may show different strengths and weaknesses at different times. For example, certain methods may equip children to perform better on one or two measures in the middle or at the end of grade 1, but when these children are followed up by further testing in later grades, their achievement may be less impressive than that of children who get off to a slower start using a different method.[4]

So for each experimental comparison, any available findings were tabulated in terms of the following eight measures of reading ability, grade by grade:

1. *Word pronunciation*—ability to read (pronounce) words on a list.

2. *Connected oral reading*—ability to read a selection aloud. Oral tests are usually scored only for accuracy, but the score may also be based on a combination of speed and accuracy.

3. *Phonics*—knowledge of letter-sound correspondences.

4. *Spelling*—skill in writing words from dictation. Some of the newer standardized tests measure spelling by having the child choose from among three misspellings of a word and one correct spelling.

5. *Vocabulary*—knowledge of word meaning. Sometimes called "word meaning" or "word reading," this is usually part of a standardized silent reading test. In grades 1 and 2 such tests usually require the pupil to select the one word out of four that matches a picture. At about grade 3 and above the child reads a "test" word and picks the one word out of four that defines it.

   A low score on such a test may mean either that the pupil does not know what the word means or that he cannot identify it (know what it says), or both. Thus, a vocabulary subtest on a standardized silent reading test measures an indeterminate amount of word comprehension, word recognition, and ability to sound out words not seen before. It also contains an element of guessing and test-taking ability. Because there is a time limit, rate of reading also may affect the child's score.

[4] This is essentially the point Guy Buswell made in 1922 in his *Fundamental Reading Habits: A Study of Their Development.* Buswell's thesis (based on eye-movement records and oral and silent reading tests of first-grade children taught by either a meaning or a code emphasis) was that each person has his own course of growth toward mature reading and that different initial teaching methods produce different patterns of growth. If we assume with Buswell and others that reading is a complex skill, we cannot accept, without further analysis, the assumption that performance on one measure of this skill necessarily represents performance on all other measures—or that one measure is necessarily the most essential at the beginning stage of reading. For example, high speed in the beginning may go with low accuracy. Further, one must consider which measures are most important at certain levels. We all agree that the *end product* of reading should be a high degree of comprehension, adequate rate, and a proper attitude. But do children taught by methods that produce such results at the beginning maintain these skills? This I hoped to learn by breaking down research results by outcomes on the different measures and by successive grades.

6. *Silent reading comprehension*—ability to understand material read. Sometimes called "paragraph reading," this is usually part of a standardized silent reading test. The child reads selections and answers questions to show that he understands them. Like the vocabulary subtest, the comprehensive subtest measures an indeterminate combination of skills and is affected by rate of reading.

7. *Rate of reading*—how quickly the child reads silently. Accuracy is not usually taken into account, although tests differ considerably on this.

8. *Interest,*[5] *fluency, expression*—these were grouped together because only one study (Currier and Duguid, 1916) reported on these measures, although no objective means of judging them was presented.

Look-Say or Phonics?

I found nine studies comparing a look-say with a phonic method—whether systematic or intrinsic. All but one were made before or during the 1930s, when the issue was mainly one of phonics versus no phonics. (After the 1930s, people were asking *how much* and *what kind* of phonics to teach, rather than *whether* to teach it.) Tables 4–1A and 4–1B present the findings of each study by measure tested and grade. In the table, "L-S" indicates that the look-say children scored higher, "SP" indicates that the systematic-phonics children scored higher, and "IP" indicates that the intrinsic-phonics children scored higher on a particular component.

What can we learn from these nine studies? First, the rather shocking fact that no studies tested beyond the second grade; even worse, *most* of the evidence—and it is limited evidence—is for the middle or end of the first grade.

Second, the different methods produced different results depending upon what was tested and when it was tested.

WORD RECOGNITION AND ORAL READING

On word recognition and oral reading, the phonics-trained children were ahead of the look-say children in both the first and second grades.

Valentine (1913) gives us some idea of why a phonic approach produced better results. Dividing test words into "taught" and "untaught"

[5] Gates (Gates et al., 1926) attempted to measure interest objectively in his comparison of "opportunistic" and "modern systematic" methods. That no one else reported results does not mean that many did not claim superior interest for this or that method.

Table 4–1A Summary of Experiments Comparing Look-Say and Phonic Methods
(Advantage in Grade 1)*

Experiment and methods compared	Oral word recognition	Connected oral reading	Silent reading: Vocabulary	Silent reading: Comprehension	Rate	Interest, fluency, etc.
Gill (1912) (L-S vs. SP)					L-S	
Valentine (1913) (L-S vs. SP)	High IQ SP (taught words) SP (untaught words) Low IQ L-S (taught words) SP (untaught words)					
Currier & Duguid (1916) (L-S vs. SP)	SP			L-S	L-S	L-S
Winch (1925) (L-S vs. SP)	SP	SP			L-S† SP‡	
Sexton & Herron (1928) (L-S vs. SP)			L-S (Jan.) SP	SP		
Tate (1937) (L-S vs. SP)			SP (Apr.)	L-S (Apr.)		
Gates & Russell (1938) (L-S vs. IP vs. SP)			IP (Feb.)	IP (Feb.)		
Tate et al. (1940) (L-S vs. IP)			L-S (March)	L-S (March)		

* Tests given at end of first grade unless otherwise specified. L-S = look-say; SP = systematic phonics; IP = intrinsic phonics.
† Irrespective of accuracy.
‡ Number of words recognized per minute.

(the latter contained the phonic elements taught to the phonics group), he found that children with phonics training generally had an even greater advantage on untaught words than on taught words. This would suggest that a phonic approach has a greater transfer value. A reanalysis of Valentine's results for the low-IQ group indicated that systematic phonics gives children the same advantage on untaught words, although the look-say approach seemed to help this group more with taught words.

COMPREHENSION AND VOCABULARY

On silent reading tests—whether of vocabulary or reading comprehension—results appear to have depended on when the test was given. The earlier the testing, the better the look-say groups performed. But by

Table 4–1B Summary of Experiments Comparing Look-Say and Phonic Methods (Advantage in Grade 2)*

Experiment and methods compared	Oral word recognition	Connected oral reading	Silent reading: Vocabulary	Silent reading: Comprehension	Rate	Interest, fluency, etc.
Gill (1912) (L-S vs. SP)					L-S	
Valentine (1913) (L-S vs. SP)	High IQ SP (taught words) SP (untaught words) Low IQ L-S (taught words) SP (untaught words)					
Currier & Duguid (1916) (L-S vs. SP)	SP			L-S	L-S	L-S
Sexton & Herron (1928) (L-S vs. SP)				SP (after 5 mos.)		
Mosher & Newhall (1930) (L-S vs. SP)			SP	SP	SP (NS)	
Tate et al. (1940) (L-S vs. IP)			IP	IP		

* Tests given at end of second grade unless otherwise specified. L-S = look-say; SP = systematic phonics; IP = intrinsic phonics; NS = not statistically significant.

the second grade, all except Currier and Duguid (who did not report test data, but only descriptive, qualitative statements) found an advantage for phonics—whether systematic or intrinsic.

I explain this as follows: Standardized silent reading tests are usually timed. They contain high-frequency words, often irregularly spelled. The children following a look-say method probably spent a greater amount of time learning these very words, while the children studying phonics were learning to associate letters with sounds. The look-say children also acquired a "set" for getting meaning; that is, using pictures and context to get the general thought. This helped them score higher on standardized silent reading tests which contain such aids. The phonics-trained children, especially those given more systematic-phonics instruction, acquired a set for accuracy in recognizing words and were preoccupied with letters and sounds (as noted in Currier and Duguid, 1916; Winch, 1925; and Gates and Russell, 1938). This kind of learning set pays off in oral, untimed tests of word recognition, but can lead to lower scores on silent, timed reading tests, especially in grade 1, when the average phonics-trained child has not yet acquired sufficient skill to "sound out" words that he cannot recognize immediately. This child concentrates on working out the words and has less time and energy left to devote to getting the thoughts. By the second grade, however, when the average phonics-trained child has mastered a sufficient amount of phonics knowledge and skill, he can devote himself more to meaning.

RATE

All studies testing rate of reading (with the exception of Mosher and Newhall, 1930) found that a look-say approach resulted in faster reading in both the first and second grades. One study, however, differentiated between rate measured irrespective of accuracy and number of words recognized accurately in one minute. Winch, testing first graders, found that the look-say group read faster when accuracy was not considered but that the phonics group recognized more words accurately per minute.

Mosher and Newhall found that their systematic-phonics group had a slight (although not significant) advantage in rate at the end of grade 2.

To sum up, our analysis of these look-say versus phonics studies indicates that an initial phonic approach (whether systematic or intrinsic) probably results in lower comprehension and rate at the beginning of grade 1 than look-say, but achieves better results in comprehension by the end of the second grade. A tenable hypothesis is that if given time, phonics is advantageous not only for word recognition but also for comprehension—one of the ultimate goals of reading instruction.

Most of the investigators making these studies—and most summarizers of these studies—did not interpret the findings as I have. The advantage for comprehension that a phonic emphasis produced at the end of the first or second grade was interpreted to mean that phonics should be delayed until then. (This seems a questionable interpretation, since a delayed phonics program was not actually tested. In fact, there is stronger evidence for the hypothesis that *early* training in phonics is required to produce higher scores on comprehension tests at the end of the first or second grade, even though it does not pay off for beginning comprehension. It is probably the cumulative effect that is crucial in producing the later advantage.)

Interestingly, only one study (Currier and Duguid, 1916) reported evidence on interest, fluency, and expression—and only in descriptive and highly subjective terms. The advantage on these, according to the investigators, went to the look-say group.

Systematic or Intrinsic Phonics?

I analyzed twenty-five studies that compared systematic and intrinsic phonics for beginning readers.[6] These are more recent than the studies discussed above. In fact, more have been reported in the decade between 1955 (when *Why Johnny Can't Read* appeared) and 1965 than in the period 1926 to 1953 (see Tables 4–2A through 4–2F).

Most of the investigators again tested only at the end of the first grade. Fewer made comparisons at the end of the second grade, and a still smaller number tested at the end of the third and fourth grades. Beginning with the fifth grade there are practically no data.

Though the evidence available on this issue is still deplorably limited, these experiments exhibit somewhat more scientific rigor than the older look-say versus phonics experiments. They show an increasing

[6] Additional studies brought to my attention after the major analysis was completed, as well as the most recent USOE-supported first-grade comparisons, are reviewed briefly later in this chapter.

Table 4–2A Summary of Experiments Comparing Systematic and Intrinsic Phonics (Advantage in Grade 1)*

					Silent reading	
Experiment	*Oral word recognition*	*Connected oral reading*	*Phonics*	*Spelling*	*Vocabulary*	*Comprehension*
Peyton & Porter (1926)						IP
Gates (1927)	E (Apr. & May)	E (Apr. & May)	E (Apr. & May)		IP (Apr. & May)	IP (Apr. & May)
Garrison & Heard (1931)	SP	IP		SP (bright) E (dull)		SP (bright) E (dull)
Gates & Russell (1938)					IP (Feb.)	IP (Feb.)
Russell (1943)	SP		SP	SP	SP	SP
Wohleber (1953)					SP	SP
Henderson (1955)					SP	SP
Sparks (1956); Sparks & Fay (1957)					SP	SP
Linehan (1958)		SP	SP		SP	SP
Bear (1959 & 1964)			SP		SP	SP
Bloomer (1960)					SP (date not given)	SP (date not given)
Bloomer (1961)					SP	E

* Tests given in May or June unless otherwise specified. SP = systematic phonics; IP = intrinsic phonics; E = equal.

Table 4–2B Summary of Experiments Comparing Systematic and Intrinsic Phonics (Advantage in Grade 2)*

Experiment	Oral word recognition	Spelling	Silent reading: Vocabulary	Silent reading: Comprehension
Garrison & Heard (1931)		SP (bright) E (dull)		E (bright) IP (dull)
Russell (1943)		SP		
Wohleber (1953)			SP	SP
Henderson (1955)		SP	SP	SP
Sparks (1956); Sparks & Fay (1957)			E	SP
Kelly (1958)			SP	SP
Daniels & Diack (1960)	SP			SP
Tensuan & Davis (1963)				IP (NS)
Duncan (1964)		SP	SP	SP

* Tests given in May or June. SP = systematic phonics; IP = intrinsic phonics; NS = not statistically significant; E = equal.

Table 4–2C Summary of Experiments Comparing Systematic and Intrinsic Phonics (Advantage in Grade 3)*

Experiment	Oral word recognition	Connected oral reading	Spelling	Silent reading: Vocabulary	Silent reading: Comprehension	Rate
Garrison & Heard (1931)			SP (bright) SP (dull)		E (bright) SP (dull)	
Agnew (1935 & 1939)	SP	SP		SP	SP (directions) SP (details) E (general significance, outcome, accuracy)	E
Wohleber (1953)				SP	SP	
Henderson (1955)			SP	SP	SP	
Sparks (1956); Sparks & Fay (1957)				E	E	
Gates (1961a)				E or IP†	E or IP†	E or IP†
Morgan & Light (1963)			E	IP	IP (Gates Basic) SP (NS) (Calif.)	
Tensuan & Davis (1963)					IP (NS) in English‡	
Duncan (1964)			SP	SP	SP	

* Tests given in May or June. SP = systematic phonics; IP = intrinsic phonics; NS = not statistically significant; E = equal.

† Several kinds of analyses were performed, two indicating approximately equal results, and one indicating somewhat lower achievement for SP children.

‡ Children were initially taught in Tagalog, the Philippine national language. Reading achievement was tested at the end of grade 2 in Tagalog and at the end of grade 3 in English.

Table 4–2D Summary of Experiments Comparing Systematic and Intrinsic Phonics
(Advantage in Grade 4)*

			Silent reading		
Experiment	*Phonics*	*Spelling*	*Vocabulary*	*Compre-hension*	*Rate*
McDowell (1953)		SP	IP	IP	IP
Sparks (1956); Sparks & Fay (1957)		E	E	E IP (accuracy)	E
Gates (1961a)			E or IP†	E or IP†	E or IP†
Wollam (1961)		SP	SP	E	SP
Edward (1964)	SP		SP	SP	SP

* Tests given in May or June. SP = systematic phonics; IP = intrinsic phonics; E = equal.
† Several kinds of analyses were performed, two indicating approximately equal results, and one indicating somewhat lower achievement for SP children.

Table 4–2E Summary of Experiments Comparing Systematic and Intrinsic Phonics
(Advantage in Grade 5)*

	Silent reading		
Experiment	*Vocabulary*	*Comprehension*	*Rate*
Gates (1961a)	E or IP†	E or IP†	E or IP†

* Tests given in May or June. IP = intrinsic phonics; E = equal.
† Several kinds of analyses were performed, two indicating approximately equal results, and one indicating somewhat lower achievement for SP children.

Table 4–2F Summary of Experiments Comparing Systematic and Intrinsic Phonics
(Advantage in Grade 6)*

		Silent reading		
Experiment	*Spelling*	*Vocabulary*	*Comprehension*	*Rate*
Bear (1959 & 1964)	SP	SP	SP (NS)	SP (NS)

* Tests given in May or June. SP = systematic phonics; NS = not statistically significant.

trend toward the use of standardized silent reading tests. The testing of reading rate almost disappears, with no reports for grades 1 and 2. Some do, however, test for spelling ability. Oral reading—both oral recognition (pronunciation) of isolated words and connected oral reading—receives relatively little attention (probably because by then these measures were already considered minor objectives). These studies do not report at all on interest, fluency, expression, etc.

Tables 4–2A through 4–2F summarize the results by different measures of reading achievement and by grade. As in Tables 4–1A and 4–1B,

I simply indicate the method that had the advantage on a particular test at a particular time, using SP and IP to stand for systematic phonics and intrinsic phonics, respectively; E (equal) indicates no difference in results with the two methods.

WORD RECOGNITION AND ORAL READING

Few investigators tested oral reading, but of those who did, all but one found the systematic-phonics group superior to the intrinsic-phonics group. Gates (1927) differed; he found both groups about equal. This might be because he tested early (in April and May of grade 1), before the systematic-phonics group had learned enough phonics to help them sound out the common, irregularly spelled words on the test.[7]

PHONICS AND SPELLING

The evidence on phonics knowledge is limited to the first grade. All studies (except Gates, 1927)[8] found that the systematic-phonics groups learned more phonics than the intrinsic-phonics groups.

Tests of spelling ability indicated either equal achievement or superior achievement by systematic-phonics groups—whether spelling was tested in grade 1, 2, 3, 4, or 6.

VOCABULARY AND COMPREHENSION

Most studies reported that children who were exposed to systematic phonics did better on standardized silent vocabulary tests at the end of grades 1, 2, and 3 than children who were learning from an intrinsic-phonics program. Beginning with grade 4, the evidence is more limited and also less clear-cut.

My explanation for this is as follows: Theoretically, the advantage that an early and heavy emphasis on phonics gives a child taking a standardized silent test of vocabulary is probably limited. In the lower grades most of the words on these tests are no doubt well within the meaning vocabularies of most children; thus a child's performance depends mainly on his ability to recognize the word. In the later grades this ability is still important, but differences in comprehension of word

[7] Recent correspondence with Gates offers another possible explanation. His intrinsic-phonics materials were extremely well programmed, teaching the alphabet along with the words. Thus, both groups probably received similar amounts of decoding practice.
[8] The reason may be that given in footnote 7.

meanings—i.e., in the child's general knowledge and experience—become more crucial.

The pattern that these studies show for silent reading comprehension is somewhat similar to that for vocabulary. Generally, systematic phonics appears to give more help than intrinsic phonics to the child taking a silent reading comprehension test in grades 1, 2, and 3. The advantage seems, however, to vary with the time of testing. In grade 1, it does not seem as great or as consistent as it does in grade 2. In fact, when children are tested early in grade 1, the intrinsic-phonics group may perform better (Gates, 1927; Gates and Russell, 1938). We can perhaps explain this in terms of learning set (discussed on page 107) and the nature of the standardized reading tests used in the studies.

By the end of grade 2, the systematic-phonics groups seem to have done decidedly better on these tests. By the end of grade 3, although systematic phonics still scores ahead, several studies report either no differences or advantages in certain aspects of comprehension only.

We lack enough evidence to be able to say anything definite about the effect of either systematic or intrinsic phonics on silent reading comprehension in grades 4, 5, and 6, except that the evidence does tend to disprove the long-accepted generalization that systematic phonics produces readers who *do not* read for meaning.

In this measure of reading ability, too, there is probably a limit on any advantage that systematic phonics might impart. In the early grades comprehension depends largely on recognizing words whose meanings are already known. Beginning in about grade 4, a child might be unable to grasp the meaning of, and the ideas conveyed by, all the words he is capable of identifying (i.e., of pronouncing). At this point his breadth of experience, his general intelligence, and other factors probably determine his reading comprehension test scores more than his ability to identify words (see Chapter 5).

RATE

The few studies that tested rate do not indicate any clear-cut trends. A systematic-phonics emphasis seems to have produced slower rates in grades 1 and 2 (see also the studies comparing phonics and look-say, which produced similar results), but not to have affected rate negatively in grades 3 and 4. In fact, two studies provide evidence (admittedly slim) that systematic phonics may contribute to a higher rate by grade 4. At least the existing evidence cannot be used to justify the often-repeated assertion that children who begin with systematic phonics become *slower* readers.

In summary, judging from the studies comparing systematic with intrinsic phonics, we can say that systematic phonics at the very beginning tends to produce generally better reading and spelling achievement than intrinsic phonics, at least through grade 3.

More specifically, the child who begins with systematic phonics achieves early superiority in word recognition. This superior ability may not always show up on standardized silent reading (comprehension and vocabulary) tests in the first grade. But, by the second and third grades, greater facility in recognizing words probably increases his ability to read for meaning, as measured by standardized silent reading tests of vocabulary and comprehension.

As for rate, systematic phonics may produce slower readers in grades 1 and 2 because it develops greater concern for working out the words. However, by the middle grades, rate seems to be about equal to that produced by intrinsic phonics.

Finally, there is probably a limit to the advantage that early facility with the code gives on comprehension tested after grade 4. After this point intelligence, experience, and language maturity probably become more important factors in success than ability to recognize words (see Chapter 5).

Additional Studies on Varying Amounts of Phonics

Three studies were called to my attention[9] after the above analysis was completed.

A 1955 study by the Committee on Research and Guidance of the Department of Public Instruction, Queensland, Australia, compared an experimental group (that I classified as intrinsic phonics) with a control group (systematic phonics). After three years the systematic-phonics group scored higher than the intrinsic-phonics group on tests of comprehension and attack on new words, and somewhat higher on tests of word recognition.

Strange as it may seem, but not unlike some previous researchers, the authors of this study concluded *for* intrinsic phonics, as follows:

> The evaluation of this experiment by objective tests does not demonstrate that either method produces clearly superior results.
>
> We are satisfied that the methods used in the experimental [intrinsic phonics] schools have produced intangible benefits that are not readily assessed quantitatively.

[9] By Theodore Clymer, of the University of Minnesota, and Mrs. Anne Hughes, former research director of the Reading Reform Foundation.

> The most important of these benefits is the arousal of interest in reading; associated outcomes are a lessening of the strain and stress on the child and a more active pupil participation in the reading programme. (p. 41)

A second study, by Santeusiano (1962), compared a heavier phonics load with the phonics component of a conventional basal-reader program. In April and June of the first grade, both groups were tested for knowledge of some aspects of phonics, silent reading (vocabulary and comprehension), word pronunciation, hearing sounds in words, and visual discrimination. The experimental group (receiving the heavier phonics load) achieved superior results on these tests.

The third study is described in an unpublished doctoral dissertation by Gold (1964). It compared 100 children in an experimental group using Phonetic Keys to Reading (systematic phonics) with 100 children in a control group using a conventional basal-reader program (intrinsic phonics) in the first grade. According to the dissertation abstract, on tests of oral and silent reading given at the end of grade 1, the group using basal readers was significantly superior in reading rate and made significantly fewer pronunciation errors. The systematic-phonics group made significantly fewer substitution errors. All other differences were "not significant."

Thus none of these three studies changed the generalizations derived from the analysis of other experimental studies. But in two cases I had to rely on the authors' findings rather than their conclusions.

Results with Linguistic Approaches

Few studies completed before 1965 involved linguistic approaches. I located only two classroom experiments testing approaches built on Bloomfield's theories (controlling material on spelling regularity) and two testing the Gibson-Richards type of approach (controlling material syntactically). In addition, three other investigations throw some indirect light on the validity of Bloomfield's theories.

THE BLOOMFIELD LINGUISTIC APPROACH

Sister Mary Fidelia (1959) compared an experimental first-grade group receiving a separate period of work-attack practice based on the Bloomfield System and a control first-grade group receiving a separate period of moderate, analytic phonics. She found no significant differences between the groups on standardized silent reading tests given after six months.

In this experiment the experimental group used conventional basal readers as well as the Bloomfield materials, and for this reason I question whether this study supports any valid conclusions about the Bloomfield approach. Using these readers violates Bloomfield's strong dictum that the child should not read irregularly spelled words until he has the alphabetic habit pretty well under control. Also, the early testing—in the middle of grade 1—weakens this study, as it weakens others.

More recently (1964), Sister Mary Edward reported on a study involving an experimental "modified linguistic" group using the Bloomfield System and a control group using a conventional basal-reader approach that included a moderate amount of phonics. At the beginning of grade 4, her experimental group tested significantly higher than her control group on standardized silent reading tests of vocabulary, comprehension, and rate. However, her description of the modified linguistic approach reveals that consonant sounds were taught.[10] This again violates Bloomfield's theory, which calls for no direct teaching of letter-sound correspondences. Thus, this study does not tell us whether using regularly spelled words controlled on common spelling patterns, *without* direct teaching of letter-sound correspondences, indeed accounted for the experimental group's better performance.

Indirect evidence against Bloomfield's assumption that direct teaching of letter-sound correspondences is not necessary when pupils practice on words with common spelling patterns comes from the early studies of Winch (1925). In one experiment Winch compared the effect of using a look-say and a synthetic sounding-blending phonic approach on success in reading such sentences as "A fat cat sat on a mat." He found the phonics-trained children superior to the look-say group. In other words, direct teaching of the sound values of letters helped these children read even regularly spelled words controlled on common spelling patterns.

In another experiment Winch compared a synthetic-phonics approach with an alphabetic spelling approach to learning these same regularly spelled words. He found that the group trained in synthetic phonics recognized words faster and more accurately than the alphabet-trained group. These findings also seem to raise a question about Bloomfield's point that a new or forgotten word should be spelled, not sounded.

A recent laboratory experiment by Bishop (1962), which simulated a beginning reading situation using adults, seems to confirm Winch's findings. Bishop set out to study the effect of previous training in letter-sound correspondences on success in learning eight Arabic words. (Sounds and

[10] Because of this, I classified the experimental treatment as "systematic phonics" and included this study in the analysis of the systematic- versus intrinsic-phonics evidence.

letters correspond perfectly in Arabic, and the eight words contained only the twelve letters learned.) The letter-trained group learned the eight words best; a word-trained group rated second; and a group without previous training scored lowest. In other words, letter training (i.e., direct phonics instruction) had more transfer value than word training. But word training did produce *some* transfer.

The letter-trained group also knew more "phonics"—that is, they could give the sounds for the letters better than the word-trained group. However, *some* subjects in the latter group had also learned the sound values of all twelve letters, and these people scored as high as the letter-trained group.

When asked how they learned the words, most of the letter-trained subjects said they had tried to apply their letter-sound knowledge. But twelve of the twenty word-trained subjects said they had tried to do the same thing; these twelve had learned the eight words as well as the letter-trained group.

Bishop's study indicates that some people are able to induce correspondences for themselves, even though not directly taught to do so. But both this experiment with adults and the Winch experiments with very young children indicate that direct teaching of sound-symbol correspondences can improve word learning. Not everyone may need such training, but it can probably help those who do not discover the correspondences for themselves. In the Bishop experiment the adults had had considerable previous experience with alphabetic languages, and yet about half of those receiving word training could *not* induce the letter-sound correspondences without direct instruction. We can probably expect children to succeed even less often (although this hypothesis needs testing). Yet in both the Bloomfield and the Fries linguistic approaches, young children are expected to do just this—and only this—at the beginning.

Levin (1963) has suggested that the Bloomfield approach is subject to another kind of limitation. In a series of laboratory experiments, he found that although, at the beginning, it takes longer to learn dual associations for letters (e.g., to learn that *g* is pronounced as in both *go* and *gem*) than to learn one association at a time, dual-association learning has greater transfer value. Levin postulated that the Bloomfield approach, which teaches single associations, may be easier for initial learning but that its transfer value in reading irregularly spelled words may be limited. Since English spelling is irregular, the Bloomfield approach may hamper the child over the long run. Levin's point, if valid, would also apply to the Fries program and others like it.

We still have little evidence on how effective the Bloomfield and

Fries linguistic approaches are.[11] These linguists' works have had a tremendous theoretical impact on current thinking about teaching children to read. However, whether their theories—which decry both sight and phonic methods—can be substantiated by laboratory and classroom experimentation is still not known.

I would hypothesize from the evidence (through 1965) that their approaches, like systematic phonics, probably give better results than approaches based on introducing sight words first and teaching moderate amounts of phonics in a varied environment of irregularly spelled words. However, to conclude from this that the Bloomfield or Fries programs will prove better than systematic phonics seems questionable.[12] I believe these approaches are effective because they put greater stress on decoding of regularly spelled words as the initial step in learning to read. Systematic-phonics programs that do the same thing but give more direct training in letter-sound relations are probably as effective. In fact, the best results probably come from using some control of spelling patterns and directly teaching their sound values.[13] Indeed, this is what several of the new "linguistic" reading programs do—the Allen Reading Materials, *Sounds and Letters, The Programmed Reading Series*, and *The Structural Reading Series.*

THE GIBSON-RICHARDS LINGUISTIC APPROACH

The studies of MacKinnon (1959) and Flinton (1962) give us some evidence on the effectiveness of the Gibson-Richards materials (controlled on language patterns and number of letters) as compared with conventional basal-reading materials.

The more provocative of the two is MacKinnon's—the only study that offers precise descriptions of, and verbatim reports on, what children do and how they behave as they read different kinds of materials.

MacKinnon found that five-year-olds taken out of their regular

[11] There is now a bit more, for the end of first grade. See the May, 1966, issue of *The Reading Teacher* and the brief reference to the USOE studies later in this chapter.

[12] See the study by Bliesmer and Yarborough (1965), discussed later in this chapter.

[13] This is what I observed in English infant classes using the Daniels and Diack phonic-word method (*The Royal Road Readers*), which resembles the Bloomfield and Fries programs quite closely. Daniels and Diack stress that their method will avoid the errors of the old phonic methods because it does not teach the sound values of the individual letters directly and then have pupils blend them to form words. Yet many of the teachers were teaching their pupils the sound values of the letters and having them blend separate sounds, even though the teacher's manual for this program says "definitely *no*" to these practices. When I asked the teachers why they did it, they said it helped.

classes, where they were using conventional basal readers, and given additional practice on the Gibson-Richards materials did better on recognition of words and sentences than those receiving additional practice on regular basal-reader materials. The Gibson-Richards syntactically controlled materials were particularly effective when used in small groups with minimal teacher instruction. They were less effective, although still more effective than the basal materials, when used individually.

MacKinnon observed that the children using the Gibson-Richards materials in small groups (without instruction from the teacher) were able to help one another identify the new words, which could be anticipated with a considerable degree of correctness. The basal-reader materials did not permit as much intelligent anticipation of new words. MacKinnon attributes this difference to the language-pattern controls in the Gibson-Richards materials. Also contributing to this group's superiority, he states, were stick-figure illustrations that "triggered off" the meaning of the sentences. Of course, we can ask whether the superior results were not due instead to a novelty effect (discussed at the end of this chapter). The control group practiced on the same kinds of books they used in class, while the experimental group had "fresh" materials.

In an unpublished study, Flinton compared reading and other kinds of achievement of one group learning with the Gibson-Richards materials plus basal readers and another group learning primarily from basal readers; she found no significant differences at the end of grade 3.

With so little evidence available, and that evidence from limited studies, it is difficult to assess a linguistic approach based on language-pattern controls. However, MacKinnon's clinical observations give the distinct impression that language-pattern control of beginning reading materials is an important variable to contend with, especially when there is little direct teacher instruction in learning new words, as in his experiments. Although basal-reader authors put much faith in the child's ability to anticipate new words from context and from pictures, MacKinnon's work tends to confirm what many teachers have long suspected—that the language and illustrations in the readers (particularly the preprimers and primers) do not seem to help the child very much in identifying new words.

Results with Modified Alphabets

We have already seen in Chapter 1 that teaching children how to read with a modified alphabet (the Initial Teaching Alphabet, or ITA) is one of the most dramatic current innovations in beginning reading instruction.

ITA, although not the only modified alphabet or spelling scheme currently being offered as a reform for beginning reading instruction (see Chapter 1), is unique in terms of the large-scale experimental tryout and public attention it has received in both England and the United States. To date, none of the other schemes has received as much attention, although Malone's UNIFON and Fry's Diacritical Marking System are currently undergoing experimental trial.

To determine the evidence on the value of using a modified alphabet as an initial teaching medium, I analyzed the annual reports of Downing on the English ITA experiment, the reports of Winch on a series of controlled experiments with Phonoscript (a diacritical-type scheme which marks certain letters for silencing), and the reports of Mazurkiewicz on the American ITA demonstration.[14]

I should note that it has been difficult to be objective about ITA. Leading newspapers and magazines have judged the English experiment a success almost from the very beginning. A newsletter designed to keep interested people informed about the experiments has become a collection of testimonials and praises; facts are reported too, but it is not always easy to identify them. It will indeed be embarrassing to the investigators to report any negative findings. At present, however, this problem seems nonexistent; most of the research results so far reported (although not all) have been positive for ITA as compared with the traditional alphabet.

THE ENGLISH ITA EXPERIMENT

The English experiment, directed by John Downing, of the Reading Research Unit of the University of London Institute of Education, began in September, 1961. The experimental design called for all possible factors other than the alphabet and spelling to remain unchanged. Thus, the reading series most popular in England was transliterated into ITA for the experimental group. The teachers were told to go on teaching as they always had, whether stressing look-say or phonics.

In a first report after nine months of instruction, Downing found the ITA-trained group significantly in the lead. (The ITA-trained children were tested in ITA, and the control group in TO—traditional orthography.) They performed better on tests of oral word recognition and were reading more advanced materials than the control group. Of special interest in this first report is the discovery that with ITA, four-year-old

[14] Several of the USOE first-grade studies discussed below tested ITA as well. See also *The Reading Teacher,* May, 1966.

beginners did as well as five-year-old beginners, while with TO, five-year-old beginners tested significantly better than four-year-olds. This seems additional evidence that ITA is easier to learn than TO.

After eighteen months of instruction, the ITA group was still in the lead. Again they were tested in ITA. This time attainment was measured by results on timed tests of silent reading (comprehension, accuracy, and speed) as well as oral word recognition and level of instructional materials read.

There is also some evidence on how well the ITA group transferred to reading traditional orthography (Downing, 1964a and 1964b). After eighteen months, about half of the ITA group were transferred to TO by their teachers. These students performed significantly better on tests of silent reading (comprehension and accuracy) in TO. They also read faster, but the difference was not significant. After two years a test of oral word recognition given in TO showed the experimental group to be a year ahead of the control group. The average reading age of ITA-trained children was 8-4, as compared with the control-group average of 7-4; both groups averaged a chronological age of 7-1. Thus, a conservative estimate of ITA's effectiveness for the average pupil, according to Downing, is that it saves one year in learning to read TO (1964a, p. 109).

How does the use of ITA affect spelling? Downing's report (1964b) includes results on a spelling test in traditional orthography administered to 318 children in the experimental group and to 602 children in the control group after 2½ years of instruction. These indicate that the ITA group was significantly better in spelling TO than the control group, even though 15 percent of the ITA-trained children had not yet transferred to TO when tested. Downing cautions, however, that these results are incomplete.

In a more recent paper delivered at the Third International ITA Conference in Cambridge, England, Downing (1966a), says this about spelling:

> Tests of TO spelling attainment in the Reading Research Unit's experiments have shown that pupils who begin with ITA are, by the third year of school, at least as competent in TO spelling as children who have learned only TO from the outset. (p. 9)

He cites as evidence the study of Peters (1966), who, in her comparison of *one* ITA class with *two* TO classes taught with differing emphases on look-say and phonics, found no difference in their TO spelling attainments in the third year of school. But Downing goes on to say that ". . . she discovered important differences in the types of spelling errors made in the ITA and TO classes. The ITA pupils made fewer errors of omission, insertion, and perseveration." (p. 10)

How much confidence can we place in the Downing reports? Generally, the research appears to be as well designed as other such experiments. Downing's analyses of the theoretical issues related to the advantages found for ITA are particularly insightful.

However, many questions remain. It is impossible to determine why different numbers of pupils were tested on different measures at different times. We are not sure of the IQ, socioeconomic background, age, or sex of the various groups who were tested; in none of the numerous, widely disseminated reports Downing has written on the experiment has he reported breakdowns of the students by IQ. Also, his reports on spelling are particularly confusing (see above). Perhaps all these weaknesses will be cleared up in his summary of the entire English experiment (Downing, 1966b), which is still in press as I write this.

Even if we assume that the children tested represented unbiased samples of the total experimental and control groups and that the groups compared had generally comparable background characteristics, we must consider other factors in weighing the superior performance of the ITA pupils.

Effect of novelty. Although the experimental- and control-group teachers in the experiment were given equal workshop and consulting time, the workshops differed considerably. At John Downing's invitation I attended one workshop for each group of teachers. In their workshop, the experimental-group teachers became beginners again, as they learned to read and spell in the new system; this process made them keenly aware of the difficulties a child faces in learning to read English. The control-group teachers, however, covered the usual topics in their workshop—how to motivate children, how to individualize instruction, etc. I leave it to you to guess whether this kind of attention was as valuable and inspirational to them as the ITA workshop was to the experimental-group teachers.

Changes in method. Although the original research design kept method unchanged, my visits to both ITA and control classes in England led me to suspect that the ITA teachers emphasized phonics more than those not using ITA. Several teachers told me that ITA made them critically examine everything they had been doing before. They said they had long suspected that a stronger phonic emphasis was needed, but did not use it because phonics was considered old-fashioned. Because ITA was so regular, they found themselves teaching phonics and word-building earlier and more effectively.

Downing himself makes a similar point in his article in *Elementary English* in 1965:

> Generally, ITA teachers in Britain have continued to use their previous eclectic approach to reading with much success. Phonics generally was taught by most teachers, but often not until the second year (age 6 plus). With ITA phonics is still postponed until after an initial look-say period, but now with ITA it comes a good deal earlier—but still *not at the start.* (p. 494)

It would seem to me that "a good deal earlier" may be change enough.

More time on reading and related activities. Downing gives no data on the amount of time devoted to reading and related activities by both groups. As I informally observed ITA classes in England, however, I got the impression of an all-out effort in reading and writing. In fact, the proponents of ITA again and again have claimed that ITA increases the amount and quality of creative writing. No doubt a more regular medium helps the child write stories, but so would putting aside more time for writing in TO. A less conscientious concern with perfect spelling in stories written by children in Grades 1 and 2—an attitude shared by ITA teachers—might also help TO teachers get more creative writing from their pupils.

WINCH'S EXPERIMENT WITH PHONOSCRIPT

Despite the questionable aspects of the English experiment, the results reported for ITA are convincing enough to essentially confirm the earlier findings of Winch (1925) on favorable results with another system, Phonoscript, which uses silencing marks. Winch tested very few children, but the smaller numbers are made up for by tighter controls, not only on pupil background but on teachers and methods as well. Both the experimental and control groups used synthetic phonics; the only experimental variable was the modified medium.

From the beginning the Phonoscript group did better than the TO group on reading untaught words when each group was tested in its own print. After two years, when tested in conventional print, the Phonoscript group was still significantly ahead, even though it had had little previous experience with regular print.

THE AMERICAN ITA DEMONSTRATION

A widespread experimental tryout of ITA began in Bethlehem, Pennsylvania, in September, 1963, directed by Albert J. Mazurkiewicz, of Lehigh University. A report by Mazurkiewicz (1964) compares progress of the experimental and control groups from the tenth week through the ninth month. Like Downing, Mazurkiewicz presents results for small samples of the total experimental and control populations only, and he gives no substantial evidence that the samples have comparable crucial background characteristics. His report, however, confirms the findings of the English experiment. In fact, the ITA group's superiority seems even more marked in the American experiment than in the British one.

What differentiates the American experiment is the conscious introduction of modifications in *method*. The American children learning ITA use the ITA Series, a new set of readers which not only emphasizes the early learning of the forty-four ITA characters and the sounds they represent but also introduces writing at the start and teaches more words, level for level, than either the English ITA readers or the American conventional basal readers (see Appendix A).

Thus the American demonstration involves:

ITA + harder readers + early and heavy phonics + early writing	VERSUS	TO + easier readers + late and less phonics + practically no writing

For this reason, we cannot attribute the results attained by the experimental group to the use of ITA alone; all other differences must also be considered. These experiments do not tell us what can be achieved by using harder readers, early and heavy phonics, and early writing without modifying the alphabet. (O. K. Moore's demonstrations seem to indicate that precocious readers can be developed with our ordinary alphabet.)

So far, the experimental evidence is still too limited to allow definite conclusions about the long-term advantages (and disadvantages) of using a modified alphabet. That ITA has its share of failures we know from a paper Sir James Pitman presented at the Educational Records Bureau Conference in 1963. We also can infer some lack of success from Downing's report (1964b) revealing that after two years, 15 percent of ITA-trained children had not yet been transferred to TO; this figure recalls the number of failures (10 to 15 percent) in grades above the first revealed by various surveys made in the United States of children taught without modified alphabets (Bond and Tinker, 1957). Furthermore, we need studies comparing ITA with other innovative methods and materials that put a greater stress on early acquisition of the alphabetic principle—the linguistic approaches of Bloomfield and Fries and the systematic phonics-linguistic programs.[15]

[15] Indeed, the USOE-supported first-grade study coauthored by Tanyzer (1966), the coauthor of the American ITA series, found that on most tests ITA-trained pupils

I make a special plea for caution concerning the use of ITA because I see it as the most expensive and drastic change that could be made in beginning reading. It is expensive, because it means developing and buying new books for grades 1 and 2—not only readers, but arithmetic, science, and social studies, as well as library books. It also means constantly retraining teachers and administrators. It is drastic, because a child moving from an ITA to a non-ITA school, or vice versa, during his first or second year will have to learn a new alphabet in midstream; this would be troublesome in the United States, where people move around a great deal. Of course, if all schools adopted ITA simultaneously there would be no problem, but educational change in this country is usually slow and sporadic.

But even if ITA goes the way of the past alphabet reforms, the experiments will have made an important contribution. They generally confirm that an early emphasis on learning the code produces better results, at least up to early fourth grade. Ironically, although ITA was offered as a way out of the old look-say versus phonics debate (or the larger one of code versus meaning), the ITA experiments may ultimately help settle the controversy by facilitating the return of a stronger code emphasis—*but* with the traditional alphabet. The American demonstration has already brought back phonics, spelling, and earlier writing, and if we read between the lines of Downing's comments in his "misconceptions" article (1965), we can infer that many in Britain as well are using ITA to reintroduce phonics or other instruction in the code as the way to start.

Different Methods for Different Children?

The evidence from the experimental studies analyzed so far indicates that unselected children taught initially by a code emphasis generally do better in reading than children taught by a meaning emphasis, at least up to early fourth grade. Is there any evidence that this generalization holds for some children and not for others? Could it be that one method is more effective for brighter children, another for average children, and

---

achieved about the same results as the systematic-phonics group (who used the Lippincott Basic Reading Program). However, on spelling and vocabulary the systematic-phonics group was ahead of the ITA group. Both groups were superior at the end of grade 1 to an intrinsic-phonics group (who used the Scott, Foresman Reading Program). All children, however, were tested on TO, which is not completely fair to the ITA children, who had not yet been given enough time to transfer to TO.

still another for children of low mental ability? Do children from different socioeconomic backgrounds learn better from different methods?[16]

DIFFERENCES IN MENTAL ABILITY

Many people concerned with beginning reading believe that systematic phonics is fine for bright children, but too hard for slow learners. The research of Dolch and Bloomster (1937) is primarily responsible for this notion. Dolch and Bloomster correlated the mental age and phonic ability (defined as ability to make phonic generalizations) of 115 pupils in grades 1 and 2 and found a substantial relationship between the two. While only *some* bright children failed on the phonic ability test, *all* the slower ones failed. From their scattergrams the investigators concluded that a child must have a minimum mental age of seven to benefit from instruction in phonics. This would disqualify the average and slow first grader.

It is important to note that the pupils in the Dolch and Bloomster study had been exposed to an intrinsic type of phonics program, not a systematic-phonics program, in which sound-letter relationships are usually taught more directly. As a result, the study does *not* tell us whether slow-learning pupils can or cannot benefit from a more direct, more concentrated dose of phonics; it tells us only that it is difficult for them to figure out and benefit from "intrinsic-type phonics."

To try to determine whether slow-learning pupils fare worse under phonics, I reanalyzed the nine experimental studies discussed above that made a breakdown by intelligence. I judged whether the findings of each study favored a look-say, an intrinsic-phonics, or a systematic-phonics approach for children of low, middle, and high IQ in each grade studied. Table 4–3 shows the results.

On the basis of these studies, it appears that the generalization about the benefits of an initial code emphasis seems to hold fairly well for all IQ ranges studied. However, some trends are evident.

[16] I shall not consider personality differences here, although a study by Grimes and Allinsmith (1961) suggests an interaction between personality and method. Their comparison of the reading achievement of third graders exposed to either a phonic or a look-say method indicated that highly anxious and compulsive children achieve better in "structured" phonics classrooms than similar children in "unstructured" look-say classrooms.

Note, however, that the reading method itself may not have accounted for the difference, since the investigators report that the "atmospheres" of the two schools differed too: the "phonic" school was more "authoritarian," while the "look-say" school seemed more "democratic." That phonics does not necessarily go with an authoritarian atmosphere, or even with greater classroom structure, can be seen from the Wilson and Fleming study described in Chap. 5.

Systematic phonics, it seems, is as effective for the slow learner as for other children, but it takes the slow learner a little longer to benefit from this approach. In this respect, the slow learner at the end of grade 1 or in grade 2 is like the normal learner at the beginning or middle of grade 1 who, when tested after six or eight months of instruction, may not do as well on standardized tests (vocabulary and comprehension) as children exposed to a more moderate (intrinsic) phonics program. But by the end of grade 3, the slow learners taught systematic phonics begin to outperform those taught by a meaning emphasis. This is especially evident on standardized silent reading tests, which require sufficient facility with the code to allow concentration on the author's thoughts—something particularly difficult for the mentally slow child.

Daniels and Diack (1960), testing after two years of instruction, concluded that IQ and method success are not significantly related. Generally they found a stronger phonic emphasis (their phonic-word method) to be better than a weaker phonic emphasis (the English "mixed" methods), for dull as well as bright children. The study by Wollam (1961), however, indicates that by grade 4 systematic phonics is a more effective beginning approach for slow learners only.

The evidence is sparse. However, if the limited findings from these nine studies are accurate and can be replicated, they may be explained as follows: Systematic phonics is probably more effective for slow-learning pupils because it can be made easier than intrinsic phonics. These nine studies indicate that when slow-learning pupils follow a systematic-phonics approach programmed so as to simplify the learning—either through direct, didactic teaching of the sound values of the letters (Bear, 1959, where Hay-Wingo was used) or by learning phonic generalizations from regularly spelled words controlled on phonic elements (Daniels and Diack, 1960)—they do better than when taught by an intrinsic-phonics emphasis (which requires them to induce generalizations from an irregular environment). Thus, Dolch and Bloomster's conclusion that a mental age of seven is a prerequisite for learning phonics is probably true only when children are taught inductively, from words selected on a meaning-frequency principle and with no control of spelling patterns or common phonic elements—i.e., by intrinsic phonics, the phonics included in most conventional basal series.

Three additional studies confirm the effectiveness of systematic phonics for children with mental ages below seven. Winch (1925) found that children with a mental age of five years on the Binet scale learned better with a synthetic-phonics approach than children of similar mental age exposed to a look-say method. Both groups used material with a high

*Table 4–3 Advantages for Look-Say, Systematic Phonics, or Intrinsic Phonics on Different Outcomes, by IQ and Grade**

Experiment, approaches compared, outcomes measures	Low IQ						Middle IQ						High IQ					
	1	2	3	4	5	6	1	2	3	4	5	6	1	2	3	4	5	6
Valentine (1913) (L-S vs. SP)																		
Word pronunciation:																		
Taught words		L-S	L-S											SP	SP			
Untaught words		SP	SP											SP	SP			
Garrison & Heard (1931) (SP vs. IP)																		
Word pronunciation	SP												SP					
Oral reading	IP												IP					
Silent reading comprehension	E	IP	SP										SP	E	E			
Gates & Russell (1938)																		
(L-S vs. IP vs. SP) Silent reading comprehension	IP						IP						E					
Sparks & Fay (1957) (IP vs. SP)																		
Silent reading:																		
Comprehension	SP	E	IP	E			SP	SP	E	E								
Vocabulary	E	E	E	E			SP	E	E	E								
Rate				E						E								
Accuracy				IP						E								

Daniels & Diack (1960) (SP vs. IP)												
Oral pronunciation		SP				SP				SP		
Silent reading comprehension		SP				SP				SP		
Bear (1959 & 1964) (SP vs. IP)												
Silent reading comprehension:												
Gates	SP				SP				E			
Metropolitan	E				SP				E			
Gates survey				E				SP				E
Wollam (1961) (SP vs. IP)												
Word recognition			SP				E				E	
Silent reading:												
Comprehension			SP				E				E	
Vocabulary			SP				E				E	
Edward (1964) (SP vs. IP)												
Phonics			SP				SP				SP	
Silent reading (comprehension & vocabulary)			SP				SP				SP	
Duncan (1964) (SP vs. IP)												
Silent reading comprehension		SP				SP				SP		

* L-S = look-say; IP = intrinsic phonics; SP = systematic phonics; E = equal.

proportion of regularly spelled words; even with a vocabulary that permitted discovery of phonic generalizations, direct teaching of the sound values of the letters helped.

Bloomer (1960), comparing a program of synthetic phonics (with vocabulary controlled as described above) and a conventional basal-reader approach for first graders, found synthetic phonics more effective. We can infer from his report that most of these children had mental ages below seven.

Joyce Morris, in an extensive study relating school and pupil characteristics to reading attainment in English schools (1959), found phonic instruction with five-year-olds and an initial phonic method significantly related to reading attainment adjusted for intelligence. (The Morris study is discussed in more detail in Chapter 5.)

John Downing's early report (1962) that ITA was as easy for four-year-olds as for five-year-olds makes the point even broader. This finding and our previous analyses of experimental studies seem to indicate that it is not solely a question of learning phonics, but rather of facilitating the acquisition of the code. Systematic phonics makes it easier than intrinsic phonics for the child to acquire the code, especially the duller child. ITA makes it easier for four-year-olds than TO.

Thus, contrary to a great deal of opinion, a code emphasis—but one that is extremely well programmed—seems indicated for slow and average pupils as well as for bright ones. In fact, bright children, the studies tend to show, are affected less by method than other children; in general they learn well under a code or meaning emphasis. Slow and average children are the ones for whom choice of method is most important.

DIFFERENCES IN SOCIAL BACKGROUND

Only two of the experimental studies refer specifically to the interaction of method effectiveness with the social and economic background of pupils. The 1956 and 1960 Daniels and Diack studies seem to indicate that stronger phonics in the beginning (the investigators' phonic-word method) is more beneficial than moderate phonics for children of lower socioeconomic background. They found this to be the case in their 1956 study of retarded readers and in their 1960 study of infant-school children.

Another relevant study (Gardner, 1942) was concerned not with varying amounts and kinds of phonics but with the effectiveness of "formal" and "informal" approaches. Working with children aged six to seven, Gardner found the informal approach (which, no doubt, included indirect instruction in phonics) generally more effective in schools with a large proportion of children from a higher socioeconomic background and of higher mental ability. For children from poor homes who were mentally younger, the formal school (which generally had more direct instruction in the mechanics of reading) produced better results in reading (as well as in arithmetic) at age seven.[17]

The very limited experimental evidence we have seems to indicate that a heavier code emphasis is more effective for children of lower socioeconomic status. It makes sense: A code-emphasis method, which tends to give early independence in recognizing words, would be of particular help to a child who is not surrounded by books and adults who help him read words he cannot figure out for himself. A middle-class child has more opportunity to "discover" what reading is all about—particularly the letter-to-sound relationships—even if the method used in his school does not go about teaching the code systematically.[18]

DETERMINING THE INFLUENCE OF THE NOVELTY EFFECT

It has long been observed that human subjects are affected by being studied—that merely paying additional attention to them, as is done in an experimental situation, makes them perform better. Furthermore, in classroom comparisons, the experimental group aften attracts the more imaginative and able teachers.[19] Thus, if the experimental, or the newer-method, group wins out—and it usually does in educational experimentation—it is still debatable whether to attribute the superior performance to a change in method, the higher quality of instruction, or the "novelty effect" (sometimes called the "Hawthorne effect").

I decided to try to determine to what extent the novelty effect influ-

[17] An earlier study by Gates (Gates et al., 1926) found a "modern systematic" method superior to an "opportunistic" method even for bright (mean IQ 116) first graders from educationally advantaged homes.

[18] As an Italian resident of Greenwich Village put it, in discussing a local "progressive" experiment: "The program of that school is suited to the children of well-to-do homes, not to our children. We send our children to school for what we cannot give them ourselves, grammar and drill. The Fifth Avenue children learn to speak well in their homes. We do not send our children to school for group activity; they get plenty of that in the street. But the Fifth Avenue children are lonely. I can see how group experience is an important form of education for them." From Carolin Ware, *Greenwich Village: 1920–30,* New York, 1935, p. 343, cited by Lawrence A. Cremin in *The Transformation of the School,* Alfred A. Knopf, Inc., New York, 1961, p. 212.

[19] One study (Tensuan and Davis, 1963b) reported that teachers of the experimental classes had a higher teacher-background index than teachers of the control classes. In this case, the investigators made statistical adjustments for the difference. However, many other investigators may not have been so careful about adjusting for the influence of teacher ability.

enced my analyses. But admittedly my examination had to be very limited,[20] since I could deal only with studies of the phonics question, which were numerous enough to allow a historical-trends analysis. (There simply are not enough studies of modified alphabet or linguistic approaches to make possible a similar analysis of them, but presumably the novelty effect would have a comparable influence on studies involving these other approaches.)

To make this analysis I judged which of the methods in my classification—look-say, intrinsic phonics, or systematic phonics—was the prevailing or the innovative method at the time it was tested. These judgments were based on Nila B. Smith's historical studies of American reading instruction (1963 and 1965).[21]

Did the innovative methods tend to produce the better results?

Table 4–4, which shows the authors' overall conclusions as "verdicts," seems to indicate a slight trend toward a novelty effect. Had the authors' findings, rather than their conclusions, been used as verdicts, the trend would probably not seem so great, as explained below. To use findings here would have required too many adjustments, since the findings depended a good deal on when the children were tested and on the tests used.

Table 4 shows that during the period 1900 to 1920, when systematic phonics was the "in" method according to Nila Smith, the authors of two

[20] For a systematic study of the influence of the Hawthorne effect on educational research, see Cook (1963).
[21] See Chap. 6, p. 161, for a more extensive reference to this material.

*Table 4–4 Authors' Conclusions from Experimental Comparisons of Reading-Instruction Methods, 1900–1965**

Period	Prevailing method	Total studies made	Found systematic phonics superior	Found intrinsic phonics superior	Found look-say superior
1900–1920	Systematic phonics	3	1		2
1920–1935	Look-say	6	4	2	
1935–1955	Intrinsic phonics	8	4	3	1
1955–1965	The debate: Intrinsic phonics still the prevailing method, with a push toward earlier and heavier emphasis on phonics	13	9	4	
Totals		30	18	9	3

* This table covers the studies summarized in Tables 4–1 and 4–2. The total number of studies is reduced to thirty because the Gates and Russell (1938) experiment is counted only once here, although it is included in both Tables 4–1 and 4–2.

of the three studies concluded that the innovative method, look-say, was better.

When look-say was the accepted method (from 1920 to 1935), in theory at least,[22] all the studies concluded for phonics—twice as many for systematic as for intrinsic phonics. But while systematic phonics may have been the "out" method then, albeit only in theory, it had probably not yet been "out" long enough to be innovative again and to bring with it the novelty effects of new methods.

Between 1935 and 1955, when intrinsic phonics was "in," we find again that the "out" method (systematic phonics) tends to win.

During the period of the debate (1955 to 1965), when intrinsic phonics was still the dominant approach (and systematic phonics old enough to be innovative again), there seems to have been a real buildup of conclusions for systematic phonics.

These trends in conclusions would seem to indicate that some novelty effect is operating. However, the verdicts (which tend on the whole to support a stronger phonic emphasis, irrespective of historical period) reflect the authors' conclusions, some of which ran counter to their own findings or were based on what I consider questionable tests for that particular stage of reading development. Indeed, had they based their conclusions on their own findings, many more investigators would have concluded for systematic phonics.

On the basis of this very limited study, I would say that the novelty

[22] A. I. Gates writes: "In your report you seem to state that the decade 1920–30 was the time when the nonphonic or low phonic or the 'look and say' approach was in widespread use. I think that this was not the case. Early in my work I made quite an extensive investigation of schools in the New York area by direct observation of teachers in their classrooms, by conferring with teachers from all parts of the country who were members of my college courses, and by analyzing all or nearly all the basal reading books in use at that time. The results were published in 'Problems in Beginning Reading,' *Teachers College Record,* March 1925. I found that extensive phonic work was provided and recommended in nearly all the basal reading programs and was in fact being done in practically all schools. This was also shown by a study made by Clifford Woody, *Practices in Teaching First-Grade Reading in the Public Schools of Michigan,* Bureau of Educational Reference and Research Bulletin 58, School of Education, University of Michigan, 1923, who reported that in 1921–2 a quarter of the teachers spent half or more of their time, one half spent 38% to 48%, and three quarters spent 27% to 38% on word study including phonics. Despite the fact that William S. Gray, I, and others, beginning about 1920, were questioning the desirability of devoting so much time to drill on phonics, the phonic method was heavily entrenched in the schools for many years thereafter. Although Nila Smith characterized 1920 as the time when the critical views began to appear, almost everything I wrote and said during the 1920–30 decade was based on the assumption that most teachers were committed to a very heavy program of phonics." (Personal communication, November, 1965)

effect probably had some influence on conclusions as well as on findings of these studies. However, the more essential factor influencing their results, I believe, was the degree of emphasis on the code afforded by the methods under examination. Even if we choose the most simple-minded way out—i.e., if we take a ballot (indeed, a risky business if no theory or explanation accompanies it)—we find that, except for the period 1900 to 1920, the stronger code-emphasis methods tended to produce the better results.

But the major evidence that a stronger code emphasis at the beginning produces better results than a weaker one (one that emphasizes meaning initially) stems not from "head counting" or "ballot taking" but from my theoretical analysis of the probable course of development of reading skill when children are given more or less instruction in the code system of English writing, discussed more fully above. The studies are used as confirmations or denials of this theoretical position—which, like all theories, will of course need refinement and revision as new evidence comes to the fore.

A recent study by Bliesmer and Yarborough (1965), published after the major portion of this chapter was written, tends to confirm my basic interpretations of the past classroom experiments as well as my judgment that a novelty effect did not have a major influence on their results.

Bliesmer and Yarborough compared ten beginning reading programs that varied in the emphasis given to code learning. Three programs (the Ginn Basic Readers, 1959; American Book, 1963; and the Scott, Foresman Reading Program, 1962) were of the conventional basal-reader type (my intrinsic, moderate phonics or meaning-emphasis classification). Three of the programs had a stronger code emphasis (Houghton Mifflin's *Reading for Meaning Series,* 1963; Economy's Phonetic Keys to Reading; and the Lippincott Basic Reading Program, 1963). Also included was a linguistic-type program, Stern's *Structural Reading Series.* Two programs involved an individual approach—one using no set of commercially prepared materials, and one using as supplemental materials the SRA Reading Lab (essentially reading-for-meaning exercises) and word games (code practice).

All the children took the same standardized tests (Stanford Achievement) at the end of grade 1. Those using the programs with heavier code emphasis—whether phonic or linguistic—scored higher than those using the conventional basal-reader programs (more moderate emphasis on the code and greater emphasis on "meaningful reading") and also higher than those using both Individualized Reading approaches (which also tend to give less systematic practice in code acquisition—see Appendix A). It is important to note that the Stanford test is supposed to measure reading comprehension.

Since the two Individualized Reading programs were also innovative programs at the time of this study, they, as well as the stronger code-emphasis programs, should have been the winners if the novelty effect was stronger than the effect of method. Instead, only the code programs, and not the *new* meaning programs, were superior to the conventional, prevailing meaning programs.

An Addendum on the USOE First-grade Reading Studies

The recently completed twenty-seven USOE first-grade reading studies (*The Reading Teacher,* May, 1966) afford an opportunity to test some of the interpretations of the classroom experiments from 1910 to 1965. Unfortunately, time did not permit my analyzing and synthezing their findings with those completed before 1965. Nor were all these studies available at the time of this writing. Therefore, I rely essentially on the progress report of Guy Bond (1966), the coordinator of all twenty-seven studies. In Bond's words:

> The major goal of the First-grade Reading Study is to explore the effects upon early reading growth of various approaches to reading under conditions that would make it possible to compare findings among a group of independent studies. As the result of a widely publicized invitation by the U.S. Office of Education, 76 proposals were received. Each research proposal submitted was reviewed by the Research Advisory Council which selected 27 for support by the Cooperative Research Branch of the United States Office of Education. The projects were selected on the basis of their individual merit as self-contained studies having unique characteristics and at the same time being directly related to the problems and differing points of view in regard to initial reading instruction. They were also selected so that in total scope a more massive body of information about various approaches to reading instruction could be obtained for further combined analysis than had ever before been possible in the field of reading. (p. 2)

Although these were twenty-seven independent studies, extending over almost all the United States, they were coordinated in terms of research design, measuring instruments, and information gathered, so that comparisons among the studies were possible "in ways that have not previously existed." (p. 2)

The major group of studies investigated the effectiveness of a variety of approaches

> . . . including those employing [conventional] basal readers, phonetic [phonic] emphasis, linguistic materials, language-experience approaches, the Initial Teaching Alphabet, and diacritical markings. (p. 2)

The Coordinating Center at the University of Minnesota, under Bond's direction, treated the data from all the individual studies as one large study.

Although the statistical analyses had not yet been completed when Bond wrote his progress report, he presented "certain specific generalizations that can be made at this time on the basis of the analyses of the combined data thus far completed." (p. 8)

His first generalization confirms one that I made from the past studies:

> We have found no one approach[23] so distinctly better in all situations and respects than the others that it should be considered the one best method nor to be used exclusively. (p. 8)

Bond generalizes further:

> There are, however, many indications that no matter what the underlying method is, word-study skills need to be emphasized and taught systematically. This is best shown by *the superiority of the approaches which augmented the basal reader with a phonetic [phonic] emphasis as compared with basal readers as usually taught.* (p. 9, emphasis mine)

The above seems to confirm my interpretation of the past research—i.e., programs that facilitate code acquisition tend to produce generally better results at the end of grade 1.

The USOE studies also found that some code-emphasis programs may not show their advantage on comprehension tests at the end of grade 1, although they do so on word-recognition tests:

> The combined data analysis tends to show that a linguistic approach develops word-recognition skills effectively, but demonstrates no superiority over other systems in developing comprehension abilities. (p. 9)

This finding is reminiscent of the earlier ones already analyzed in this chapter. Now it remains to be seen whether these "linguistic-trained" children will catch up in reading comprehension and, if they do, when?

It will also be important to see whether the second-grade studies, scheduled to be completed in 1967, will necessitate a modification of the generalizations from the earlier studies presented in the following summary.

A Summary, Particularly for Researchers on Method

We have viewed the experimental studies analyzed in this chapter as sources of evidence on the basic question: Does an initial code emphasis produce better results than an initial emphasis on reading for meaning?

[23] Bond refers here to the specific programs rather than to my basic categories of meaning emphasis and code emphasis.

I cannot stress sufficiently that this dichotomy is only one of *emphasis*. All code-emphasis programs give some practice in reading for meaning during the initial stages. Many put great stress on it. Reading for meaning really cannot be avoided unless, of course, only nonsense syllables are used, and no code-emphasis program has ever gone to that extreme.

Similarly, the meaning-emphasis programs give some practice in code learning. Reading could not take place without some attention to the code. But compared with code-emphasis programs, the meaning-emphasis programs provide less practice, and they give it later.

When we view the analyses given above in terms of this code-meaning dichotomy, the following generalizations—which I present as hypotheses to be tested further—seem tenable:

1. A code emphasis tends to produce better overall reading achievement by the beginning of fourth grade than a meaning emphasis.

2. Growth in reading skills seems to take different courses under the two emphases.

a. Under a code emphasis, the child shows, from the very beginning, greater accuracy in word recognition and oral reading; this may or may not give him an immediate advantage on reading-for-meaning tests (standardized silent reading tests of vocabulary and comprehension). However, by the end of the first or sometime during the second grade, the early advantage in word recognition produces better vocabulary and comprehension scores on silent reading tests. These advantages persist through about the third grade.

With a code emphasis, the child seems to read more slowly at the very beginning because of the greater stress on accuracy. However, by the third (or fourth) grade, when he is more fluent, his rate is equal to (and may ultimately exceed) that produced by a meaning emphasis.

b. Under a meaning emphasis, the child has an early advantage (in the middle of grade 1) on reading-for-meaning tests (standardized silent reading tests of vocabulary and comprehension). However, he has an early disadvantage in accuracy or oral word recognition (pronunciation) and connected oral reading tests (when rate is not included in the score), which ultimately dissipates the early advantage on the standardized silent reading tests. At about the end of the first grade (or the beginning of the second grade), and continuing through about the third grade, meaning-emphasis programs tend to affect comprehension and vocabulary test scores adversely, mainly because the child does less well in word recognition.

In the beginning, the child reads faster under a meaning emphasis, but he may lose this advantage by about the third or fourth grade.

3. There is more than one way to facilitate learning of the code; systematic-phonics programs that rely on direct teaching of letter-sound relationships are as successful as, or perhaps more successful than, programs that rely on "discovery"—the so-called linguistic approaches that *do not* teach letter-sound correspondences directly.

4. Modified alphabet schemes and linguistic approaches that control words on spelling patterns to permit discovery of letter-sound correspondences tend to help the child master the code. They are probably superior to approaches that expose the child to high-frequency, irregularly spelled words with "late and little phonics" (the phonics programs of the conventional basal readers). However, even the modified alphabet schemes and the linguistic approaches appear to benefit from direct teaching of sound-letter correspondences.

5. With regard to individual differences:

a. Children of below-average and average intelligence and children of lower socioeconomic background probably learn better in the end with a code emphasis than with a meaning emphasis, although this advantage does not show immediately.

b. Children of high mental ability and children of middle and high socioeconomic background appear to gain an immediate advantage from a code emphasis. However, because they are bright they are generally better able to discover sound-letter relationships for themselves. Thus, the differences between results from a meaning or a code emphasis are probably not ultimately as great for them as for average and slow learners and for children of lower socioeconomic background.

The experimental comparisons do not provide enough evidence to generate tenable hypotheses about differential growth patterns at the fourth grade and beyond. However, I would like to present the following set of second-order hypotheses:

1. Whether an initial code emphasis keeps its advantage in the middle and upper elementary grades, and later, depends on how reading is taught in these grades: how much the reading program stresses language and vocabulary growth and provides sufficiently challenging reading materials. If the reading programs are not challenging enough in these respects, the early advantages will probably be dissipated.

2. Generally, aspects of reading comprehension such as "reading to predict outcomes," "making inferences," "reading for appreciation," and the like may not show substantial differences in later years when initial mean-

ing and code programs are compared, since the reader's intelligence and general knowledge put a limit on performance in these areas. However, a code emphasis should still maintain its advantage, even in later years, in those aspects of literacy which depend less on language, intelligence, and experience and more on "reading skill": accuracy in recognizing "unknown" words, accuracy and rate of connected oral reading, rate of silent reading, and some kinds of reading comprehension—e.g., reading for details and following directions. A code emphasis will tend to maintain its early advantage in spelling.

It should be made clear that the above hypotheses concern groups, not individuals. Obviously, every method produces ranges of attainment, and every method has its failures. And it may very well be that certain individuals find one or another method particularly suitable—or impossible.

FIVE

The ABC's of Reading: Is the Alphabet Necessary?

WE GAIN FURTHER insight into the value of an initial code approach to learning to read from examining correlational studies relating children's knowledge of the letters of the alphabet and the sounds they represent to various aspects of reading achievement. Correlational studies in themselves do not give evidence of cause and effect, but when placed alongside the findings of the experimental comparisons, they can help illuminate causal relationships.

In essence, the correlational studies summarized here help to answer the question: Do children need to know the alphabet (and/or the sound values of letters of the alphabet) in order to learn to read? This question may seem but another twentieth-century manifestation of the same pedantry that kept medieval scholars worrying about how many angels could fit on the head of a pin. Of course, you might say, everyone agrees that a child must know the letters before he learns to read words.

Well, you would be mistaken. Oddly enough, it *is* possible to learn to read without knowing the letters of the alphabet. In fact, since the early 1920s the accepted theory and practice have called for *not* teaching letter names and their sound values until the child has learned to read words. Even today most children learn to read words before they learn the letters; the teachers' guidebooks for the most popular basal-reading series suggest that letters and their sound values be taught when the child can read about fifty to one hundred words by sight—that is, as wholes (see Chapter 8). (The average child reaches this point about halfway through the first grade.) Indeed, most methods textbooks currently used in graduate and undergraduate courses in teaching children to read suggest that letters be taught even later—after about one hundred or more sight words are learned. Some even suggest that the child need not learn the letter names, or the proper order of the letters, until he starts to use a dictionary in the third grade.

THE CORRELATIONAL STUDIES

I analyzed seventeen studies (all that I was able to locate) that related knowledge of the letters and/or of letter-sound relationships (phonics knowledge) and reading achievement. Seven[1] were predictional studies relating pupils' knowledge of letter names and/or sounds *before they began to learn to read* and their reading achievement in grade 1, 2, or 3. The remaining studies (and also some of these seven) tested letter and/or phonics knowledge and reading achievement at the same time in the primary or intermediate and upper elementary grades. Two reported correlations between phonics knowledge and reading achievement among college students.

Table 5–1 presents the relevant data from these studies: the population covered (grade, number, and kinds of children); how the subjects learned to read initially (when reported); the correlation coefficients between the various tests of letter and/or phonics knowledge and reading achievement; and the correlation coefficients between mental ability (MA or IQ) and reading achievement (when reported). Table 5–2 shows only the correlation coefficients between knowledge of letters and/or phonics knowledge and reading, by grades.

THE FINDINGS

From Table 5–1, we see that a child's ability to identify letters by name (letter knowledge) in kindergarten or the beginning of grade 1 is an important predictor of his reading achievement at various points in the first and second grades (r's from .3 to .9).[2] In fact, letter knowledge has

[1] Wilson et al. (1938), Gates et al. (1939), Durrell and Murphy (1953), Olson (1958), Gavel (1958), Nicholson (1958), and Weiner and Feldmann (1963).

[2] An r, or correlation coefficient, of zero indicates no relationship; an r of 1.0 indicates a perfect correlation.

Table 5–1 Summary of Studies Relating Letter and/or Phonics Knowledge and Mental Ability to Reading Achievement

Study	Population		Beginning reading method	Correlation between letter and/or phonics knowledge and reading achievement	Correlation between mental ability (MA or IQ) and reading achievement
	Grades	Description			
Wilson et al. (1938)	K	54 (high SES; average IQ, 120)	Informal, functional, part of rich broad experience; letter names and sounds taught functionally	r = .61 (Stanford-Binet MA held constant) between recognition of small letters and word recognition (Gates Primary, Type 1); .69 (Stanford-Binet IQ held constant). Both tests given in autumn	
				r = .74 (Stanford-Binet MA held constant) between recognition of small letters and word recognition (Gates Primary, Type 1); .76 (Stanford-Binet IQ held constant). Both tests given in spring	
	1,2	Number not given, presumably 1 class followed into grade 2; SES and IQ as above		r = .70 to .79 between letter and phonics knowledge in Oct. of grade 1 and reading (Gates Primary) in spring of grade 1	
				r = .60 to .89 between letter and phonics knowledge in Oct. of grade 1 and reading (Stanford Achiev.) in spring of grade 2	
Wilson and Fleming (1938)	K	48	Same as above	*Rho** = .49 to .79 between 6 tests of letter knowledge and word recognition (Gates Primary, Type 1); .41 to .78 with IQ held constant	

	1	25		*Rho* = .34 to .82 (average .52) between 30 tests of letter and phonics knowledge and 14 reading tests	*Rho* = .37 (average) between 21 measures of mental ability and 14 reading tests; .51 between MA (Stanford-Binet) and 14 reading tests; .33 between IQ (Stanford-Binet) and 14 reading tests
	1	83		*Rho* = .60 between phonics knowledge and word recognition (Gates Primary, Type 1); .62 with IQ constant; .55 between phonics knowledge and paragraph reading (Gates Primary, Type 3); .56 with IQ constant. All tests given in spring of grade 1	*Rho* = .42 between MA (Stanford-Binet) and word recognition (Gates Primary, Type 1); .46 with paragraph reading (Gates Primary, Type 3)
	2	Number not given; presumably two classes		*Rho* = .86 (from .75 to .93) between 2 phonics tests and 14 reading tests for 1 class; .50 (from .37 to .72) in other class	
Rogers (1938)	college freshmen	72 poor readers (20th percentile or below on Iowa Silent Reading)	Not stated	*r* = .45 between phonics ability test and reading achievement (Iowa)	
Gates et al. (1939)	1,2	4 classes, 97 children; mean IQ about 100	Sight, meaning emphasis first, then moderate phonics	*r* = .31† between reading letters of alphabet at beginning of grade 1 and reading achievement‡; *r* = -.41 between errors in giving words beginning with the same sound, tested at beginning of grade 1; *r* = .43 between giving words ending in the same sound, tested at beginning of grade 1	*r* = .40 between MA (Stanford-Binet) and reading achievement *r* = .23 between reproduction of ideas and reading achievement *r* = .20 between range of information (Van Wagenen) and reading achievement *r* = .54 between rated quality of story completed by pupil and reading achievement

Table 5–1 (Continued)

Study	Population		Beginning reading method	Correlation between letter and/or phonics knowledge and reading achievement	Correlation between mental ability (MA or IQ) and reading achievement
	Grades	Description			
Tiffin & McKinnis (1940)	5,6,7,8	155 children	Not stated	r = .70 between individually administered phonics test and reading achievement (Stanford) r = .66 with silent reading comprehension (Iowa) r = .55 with rate (Iowa)	
Durrell & Murphy (1953)	1,2,3	Several hundred children	Sight-meaning emphasis, moderate phonics	r = .52 to .56 between ability to notice separate sounds in words and reading achievement (Gates)	
Templin (1954)	4	318 children; mean IQ slightly above average	"Most teachers reported that they used phonics training when they felt it was necessary," but no reliable estimate of amount of phonics instruction	r = .22 to .47 between various phonic measures and reading achievement r = .23 to .57 between various phonic measures and spelling	
Rudisill (1957)	3	315 children	Not stated; by inference, "functional phonics," not separate or systematic	r = .71 between phonics knowledge and reading achievement (Stanford) r = .69 between phonics knowledge and spelling	r = .52 between MA (Otis) and reading achievement (Stanford); .29 with spelling
Cottrell (1958)	college	1652 students from 3 California colleges	Not stated	r = .67 between phonics knowledge and reading comprehension (Cooperative Test)	
Nicholson (1958)	1	2188 children	Early emphasis on letter names, ear training (hear-	r = .47 between naming lower case letters in Sept.	r = .37 between MA (Otis or California) and ability to

			ing separate sounds in words), then sight-meaning emphasis	and rate of learning words in Sept.	learn sight words
				r = .36 between giving sounds of lower case letters in Sept. and rate of learning words in Sept.§	
Olson (1958)	1	1172 children	same as Nicholson	r = .53 between naming lower case letters in Sept. and reading achievement‖ in Feb.	r = .41 between MA (Otis) and reading achievement
				r = .40 between giving sounds of lower case letters in Sept. and reading achievement‖ in Feb.	
				r = :57 between naming lower case letters in Feb. and reading achievement in Feb.	
				r = .65 between giving sounds of lower case letters in Feb. and reading achievement in Feb.	
Gavel (1958)	1	1506	same as Nicholson	r = .54 between naming lower case letters in Sept. and reading achievement in June	r = .44 between MA (Otis) and reading achievement in June
				r = .39 between giving sounds of lower case letters in Sept. and reading achievement in June	
				r = .51 between naming lower case letters in Feb. and reading achievement in June	
				r = .61 between giving sounds of lower case letters in Feb. and reading achievement in June	

Table 5–1 (Continued)

Study	Population		Beginning reading method	Correlation between letter and/or phonics knowledge and reading achievement	Correlation between mental ability (MA or IQ) and reading achievement
	Grades	Description			
Chall (1958)	2	48 (low SES)		r = .91 between phonics knowledge and oral reading (Gray)	
		44	Sight-meaning emphasis, moderate phonics	r = .92 between phonics knowledge and silent reading (New York Test of Growth in Reading)	
		27		r = .90 between phonics knowledge and spelling (Metropolitan)	
	5	50 (low SES)		r = .71 between phonics knowledge and reading (Metropolitan)	
	3–11 (retarded readers)	46 (low SES)	Sight-meaning emphasis, moderate phonics	r = .73 between phonics knowledge and oral reading (Gray)	
		44		r = .64 between phonics knowledge and reading (Metropolitan)	
		25		r = .57 between phonics knowledge and spelling (Metropolitan)	
Tierney (1961)	8	43	Not stated	r = .68 between phonics knowledge and reading achievement (Nelson)	r = .60 between IQ (Pinter General Ability) and reading achievement
Feuers (1961)	1	130 children; mean IQ of 109	Not stated	r = .62 to .81 between various measures of letter knowledge and sight word recognition (all tests given at the same time)	r = .45 to .57 between IQ (California) and word recognition

				r = .58 to .74 between knowledge of "letter sounds" and sight-word recognition (tested at same time)	
Forman (1962)	4	82 poor readers; low SES; mean IQ of 87	Not stated	r = .58 between phonics knowledge and reading achievement (Metropolitan)	r = .46 between IQ (Otis) and reading achievement (Metropolitan)
Weiner & Feldmann (1963)	1	126 children; 72 lower class, 54 middle class	Not stated	r = .70 (lower case) and .72 (upper case) between letter knowledge in Oct. and paragraph reading (Gates) in June; .75 (upper case) and .76 (lower case) letters in Oct. with sentence reading (Gates) in June	r = .67 between meaning vocabulary (no reading required) in Oct. and reading (Gates Primary, Paragraph Reading) in June; .29 with story-telling; .56 with subtest including vocabulary and story-telling

* *Rho* = rank correlation.
† Nearly half scored zero on reading letters.
‡ Reading achievement was measured by averaging the scores of 6 equally weighted tests, 2 given in the middle of grade 1, 2 given at the end of grade 1, and 2 in the middle of grade 2.
§ More than half scored zero on "sound" test in September.
‖ Reading achievement measured by oral reading test using basal reader vocabulary (Scott, Foresman).

Table 5–2 Correlation Coefficients among Various Tests of Letter and/or Phonics Knowledge and Reading Achievement, by Grade

Study	K	1	2	3	4	5	6	7	8	9	10	11	12	College
Wilson et al. (1938)		.6–.9												
Wilson & Fleming (1938)		.3–.9												
Rogers (1938)														.5
Gates et al. (1939)		.3–.4												
Tiffin & McKinnes (1940)								.6–.7						
Durrell & Murphy (1953)		.5–.6												
Templin (1954)					.2–.5									
Rudisill (1957)				.7										
Cottrell (1958)														.7
Nicholson (1958)		.4–.5												
Olson (1958)		.4–.7												
Gavel (1958)		.4–.6												
Chall (1958c)			.9					.6–.7						
Tierney (1961)									.7					
Feuers (1961)		.6–.8												
Forman (1962)					.6									
Weiner & Feldmann (1963)		.7–.8												

a generally higher association with early reading success than mental ability as measured by various intelligence tests and other tests of language and verbal ability (r's from .2 to .7).

Where letter knowledge, *before* learning to read, correlates below .5 with early reading achievement, substantial proportions of the children (about half) knew no letters at all (Gates et al., 1939). (A complete lack of knowledge on the part of some children in the group tested lowers the chances of finding a high correlation.)

A child's ability to give sounds for the letters *before* learning to read is also related to his early success in reading. But the correlations tend to be lower than those discussed above. Again, this may be because most children scored zero or very low on tests of this ability (Olson, 1958; Nicholson, 1958; Gates et al., 1939). However, on tests of detecting rhymes, giving words beginning with the same sounds, and auditory blending (giving words that are made by such separated sounds as *m-a-n*, *b-a-t*, etc.), the correlations with early reading success are higher; knowledge of the visual forms is not required on these tests, and more children can therefore score above zero on them (Gates et al., 1939).[3]

Once the children have learned to read, the correlations between their letter and/or phonics knowledge and their reading achievement are quite high. At every level tested—from kindergarten through college—letter and/or phonics knowledge is positively associated with reading achievement (whether measured by oral word recognition, connected oral reading, silent reading comprehension, or rate of reading) and also with spelling.

At the beginning stages of reading—in grades 1, 2, and 3—the relationship appears to be generally higher than at the intermediate and upper elementary grades. However, even in the upper elementary grades, the relationship is substantial, especially among poor readers. At the college level, and particularly among poor readers, knowledge of the sound values of letters still has an important relationship to reading ability.

WHAT THE FINDINGS MEAN

Since the tests given in these studies and the children who took them differed a great deal from study to study, drawing simple conclusions is hazardous. However, I think we can state some tenable generalizations:

1. Knowing the names of the letters *before learning to read* helps a child

[3] See Chall et al. (1963) and Chall et al. (1965). These studies found auditory-blending ability in grade 1 to be a significant predictor of reading achievement in grades 1, 2, 3, and 4.

in the beginning stages of learning to read, whether he learns from an approach emphasizing code or meaning.

2. Knowing the sound values of the letters and being able to hear similarities and differences in the spoken words *before learning to read* also helps a child learn to read in the beginning stages. This generalization too seems valid whether the beginning method is a code or a meaning emphasis one.[4]

3. In the primary grades (1, 2, and 3), letter and/or phonics knowledge appears to have a greater influence on reading achievement than mental ability (MA, IQ, or language measures similar to those used on general intelligence tests). Almost every study that correlated letter and/or phonics knowledge *and* mental ability with reading achievement reported higher correlations for letter and/or phonics knowledge. Even when IQ was held constant, a significant relationship between letter and/or phonics knowledge and reading achievement was reported.

The above generalization, although applicable in cases where children are exposed to both types of initial teaching methods, seems more valid when a code emphasis is used. Thus, mental ability seems to have an even lesser influence on reading achievement in the primary grades than knowledge of letters and/or phonics knowledge when the child learns from a method that emphasizes decoding.

4. Beyond the third grade, the relationship between phonics knowledge and reading achievement is still positive and substantial:

a. A low level of phonics knowledge tends to be consistently associated with a low level of achievement in reading.

b. A high level of phonics knowledge may or may not be associated with a high level of reading achievement.

This is easily understood if we remember that as the child grows older, intelligence plays a greater role in determining his reading achievement. The studies summarized in Table 5–1 tend to indicate this. They are confirmed by Lennon's analysis (1950) of the relationship between intelligence and achievement tests, which found increasing correlations between reading ability and intelligence, from .34 for the second grade to .85 for the eighth grade.

5. It was not possible to analyze correlations by components of reading (e.g., oral word recognition, connected oral reading, silent reading comprehension) because many studies did not report the types of tests used. Nevertheless, there are indications that letter and phonics knowledge is

[4] As we see later, Gates, Bond, and Russell would disagree with this and the above generalization on the basis of their own study (1939) and the Wilson et al. (1938) and the Wilson and Flemming (1938) studies.

more highly related to the more mechanical or "code-related" aspects of literacy—oral word recognition, connected oral reading, spelling, and rate of reading—than to such "conceptual" aspects as silent reading comprehension and vocabulary (word meaning) knowledge as measured on standardized silent reading tests. Remember, however, that the analysis of experimental studies showed that the decoding aspects influence outcomes on the conceptual aspects; thus, we can say that letter and phonics knowledge is also important for the ultimate goals of reading.

INTERPRETATIONS OF THE EVIDENCE

So much for my own conclusions from these studies. The authors, however, did not always conclude as I did. To understand how I reached my conclusions, you must look at the earlier studies in the settings in which they were made and originally interpreted, and also briefly consider some newer evidence only recently made available.

The earliest study analyzed (Wilson et al., 1938) presents convincing evidence that knowledge of letters and their sound values affects reading achievement. Wilson and his coinvestigators conducted a series of studies of kindergarten and first-, second-, and third-grade children in the Horace Mann School of Teachers College, Columbia University, during the early 1930s. From the results they concluded:

> The relations between abilities with letter forms and sounds on the one hand and reading ability, in terms of word, sentence, and paragraph reading, on the other hand are remarkably close for children learning to read in the Horace Mann School. . . . Ability with the letter symbols is to a large degree a causal factor in ability to read words and sentences. (p. 442)

Thus, they strongly defended teaching letters in kindergarten, citing evidence from the study that some children are ready for such instruction and are interested in it.

Wilson and his coauthors were well aware, however, that their findings—and especially their conclusions—went counter to the conventional wisdom of the period. They took pains to make clear that although letter forms and sounds were taught in the Horace Mann School, the reading program still met the "felt needs" of the children and that such teaching did not necessarily have to involve formal drill. They proposed, instead, a "functional" approach to teaching letters and sounds.

In view of their findings, Wilson and his coauthors were quite critical of prevailing teaching practices:

> It seems probable that most teachers far underestimate the long and difficult processes involved in mastering letter forms and sounds. In testing the children in this study the examiners were impressed with the intense effort put forth by most of the children in trying to name or to write letters. The efforts were often painful to

> observe: sustained frowning, alternate squirming and rigidity of body, pointing tensely, labored breathing, grunting, whispering, and even weeping. There are more than fifty-two printed letter forms and more than fifty-two script forms. These are complicated by varieties of type and by variations in written style more or less individual with every writer. It seems irrational to suppose that children can learn these many forms easily and painlessly. Still more irrational seems the theory that these confusing, and to the young child well-nigh numberless, forms should be learned without bringing attention directly to them. Such a theory, however, lies behind some current methods of teaching reading. The child must read sentences first, it is maintained, then break these up into phrases and then into words; but the idea unit must not be violated by any perception of letter elements. "Hat" will be "hat" and not "hot," "bed" will be "bed" and not "bad," by context, not because the child sees letter differences in the words. It would seem as if teachers who follow such a theory conspire against pupils in their efforts to learn; these teachers appear to be determinedly on guard never to mention a letter by name, to give a letter sound, or to show how to use either letter forms or sounds in reading. Further, such teachers compound confusion by directing attentions from the beginning to complicated patterns of forms and sounds which are forever changing their combinations in words, phrases, and sentences. Such a method may produce results (as almost any consistently used method will), but the reason may be mainly that the children attend to and learn the letters in spite of the teachers and the method. (p. 449)

As we shall see in Chapter 8, this description of first-grade teaching practices in 1938 is still appropriate today for teachers following the procedures suggested in the teachers' manuals of the most widely used basal-reading series. Clearly, then, the findings of these studies were not incorporated into practice; even now, a quarter century later, Wilson's criticisms and recommendations are still not generally heeded.

One reason is that other studies made later, most notably the work of Gates, Bond, and Russell, published in 1939, obscured Wilson's findings. These investigators, studying a public school population, found a lower correlation between letter knowledge and reading ($r = .3$) than Wilson had ($r = .3$ to $.9$). They ascribed the disparity to differences in the populations and in the initial reading instruction.

Gates noted that Wilson's Horace Mann children were brighter by about eighteen IQ points and came from more advantaged homes than his public school children. Thus, they had had more opportunity to learn the letters and sounds from books, ABC blocks, and so on. In addition, their school gave them early training in letter-sound correspondences.[5] The public school children tested by Gates did not know letter sounds and could not name the letters when they entered school. Once there, they were taught by a meaning-emphasis method.[6] And yet they too learned to read.

[5] In Gates's words, a "letter-first" emphasis.

[6] In Gates's words, "word-first with later analysis of letter combinations and single letters" emphasis.

Gates concluded from his observations of these differences that letter and phonics knowledge *before* reading will help a child learn to read only if he has some of this knowledge *before* he enters school and if, in school, he is exposed to a method that stresses developing it. Conceding that teaching the letters and their sound values first might be helpful to the Horace Mann pupils, who already had some mastery of letters, he nevertheless thought that public school pupils, with little training in letters and generally lower IQs, would find this course too difficult. He cites as evidence Wilson's description (quoted above) of the difficulty children experience in learning the letters. Like many others at the same period, Gates was greatly concerned that learning not be arduous. Although Wilson also mentioned the natural and keen interest most children show in learning the letters, Gates was most impressed by his observation of the difficulty that some children experienced.

In summing up, Gates wrote:

> We can agree with the Horace Mann investigators that knowledge of letters and letter sounds helps the pupil to work out the recognition and pronunciation of words, that acquiring this knowledge is difficult and time-consuming, that such learning should enlist the skilled assistance of the teacher and should not be left to chance and trial and error, and that it should be functional and not formal. But the suggestion that it should usually be given such early and emphatic attention as to become the major approach to learning to read is one we cannot accept. (p. 40)

Since Gates was the more prominent researcher (indeed, since the 1920s he has been the most productive and creative research scholar both in reading and in other areas of educational and psychological research) and since his conclusions fit the meaning-emphasis approach supported by Gray, his interpretation prevailed. The conclusion that early knowledge of the letters and their sound values produced superior results "disappeared" for some time from the stream of thinking about beginning reading, only to be discovered again by Durrell and his students in the middle 1950s.

Durrell's conclusions (1958) differ in two essential respects from Wilson's. First, Durrell proposed not only that letter and phonics knowledge has a positive influence on learning to read but also that *separate, systematic* (formal) instruction in letters and sounds has a greater effect than informal instruction. Second, he believed that such instruction should begin before or at the same time that pupils learn a sight vocabulary and that this instruction helps them learn a sight vocabulary.

Durrell's conclusions are based on a large-scale cooperative study by the language arts staff of Boston University.[7] The studies covered more

[7] Various students undertook separate aspects of the study: Nicholson (1958), Gavel (1958), Olson (1958), and Linehan (1958). Findings of the first three are summarized in Table 5–1. The Linehan study is summarized in Table 4–2.

than two thousand first-grade children in four communities of greater Boston with a mean chronological age in September of six years, three months, and a mean IQ of 110. Children were grouped by initial "readiness" as measured by a test of learning rate (ability to learn sight words), knowledge of letter names, and ability to hear sounds in words. They were given three different programs of instruction, all of which stressed learning the letters and sounds. Overall conclusions from the studies were as follows:

1. Most reading difficulties can be prevented by an instructional program which provides early instruction in letter names and sounds, followed by applied phonics and accompanied by suitable practice in meaningful sight vocabulary and aids to attentive silent reading. Among the 1,500 children measured in June, only 18 had a sight vocabulary of less than 50 words; this is slightly more than 1 percent of the population. Four percent, or 62 children, had a sight vocabulary of less than 100 words (Gavel, 1958).

2. Early instruction in letter names and sounds produces a higher June reading achievement than does such instruction given incidentally during the year (Linehan, 1958).

3. Children with high learning rates and superior background skills make greater progress when conventional reading readiness materials are omitted from their reading programs (Gavel, 1958).[8]

4. Children entering first grade (in the Boston area, mean IQ, 110) present wide differences in levels of letter knowledge.[9]

5. Tests of knowledge of letter names at school entrance are the best predictors of February and June reading achievement (Olson, 1958; Gavel, 1958). They relate most closely to learning rate in September (Nicholson, 1958).

6. Chronological age shows little relationship to any of the fa tors measured at any testing period. *It correlates negatively with reading achievement* (Olson, 1958; Gavel, 1958). A difference of nine months of chronological age produces a difference of only three months of mental age (Nicholson, 1958). Apparently no solution to reading difficulties is to be found by raising the entrance age to first grade.

[8] It is important to note here that the usual, conventional reading-readiness materials give practice in interpreting pictures, in speaking, and in observing similarities and differences in pictures and some geometric forms, but *no* instruction in identifying the letters of the alphabet.

[9] Durrell's public school children were superior (with a mean IQ of 110) to Gates's (mean IQ of 101), and they came to the first grade with considerably more knowledge (half of Gates's population could name no letters). It is interesting to speculate why Durrell's group had superior letter knowledge. Americans were, of course, generally better educated in the 1950s than in the 1930s; was this reflected in parents' attitudes? Had more of these children attended kindergartens and nursery schools? Or were parents already influenced by the Flesch book that urged them to teach the children at home and to start with the alphabet and sounds? Higher IQs alone should not be the crucial factor, since Durrell, like Wilson and others, found that letter knowledge and mental ability are not strongly related.

7. *Mental age,* as measured by the Otis Quick-scoring Tests of Mental Ability, *has a low relationship to reading achievement and to letter- and word-perception skills* (Nicholson, 1958; Olson, 1958; Gavel, 1958; Durrell, 1958, pp. 5–6). (emphasis mine)

Although Helen Robinson (1959) is justified in raising questions about the design of the Boston University study, particularly with regard to the equating of experimental and control groups (the experimental-group teachers seem to have received more supervision and guidance than the control-group teachers), most of the questions she raised may be applied to the bulk of the educational research in existence (see Chapter 4). Were we to use the strict methodological criteria Robinson proposes, there would be no research to summarize. The Boston University study seems to me as good as most studies of its kind, and Durrell's conclusions appear to be more grounded in the actual findings than is characteristic of most studies in beginning reading. At any rate, Durrell's study is only one of many other similar studies, conducted before and after his, that tend to find the same thing.

Durrell and the other investigators cited above all agree that letter and letter-sound knowledge is important for progress in learning to read. The only questions concern the nature and significance of the relationship: Is it causal? If it is causal, should children learn the alphabet and sounds before learning to read words? Gates, of course, thought the relationship causal only when the initial teaching method emphasized letters first, when the pupils were advanced intellectually, and when they had learned letters and sounds at home. Even then, letters and sounds, he believed, should be taught functionally, as part of and after initial reading. Wilson and Durrell, on the other hand, concluded that early knowledge of letters and sounds is causally related to reading achievement irrespective of the initial teaching method. Therefore, the alphabet and sounds should be taught *early,* either before or as children learn words. Durrell advocated systematic teaching of letter names and "ear training"; Wilson, like Gates, favored teaching letters and sounds functionally from words.

The additional evidence now available to us indicates, I believe, that Wilson and Durrell were probably more correct than Gates. The high correlations ($r = .7$ to $.9$) found by Weiner and Feldmann (1963) among both culturally disadvantaged and middle-class Negro and white children contribute to this evidence. Weiner and Feldmann did not report how their children were taught to read. However, we are probably safe in assuming that the prevailing method of the period was used, i.e., that the first and major stress was on acquiring a sight vocabulary and reading for meaning, with later and moderate emphasis on letters and sounds. The method, therefore, was probably not essentially different from that used with Gates's public school group in the 1930s. If this is true, the Weiner and Feldmann prediction study would confirm the importance of knowing letters first, before learning to read, even with pupils of average and below-average ability taught with a word or meaning emphasis.

Most of the first-grade cooperative studies sponsored by the USOE also found that children who knew the letters (and could hear the separate sounds in words) before they learned to read did better in reading at the end of the first grade. Indeed, Shirley Feldmann and I found this to be so among culturally disadvantaged first graders who were taught in classes where the "approved" method had a meaning emphasis (a modified, eclectic, conventional basal-reader approach), but where the teachers were observed to pull it toward either the code end or the meaning end of the continuum (Chall and Feldmann, 1966).

A recent laboratory study (Marchbanks and Levin, 1965) further strengthens the hypothesis that letters should be taught first, or at least early, as Durrell suggests. To discover the bases on which nonreaders and beginning readers recognize words, these investigators had fifty kindergarten and fifty first-grade children select from a group of pseudowords the one similar to a word they had just seen. Three- and five-letter pseudowords were used, all in lowercase type. Results indicated that the first letter of both the long- and short-word forms was the cue most used by both nonreaders and beginning readers in word recognition. The last letter in both word forms was the second most utilized cue for all subjects except the first-grade girls, who tended to work their way through the word letter by letter.[10]

In fact, the investigators observed that the girls tended to vocalize the letters, showing the effects of instruction in the alphabet, and to use their knowledge as "verbal mediators" in remembering the original word. The least-used cue in all cases was word shape.

The authors conclude:

> Theories which propose that beginning readers recognize words as wholes by their shape have not been supported by this study. . . . Rather, this study indicates that recognition is based on individual letters. . . . (p. 61)

If we assume again that the first graders in the Marchbanks and

[10] Most studies of reading achievement, especially at the lower elementary grades, have found that girls perform better than boys. Reading failures are also more characteristic of boys. The reasons given vary; some writers favor a social-cultural explanation, mentioning, for example, that most teachers are women or that reading materials and methods are more interesting to girls. Others cite developmental differences, stating that girls at the same chronological age have more advanced "brain organization" or are more mature physiologically.

Levin study also learned to read by the methods prevalent during the early 1960s, the evidence becomes even more significant, for their first graders, who had already received reading instruction, also used letter in preference to shape cues.

The extensive correlational work done by Joyce Morris in England (1959) also supports an initial emphasis on letters and their sound values. In a unique study sponsored by the National Foundation for Educational Research in England and Wales, Morris correlated various school characteristics with reading attainment, using more than seven thousand children, aged seven to eleven. She found a significant correlation ($r = .47$, $P<0.001$) between phonics as the beginning method and reading achievement after adjustment for intelligence (nonverbal). A significant correlation was also found for phonics with five-year-olds and reading achievement after adjustment for intelligence ($r = .36$, $P = 0.01$). Furthermore, after eliminating the effects of urban-rural location, socioeconomic status, and school size, "variables which cannot readily be altered," the correlation between phonics as a beginning method and reading achievement after adjustment for intelligence was still significant ($r = .48$), and that between phonics with five-year-olds and reading achievement was also significant ($r = .35$).

Although she was extremely cautious in presenting her conclusions, prefacing them with many reservations, Morris wrote:

> With these reservations, the results of the present inquiry lend little support to those who advocate an informal approach to reading without emphasis on systematic phonic instruction. . . . The fact that it was a test of reading comprehension ability which produced the results is also worthy of comment, for a summary of previous studies . . . indicated that the phonic method appears to improve word recognition, whilst the whole word approach promotes reading comprehension.
>
> Results of the Kent study also seem to conflict with previous evidence of the need for children to have at least a mental age of six years six months to seven years before phonic instruction is introduced. . . . (p. 128)

Four recent and significant studies support the hypothesis that children use different skills in reading at different levels and that early knowledge of sound-letter relationships helps the child master the earlier stages of reading, so that he can progress more quickly to the later stages.

The work of Holmes and Singer (1961) and Singer (1962) seems to indicate that the factors underlying power and speed of reading undergo a change between the fourth-grade and the high school level. At the fourth-grade level more auditory word recognition (phonetic association) is involved in reading, while at the high school level visual and conceptual factors play the more important role. Even at the fourth-grade level, different "substrata-factor sequences" are used for speed and for power of reading. Thus, Singer found that a fourth grader when reading for speed

> . . . tends to mobilize a working system undergirded by the processes of *visual* word recognition, concrete and functional concepts, rather than abstract levels of word meaning. However, when reading for power, his working system is organized to utilize more *auditory* word recognition processes (phonetic associations), auding (listening comprehension), and visual vocabulary abilities. (p. 230)

While Holmes and Singer (1961) also found an auditory word-recognition factor (phonetic association) among high school students, it was considerably less important than at the fourth-grade level.

Loban (1963) and Strickland (1962), who correlated children's oral language ability (in terms of complexity of language patterns used) to their reading achievement, found no significant relationship between oral language and reading achievement in the primary grades, although significant correlations were found for the intermediate grades. Thus, Strickland found a significant correlation between reading and oral language at the sixth-grade, but not at the second-grade, level. Loban reported that at the third-grade level, the best readers always had good oral language ability but that this did not necessarily go with good reading achievement. Like Strickland, he found that the relationship between oral language and reading increases from grades 4 through 6; by grade 6 the relationship is substantial.

We are now ready to answer the question posed at the beginning of the chapter: Do children need to know the alphabet (and to have a knowledge of letter-sound relationships) in order to learn to read?

Although we are dealing here with correlations only, and although the correlations found in almost all such studies could be attributed to a more fundamental cause, our answer, based on the research *as of now,* is *probably yes,* especially when the correlational studies are backed up by the experimental studies reported in Chapter 4 and by the Marchbanks and Levin (1965) laboratory experiment. Perhaps the crucial point is not that children must know *all* the letters *before* they learn to read words, but instead that they should *pay attention to* the letters, and naming or sounding them helps them pay attention. In fact, interest in, and concern with, letters among preschool children have been found positively associated with early success in reading; see, for example, Almy (1949) and Durkin (1964).

The importance of letters and letter-sound knowledge, however, changes through the years. They appear to be more essential for success in the early stages of reading than high intelligence and good oral language. In the middle grades, however, when the reading-matter content begins to tax the pupils' intellectual and language abilities and when most of them have a good knowledge of the alphabet and of letter-sound relationships (i.e., they have control over the "mechanics" of reading), intelligence and language ability begin to play a larger role in reading achievement. But the child who fails to master the first stage will find it difficult to reach the second.

I want to make one other point about the value of early knowledge of the alphabet, admittedly a speculative one. Doesn't an early knowledge of, and interest in, letters mark a new step in the child's intellectual development? The alphabet is a code, an abstraction, perhaps the first that the child learns (and one that is valued because adults value it). Pointing to and naming a letter, or writing a letter, at an early age is quite different from pointing to or drawing a picture of a cat, a truck, or a tree. The child who can identify or reproduce a letter engages in symbolic representation, to borrow a phrase from Jerome Bruner, while the child who is working with a picture of an actual object engages in iconic representation. When the child engages in symbolic representation, he is already practicing a higher form of intellectual behavior. Perhaps early mastery of this first step contributes to building the abstract attitude so necessary in our highly scientific and automated world.

SIX

Reading Failure—Is Method at Fault?

IN ALMOST EVERY class, there are some children who do not learn to read along with their classmates. These are the reading failures.

It is generally agreed that the true reading failure is not the child whose intelligence holds him back. Rather, he has all the necessary intellectual equipment, but has not been able to learn, or he does so slowly and with great difficulty.

My analysis of the research evidence on approaches to beginning reading would lack depth if I did not consider what is known about the relationship between method and reading failure as well as success. Does one approach produce more failures—or different kinds of failures—than another? Is one approach more successful in treating reading problems than another? Is there any action we can take to reduce the number of reading failures in the future?

To learn more about these questions, I analyzed six reports, veritable classics in the field, on case studies of pupils with reading problems. For further insight into how reading failures and retarded readers can be helped, I also examined four experimental studies of results with various remedial methods.

The Case-study Reports

During the time span covered by these six reports (1922 to 1946), the approach to teaching reading changed considerably. Thus, the children discussed in some reports received initial reading instruction that strongly emphasized phonics, while those in others received much less phonics. As a guide to what approach was most common at a given time, I used the historical account of Nila B. Smith (1963 and 1965). She indicates the following initial reading methods for the period 1890 to 1955:

> 1890–1920: Elaborate, synthetic phonic systems [were used] in which the child was started out immediately with practice on sounds of isolated letters and "family words" [hall, ball, tall, etc.].
>
> 1920–1935: The new emphasis became that of reading silently to get the thought and the use of phonics was looked upon as an outmoded procedure.
>
> Experience charts were first introduced during this period. With the use of the experience chart children were initiated into reading instruction by reading, as a whole, a small unit of text which they had composed, after which the teacher called for the reading of sentences, phrases and words as she broke down the composition into smaller parts.
>
> 1935–1955: Phonics began to come back gradually . . . supplemented, however, with the use of picture clues, context clues, structural analysis and dictionary skills. Charts continued to be used for initial instruction in reading. (1963, pp. 1–2)

Two of the clinical reports (Gray, 1922; Gates, 1922) were published when phonics was being abandoned as a beginning method. However, since it takes a year or two to write up a study, and since the children involved probably received their initial reading instruction several years before, we may infer that most of them learned by a code-emphasis method, using some elaborate, synthetic-phonics system.

When the third study (Monroe, 1932) was published, "thought" methods were more common. Monroe's pupils probably received their initial instruction under a heavy meaning emphasis.

Although the next two reports (Orton, 1937; Fernald, 1943) were published during a period when phonics was coming back gradually, supplemented with "picture clues, context clues, structural analysis and dictionary skills," the pupils studied probably also received their first- and second-grade instruction during the silent reading, meaning-emphasis period. It is important to note, however, that both of these investigators formulated their views considerably earlier than the publication dates of their books indicate, Fernald probably as early as 1915 or 1916.[1]

Pupils described in the last report (Robinson, 1946) were probably in the first and second grades when phonics was coming back "gradually, with supplements."

The reports vary considerably; they demonstrate a growing depth of analysis, with time, into the study of both the causes and the treatment of reading disability.

WILLIAM S. GRAY (1922)

Gray, writing in 1922, acknowledged a relationship between method and failure. He wrote in his introduction:

> Regular classroom instruction frequently fails to provide adequately for pupils who encounter unusual difficulties in reading. There are thousands of boys and girls in school each year who make little or no progress because of inaccuracies and personal handicaps which could be eliminated. (p. 2)

His solution was that teachers should "make systematic, detailed studies of the reading difficulties of children, and they must provide appropriate remedial instruction." (p. 2)

In his book, Gray presents twenty-five such case studies of pupils aged seven through twenty, grouped by type of remedial case, and he outlines the steps taken to overcome their difficulties. Although some of his descriptions of reading problems sound outdated today, his remedial steps are very similar to those given in current manuals on diagnosis and treatment.

When we analyze Gray's remedial cases and eliminate those with low mental ability, we find one characteristic common to almost all: *poor word recognition and analysis.*

Why did these children fail? On the basis of previously published studies as well as his own case studies, Gray listed fourteen causes. The list strikes us as unsophisticated today, since he gave parallel *causal* weight to general personal characteristics (e.g., "defective vision") and specific reading difficulties (e.g., "narrow span of recognition.")

Two of the fourteen causes concern initial teaching method. The

[1] I am indebted to Arthur Gates for this point. He referred me to an early article by Fernald and Keller in the *Journal of Educational Research,* December, 1921, entitled "The Effects of Kinesthetic Factors on Development of Word Recognition."

first of these is inadequate training in phonics. Gray further amplified this as follows:

> Recent experiments have shown that some children are able to learn very well without any systematic training in phonetics.[2] Other children in the same class fail because they are unable to recognize words independently, but when given supplementary training in phonetics and word analysis, they are able to make up their deficiencies. (p. 16)

The second cause is inadequate attention to content:

> Phonetic drill had been carried beyond the point where it was useful. Instead of being the means to the recognition of word meaning, it had become an end in itself, and really blocked the recognition of the meaning. (p. 17)

Gray postulated these two causes from the errors his pupils made. He did not try to discover whether those who did not know phonics had actually received any phonics instruction. Similarly, he did not determine whether those who seemed to use too much phonics had been over-drilled in it. According to Nila Smith's historical analysis of trends, most of his backward readers probably learned initially by a phonic method. Yet, since one cause reported by Gray was *too little* phonics, schools and teachers at that time were probably like those of today—not all followed the prevailing method.

Clearly, it is dangerous to guess what method resulted in failure on the basis of errors and broad historical trends. Nevertheless, I believe we may chance at least one inference from Gray's case studies: Too little or too much phonics may contribute to failure. Perhaps more fundamental is the possibility that some pupils are strongly predisposed toward difficulty in word recognition and analysis; if this is the case, neither the code emphasis of the early 1900s nor the meaning emphasis brought in since the 1920s can be said to have entirely overcome this problem.

ARTHUR I. GATES (1922)

Gates's report, based on a more thorough study of good and poor readers in grades 3 to 8 (median IQ 117), is considerably more analytical. He correlated various aspects of reading, spelling, handwriting, and school achievement with scores on tests of visual perception and intelligence to get at the *what* and *why* of both reading and spelling failure.

Gates concluded that the one characteristic distinguishing the poor from the more able readers was *an unsatisfactory method of attacking a new or difficult word.* Poor comprehension, slow rate, irregular eye movements, and so on were *results* rather than causes; they developed because

[2] Gray is referring here and elsewhere to what I call *phonics.*

the pupil had been grappling unsuccessfully for a long time with word recognition and analysis.

Gates concluded that the major causes of this difficulty with decoding had to do with unfavorable training and environmental influences. The first among these was:

> Learning wholly by the "natural" method or "word" method or otherwise without training in visual perception analysis [which] results frequently in inappropriate methods of observing words. This occurred among pupils who had superior intelligence and no organic or physical defects that could be discovered; who were anxious to learn. (p. 89)

Gates believed the second important cause of backwardness in reading to be:

> Inappropriate forms of phonic or phonetic or other types of analytical training. . . . (p. 90)

The third cause he described as:

> Changes from one form of phonic, phonetic, or visual training to another, [which] may result in confusion and prevent the formation of effective perceptual habits. (p. 91)

Thus, many of Gates's backward readers, like Gray's, had originally learned by a "natural" or "word" method, although when they were in the first and second grades the prevailing method was, according to Smith, synthetic phonics. Again this shows the hazards of making inferences from historical trends.

Both Gates and Gray found that no phonics was bad and that wrong phonics was also bad. However, in describing two children who had received so much phonics that they exhibited "overemphasis on articulatory responses" and could attack words far beyond their comprehension, Gates noted:

> In the two cases observed, there was but little difficulty in securing a transition to more appropriate reading habits. (p. 55)

Thus, it would seem that Gates's backward readers were suffering mainly from lack of training, especially consistent training, in phonics. Those who had had too much phonics could easily be helped. The more serious problem was posed by those who had had no phonics or inconsistent phonics.

For these children Gates outlined a program for training in word perception. With it he included some general principles on providing such training for backward readers:

> 1. The method should be simple enough for the subject to employ himself.
> 2. The method should be such as not to yield readily to overuse. Analytical work

should not be done for its own sake; no word or practice should be introduced for the sake of the system, a common defect of most phonetic[3] practices.[4]

3. The method should provide against the teaching of what is already known, what will be known without teaching, or what ought not to be known. For example, little time should be devoted to phonetic training for the mass of pupils. The associations between letter combinations and sounds come, as a rule, without special effort. The difficulty is not in the association between the word and the sound but in acquaintance with the form of the word. This distinction is important. Some of our backward cases who were said to have no "phonic ability," were found to have extraordinary capacity for representing sounds by letters; in fact, they could give many different combinations of letters which were phonically adequate. That they did not know which one of these the English race had adapted, was no reflection on their phonic ability.[5] The futility of much phonetic drill is that the pupils already know or soon will know it without the daily articulatory gymnastics. . . .

4. An acquaintance with many small words as wholes should precede training in word analysis.

5. It should be understood that the purpose of analytical work is not the perception of longer words piece by piece, nor a fund of information about the composition of words nor a stock of serial recitals. What is wanted is the *habit* of seeing a word as a group of familiar and simpler parts and of seeing it more clearly, rather than seeing it confusedly or vaguely as one would at first perceive a complicated Chinese character. (pp. 45–46)

[3] *Phonic,* here and elsewhere in this quotation.

[4] This principle and the two preceding it illustrate my observation in Chap. 3 that researchers in reading have been influenced by the theories and philosophical assumptions of their times. Gates accepted the connectionist theory of E. L. Thorndike, according to Hilgard (1948) the dominant theory of learning in America for at least half a century after Thorndike announced it in his *Animal Intelligence* (1898). As Gates wrote in the 1927 experimental study cited in Chap. 4, "In the light of the theory which considers all learning to be the establishment of definite reactions to specific situations and in the light of established facts concerning the transfer of training, the validity of phonetics and other supplementary devices may well be questioned. Their probable weakness lies precisely in the fact that they are supplementary and not intrinsic. They depend upon the transfer of training which probably occurs in small degree, if at all." (p. 218)

[5] The concern with the irregularity of English spelling that Gates reveals here has been widespread. From 1920 on, most reading theory and practice has stressed irregularity, and methods textbooks have cited words like "cough" and "though" to illustrate the futility of using a phonic method. Only the phonics proponents continued to emphasize the basic regularity of English. Thus, Hay and Wingo stated that 85 percent of English is regular (1954). More recently, John B. Carroll (1964) has written: "These [grapheme-phoneme] correspondences, in English, are more regular than irregular, contrary to the impression often given. It may be estimated that a computing machine could be programmed to translate a printed text into phonemes with better than 95 percent accuracy even without building into the computer program information about irregularly spelled words. The program would simply incorporate a large number of rules for translating graphemes in conjunction with other graphemes in their immediate environments. Now, the number of such rules might be much larger than the number it would be feasible to embody in a procedure for teaching reading to children, but many of them are of considerable power. There is evidence, in fact, that mature readers behave as if they had acquired a large number of these rules." (p. 340)

Thus Gates, like Gray, prescribed for most of his backward readers (who lacked skill in word perception) training in decoding, but training that was not separate from the "process of reading." Interestingly enough, the word-perception program outlined in Gray's 1948 book, *On Their Own in Reading* (and incorporated into other conventional basal series since then), is basically that proposed by Gates in 1922 for backward readers: first the teaching of whole words, followed by analysis of sound-letter correspondences from words learned as wholes, with emphasis on visual aspects of words (no direct learning of the sound values of letters), no blending of letter sounds, and primary stress on larger units. Gray called this "structural analysis," while Gates simply said: "Begin with syllables as the smallest unit." Above all, Gray followed through on Gates's suggestion about "not teaching analysis in isolation."

MARION MONROE (1932)

Monroe's correlational study of 415 pupils, ranging in age from seven to seventeen, resembled Gates's in method and scope. Since it came ten years later, however, most of her children probably had received their initial instruction under a heavier meaning emphasis. Monroe, too, found that her severe cases (average reading grade of 2.5) had extreme difficulty with word recognition and analysis.

Monroe looked more toward the personal characteristics of her backward readers for causes than Gates had; in fact, she seemed to favor the possibility of a constitutional factor. At the same time, she did not rule out method as a possible cause:

> In individual cases, we found evidence of deleterious effects of certain methodological practices, such as over-speeding or some methods of developing word recognition. We did not, however, study the methodological factors quantitatively. (p. 102)

Monroe's remedial program for the severe cases—those reading below the second-grade level—made much use of procedures considered outmoded and even harmful for ordinary beginning instruction: a heavy dose of synthetic phonics and motor responses like "finger pointing," "articulating," and "grunting and groaning." Monore explained:

> The very complexity of the reading process offered the possibility of a variety of methods of learning. Reading, like thought, may be accomplished in many ways. . . . We tried to teach the children who had trouble in learning to read to utilize the possible secondary or vicarious steps in word-recognition which are not usually presented in ordinary instruction. . . .

As reasons for stressing overt motor responses she gave:

> (1) The overt motor response is more easily observed by both the teacher and the child than an ideational response. . . .

(2) The overt motor responses are probably a part of the normal reading process, but the movements soon become incipient or fragmentary with unselected children and are not easily observed in the learning process. . . . The reading-defect cases . . . may not be able to relinquish the overt responses until a later stage of learning. By exaggerating the movements we may intensify at least one of the components of the learning process.

(3) The overt motor responses, when carefully controlled, may assist in discrimination. Many of the reading-defect cases had no observable deficiencies in sensory organs and yet failed to discriminate . . . sounds of vowels or the spatial position of patterns. It is probable that, in cases of no sensory defect, the difficulty in discrimination lies in the central co-ordinating mechanisms.[6] By forcing the child to make different motor responses to the different sensory characteristics, and thereby reinforcing the visual and auditory stimuli with discriminable kinesthetic cues, we may ultimately develop more precise discrimination of the visual and auditory characteristics.

(4) The overt motor responses, directed toward the sensory stimuli, may also assist in attention. . . . By bringing into play a larger number of movements, all of which are directed toward the visual and auditory stimuli, the child may be able to prolong the attentional adjustment. (pp. 111–113)

In defense of these special remedial methods, which differed so markedly from classroom methods that were opposed to a mechanical approach and sought for smooth, silent reading from the start, Monroe noted:

To the usual child, the emphasis on motor responses as outlined here, and the placement of secondary links in the learning process, may be an unnecessary procedure, detracting from the enjoyment through the mechanical devices for recognition of words.[7] The child who has not learned to read, however, and who for the first time finds that he can succeed in reading simple words and sentences, even if by somewhat laborious methods, finds a new interest and enthusiasm for reading, and a new respect for his own capacities. (p. 113)

Once the word-recognition problem was cleared up, she observed, the mechanical reading disappeared, and the reading-defect child read like a normal reader, except when he met an unfamiliar word. Monroe's reading-defect cases seem to have followed the probable growth pattern we hypothesized for "unselected" children taught by a code-emphasis method (see Chapter 4). For them, emphasizing the code did not lead to the mechanical, word-by-word reading so many fear.

To quote Monroe again:

Re-examinations of children taught by these methods show that after the initial start in reading is made, the children become more and more like normal readers. The secondary links, while utilized extensively by the children at first, become less in

[6] Compare M. D. Vernon (1957). Vernon, after reviewing the entire literature to 1957, came to essentially the same conclusion.

[7] As we saw in Chaps. 4 and 5, there is no substantial evidence for this very common assumption.

> evidence and seem to disappear. Speed of reading develops gradually without specific pressure. Words are grouped into phrases and larger thought units. After remedial training, reading takes on the character of normal performance until the child meets a strange, unfamiliar, or forgotten word. The mechanical links thereupon immediately become evident as the child attacks the word. Incipient tracing or articulatory movements appear until the word is recognized, and the child proceeds with the reading.[8] Thus, it appears that the child ultimately builds up an organization of responses which is very similar to the usual performance of unselected children, although the underlying steps in building the organization are somewhat different. (p. 114)

You will remember that Gates, too, found it easy to help the few backward readers who were able to sound out words beyond their own understanding, and who overarticulated, simply by encouraging reading for content.

SAMUEL T. ORTON (1937)

In his 1937 volume, Orton, a neurologist, summarized his findings from

> . . . a ten-year period of intensive study of some disorders in the acquisition of the language faculty encountered by certain children, as interpreted from a much longer period of interest and study from the literature, in the clinic, at the autopsy table and in the laboratory, of cerebral localization and of the aphasias. (p. 11)

His studies covered several hundred cases diagnosed and retrained.

"Obviously," Orton wrote, "there are multiple causes for a delay in learning to read." Among those he cited were marked defects in vision, in hearing, and in general intellectual ability and emotional disturbances.

> When, however, all of such factors are excluded there remains a group of very considerable size in every school who have shown no evidence of any delay or abnormality in either their physical, mental, or emotional development until they have reached school and are confronted with reading, and then they suddenly meet a task which they cannot accomplish. (p. 73)

Why? Orton's theory was that such children fail to develop consistent dominance of one side of the brain over the other; this leads to confusion and conflict, resulting in various forms of language disability.[9]

[8] Edfeldt (1960) found essentially the same thing in a study of eighty-four students during their first term at the University of Stockholm. With the electromyograph, which electronically measures muscular activity, he found that good readers engage in less silent speech than poor readers and that both good and poor readers engage in less silent speech when reading an easy or clear text than when reading a difficult or blurred one. Silent speech, says Edfeldt, occurs to some degree in everyone's reading. It is not necessarily a habit detrimental to reading; it merely indicates that the reader is reading something difficult for him to grasp (p. 152).

[9] Orton's theory of cerebral dominance has not been substantiated, but his general view of specific language disability has been accepted by many current investigators of reading disability. See Bender (1951 and 1958), de Hirsch (1954 and 1957),

During the first two years of exposure to reading, the child is unable to learn to recognize words at sight as readily as normal readers do. Spelling is almost always poor, as well as handwriting. In older children, silent reading has usually improved, but oral reading, spelling, and the mechanics of language are poor, and the child finds it particularly difficult to learn a foreign language.

According to Orton, one factor is common to these cases of specific language disability:

> . . . a difficulty in repicturing or rebuilding in the order of presentation, sequences of letters, of sounds, or of units of movement. . . . (p. 145)

Thus, although Orton's theory of causation differed from those of Gray, Gates, and Monroe, he found the same kind of difficulty—a difficulty with the decoding or mechanical aspects of reading rather than with comprehension.

Could the "proper" initial teaching method have made a difference? Orton tended to think so:

> In those children whose training in reading has been exclusively by the "whole word" or "sight method" . . . order (sequences of letters, sounds, and movements) remains as an obvious difficulty much longer than in those who have been taught the sounds which each letter represents and hence have an auditory clue to the proper sequence. (pp. 145–146)

His remedial training for children with a language disorder, particularly in reading and spelling, was a systematic-phonics program buttressed by kinesthetic aids (finger pointing, tracing, and writing)—procedures quite similar to those Monroe advocated. Noting that such mechanical approaches are frowned upon, Orton commented:

> This method of finger pointing while reading is a spontaneous act with some children and has been criticized as retarding the rate of reading seriously. There remains, however, the very pertinent question as to whether children who use finger pointing while reading are slow readers because of the strephosymbolic confusions (seeing *b* as *d*, *saw* as *was*, etc.) and make use of the finger to overcome their difficulty. It must be remembered here, moreover, that in the case of extreme degrees of reading disability our choice may not lie between rapid and slow reading but between slow reading or not at all. (pp. 163–164)

Acknowledging that these methods are diametrically opposed to those used in many schools, he says:

---

de Hirsch et al. (1966), Rabinovitch et al. (1956), Money (1962), Silver and Hagin (1960), and Roswell and Natchez (1964). See particularly Brewer (1963) for a comprehensive summary of the literature on specific language disability from 1896 to 1963. Two reading programs have been developed from Orton's remedial procedures: the remedial program of Gillingham and Stillman (1940) and the writing-reading-spelling method of Spalding (1962).

There has been in recent years a striking swing toward the use of the sight or flash-card method of teaching reading and away from the use of phonetics [i.e., phonics]. The writer is not in a position to offer an opinion as to the efficacy of either of these methods as a general school procedure but their effect on children suffering from varying degrees of strephosymbolia has come under his immediate attention and he feels that there can be no doubt that the use of the popular flash method of teaching reading is a definite obstacle to children who suffer from any measure of this disability. We have no new numerical data to offer here since our work recently has dealt exclusively with referred cases and we have made no general surveys of the number of cases of the reading disabilities in schools using different methods. At an earlier period, however, some such surveys were undertaken in Iowa and they indicated strongly that where the sight or flash-card method of teaching reading was exclusively used, the number of reading disability cases was increased by three times that found in schools which used phonetic [i.e., phonic] training for those children who did not rapidly progress by the flash-card method. . . . (pp. 175–176)

But Orton also stated that a phonic method in the initial stage does not guarantee success. He cites reading-disability cases who had learned to give the sounds for the letters and phonograms, etc., but still could not read:

In these cases, examination has revealed the fact that while the teaching of the phonetic [i.e., phonic] equivalents may have been fairly complete, the next and most cardinal step, that of teaching the blending of the letter sounds in the exact sequence in which they occur in the word, had not been attempted or had been poorly carried out. It is this process of synthesizing the word as a spoken unit from its component sounds that often makes much more difficulty for the strephosymbolic child than do the static reversals and letter confusions.[10] (p. 162)

GRACE M. FERNALD (1943)

Grace M. Fernald, writing in 1943, also found that her backward readers were unable to identify and analyze words, and her famous kinesthetic method was designed specially to help them overcome this deficiency. With regard to whether their initial training contributed to this weakness, Fernald states:

It seems that most cases of reading disability are due to blocking of the learning process by use of limited, uniform methods of teaching. These methods, although they have been used successfully with the majority of children, make it impossible for certain children to learn because they interfere with the functioning of certain abilities that these children possess.

At present one of the main blocks is the use of extremely visual methods of presentation with suppression of such motor adjustments as lip, throat, and hand movements. . . .

[10] In a series of studies going back as far as Gates et al. (1939), auditory blending has been found positively related to reading achievement. See also Chall et al. (1963), Huset (1961), and Chall et al. (1965).

> We do not claim that all cases of reading disability are due to the use of methods that omit kinesthetic factors, but merely that such cases exist and that under our present system of education, a large percentage of the cases of extreme disability are due to the above. . . . It seems also to be true that many cases of partial disability are due to the same general situation, though the individual is not so dependent on kinesthetic factors as is the individual of total disability. . . . (pp. 175–176)

Although Fernald did not use the word *phonic* in describing her remedial techniques (and in fact was opposed to formal phonics), some of the steps she proposed resemble quite closely the methods of Monroe and Orton, which strongly emphasize phonics. In Fernald's view, the first step in learning to read is to master the printed code for the spoken language. Throughout, her program shows a great sensitivity to, and compassion for, children with reading disability who, although they are of normal or sometimes superior intelligence, are deeply hurt and embarrassed by their failure at something that seems to come naturally to many of their peers.

Fernald divided her remedial program into four stages. In the first stage, the child traces the word with his finger, saying each part out loud as he traces it until he can write it without looking at the copy. By the second stage, he can learn any new word by looking at it, saying it to himself, and then writing it while repeating each part to himself. He is urged to say the parts of the word to himself, Fernald explains, to "establish the connection between the sound of the word and its form."[11]

In the third stage, the child can look at a word (even a long one), say it once or twice, and then write it without looking at the original; once he writes the word he will recognize it at sight when he meets it again. By the final stage, he can begin to generalize about words and identify new ones from their resemblance to words he already knows.

By this last stage, Fernald's remedial-reading case is eager to read. His enjoyment is the *result*, not the *cause*, of his reading skill. Note also that Fernald stressed using, from the beginning, reading materials suited in terms of vocabulary and content to the child's intelligence level rather than to his reading skill. She explains:

> The child is much more interested in writing and reading fairly difficult material that is on the level of his understanding than simpler material which is below his mental age level. . . . (p. 44)

Fernald made some cogent observations about the course of growth of the various components of reading, specifically word recognition, comprehension, and reading rate.

[11] The practice of saying words out loud or to oneself is discouraged as early as possible in today's prevailing beginning reading methods.

> Many teachers will carry a reading case through the first stages with great enthusiasm and encounter no difficulty but will expect some miracle to complete the process and give the individual that flexible, immediate recognition of various word groups with words arranged in all the combinations in which they occur in printed material. It is certain that the failures reported in many remedial reading cases are due to the failure to give the individual the wealth of experience necessary for intelligent and rapid reading. (p. 55)

Like Monroe and Orton, Fernald indicated that, contrary to widespread belief, a child who learns to read mechanically need not read in this fashion forever:

> Although these children learned by a peculiar method until they had acquired a certain degree of skill, they were normal in their adjustments after that stage had been reached. They were able to go on with the group and in many cases were distinctly superior to the group. (p. 145)

In fact, Fernald proposed (as did Monroe) that suppressing such "adaptive movements" as saying and writing the words during the initial stage of learning may in fact impede progress later, even for normal readers:

> In reading, just as in other learning, the adaptive movements drop out as skill is perfected and final smooth performance shows none of the activities that characterized the initial learning process. We are of the opinion that in reading, just as in other activities, the suppression of adaptive movements in the initial stages of learning leads to the continuance of these movements in the more advanced stages and slows down the entire reaction.[12] (p. 169)

HELEN M. ROBINSON (1946)

In her case studies, Robinson departed from the practice of making detailed analyses of the failing child's specific reading strengths and weaknesses and turned instead to physical, psychological, and social factors for an explanation. Her cases were examined by a team of specialists including

> . . . a social worker, a psychiatrist, a pediatrician, a neurologist, three ophthalmologists, a speech-correction specialist, an otolaryngologist, an endocrinologist, a reading specialist, and the investigator, who acted as psychologist and reading technician. (p. 3)

Judging from their scores on the Gray Oral reading test, we can infer that most, if not all, of Robinson's children had word-recognition and word-analysis difficulties. The most prevalent causes of reading failure in

[12] Most code-emphasis methods permit more adaptive movements than meaning-emphasis methods, which caution the child against whispering, finger pointing, etc. Indeed, use of tracing and writing (typing) for unselected first-grade children seems generally beneficial. Some evidence for this is suggested by findings of the USOE first-grade studies (*The Reading Teacher,* May, 1966).

the thirty cases were found to be maladjusted homes (55 percent of the children came from such homes), visual anomalies (in half of the cases), and emotional problems (in 32 percent). Incorrect reading methods, pertinent for 18 percent of the children, were fourth in importance.

Robinson stated that she did not evaluate the reading methods that had caused problems in 18 percent of the cases because she lacked the necessary information. But she also noted:

> Since a large number of these severely retarded readers improved, it seems logical to assume that better adaptation of methods of teaching reading to some of the deviating cases has greater value than the number of such cases reported in this study indicates. (pp. 226–227)

In contrast to previous investigators, Robinson paid little attention to the "phonics versus sight" or decoding-emphasis versus meaning-emphasis issues, probably because by the middle 1940s there had been a return, *at least in theory*, to a combined sight-phonics approach. Her findings on emotional causes, buttressed, of course, by the writings of other psychologists, education specialists, and psychoanalysts, formed the basis of what became, in the late 1940s and 1950s, and remains to some extent today the prevalent approach to reading disability. Indeed, in 1960 the national sponsors of American Education Week (the National Education Association, the American Legion, the USOE, and the National Congress of Parents and Teachers), in a suggested advertisement for local newspapers based on the theme "What Teachers Know about Your Child," said:

> Typically, an elementary-school teacher, during a thirty-year career, will live with, work with, and love more than 1,000 children. . . . Teachers receive extensive training in child psychology. They learn to recognize signals of potential delinquency. . . . They learn that reading difficulties often result from emotional problems. . . .

The Experimental Studies

Four experimental studies tell us something about the effectiveness of different approaches for helping children who have had difficulties in learning to read.

The earliest (Currier, 1923) is only suggestive, describing what the author did with her own third-grade class. Dividing the class into three groups according to reading achievement, she gave the advanced children no phonics, the middle group ("careless, inattentive readers") intensive phonics drills, and the lowest group ("foreign, poor, and retarded children") an easy reading program designed to restore their confidence, followed by intensive phonics and word drills. All groups made good progress.

Currier concluded that not all children learn best from the same system; what is food for one can be poison for another. In essence, however, she did not vary the method according to the individual pupil's IQ, but according to his stage of reading attainment. Her treatment of the poorest-achieving group indicates that her conclusions were the same as mine on the interaction of IQ and method (see Chapter 4): For immediate results, a look-say method is a good choice because it is easier. But for more lasting results, even poor achievers must master phonics.

Burt and Lewis (1946) caution the reader not to generalize too much from their study, since they were concerned mainly with trying out a new statistical technique—analysis of variance. They compared four groups of eleven-year-old English children of low intelligence (IQs 79 to 83) who were retarded in reading, even considering their mental ages. Each group received one year of reading instruction with a different approach: visual (sight or whole word), kinesthetic (tracing and writing the words), alphabet (spelling), and phonic (sounding).

All the pupils improved. The visual group improved more than the others, but only 10 percent more than the least improved group. The kinesthetic approach was also more effective than the alphabet and phonic approaches. The authors cited the teachers' opinions that for the dull and backward, the best procedure is "active learning" based predominantly on a visual approach. They further noted that a mere change of method made for improvement. Their overall conclusion was that for ordinary dull and backward pupils, a phonic approach is too hard.

It is significant that the phonic method used in this experiment was quite difficult, even for normal children; for phonics instruction it used common, irregularly spelled, high-frequency words containing many exceptions to the phonic generalizations taught. Also, most of the pupils had received their initial instruction from a program emphasizing phonics; these children were denied the novelty effect experienced by the others.

Mills (1956) compared four methods of teaching word recognition to seven- to nine-year-olds in the second and third grades who were retarded in reading by six months. The four approaches were kinesthetic, phonic, visual, and a combination of these three. The children were compared on their ability to learn ten words in a fifteen-minute period. The words were selected on the basis of the frequency of their use in basal readers and were equated for difficulty on this basis.

Mills found some differences in effectiveness of methods by IQ: The children with IQs between 65 and 80 generally did best with the kinesthetic approach, but not significantly better than with a visual or combination approach. The phonic approach, which was the least effective overall, was significantly less helpful for these low-IQ pupils. For the children with IQs between 85 and 100, the visual and combination approaches worked best; the phonic approach worked less well, but not significantly so. The kinesthetic approach was the least effective.

For the children with IQs between 105 and 120 all approaches seemed equally effective.

Thus, Mills found that the effectiveness of a phonic emphasis in particular depended on IQ—the lower his IQ, the less readily a retarded reader learned by a phonic approach compared with other approaches.

Again, however, the phonic approach used in this study relied on words of high frequency, many of which were irregularly spelled. The teacher sounded each letter separately, said the word, and then asked the pupil to do the same. Since many of the ten words to be learned in fifteen minutes could not be sounded letter by letter, and since the phonic elements of those which could be were not limited, learning from Mills's phonic method was a difficult task, especially for retarded readers of below-average intelligence.

The most extensive experimental study of methods of teaching retarded readers was made by Daniels and Diack (1956). They compared their phonic-word method with a mixed method (sight, then gradual phonics) using eight-year-old nonreaders. The Daniels and Diack method is probably easier than the phonic method used in the Burt and Lewis and the Mills studies. The method used by Daniels and Diack's control group also included phonics, but contained words selected on a meaning-frequency principle and often irregularly spelled. After one year, the phonic-word group tested higher in oral word recognition and sentence reading than the other group.

In summary, the research evidence tells us the following about the relationship between initial teaching method and failure to learn to read and about what we can do to help reading failures:

1. In answer to the overall question of whether reading failure stems primarily from the initial teaching method or from various characteristics of the child, I would say that both are involved. Analysis of the research evidence presented in this chapter (supported by analysis of other studies, my knowledge of current theories of disability, and my own experience in the diagnosis and treatment of reading and spelling disability) leads me to believe that we cannot blame reading failure—especially extreme disability—on either the child or the initial method alone. Severe disability seems to result when a child has a predisposition (a set of characteristics that make it difficult for him to associate printed symbols with their spoken counterparts) *and* is exposed to an initial method that ignores this predisposition.

2. The six clinical studies analyzed do not prove that any one method used during the initial stages of reading instruction produces more reading failures than any other. I am not really sure what method was initially

used with these cases. Also, none of the investigators indicated what proportion of the general school population his cases represented. To add to our difficulty, each investigator defined failure to learn to read differently. Gray even studied children with IQs as low as 53; today these children would not be considered reading failures.

Unless national surveys are taken in which the initial reading methods are described (not only by teachers and administrators, in their reports, but also by impartial observers) and in which pupils are tested over a long period, we will lack sufficient data to say how beginning methods influence general reading attainment and to what extent they cause reading failure.

3. The six case studies do indicate, however, that both broad approaches to beginning reading—a code emphasis and a meaning emphasis—produced *some* failures. In fact, dipping into the wealth of literature in this field, we find cases of severe reading and spelling disability described as early as 1896 (Wyckoff) and 1907 (Witmer) in the United States and 1893 (W. P. Morgan) in England, when the predominant beginning methods stressed a code start. Thus, a "wrong" or "inadequate" method cannot be the only cause of severe reading disability.

4. No matter how the readers in the six case studies had been taught initially, they all shared the same problem: extreme difficulty with *decoding* (not with comprehension). Indeed, the true reading-disability pupil can be described as follows: He is intelligent enough to understand the stories that other children of his age and mental ability can read (when these are read to him), but he cannot read them himself—because he cannot identify the words. Even if he learns to read silently, he often does poorly with spelling and oral reading, both of which have stronger decoding components than silent reading.

5. Most of the authors of these case studies noted that lack of interest in reading and in schoolwork were the *results*, not the *causes*, of reading difficulty. Specific reading problems like poor comprehension and slow rate were also noted as results of lack of skill in decoding. Most of the children with reading difficulties were interested in learning to read. Once they achieved some success in decoding skills, they acquired an interest in reading and in schoolwork, and they were able to overcome their specific reading problems.

6. There is *considerable* evidence from all the case studies except Robinson's (and she admittedly was not concerned primarily with method) that an initial reading method that emphasized "word," "natural," or "speeded" reading at the start and provided insufficient or inconsistent training in decoding produced *more serious* reading failures than one that emphasized the code. Three of the authors (Orton, Fernald, and Monroe) were firmly convinced that sight methods that inhibit oral responses and other kinds of movements and articulation in their immediate pursuit of smooth, speedy silent reading had caused many of the failures they diagnosed and

treated. They concluded that at least some children need to learn the written code for the spoken language in a more systematic way and to be encouraged to use "lower-order" responses such as tracing, writing, pointing, sounding, etc.

Gates, who has erroneously been associated with a "pure sight" approach to beginning reading, wrote in 1922 that the first cause of backwardness among his cases was probably "learning wholly by the 'natural' method or 'word' method." And Gray, who since the 1920s has called for a meaning-emphasis approach to regular classroom instruction of beginners, listed inadequate (insufficient) training in phonics in his 1922 report as the seventh most important cause for failure among his cases, before inadequate attention to content, which he ranked eighth.

7. There is some evidence that a heavy emphasis on phonics (or "wrong" phonics) as a starting method produced problems in some children. Thus, Gates noted the slow rate and poor comprehension of children who overarticulated and overreacted to individual letters and sounds, and he thought these difficulties might have been the result of too much phonics training in the first grade. However, he appears to have solved this problem rather easily by encouraging the pupils to concentrate more on content in reading.

Orton noted that merely teaching the sound values of the letters—which some teachers called "following a phonic method"—was ineffectual for some students. Such training, he believed, was not valuable unless followed by adequate practice in blending (or fusing) the separate sound values to form words.

8. The remedial-reading treatments described in these six case-study reports concentrated on teaching the child to decode printed words. That is, all cases received some kind of training in learning how to recognize and identify words independently. This training ranged from a primarily visual type of analysis, starting with syllables and progressing to larger units, to remedial procedures of a more mechanical nature, using kinesthetic aids. Some used phonic procedures involving blending. All investigators reported success with their treatments. Especially significant is the fact that once the hurdle of learning the code was overcome, the formerly disabled reader was able to read with understanding, speed, and enjoyment.

9. The experimental studies that compared phonic approaches with other approaches to helping disabled readers also showed that such approaches, if properly designed, achieve good results. Progress may be slower with a phonic emphasis than with other approaches, but the end results are probably more satisfactory. However, my analysis of these studies indicated that the difficulty of the phonic method makes a difference in its effectiveness with poor readers. A simplified phonic approach which uses words controlled for spelling regularity is more effective than a phonic emphasis that uses common, irregularly spelled words for practice.

After long and sometimes arduous travels through the mass of research on beginning reading, we are left with two questions: Why did those responsible for teaching children how to read ignore the evidence? Where does this evidence leave us?

The first of these questions raises the subject of what other factors besides research results determine how children are taught to read. In Sections 3 and 4 we move away from the world of numbers and percentages and into the world of classrooms, publishing houses, and PTA meetings. First we examine the basal-reading programs—the most widely used reading materials. Then we look at the environment in which reading programs are written, sold, adopted, and used. Research findings, we shall discover, are probably only a minor influence on the choice of beginning reading materials and methods.

As for the second question, my recommendations, which grow out of the entire inquiry, are presented in Section 5. Here I can say briefly that it would seem, at our present state of knowledge, that a code emphasis—one that combines control of words on spelling regularity,[1] *some direct teaching of letter-sound correspondences, as well as the use of writing, tracing, or typing—produces better results with unselected groups of beginners than a*

[1] Although not complete control of one sound for one symbol (see Levin, 1963).

meaning emphasis, the kind incorporated in most of the conventional basal-reading series used in schools in the late 1950s and early 1960s.

A similar code emphasis, clinical studies indicate, also helps children who are predisposed to reading and spelling difficulty. The clinical studies also indicate that such children need to use responses other than purely visual (ideational) ones at the beginning stages of reading and spelling and that the use of more oral, articulatory, and kinesthetic responses at the beginning does not prevent the child from becoming a normal reader later on, as so many have feared.

For children predisposed to severe reading disability, there are strong indications that schools should use diagnostic techniques to identify them early so that they may receive the special training they require and be spared frustration and failure in later years of learning. We have reason to believe, however, that other children who might fail can be helped—and that normal children can become better readers—with classroom instruction that concentrates more on breaking the code than most current programs do.

3

THE BASAL-READING SERIES—AS BAD AS THE CRITICS SAY?

*D*ESPITE *recent innovations, most children in America still learn to read from a few widely distributed sets of instructional materials called* basal-reading series. *Critics of the prevailing view are, in effect, criticizing these materials.*

If you read the angry words of critics and defenders in the reading controversy—even if you read them carefully—you are not likely to gain any consistent picture of what a basal series is like. Thus, Flesch made the flat statement that American children learn by the "word" method—that they are not taught any phonics at all. This statement was wholeheartedly denied in the educational press, where every reviewer of the book affirmed that phonics, as well as "other means of identifying words," was in fact being taught. However, half of the book reviews in the mass magazines agreed with Flesch that phonics was not being taught. The other half were noncommital.[1]
Among other accusations made by Flesch (also made in 1962 by Trace in What Ivan Knows That Johnny Doesn't) *was that the basal readers are dull and repetitious because of their rigid vocabulary control. Reviewers in the mass magazines unanimously agreed. Most of the educational reviews—two-thirds of them—again dissented (Riedler, 1962).*

[1] Terman and Walcutt, later (1958) critics of prevailing methods, were less drastic, reporting that phonics was taught in American schools, although neither sufficiently nor well.

What is the evidence for these claims and counterclaims?

To find out, I asked the authors and an editor of three widely used basal-reading series a number of questions about the philosophy behind the basal-reading programs. (These were the same four people whose general views on issues in the debate are given in Chapter 2.) I present their answers in the next chapter, along with a brief discussion of what the basal series contain and their importance in beginning reading instruction. In Chapter 8, I report on an analysis of the two series most widely used during the height of the debate—the late 1950s and early 1960s. This analysis was aimed at obtaining quantitative information on the teaching methods proposed by the basal series in wide use. Such information, I hoped, would allow me to form more substantial qualitative judgments than either side in the debate has yet been able to supply. I also analyzed a newer series with a stronger phonic emphasis and investigated a more recent edition, as well as previous editions, of one of the two leading series to determine trends in several characteristics over the years.

Before we begin the detailed analysis of the basal series, here are a few of the major findings of this effort. (Again, however, I urge the reader to go through the data presented in this section to gain an understanding of the bases for these findings as well as for my conclusions about the basal series, which appear at the end of the section.)

Children using the leading basal readers of the late 1950s and early 1960s are taught by a sight or word method. The preprimers start the child off on learning to read words, and throughout the primary grades—up through the 3–2 book for the end of the third grade—words are pretaught. What about phonics and the alphabet? They are taught too, but they receive much less emphasis. Indeed, one has to look rather hard to find any phonics (or code-learning) exercises, so well are they integrated with the other "follow-up" activities.

Most of the practice suggested is on "understanding the stories." Questions and answers on the stories and the pictures take up most of the time the class spends on the readers. The follow-up activities, too, reflect this strong meaning emphasis.

Throughout the primary grades, the programs of both series lean heavily on the teacher. Very few self-directed pupil activities are provided or suggested.

Of the three major modes of responding to questions, practicing skills, and engaging in follow-up activities—silent reading, oral reading, and writing—silent reading predominates; the pupil does little oral reading or writing.

The newer basal readers that have a phonic start incorporate some changes, but they also retain many of the features of the conventional basals.

My comparison of the 1962 and 1956 editions of one of the conventional basal series shows a trend toward a heavier code emphasis; phonics is taught earlier, and more practice is devoted to it.

SEVEN

What Is a Basal-reading Series?

LET US SAY that you have never seen a basal-reading series, but have only read about them in the newspaper, *Life,* or *Look.* You would have no reason to think that such a series is anything more than a collection of silly sentences like "Look, look, look," or "Go, go, go!"

Actually, a basal-reading series is one of the most expensive and extensive ventures a publisher can undertake. It attempts to give teachers and pupils a "total reading program" embodying a system for teaching reading (in the teachers' manuals), a collection of stories and selections for pupils to read (the readers), and exercises for additional practice (the workbooks).

The series generally starts with a prereading program (one, two, or three "reading-readiness" books for kindergarten and/or grade 1). Then come the "graded" readers: three or more small paper-covered books (the preprimers), which are followed by the first hard-covered book (the primer) and then a first reader (the 1–2 book). Typically, these five (sometimes six) books are used by children in the first grade, although some advance through them faster, and some slower. The typical basal-reading series has a book for each half of the second grade—the 2–1 and 2–2 books. Similar breaks are made for the third through the sixth grades.

Some companies have readers for the seventh and eighth grades of elementary school or the ninth grade of junior high school.

With each reader goes a workbook—a "consumable," paper-covered book containing a variety of exercises. Each reader also has a teachers' guidebook (a manual on how to teach from the readers and workbooks). Schools can also purchase accompanying charts, tests, and other aids with each series. In addition, some publishers offer supplementary readers and subject-matter textbooks coordinated with the basal-reading program.

I was reminded of how bulky a basal series and related materials can be when the generous editor of one of the series I analyzed wanted to know how much space I had in my office before sending his complete reading program for grades 1, 2, and 3. Fortunately, I decided that only the *core* of the program was required. Had I wanted to analyze the complete program, including all the various aids, I would have needed a storage room!

INFLUENCE OF THE BASAL SERIES

The basal series are very widely used. Two studies—the Columbia Reading Study by Allen Barton and David Wilder (1964) and the Harvard Report on Reading by Mary Austin and Coleman Morrison (1963)—found that these materials are used almost universally by American classroom teachers of the first three grades. After surveying over fifteen hundred elementary school teachers, Barton and Wilder wrote:

> Reading instruction in almost all schools starts from a similar basis: basal readers from a graded series are used by 98 percent of first grade teachers and by 92 to 94 percent of second and third grade teachers on "all or most days of the year." (pp. 378–379)

Even more impressive than their widespread use is the influence these materials have on teachers and administrators. Barton and Wilder note that 63 percent of the teachers they studied in grades 1 through 3 considered the reading series and their accompanying teachers' manuals a "very important" influence on their beliefs about the teaching of reading—even more important than their practice teaching experience, their own reading of books and articles on reading, and their undergraduate courses on teaching methods.

The Columbia Reading Study findings on attitudes toward the teachers' manuals substantiate this influence. From 66 to 70 percent of elementary school teachers either "strongly" or "mostly" agreed with the statement: "The suggestions to teachers found in reading manuals are based on definite scientific proof." Only 7 percent either "mostly" or "strongly" disagreed.

Elementary school principals followed the same pattern: 58 percent either "strongly" or "mostly" agreed with the statement. Only 9 percent either "mostly" or "strongly" disagreed. Indeed, during my own school visits I found more than one principal who believed strongly that if his teachers would only follow the basal-reader manuals, he would have no reading problems in his school.

Interestingly, reading experts were not as convinced as teachers and principals of the "scientific basis" of the teachers' manuals. Only 32 percent either "strongly" or "mostly" agreed with the statement; 46 percent either "mostly" or "strongly" disagreed.

Barton and Wilder (1964) summarize their findings as follows:

> The teachers believe that the suggestions to teachers found in reading manuals are based on "definite scientific proof": almost no teachers disagree. But the experts . . . are much less impressed by the scientific status of reading manuals; almost half disagree with the statement that they are based on "definite scientific proof," and only a third agree "mostly."[1] The experts thus think much less highly of their own product, in a sense; perhaps the teachers have been oversold—and the principals are almost as sold as the teachers. (p. 382)

In any event, for all practical purposes American reading instruction is basal-series reading instruction.

PRODUCING A BASAL SERIES

A series is written by a team of specialists. The head of the team, the senior author, is usually a person of recognized authority and stature in the reading field. Most often he is a professor of education.

The basal-reader "teams" work differently. Some series are planned and supervised by the senior author, with different team members assuming responsibility for different assignments. Under such an arrangement, professional writers, teachers who have become writers, and regular

[1] I quote, in this connection, the reaction of an editor of a leading basal series: "It does not seem surprising to me that the reading experts are not convinced of the scientific basis of the teachers' manuals. Most of them are aware of the lack of solid research for building a basal reading program. Also, many of them are relatively modest people who would not be aggressive in promoting a scientific basis of their own materials. They know that various methods are successful. They believe in change and try to maintain an open mind. School people, on the other hand, are constantly asking for the research behind a particular published program. They seem to need assurance for decisions to purchase or use a program. Belief in the existence of definite scientific evidence is undoubtedly based on promotional methods, and also on the continuing request from school people for 'proof.'" (personal communication)

classroom teachers write, adapt, and select the stories that are included in the readers. Usually, the classroom teachers write the manuals.

In one of the larger companies, a permanent staff writes the stories in the readers, the workbook exercises, and the teachers' manuals. Their "head" does not work on a royalty basis, as do the senior authors of other series, but acts as a consultant. However, he too plans and approves all parts of the program.

All basal-series teams pride themselves on cooperative effort. The larger the company, the more specialists involved—reading experts, psychologists, linguists, people with degrees in literature, and so on.

The editor of one series emphasized that producing a basal series is such an extensive enterprise that no one author could possibly do it:

> Creative ideas must come from different people. Even the books suggested as supplementary reading at the end of the various lessons in our series are gone over by five people before they are listed. The books and the manuals are composites. About ten full-time writers, editors, and artists are involved. No one person is responsible.

The financial investment in a series is, of course, enormous. No one whom I or my associates interviewed would give an actual cost figure. However, when I mentioned 1 million dollars (a figure the American Textbook Council gave in 1950 as the basic investment in a basal-reading series), the editor of one series said that this amount may cover the primer—*one* of the *six* basic books in his first-grade program! "It is hard to give a definite figure," he explained, "because we don't know what to include. We have a staff. Others pay royalties, so their investment may seem lower. The cost for an entire series is probably within the range of 10 to 20 million dollars."[2]

One large publishing house devoted five years to its series' first-grade program alone. It took an illustrator two full years to do just the primer. He produced one illustration a week, a painting from a photographer's model. In the words of the editor: "You can't put that kind of quality into something that you sell one copy of."

USE OF THE SERIES

Although the basal-reading systems are, to date, the most complete reading programs available, the basal authors interviewed saw their series as only part of a "total reading program." In the words of one author:

[2] These figures check quite well with an estimate given to me in 1966 by the editorial head of the elementary school division of one of the largest publishing houses. He said that a full reading system for kindergarten through grade 6, including books, tapes, films, and tests, probably represented an investment of about 25 million dollars.

I don't see it as a total reading program. It is part of one. In fact, I believe it is too much a part of the total program in some schools. Our manuals suggest that there is a lot of reading to be done in content fields and in library books. In practically every lesson in the manuals, we recommend supplementary, related reading—references to children's books.

Another author stated it this way:

The problem of the basal-reading program is to select that which is most likely to help the child develop the basic skills that are common to all areas of the curriculum. Map reading is not taught in our reading series. We don't attempt to develop the reading of numbers and number words, because we think it is best done in arithmetic. We don't attempt to teach "percentage" in the reading program. We try to avoid these concepts until they are definitely taught in the specialized areas. We don't believe that precious time should be taken from reading for building sentences and for spelling.

Thus, the authors of basal series see teaching of the basic reading skills as the main purpose of their series. They leave some of the special reading skills required for arithmetic and social studies to the textbooks in those areas. Also, they recognize that their readers cannot possibly provide for all the child's reading needs—especially in the content areas, which are covered by textbooks, literature anthologies, and library books.

At the same time, the authors interviewed were well aware that schools differ widely in their use of the series. According to one author:

In schools of a high cultural level the basal readers play a smaller part because they have lots of other books, lots of children's literature. For schools with fewer facilities, the basal readers play a larger part. For most children, it is the actual specific work on basic skills that is important.

SIMILARITIES AND DIFFERENCES

Generally, the three authors interviewed agreed that the basal-reader series available in 1962[3] were quite similar, although they would not agree with the critics that they were all alike. They did concede, however, that these series were based on a common philosophy and common goals. One author was more outspoken about the similarities than the other two:

My basal series is pretty much the same as three or four leading basals. They are alike in that they have a controlled vocabulary through the sixth grade, and a three- or four-strand program concentrating on (1) developing a sight vocabulary, (2) a word-analysis skills program, which is eclectic, (3) comprehension and critical thinking, (4) study skills starting at the third-grade level.

Similar to other basals, we created a family and maintained it through the first grade. Similar to others, we used the social studies curriculum—the family, and com-

[3] The "phonics-first" basal-reader series, the Lippincott Basic Reading Program, was not published until 1963.

munity—for our readers for grades 1, 2, and 3. Another likeness is in the manual—step-by-step, direct instructions for the teacher.

We do differ somewhat in having introduced diagnostic tests and some fresh material in science at an earlier level. But this was just a commonsense thing, and it seems to appeal to teachers. Also, I would say that the material is generally fresher, and that is why our series is becoming popular.[4]

Another author pointed to differences not so much in the content of the readers and manuals in his series as in the way they are produced. His company sets aside more money for research, he said, and hires more specialists to work on its series than other companies.

BASAL SERIES PHONICS PROGRAMS

All the authors interviewed agreed that, compared with the supplemental, systematic-phonics programs available,[5] the phonics programs in the basal-reading series were similar to one another. All mentioned that in their series, phonics was "integrated" with the rest of the material. As one author put it:

Phonics is part of word study, which is only one of six divisions in a lesson. The first job is developing concepts and building readiness for understanding the story. This is especially important for children of limited backgrounds, for slow learners, and for slow readers. . . .

Then there is a division in each lesson on reading to answer questions; then word study, which we see as only part of the total picture. Our word-study program differs in minor ways from the word-study programs of other basal series.

As seen by another author:

We believe, as do most other basal series, in having the child master, through a variety of approaches after lessons in auditory and visual discrimination (the reading-readiness books), about fifty to sixty words. He learns these words in the three pre-primers. On the primer level, we begin a few lessons in structural and phonetic analysis. But basically, a contextual approach[6] is used. Our emphasis, in contrast to the separate systematic-phonics programs, is that reading is a meaningful process, not just word recognition. The phonics people present words as combinations of discrete parts, and then meaning, if they do it at all.

[4] The chief editor of a reading series in England I spoke to was quite upset that sales of his book were dropping off because the English infant schools were ordering the English editions of American basal-reading series. Why? According to the editor, the teachers were not dissatisfied with results from the older series; in fact, the new series were quite similar in content and method. But the teachers found the new series "more colorful" and "fresher." "Teachers want something new, although not basically different," he said.

[5] See Chap. 8 and Appendix A for comparative data.

[6] In a "contextual approach," the child is encouraged to use illustrations and the rest of the story in identifying a word he does not recognize "at sight," i.e., immediately as a whole word.

Thus, the first step is reading for meaning. Later, after the child learns to read for meaning and masters a sight vocabulary, phonics is begun.

All the basal authors interviewed emphasized that their phonics programs are analytic, *not* synthetic—that is, they are designed to teach the child to arrive at generalizations and rules about phonics inductively, from known sight words. The authors also emphasized that phonics teaching in the basal series is "functional"; i.e., the sounds learned come from the words used in the stories. As one author put it:

> Children generalize phonic rules from examples of known words, i.e., words they have learned as wholes. Some of these generalizations come as discoveries. Some are teacher-directed.

Only two of the authors interviewed were definite about how they decided on the amount and kind of phonics to include in their reading programs. One frankly said:

> From tradition. We included those used by primary teachers over the past fifty years. We believe it has "consensual validity." We got our team together and talked about it. Those of us who knew a lot about phonics hammered it out. Two of us who knew the research found no specific knowledge about what elements should be taught first or second. Therefore, we thrashed through what we thought should be included, mapped it out roughly by grades to see whether it was logical, and made our decision.

Another author candidly said that he modeled the phonics component for his series after those of the other basal series, especially the Scott, Foresman Reading Program, the best seller:

> I made an analysis of when various phonetic and structural elements were introduced in five leading basal series, and I pretty much did the same thing. Consonants in the first grade; vowels in the second grade; vowel digraphs and diphthongs in the second and third grades; vowel rules developed inductively in the second grade. Syllabication is developed from the second grade on, and given heavy emphasis in the third grade. It is continued through the fourth, fifth, and sixth grades. We repeat and emphasize phonic rules through the sixth grade. In the seventh grade the first lessons review everything.
>
> After we set up our plan, if something differed markedly from Scott, Foresman, we looked at it closely. Another source was Bloomfield[7] and other linguistic scientists.

The third author said that he was being put under considerable pressure to include more phonics in his series, but as senior author he was resisting:

> I believe that phonics can be overdone. It is a tool for learning to read. It is needed

[7] See Chap. 8 and Appendix A for a comparison of the sequence and pacing in conventional basal-reader phonics programs and in the Bloomfield System and other "linguistic" programs.

> only to the stage of being useful. But it becomes less important in the higher grades.[8] My own theory is that there is no one best way and that each teacher who has good training will develop her own style. So long as there is no particular method, no royal road to reading success, and children are different and learn in different ways, the successful teacher adapts every program.

With one or two dissenters—Houghton Mifflin's *Reading for Meaning Series* (McKee et al., 1963) was teaching phonics earlier—basal-reader authors in 1962 to 1963 generally agreed not only on *how* and *when* phonics is to be taught, but *what* phonics to teach, with the smaller sellers tending to model themselves after the largest seller.[9]

FOR ALL CHILDREN, EXCEPT . . .

Two of the authors stated that their series were designed for the middle two-thirds of the general population of English-speaking children. One said:

> Our series was not designed for the slow learner, the non-English-speaking child, nor for those with IQs of 160, although suggestions for enrichment for faster-moving children, and additional practice for slow learners, are given in the manuals.

[8] One unfortunate outcome of the present phonics controversy may be the spread of phonics teaching into advanced levels (even junior and senior high school), where the great majority of children (except backward readers still in need of help in identifying words) cannot benefit at all from it. This indiscriminate extension of techniques newly in vogue characterizes the teaching of reading (and probably other school subjects as well). For example, in the early 1900s it was found that many pupils in grades 4 through 8 were deficient in silent reading comprehension (see, e.g., Thorndike, 1917). The reaction was a strong "push" on silent reading, one so strong that it spread down into the early grades, and nonoral methods were used even with first graders on the assumption that what was good later should be stressed earlier. Fortunately, oral reading was reintroduced to some extent in the early grades, but as Chap. 8 shows, only within the framework of a major emphasis on silent reading (see Hyatt, 1943).

[9] Compare these "criteria" for phonics instruction with those used for vocabulary control. In analyzing the research basis for the low vocabularies of basal readers in 1958, I found that by the early 1950s the vocabulary control of the basal readers was much stricter than the limited research evidence then available justified. In fact, by the 1940s basals repeated words more often than Gates (1930) found useful even for slow-learning pupils, and three times as often as needed by pupils of above-average ability. Yet, until the early 1960s each succeeding edition of a series had a lower vocabulary load. Why? Probably because the authors all looked at what the others were doing, rather than at the experimental evidence, albeit limited. True, classroom procedures were investigated and courses of study were examined, but by then schools and teachers were convinced that a low vocabulary load was desirable. They were convinced by the "research" articles in the educational periodicals—research that was comparative rather than experimental. These articles reported the number of different words used in the different basals, with statements on "averages"; none (except the Gates 1930 study) gave any *evidence* that a lower vocabulary load really produced better results. In this connection, see also Mayer (1962).

The other author said:

> My series suffers like the others in not having much appeal for the culturally disadvantaged. It is middle class, white, and sometimes I am a little ashamed. Publishers say that two sets are needed, that different pictures and content are needed for the culturally disadvantaged and for Negroes. I don't know if this is the answer.[10] Some linguistic people have started with *Frog Fun,* avoiding people altogether.[11] I also think we do a rather poor job of appealing to New York City and other large-city children.[12] The settings of our readers are definitely suburban. But then, over 60 percent of the children in the United States are living in suburbia. I personally agree with the viewpoint of Otto Kleinberg in a recent issue of the *Saturday Review*[13] that the readers present a distorted view of American life. But because the publisher aims for numbers, we do it.

The third author, however, was not at all concerned about any possible lack of appeal for some children. Although in content his series is essentially the same as the other two, he was convinced of its universal appeal:

> Our series is printed all over the world—Indo-China, England, France. Props are unimportant. The human relationships are the important thing—and the cleanliness of the children. Every dress worn by the girls in our readers comes from a mail-order catalogue. The furniture can be bought at any discount furniture store. The car is not this year's model. We keep everything clean and attractive. The foreign editions sometimes change our illustrations. In the Indo-Chinese edition ——— looks different and his hair coloring is changed. In the Muslim edition (in the United States) the children are a different color.
>
> But the emotional identification and American ideals are the same. In the British edition words such as "cookies" had to be changed to "biscuits."
>
> Our stories are frankly selected for their reflection of the American way of life.[14] It is an idealistic representation. We know that children in deprived areas do not experience the same things, but why should they be surrounded by ugliness and ugly language? Wouldn't they feel better if they identified themselves with the lives and the family depicted in our readers? Children's first impressions are strong. Our standard is—if you have a child, would you like to have him live with this family for a

[10] In 1965 Scott, Foresman, the leading basal-reader publisher, published an "integrated" edition of their basal series. Other publishers have produced or are producing similar editions of their own series.

[11] The reference is to *The Linguistic Science Readers* (Stratemeyer and Smith, 1963).

[12] Two new series based generally on conventional basal-reader methods have been designed specifically for the urban and ethnically different child—the Bank Street Readers and the City Schools Readers. The Chandler Readers, which use an urban setting, incorporate a slight change of methodology, but this too is basically a meaning-emphasis reading program.

[13] Feb. 16, 1963.

[14] See in this connection DeCharms and Moeller (1962), who found that the content changes in the basal readers between the late 1800s and the present reflect a change from the "Protestant ethic" to the "social ethic," as found by David Reisman and others.

> little while? We want to relax children's fears and tensions and create a desire for correct living.
>
> In the new stories, we have a strong father-son relationship. We got our cue from psychologists who worked with deprived children. They say you have to build up these children. We don't know if this will help the boys. It is still experimental. But the stories have been okayed by the psychologists. We also have male artists. Very seldom do the girl and the boy do the same thing. Their facial reactions are different. In picture after picture, the boy is emulating his father.[15]
>
> Throughout, we select content with which all children can identify. Our readers are for all the children who live in the slums, too. If we don't show them something better, how will they learn about it? This is what the parents want. They want the children to get out of the slums. We have gone on the philosophy that the child wants to identify with the prevailing environment—a clean home, etc. If not, we would have to have different books for different children. The philosophy we accept is an important one. Children respect books in the first grade, and if you put it in the book, it gives it a stamp of approval.

The above excerpts show the basal-reader authors interviewed to be primarily concerned with the suitability of content—whether the stories *appeal* to all kinds of children. They did, however, also voice some concern about how appropriate the basals were for all children in terms of difficulty. When the author of the series that is meant for "all the children of all the people" was asked for what kinds of children the grade levels were suitable, he said that his series was aimed at children in the middle range of ability. For the others, he said, materials can be differently paced: an advanced second grader can use the third- or fourth-grade reader, while a slow one can use the first-grade reader or the primer.

The other two authors were less convinced that children of all levels of ability could use their readers effectively. They were very much aware that a slower third-grade child would no longer find the *content* of a first-grade reader appealing when he was ready to cope with its difficulty. They hoped, in fact, that teachers would not use their basal readers with such children, but would find more suitable books.

As for the brighter pupils, the two authors agreed that their readers introduce words at too slow a rate for these children and, also, that extensive preteaching of words allowed little room for discovery. They hoped that the teachers took brighter children through the books faster, for theoretically a child with an IQ of 160 should be able to do the six-year reading program in three years. However, both authors noted that the teachers' manuals do not suggest this kind of adjustment. "I say this publicly," said one author, "and to teachers in my classes. But not in the manuals of the readers. The publisher would not want me to make this statement, but they should, and probably will."[16]

[15] Note the importance given to illustrations. We shall see why in Chap. 8.

[16] See Chaps. 9 and 10 for a discussion of school policy on giving children readers beyond their grade placement.

Generally, all three authors interviewed hoped that the teachers would gear the instruction to the child—and not hold a child back with too easy a reader. However, two were also concerned lest the bright child be advanced too fast, for "even the brighter children often lack the skills presented in the workbooks and teachers' manuals." The authors themselves would like to dispense with the "grade levels" on the readers altogether, but they cannot, they said, because the twenty-six states that still have state adoption policies require this system. One author said:

> If we encourage faster pacing, the danger is that teachers will push too far, and not give needed, extended reading. But we are against too slow pacing, too. Some schools make children read five first preprimers (one from our series and four from other series) before they go on to the second or third preprimer (of any series). We think this is not good and have suggested that in our latest revision.
>
> Generally, we think the pacing is a job for the administrator. We say, "If you believe that the child should progress at his own pace, you must remove the ceiling at the upper end as you do at the bottom." Having two readers (a first-semester and a second-semester level) for each grade has made it easier to give children the levels they need. We say nothing in the manuals that prevents the teacher from using a fourth-grade book in the second grade. We never say *not to.* Although we think pacing can be faster for the brighter children, we do not favor skipping readers.

This author also said that in his experience, series users are generally pleased with an "easier" program. When by error his company sold only part of the first-grade program—the preprimers and primers—to one school system, the principal wrote a letter saying how pleased he and the first-grade teachers were that they did not have to take the children so far. In another school, he related, the teachers had followed the teachers' guidebooks and their suggestions for activities so thoroughly—having the children do all the exercises and all the supplementary reading—that the children were still on the first-grade program in the fourth grade.

HELPING THE TEACHER

The basal series all provide guidebooks for the teacher. I wondered whether the authors thought all teachers need to use these guides.

One author said that the guidebooks were designed for the "middle teachers," not for the superior ones:

> However, I find that the best teachers are the strongest advocates of the guidebooks because they find in them what they need, and they are not didactic. The guidebooks actually teach the teachers how to teach reading. Teachers find them more valuable than basic textbooks in reading.[17]

Another author noted, however, that the guidebook in his series was designed for the inexperienced teacher:

[17] The Barton-Wilder study (1964), cited above, confirms this.

Our theory has been to have the manual provide more material than any one teacher can use. We have aimed at the inexperienced teacher, hoping that when she gains confidence and experience, she will adapt and select according to the needs of the children. The manual is based on a "cafeteria theory." The good teacher becomes increasingly independent of the manual. But even quite experienced teachers hold the manuals in their laps while teaching.[18] We have tried to put practically everything in the manual that she might need.

The third author said that his series "shoots" for the "artist" teacher. "However," he noted, "there is also help for the beginning teacher, in that our manual tells why things are to be done. But," he continued, "the inexperienced teacher will not understand it completely the first year. She needs at least another year to understand it. Most of the teachers follow it blindly. The teachers should really learn how to use the guides in college courses. Most of them start their first year of teaching using it as a Bible. It should not be used as a Bible or as a cookbook, but as a philosophy."

The problem of how much to include was expressed vividly by the same author:

Something is definitely needed by the high school teacher who enters elementary school teaching and by the older teacher coming back after many years to the classroom. It is hard to know how much to give in the manual. We are not really sure how much to tell them—the philosophy, the why, and the how. They get philosophy in the teachers' colleges, so we must give specific procedures. The function of the guidebook is to present the teacher with procedures to implement the philosophy of the authors.

Since the manual has so much material, who helps the inexperienced teacher distinguish essentials from nonessentials? On this point the authors were not too clear, tending to put the responsibility on the teacher. When I asked whether selectivity is built into the program, one author said:

Not specifically, although there are suggestions in the manuals. In a sense, we have never accepted the fact that teachers don't have to think when they use one of the manuals. They have to think more, in fact.[19]

[18] I cannot help reporting that at a recent reading conference a teacher asked the speaker (a well-known reading expert and coauthor of a leading basal-reading series) what he thought about the use of a spiral binding compared with a cord binding for the teachers' manual. The speaker jokingly answered that it would give the teacher another hand. She would not have to keep the place with her finger.

[19] Here is another dilemma: In trying to be all things to all teachers, the manuals include a tremendous amount of material. It takes considerable experience to know what is a *must* and what may be omitted. Yet it is the inexperienced teacher, the one who does not know enough to tell essentials from nonessentials, who needs the manual most.

CLASSROOM ORGANIZATION

All the basal-reader authors interviewed felt that the success of their programs did not depend on any particular kind of classroom organization, although all assumed that pupils would be grouped in some way. One of the authors said that he suggests three groups but that the teacher does not have to have three. Another said, "We assume that the teacher will group in some way, but we have no fixed system. We even suggest having a few whole-class activities, and also ways of helping the individual child. But the fundamental organization is some kind of within-class grouping." The third stated: "The grouping is for local administration to decide."

READINESS AGE

The authors I talked to were quite hesitant on the question of readiness age. They agreed, however, that the school administration rather than the author or publisher must decide when to initiate a basal-reader program. One said:

> We have two readiness books that present a guide and a checklist to tell when a child is or is not ready.

Another said:

> We are getting millions of letters from principals and teachers asking whether they can use the beginning books for kindergarten. We just say, "They are beginning books. Use them when you wish."

The third author said that his series can be used at age five and, for some children, even at age four:

> One mother taught her three-year-old daughter to read from our books and charts. This child, at the age of three, could read 200 words.[20] I am aware of the push for starting earlier. It can be done, but we think of children as being ready for our books at age five. The extra readiness books and games can be used by the four-year-old.[21]

[20] Two hundred words by present-day standards would be upper-first-grade achievement. The entire first-grade program of the typical basal-reading series contains about 350 different words.

[21] This author's point was particularly interesting since his series, even the reading-readiness (prereading) books, is generally introduced at age six (grade 1) in most schools.

EIGHT

A Look at the Basal-reading Series

IN THE LAST chapter, authors and editors told us what they wanted to put into their reading series, and each one said how he thought his differed from the others. With these statements in mind, we can now take a careful look at the series themselves to gain a more complete and objective picture of what they actually contain.

A comprehensive analysis of all conventional reading series in use in American schools would take many years and, since new series come out periodically, would of course be chronically obsolete. Thus, I investigated only a sample of the series (and a sample of the lessons within the series), taking care to choose these samples so as to reveal the main characteristics of the material in question. Even limited in this way, the analysis reported on in this chapter may seem laboriously detailed. For this I apologize. I have attempted to present only the amount of data required to give the reader an adequate basis for making judgments about these series and to substantiate my own evaluations.

WHY THESE SERIES?

To discover what basal-reading series representing the prevailing view are like, I analyzed the two series most widely used in the late 1950s and early 1960s—Scott, Foresman's 1956 edition[1] of *The New Basic Reading Program* and Ginn's 1961 edition of the Ginn Basic Readers—which probably accounted for around 80 percent of total reading-series sales during this period. According to the Barton and Wilder survey made in 1964, about 77 percent of 900 reading experts felt that for all practical purposes, the basal series were pretty much alike.[2] Thus, a study of these two series should give us a good idea of what the others that follow the prevailing view contain and should allow us to make some generalizations about basal-reading series used during this period.

To discover how a series inspired by the newer emphasis on increased use of phonics differs from the conventional series, I also analyzed the first-grade program of the Lippincott Basic Reading Program, published in 1963. This series was coauthored by Charles Walcutt, one of the first critics of the prevailing view and a vocal proponent of early phonics.

Finally, since I am also interested in how the great debate has affected the prevailing view, I analyzed the first-grade reader of the 1962 revision of the Scott, Foresman series, looking for any changes that might reflect a trend. I also compared this edition with earlier editions from 1920 to 1950.

HOW THE SERIES WERE ANALYZED

Two schedules were devised for analyzing the readers, teachers' manuals, and workbooks (see Appendix B). As the schedules indicate, my associates and I counted the number of running words in stories as well as the number of new words; we counted the number of words of verbal instruction given the teacher; we determined the number of exercises for each lesson and classified them by kind; we counted the number of pictures per story and estimated the size of the pictures; and we even classified the kinds of questions the teacher was to ask the pupils. In short, we tried to get as objective a picture as possible of *what* is taught, *how*, and *when*.

Most of the classification items on the schedules represent issues in the debate and also significant research issues—for example, the value of illustrations. Other items were suggested by my early observations in

[1] Only the first-grade program of the Scott, Foresman 1962 edition was available when I began the analysis. Hence, I decided to analyze the 1956 edition, which was still being used in classrooms in 1962.

[2] One series available during this period did differ from the others in that it has a stronger phonic emphasis at the beginning: *The Reading for Meaning Series* (McKee et al., 1963), published by Houghton Mifflin. Some of the newer series differ substantially, as we shall see later on.

classrooms. I seemed to find more talking than reading (with the teacher doing most of the talking) during basal-reader lessons. Why? Could it be that I just happened to observe talkative teachers, or were the teachers following what the manuals suggested? I had to find out. Hence the tedious counting of "words the teacher speaks" for each lesson.

I was, of course, working only with published materials; these indicate what the teacher is *expected* to do, but cannot tell us what she actually does.[3]

Series That Reflect the Prevailing View

My analysis of widely used traditional basal-reading series is based on a sample of the material in the readers, workbooks, and teachers' manuals of the Scott, Foresman 1956 edition and the Ginn 1961 edition series[4] for the first three grades.[5]

LESSONS BUILT AROUND STORIES

Each lesson in Scott, Foresman (1956) and Ginn (1961) revolves around a story. The teachers' manuals of the two series suggest a similar four-part procedure for all lessons—from the very first lesson in the first preprimer through the last one in the 3–2 reader for the third grade.

Preparation for reading the story. Here the teacher establishes the background, making a few relevant statements and asking questions to arouse interest. The guidebooks usually provide exact phrases for the teacher to use.

Presentation of the new words and practice on them. The guidebooks tell the teacher which words to teach and how they should be practiced.

Guided reading and interpreting the story. Here the teacher is given specific questions to ask and is told what points to emphasize while the children read the story. This section also includes suggestions for rereading the story, usually indicating a definite purpose for rereading and providing questions to ask the pupils for further interpretation.

Follow-up activities. A series of suggested activities and exercises follow each story (lesson). These usually include one or two exercises in the correlated workbook.

[3] In this connection, see Chall and Feldmann (1966).

[4] In this chapter I call these two editions simply Scott, Foresman (1956) and Ginn (1961).

[5] For Ginn (1961) I analyzed every fourth lesson of the reading program for these grades (excluding reading-readiness, or prereading, books). For Scott, Foresman (1956) I analyzed every eighth lesson, which produced substantially similar results.

EMPHASIS ON A WORD METHOD

In the main, the basal readers prominent in the late 1950s and early 1960s use a sight or word method to teach reading in grades 1, 2, and 3. That is, although the total program includes some instruction in letters and sounds, children are taught to recognize words as wholes first. This emphasis is evident in the rate at which words are introduced and in the way they are taught throughout the first three grades.

Analysis showed that, on the average, the preprimers introduced the child to one or two new words per story (see Table 8–1). In the first grade he confronts more new pictures per story than new words. By the third grade, he meets about twelve new words per story. Because stories for older children are longer, however, the number of new words per 100 running words of text remains about the same, or even decreases, as we move from the preprimers to the 3–2 books.

Not very rapid progress, you might say. But to realize exactly how diluted the lessons are you have to know that these "new" words are merely words that the child has not yet been taught to recognize *in print*. If English is his native language, he can most likely use correctly and understand any of these words in conversation. The average *first grader* can probably use accurately and/or understand about four thousand different words.[6]

Yet the typical *third-grade* basal reader of the 1950s and early 1960s contains a total reading vocabulary of about fifteen hundred different words (words ending in *s, ed, ing, ly, er,* or *est* are not counted separately from their roots), a small fraction of the total meaning (receptive and speaking) vocabulary of the typical third grader.

The teacher following the teachers' manuals uses essentially the same techniques in teaching new words throughout the first three grades. She preteaches the new words in each lesson before the children read the story, placing the words on the blackboard or in a pocket chart. For first graders the words are usually presented within sentences and phrases; beginning with the second grade, they are more often taught alone. In either case the teacher is to place them in an "oral, meaningful context," i.e., tell a little story while she writes the appropriate sentences, phrases, or words. The manual usually tells her exactly what to say.

Next, the children practice reading the words from the board or

[6] Estimates of the number of words first graders know vary from 2,000 to 25,000. See Lorge and Chall (1963) for a review of these studies and some of the methodological "errors" that have resulted in the 25,000 figure. Even the most conservative estimate (2,000), however, indicates that the words in the readers are new only to the child's eyes.

Table 8–1 Comparison of Story Content in Two Basal Series: Scott, Foresman (1956) and Ginn (1961)

	Preprimer		Primer		1-2		2-1	
Average story	SF	G	SF	G	SF	G	SF	G
Running words	64	87	165	188	305	270	483	493
New words	1.0	1.8	3.0	2.9	4.3	3.8	5.2	4.7
New words per 100 running words (vocabulary load)	1.6	2.1	1.8	1.5	1.4	1.4	1.1	1.0
Pictures	4.2	4.3	4.6	5.0	4.8	4.6	4.8	5.4
Pictures per 100 running words (picture load)	6.6	4.9	2.8	2.7	1.6	1.7	1.0	1.1

chart. Table 8–2 shows how the teacher is instructed to help them. In the first- and second-grade programs, she is supposed to tell the children to "just read" the word, phrase, or sentence and to ask them what the words mean. She also has the children note the shape of the word.

All these are techniques for teaching children to recognize words as wholes. By comparison, only minor attention is directed to the alphabetic, phonic, or structural aspects of the word (which might help the child recognize new words without preteaching). Not until the third grade do these aspects begin to take on importance in the preteaching of new words. But even then, the look-say (just-read) approach receives about equal emphasis in Scott, Foresman (1956).

Although theoretically the basal-reader word-perception program leans heavily on the use of context and picture clues (learning or remem-

Table 8–2 Comparison of Ways in Which Pupils Are Instructed to Practice New Words in Two Basal Series: Scott, Foresman (1956) and Ginn (1961)

	Preprimer		Primer		1-2		2-1	
Average lesson	SF	G	SF	G	SF	G	SF	G
Total questions, directives, statements suggested in manual	11.0	12.4	8.2	9.7	11.0	5.2	11.7	8.5
Percentage of total questions, directives, statements instructing child to:								
Just read	65	64	66	47	50	39	80	43
Give meaning	24	13	15	24	25	9	0	18
Note visual form	11	22	19	10	14	26	0	7
Engage in phonic and/or structural analysis	0	0	0	9	9	23	20	28
Use context as clue to recognition	0	1	0	10	2	3	0	4
Total	100	100	100	100	100	100	100	100

2-2		3-1		3-2	
SF	G	SF	G	SF	G
619	564	702	658	808	1,024
7.6	6.2	11.0	10.0	12.7	12.4
1.2	1.1	1.6	1.5	1.6	1.1
4.6	6.1	5.8	6.4	4.8	7.4
0.7	1.1	0.8	1.0	0.6	0.7

bering a word because it makes sense in relation to the surrounding words or pictures), the guidebooks suggest almost no such practice.

Thus, children using these series are expected to approach a new word primarily by learning to recognize it by sight (as a whole) or are asked to think of its meaning—at least through the upper second grade—even though, as we shall see, by the end of the second grade a considerable amount of phonic and structural analysis has been taught.

EMPHASIS ON UNDERSTANDING THE STORY

The basal-reading programs, right from the start, emphasize practice in reading stories for understanding and enjoyment.

Our first indication of this was the insistence on preteaching new

2-2		3-1		3-2	
SF	G	SF	G	SF	G
11.4	10.6	17.0	8.2	18.3	7.0
63	25	48	32	46	11
0	26	0	2	0	0
0	12	0	0	0	0
37	33	52	66	54	89
0	4	0	0	0	0
100	100	100	100	100	100

Table 8–3 Comparison of Establishment of Background in Two Basal Series: Scott, Foresman (1956) and Ginn (1961)

	Preprimer		Primer		1-2		2-1	
Average story	*SF*	G	*SF*	G	*SF*	G	*SF*	G
Questions or statements teacher uses to establish background	6.8	2.2	7.2	5.7	3.5	5.6	5.0	6.3
Words in story	64	87	165	188	305	270	483	493

words by placing them in a meaningful context. Also, in practicing words children are often asked what the words mean—even more often in the first grade than in the second and third (see Table 8–2).

Further evidence is the attention the manuals give to preparing children for each story by establishing background and arousing interest. One gets the impression from the manuals that children do not really want to learn to read and will do so only if they are promised an enjoyable story full of surprise and fun. This emphasis does not change much from the preprimers through the 3–2 reader (see Table 8–3). Story length and characteristics, of course, do change—from the rather thin picture-stories of the preprimers (averaging about seventy running words) to the substantial stories of the third-grade readers (averaging about one thousand running words)—but the amount of preparation does not.

We become thoroughly convinced that meaning and enjoyment receive the major emphasis when we look at the guided-reading section—the heart of the basal-reading program. Here the manuals go into the greatest detail in instructing the teacher, in some cases literally putting words into her mouth.

In the preprimers the teacher helps her pupils interpret *each line of print.* Generally the number of "guidance units" (the portion of the text to be read alone by the child) increases as the child grows older. By the third-grade readers, the pupil may read an entire page without questions or comments from the teacher.

Table 8–4 Comparison of Amount of Guidance Material in Two Basal Series: Scott, Foresman (1956) and Ginn (1961)

	Preprimer		Primer		1-2		2-1	
Average story	*SF*	G	*SF*	G	*SF*	G	*SF*	G
Words in story	64	87	165	188	305	270	483	493
Questions, statements, directions suggested in guidebook	54	25	41	22	46	20	48	26
Words teacher speaks in guiding	444	268	376	230	403	161	455	273

2-2		3-1		3-2	
SF	G	SF	G	SF	G
6.0	6.3	8.8	5.8	7.3	5.2
619	564	702	658	808	1,024

The number of questions, statements, and directions suggested for guiding pupils in reading a story remains rather stable in both series from the preprimers through the third-grade readers, although one series tends to "suggest" twice as many as the other (see Table 8–4). The Scott, Foresman (1956) guidebook suggests that the teacher ask an average of about fifty questions per story, irrespective of story length, substance, or content. Thus, for the typical preprimer story, with an average of sixty-four running words, the teacher is to use fifty-four separate questions, directions, or statements to guide the pupil, or almost one question for each word the child reads. In fact, the teacher is to speak about seven words to one word read by the pupil. Throughout the first grade, the teacher following this manual would speak more words per story than the child would read.

The Ginn (1961) guidebook suggests less questioning and directing. But the teacher is still to speak more words than the pupil reads in the preprimers and primer.

I classified the questions, directions, and statements suggested for guiding the pupils' interpretation of the stories as follows:

1. Those not primarily concerned with the text, e.g., questions about the pictures, about stories previously read, and about the pupil's experiences.

2. Those telling the pupil to "just read" the next line or so.

3. Those directing the pupil's attention to understanding the text (a literal understanding and also interpretation, evaluation, etc.).

2-2		3-1		3-2	
SF	G	SF	G	SF	G
619	564	702	658	808	1,024
49	28	48	24	40	26
456	258	560	258	417	266

Table 8–5 Percent of Teacher Directions and Questions to Various Aspects of Stories in Two Basal Series: Scott, Foresman (1956) and Ginn (1961)

	Preprimer		Primer		1-2		2-1		2-2		3-1		3-2	
Average story	*SF*	*G*	*SF*	*G*	*SF*	*G*	*SF*	*G*	*SF*	*G*	*SF*	*G*	*SF*	*G*
Nontextual aspects:														
Pictures	30	22	27	18	10	17	11	11	10	12	7	9	8	2
Pictures and print	2	4	5	6	6	4	4	5	2	4	6	5	5	4
Previous stories	1	1	1	1	2	0	3	0	2	1	1	0	2	1
Personal experience	18	14	24	14	10	13	15	13	18	16	15	19	11	7
Total nontextual	51	41	57	39	28	34	33	29	32	33	29	33	26	14
Textual aspects:														
Just read	26	19	17	4	23	8	3	2	7	3	8	9	5	7
Meaning (from reading the text):														
Literal	19	35	15	42	30	38	34	45	35	43	30	38	35	59
Interpretation	4	5	11	15	16	19	30	23	26	21	33	19	34	19
Total meaning	23	40	26	57	46	57	64	68	61	64	63	57	69	78
Print as "code":														
Word form	0	0	0	0	1	0	0	0	0	0	0	0	0	0
Structural analysis	0	0	0	0	1	0	0	0	0	0	0	0	0	0
Phonetic analysis	0	0	0	0	1	1	0	0	0	0	0	0	0	0
Context clues	0	0	0	0	0	0	0	0	0	0	0	0	0	0
Picture clues	0	0	0	0	0	0	0	1	0	0	0	1	0	1
Total "code"	0	0	0	0	3	1	0	1	0	0	0	1	0	1
Total textual	49	59	43	61	72	66	67	71	68	67	71	67	64	86
Grand total	100	100	100	100	100	100	100	100	100	100	100	100	100	100

4. Those directing the pupil's attention to the print as a code—to the word form, structural aspects, phonic aspects, verbal context, and picture clues.

As Table 8–5 shows, much of the guidance focuses the pupil's attention on the nontextual aspects of the story. In the first-grade program a large portion of the guidance material aims at getting the children to "read" and "interpret" the pictures. In fact, in the preprimers of one series, the children are asked more questions about the pictures than about the text. Many of the questions about the pictures are so subtle that even adult analysts are not always sure of the correct answers.

The number of questions directed to the pictures decreases steadily after the first-grade readers. However, even in the third-grade readers, from 5 to 8 percent of the questions concern pictures exclusively. Furthermore, the *first* question asked on each page, from the preprimers through the second-grade readers, is generally concerned with a picture. Only in the third-grade readers is the child's attention first called to the text.

From the first through the third grades, a considerable, though decreasing, proportion of the guidance material is aimed at eliciting judgments, evaluations, and expressions of feeling removed from both pictures and text. Even in the 3–1 readers about 30 percent of the questions can be answered without reading the words.

As the number of nontextual questions decreases, the proportion of questions directed to the text increases—faster in Ginn (1961) than in Scott, Foresman (1956). In the latter it is not until the 1–2 level that the child can answer more questions by reading the text than without reading it.

The questions based on a reading of the text tend to be heavily weighted toward literal reading, especially in the first few grades. The higher the level of the reader, the higher the percentage of questions that go beyond the literal understanding of the text to interpretation, critical reaction, and the like.

If the teacher relies entirely on the guidebook's suggestions, she almost never calls the children's attention to the printed words as symbols (i.e., to their visual, structural, or phonic characteristics) during the guided reading. Nor do verbal context or picture clues receive much notice.

In summary, then, we see a great concern for reading for meaning and enjoyment. But meaning here is rather vaguely defined. There is, especially in the first grade, a constant dialogue between the teacher and the pupils—a dialogue that could well distract the child from the task at hand: reading the text. In fact, the teacher at the beginning of grade 1

Table 8–6 Follow-up Activities in Two Basal Series: Scott, Foresman (1956) and Ginn (1961)

	Preprimer		*Primer*		*1-2*		*2-1*		*2-2*		*3-1*		*3-2*	
Average lesson	*SF*	G	*SF*	G	*SF*	G	*SF*	G	*SF*	G	*SF*	G	*SF*	G
Total follow-up activities	7.6	12.3	8.0	13.3	8.0	13.5	6.0	16.0	7.2	18.0	7.2	17.0	7.5	20.4
Percentage of total follow-up activities involving:														
Reading comprehension	28	24	27	35	19	26	36	25	22	20	28	25	31	20
Word meaning	5	7	7	5	0	5	0	4	5	5	6	5	4	10
Whole-word recognition	8	8	7	6	13	3	3	3	3	0	3	0	2	0
Phonic and structural analysis	19	13	13	15	13	20	17	18	22	19	25	20	16	15
Independent silent reading	3	0	10	1	9	0	5	7	6	6	8	4	5	5
Oral language	13	22	13	25	13	11	16	15	19	17	14	12	13	16
Literary appreciation	13	8	13	3	13	12	14	8	14	12	11	13	13	9
Art	8	4	5	3	6	7	3	8	0	7	0	7	0	9
Music	3	7	5	4	6	7	3	6	3	4	0	4	2	5
Social studies	0	3	0	0	0	1	0	0	0	2	0	4	5	2
Science	0	0	0	0	0	0	0	0	3	1	0	0	0	1
Films & film strips	0	1	0	3	0	4	0	4	0	4	0	3	0	3
Creative writing	0	0	0	0	0	0	3	1	0	2	0	1	0	3
Miscellaneous	0	3	0	0	8	4	0	1	3	1	5	2	9	2
Total	100	100	100	100	100	100	100	100	100	100	100	100	100	100

talks more than the child reads, and she asks the child to devote as much time to "reading" pictures and to discussing his personal experiences as to reading words.

FOLLOW-UP ACTIVITIES THAT STRESS COMPREHENSION

Even the last part of the lesson—the follow-up activities—emphasizes reading for meaning.

I classified these activities according to whether they were concerned primarily with reading comprehension, word meaning, whole-word recognition, phonic and structural analysis, independent silent reading, oral language (no reading), literary appreciation, art and music, or various other activities (see Table 8–6). Clearly, reading comprehension receives the most attention. If we add the word-meaning exercises to those on comprehension, the proportion of time and energy devoted to meaning activities is even larger.

This proportion remains quite stable for both series from the preprimers through the 3–2 books. You might well ask how the typical preprimer story, which has about seventy running words and is really told by pictures, can inspire such a high proportion of reading-for-meaning and word-meaning exercises. What is there to understand, for even the dullest child?

The concern with meaning is further illustrated by the high percentage of exercises devoted to oral language (discussion, listening) that requires no reading at all. In fact, in some instances more exercises are devoted to oral language than to phonic and structural analysis. Most of these, however, are not considered to deal with "essential skills," but rather are classified as "enrichment activities."

With only minor exceptions, follow-up activities change very little in character from the beginning of the first grade to the end of the third grade. True, the number of independent reading activities tends to increase, but even these do not seem to take full advantage of older pupils' more advanced reading skill. In fact, only about 5 percent of all follow-up activities could be classified as "independent silent reading" at the 3–2 level, when the child's skill is at its highest point in the primary grades and when he can truly begin to engage in independent reading.

Nonreading follow-up activities—e.g., those involving art, music, or science—vary more in kind and in amount between the series and by grade. However, when combined, these activities make up quite a substantial proportion of total follow-up activities, often as high as the proportion of those devoted to word recognition (whole word) and to word analysis (phonic and structural).

PHONICS—TAUGHT LITTLE, PRACTICED LESS

In the conventional basal-reading series, phonics is usually buried under masses of other material, and children are not always given a chance to put what phonics they learn to use. In the basal series discussed here, phonics is a follow-up activity. Phonics exercises are but one of a great variety of activities, all of which follow preparing for the story, learning new words, and reading and rereading the story—the core of the lesson.

Overall, as Table 8–6 indicates, less than 20 percent of the follow-up activities in grades 1 through 3 concern some aspect of phonic or structural analysis; comprehension and word-meaning exercises consistently receive more attention. Exercises concerned with phonic and structural analysis seldom receive first priority, but are generally the second or third out of seven or eight activities or the fourth or fifth out of fifteen. The follow-up activities concerned with reading comprehension or word meaning usually come first.

Since phonics exercises are *one*, and *not the first*, of many activities following the main part of the lesson, how likely is it that teachers using the basals will get to them at all? Most of these teachers are extremely busy. They usually divide their pupils into three instructional groups and give three separate lessons from three different books. Since children can read the stories with no knowledge of phonics (owing to the continuous preteaching of new words) and, as we shall see, since little of the phonics taught (particularly in the first two grades) can be applied in reading the stories, we can guess that many teachers either eliminate phonics entirely or do not take the phonics lessons too seriously.

To determine how much of a typical basal-reader lesson a teacher can be expected to cover, I gave ten experienced teachers photocopies of one story from the Ginn (1961) primer, the relevant passages in the teachers' guidebook, and the children's workbook, and I asked them to estimate how long each section would take. The lesson was one of 122 such lessons in the first-grade program (preprimers through the 1–2 book), not including the reading-readiness activities. Table 8–7 shows the results.

These teachers said that they spend from 1 to 1½ hours daily on all reading activities. Of course, they use different readers with slow, average, and above-average groups, but the lesson plans, as we saw from the previous analysis, are essentially the same at all levels in the primary program. I leave it to you to judge how it is possible to complete even the core of these lessons with three different groups, not to speak of covering the follow-up activities.

Not only is scant attention paid to teaching phonics in the basal

Table 8–7 Estimates of Time Required for Teaching a Primer Lesson, in Minutes*

Lesson part	Slow group	Average group	Above-average group
I. Developing readiness for reading			
A. Meaningful presentation of vocabulary	16	12	6
B. Setting up reading purposes	8	4	3
II. Reading the story			
A. Guided reading	26	17	11
B. Rereading for specific purposes	17	12	9
Total for I and II (the "core" of the lesson)	67	45	29
III. Building essential habits & skills			
A. Comprehension			
1. Main idea	10	7	3
2. Creative reading	12	7	6
B. Word study			
1. Phonetic analysis	25	17	10
2. Visual-kinesthetic	2	1	1
C. Workbook			
1. Instructing children & having them do exercises	27	15	10
2. Checking the work	17	14	6
Total for essential habits & skills	93	61	36
IV. Related language experiences			
A. Reports	18	12	12
B. Name charts	14	10	9
Total for related language experiences	32	22	21
V. Enrichment activities			
A. Construction	34	32	22
B. Imitative play	19	13	10
C. Stories to enjoy	31	24	21
Total for enrichment activities	84	69	53
Grand total for entire lesson	276 (4½ hr)	197 (3¼ hr)	139 (2¼ hr)

* "Come Down, Frisky," from the Ginn, 1961, primer, pp. 39–42. Relevant passages in the guidebook are on pp. 143–149, and those in the workbook are on pp. 24–26.

series, but what is taught is often not applied. According to their proponents, basal-reading programs are total programs in which all aspects of reading are integrated. However, I could find little evidence (except in the third-grade program) that previously taught phonic generalizations are used to teach the new words for the next story (see Table 8–2) or to facilitate the transfer and application of what has already been learned. Nor do the basals alert the child to apply the phonic elements previously taught to his reading of stories.[7] Generally speaking, until the third grade the phonics lessons seem almost an afterthought.[8]

Recognizing words as wholes remains the prime means of word recognition; ways of doing so are stressed and even developed all throughout the first few years, often in preference to phonic analysis. Thus the Ginn (1961) second-grade program (2–1 guidebook, p. 243) still teaches the child to block chatter and toddle. In the 2–2 guidebook of Scott, Foresman (1956) we read: "In attacking new words, the child's first and best aid is the context clue" (p. 181). At the 1–2 level, the teacher finds the following in the Scott, Foresman (1956) guidebook:

> Point up specific details through such comments and questions as, "One of these words has a letter below the line and no tall letters. Which word is it?" [way]. . . . This valuable technique should be applied frequently, especially to those words that pupils have failed to recognize or have tended to confuse. . . . (pp. 72–73).

The phonics teaching in the basals seems designed to give the child a sense that letter-sound correspondences are highly irregular and inconsistent. For example, on the preprimer level, where auditory perception alone is taught, some of the rhyming words used for practice in Scott, Foresman (1956) are *one* and *run; key* and *see; bed, head,* and *said;* and *rains* and *canes.* The words rhyme, but the spellings vary. Although these activities are auditory only, they will reinforce the idea of irregularity and high inconsistency for any pupils who know how to spell these words. Almost from the beginning, the plan seems to be to have the child expect numerous sounds for the same symbols and numerous symbols for the same sounds.

After the preprimer level, when the single consonants (which are highly consistent) are taught in their initial positions, no direct statement is made that a certain letter stands for a certain sound, nor is the child asked to make the inference. Evidently it is assumed that the child can apply this knowledge as an additional clue to the recognition of a new word, although he has received no guided practice in doing so.

On the second-grade level, when vowels and their sound values are presented, Scott, Foresman (1956) provides four consecutive lessons on the various sounds of the letters *i* and *y.* This is followed by the combinations employing the letter *a: ai, ay, ar, al, aw,* and *a* as in *as.* Known

[7] Beginning with the 1–2 book, Scott, Foresman (1956) divides new words into those to be pretaught as sight words and those which can be identified independently. However, the latter follow no definite pattern, and the guidebook gives no suggestions as to how to practice them.

[8] I found only two forms of "integration." Often the theme of the story is used to motivate the phonics lesson, and the lesson sometimes uses previously taught sight words from which principles on sound-symbol relationships are to be generalized.

words are presented to demonstrate the many sounds of the vowel letters. But *no* exercises are given to show how children can apply this knowledge in recognizing strange words. Instead, practice words appear in sentences so that the child can use context clues in recognizing them.

The following excerpt from the Scott, Foresman (1956) guidebook for the 2–1 reader (p. 184) will serve to illustrate these points. Note that so many rather disconnected items are taught that it is difficult to know whether any one letter-sound correspondence is really learned. Also note that the generalization taught, to try the "short sound of the vowel first," does not follow from the previous teachings of the sound values of the letters in the same lesson.

> *Phonetic Analysis:* To strengthen ability to combine context clues and phonetic analysis in attacking new words, write *sit, night, bird,* and *hand, rain, car, ball.* Have pupils pronounce each word and tell which *i* or *a* sound they hear. Then explain that *i* and *a* are called vowel sounds and that the letters that stand for these sounds are called vowel letters. Next point to *bird, car, rain, ball* and discuss the visual clues to the vowel sounds (*r,* silent *i* and *l*).
>
> Continue: "When we talk, we use the short sounds heard in *it* and *cat* more than the long *i* sound and the long *a* sound; so when we see new words that don't have a sign that tells what vowel sound to try, we try the short sound first.
>
> "If the short sound doesn't make a word that fits in the sentence, we try the long sound." Then write these sentences; have them read:
>
> Father put a *stamp* on the letter.
> The little child played *with* her toys.
> Some birds are building a nest in the old *tin* can.
> Mother baked a *cake* for the party.

One wonders what is actually the point of the above phonics lesson. When words are so richly surrounded in context, there is no need to use whatever phonics knowledge has been gained.

In short, the basal series do not really seem to expect the pupil to use the letter-sound correspondences taught.

How could it be otherwise? Since those producing the basal readers assume that the major focus should be on meaningful reading right from the start, they have had to write understandable stories that use common words already known to the pupils. These words are among the most irregularly spelled in English. Neither the workbook exercises nor the exercises suggested in the teachers' guidebooks depart from this vocabulary. If you set out to write a meaningful story for beginning readers you will find it extremely difficult to put in words to illustrate a given phonic principle and still keep the story alive. To integrate phonics and reading, the basals would need to include at least some words selected on the basis of phonic or structural elements previously taught. Scott, Foresman (1956) and Ginn (1961) do not do this.

*Table 8–8 Sequence of Teaching Major Phonic Elements in Five Programs**

Grade	Bloomfield System	Phonetic Keys to Reading	Hay-Wingo†	Phonovisual Method‡	Scott, Foresman (1956)
Readiness & preprimers	Letters of alphabet; left-to-right visual progression Single consonants Short vowels	Long vowels Vowel digraphs Short vowels Single consonants Consonant digraphs Consonant blends (several)	Short vowels 10 single consonants	Single consonants Consonant digraphs Long vowel *ee*	Auditory perception of initial consonants
Primer (1–1)	Consonant blends Consonant digraphs Vowel digraphs Diphthongs	Consonant blends Diphthongs Silent letters	Single consonants Consonant digraphs Consonant blends	Short vowels Consonant blends Long vowels	Visual-auditory perception of single initial consonants
First (1–2)	New sounds for letters taught (semiregular) Long vowels	Irregularities	Long vowels Vowel digraphs Diphthongs Silent letters	Vowel digraphs Diphthongs No silent letters	Visual-auditory perception of final consonants Consonant digraphs
Second (2–1)	Silent letters Irregularities	Review and irregularities			Consonant blends Long and short *i, y, a*
Second (2–2)		Same as above			Long and short *e, o, u* Diphthongs Vowel digraphs Silent letters Alphabet in sequence (for alphabetizing)

* There is considerable overlapping in the teaching of these elements from one level to the next; this breakdown is intended to give a general view of sequence.

† The breakdown of lessons at each level was based on the researcher's estimate and the authors' suggestion that each page of the book constitutes one lesson.

‡ This system does not define lessons. The breakdown here is based on the authors' statement that all the sounds should be learned in first grade.

With these limitations, how much phonics do the conventional basals actually teach?

Table 8–8, from Mildred Bloomfield (1962), compares the sequence of teaching phonic elements in the first and second grades of Scott, Foresman (1956) with three special systematic phonics programs and the Bloomfield System linguistic program. (The latter does not teach the sound values of the letters, but the child practices his reading on words arranged so that he can "discover" these values for himself.)

Scott, Foresman (1956) starts phonics instruction more slowly than the other programs shown in Table 8–8. Some training in listening to sounds in words (auditory perception) is begun at the readiness and preprimer levels, but children do not associate sounds and letters until they are reading primers. While most of the other programs teach both consonants and vowels, and even vowel digraphs, in the first grade, Scott, Foresman (1956) concentrates on single consonants and some consonant digraphs.

Most of the other published supplemental phonics programs of the same date teach vowels in the first grade, while Scott, Foresman (1956) does not teach vowels until the second grade.

The Ginn (1961) phonics program moves faster than that of Scott, Foresman (1956); for example, it covers consonant blends and vowel sounds in the first grade. However, Ginn (1961), too, is considerably slower in introducing phonics than the supplemental phonics programs and the Bloomfield System linguistic program.

HEAVY DEPENDENCE ON THE TEACHER

Both basal-reading programs lean heavily on direct guidance from the teacher. According to the guidebooks, the teacher is needed for all parts of all the reading lessons to establish background, preteach the new words, guide the silent reading of the story, and guide the rereading of the story.

She is also needed for most of the follow-up activities (see Table 8–9).

In Scott, Foresman (1956) the proportion of activities requiring the teacher's complete attention (about 60 percent) remains about the same from the beginning of grade 1 to the end of grade 3. In Ginn (1961), too, most of the follow-up activities require the teacher's full attention, although she is somewhat less important in the third grade than in the first. But even at the 3–2 level more than half of the follow-up activities require total teacher direction and guidance.

Pupils using both series can engage in only a few activities—from 1 to 9 percent—with complete independence. About 30 percent require the

Table 8–9 Percentage of Material Directing Follow-up Activities in Two Basal Series: Scott, Foresman (1956) and Ginn (1961)

	Preprimer		Primer		1-2		2-1	
Average lesson	SF	G	SF	G	SF	G	SF	G
Teacher directs completely	61	70	65	63	72	67	69	59
Teacher directs partly	34	30	35	36	19	33	28	36
Pupil does independently	5	0	0	1	9	0	3	5
Total	100	100	100	100	100	100	100	100

teacher's direction initially, although they can be continued independently to some extent.

To me this dependence means that the teacher who follows the lesson plans suggested in the manual is virtually enslaved to the program. These lessons seem to take no advantage of the pupil's increasing skill and facility for independent work as he progresses from the first through the third grades. Because the teacher is so indispensable for motivation, explanation, guidance, and discussion, as well as for many follow-up activities, she is forced to leave out a great deal of each lesson. What is omitted can only be conjectured, but we can guess that some bread and butter may be discarded in favor of frills.

SILENT READING, LITTLE WRITING

The guidebooks of both series suggest that stories be read silently first, from the preprimers on. Pupils read out loud to answer the teacher's questions and sometimes for other reasons. But straight oral reading as a

Table 8–10 Percentage of Follow-up Activities by Mode of Response in Two Basal Series: Scott, Foresman (1956) and Ginn (1961)

	Preprimer		Primer		1-2		2-1	
Activity	SF	G	SF	G	SF	G	SF	G
Reading:								
Silent	37	23	28	33	28	27	36	34
Silent & oral	8	14	5	14	6	14	11	7
Oral	3	8	23	9	18	11	14	18
Total reading	48	45	56	56	52	52	61	59
Listening and discussing	45	50	35	38	39	41	36	36
Construction and other nonlanguage activities	7	5	9	6	9	7	3	5
Total	100	100	100	100	100	100	100	100
Writing (in addition to other modes of response)	0	1	0	1	0	10	11	8

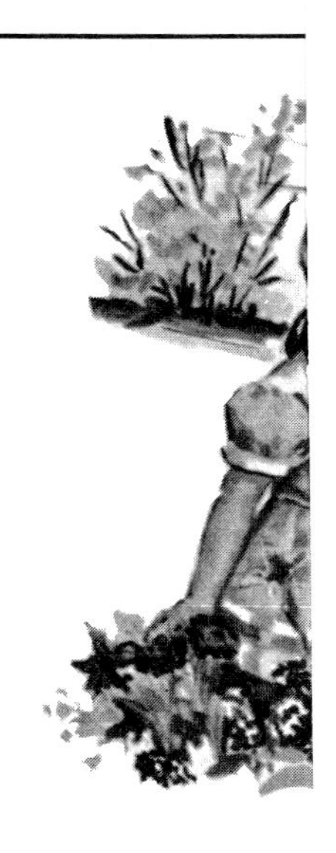

"Look, !
"Here i
Somethi
"Oh, Ja
"I want
I want s
I want s

2-2		3-1		3-2	
SF	G	SF	G	SF	G
64	56	64	55	67	52
30	40	28	41	29	42
6	4	8	4	4	6
100	100	100	100	100	100

form of practice is discouraged. Basal-series authors seem to have a great fear that if the child reads a good deal orally, he will concentrate on the words only and not understand what he reads. In the jargon of the field, he may become a "word caller."

The introductory section of the guidebooks advises the teacher to encourage the child to read with expression—to show that he appreciates the meaning of what he reads and sympathizes with the feeling of the characters who express the thoughts. Word-by-word reading is to be discouraged because it interrupts the flow of expression and impedes comprehension.

As for other means of responding, the basal series seem to discourage writing in favor of speaking. If we look at the responses called for by the follow-up activities (see Table 8–10), we see that a good proportion, from one-third to one-half, are nonreading activities like listening and discussing. (A considerable proportion—up to 9 percent—are nonlanguage activities such as constructing and drawing.)

The basal programs call for little writing before the beginning of

2-2		3-1		3-2	
SF	G	SF	G	SF	G
42	37	36	38	44	34
3	3	11	0	2	5
13	7	19	11	22	12
58	47	66	49	68	51
42	46	34	45	32	40
0	7	0	6	0	9
100	100	100	100	100	100
11	17	6	24	11	23

Mot

See

"Oh

"It

"Ye

"Mc

21

To illustrate many of the p
and guidebooks, we reprod
The New Fun with Dick
Basic Readers, *together wi*
the Guidebook for The Ne
Arbuthnot, and Gray. Cop
Glenview, Ill.

"I want this," said Jane.
"And this and this.
Three for me.
Three for you.
Something yellow.
Something red.
Something blue."

23

"Look, Mother," said Sally.
"Red, yellow, blue!"

"Look, Mother," said Jane.
"We look pretty."

"Oh, yes," said Mother.
"Yes, Jane, yes!
You look pretty.
Sally looks pretty, too."

24

ities. Now, for a purely interpretative rhythm, present Phoebe James' record "Garden Varieties." This record offers "mood music" portraying wind, rain, sun, and growing plants. The mimeographed suggestions that accompany the record show how this rhythm can be developed with young children. Capitalize, too, on the youngsters' own ideas.

Something Pretty PAGES 21-24

New Words: *pretty* *too*
Word Cards: 32, 43, 74, 85, 102, 103, 112, 123, 139
Phrase Card: 74

PREPARING FOR READING

Establishing background: Comment on some of the pretty things the youngsters are wearing—Nancy's red hair ribbon, Bob's new tie, Susan's bright-colored sweater. Children will respond eagerly with descriptions of other pretty things they own or want.

Presenting vocabulary: Display a painting that a pupil has made during the activity period and put this line below it: *This is pretty.* Present the line and ask someone to choose another painting that he thinks is pretty. Display the chosen picture and present this sentence: *This is pretty, too.* In each case, have children read the line silently and orally.

In The New Basic Reading Program the child's approach to reading is based on the understanding that written language represents meaning as well as sound—that spoken and printed words are the basic meaningful elements in our language. Throughout the Primer level, the child continues to use the basic sight vocabulary that he has developed at Pre-Primer level and gradually adds to this stock of printed words with which he can instantly associate meaning. Likewise, he continues to develop in his ability to analyze spoken language as he identifies specific sound units in spoken word wholes. At this level he also learns to associate sounds in words with specific printed letter symbols in printed word wholes. The emphasis given in this and the preceding Guidebook *to the correspondence of meaning, sound, and symbol thus forms the foundation for independent word attack at the next level. At Book One level, then, he is ready for the all-important step of independent analysis of printed words into their component sound units, a process that enables him to derive the sound and meaning of many new words. At all times his attention is focused upon both oral and written words as language symbols that communicate meaning in context.*

This meaningful approach to reading is in sharp contrast to that in which the child first drills on isolated speech sounds and associates them with letter symbols. With the latter approach, as the child learns the basic phonemic elements, he combines and recombines them into isolated word wholes; this places the emphasis upon synthesis of separate sound units or nonsense syllables into words that are pronunciation units, which may be devoid of meaning. Such a mechanical approach in the early stages of reading slows down the recognition of words in running context and delays development of the basic understanding that printed words are meaningful language units.

Checking the presentation: Ask pupils what they say when they like the way something looks. "Can you find a sentence in the chart that says something is pretty? Can you frame the word *pretty?* How many times do you see that word? Frame it each time. What word says that something else is also pretty? Frame the word that says *too.*"

INTERPRETING THE STORY

Guided reading: Write the title "Something Pretty" and say, "Today we are going to read a story called 'Something Pretty.' Let's find the story."

Page 21: When youngsters have turned to page 21, ask them what they think "something" means in this title. Mother's hat will be the obvious answer. After comments on the hat and how pretty Mother looks, establish the setting by asking, "Where are Mother and the two girls?" Next, talk about the way the three are dressed: "Are they all wearing the same kind of dresses? the same kind of hats? What's different about Mother's hat?"

Guide the reading in thought units and check understanding with such questions as "What did Mother want Jane and Sally to see? What did Mother mean when she said *this?* What did Sally say about the hat? What did Jane say about Mother? [The last question brings out the "appears to be" meaning of the known word *looks.*] Who will read the page aloud to show us how much Jane and Sally like Mother's new hat?"

Page 22: Bring out the idea that Sally and Jane have gone outside, perhaps to wait for Mother, and ask, "Do you sometimes have to wait for your mother?" Point up details by asking what Jane and Sally see in the yard. "Why do you suppose Jane is pointing to the flowers? Can you guess what she might be thinking? Read what she said." Ask someone to tell what the "something pretty" is. "What do you suppose Jane is planning to do?" Have the next section read silently to see what Sally wanted. "What do you suppose Sally might want to do with the flowers?" Conclude by having children describe the pictured action and then read both speeches aloud.

Page 23: Discussion of the picture will bring out the idea that Jane has already selected red and blue flowers for Sally and herself. "What color do you think Jane and Sally want now? Let's read to find out." After silent reading, ask, "What did Jane mean when she said *this?* What were the colors of the flowers Jane was picking?" The rhythmic quality of these lines will warrant several oral readings. After youngsters have enjoyed the way the words sound, ask, "Did Jane say what she planned to do with the flowers? What do you think she will do? Why do you suppose that Sally has taken her hat off? Turn the page to see whether you're right!"

Page 24: Some pupils may have decided opinions about whether the girls' hats are prettier this way and all responses should be respected. "Do the girls look pleased with their flowered hats? Read what they said. Now read what Mother said. Did she like Jane's and Sally's hats? Did Jane think she and Sally looked pretty? Read the line that says so." Three pupils may read the page as they think Mother, Jane, and Sally talked.

Rereading: Choose a narrator and three girls to retell and reread "Something Pretty." Later, try a different plan. Suggest, perhaps, that each character tell what she did as well as what she said. For instance, for page 21, Mother might say: "Sally, Jane, and I were going out one afternoon. We had on new dresses that looked very much alike, and Jane and Sally had on their new hats. I sat down at my dressing table to put on my new flowered hat, while Jane and Sally watched. They had never seen this hat before; so I said . . ." Here, Mother reads from the book.

Sally can go on with: "I liked Mother's new hat. It had pretty colored flowers on it. I said . . ." Sally adds her speech from the book.

Jane continues, "Mother looked beautiful in her new hat. Some of the flowers matched her dress. I said . . ." Jane reads her two lines of text.

EXTENDING SKILLS AND ABILITIES

Comprehending sentence meaning: This exercise is designed to strengthen the ability to comprehend sentence meaning in light of pronoun reference and to promote the ability to associate meaning with the words *I*, *me*, *you*, and *we*. Place the word cards *Dick*, *Jane*, *Sally*, *Puff*, *Spot*, *Mother*, and *Father* on the chalk ledge and write the following three-line units.

"Look, Spot," said Sally.
"See me run.
Can you run, too?"

"Oh, Dick," said Jane.
"You and I can run, too.
We can run with Sally."

"Look, Jane," said Mother.
"I see something pretty.
Something pretty for you and me."

"Oh, Sally," said Dick.
"I see Father in the house.
We can run to Father."

Have children read the first three lines silently. Then point to the word *me* and ask, "Whom did Sally mean when she said *me?* Find that name on the chalk ledge. Look at the next line. Whom did she mean when she said *you?* Find that name on the ledge." Continue with the other groups.

Finally, have children open their books to page 22 and read the first three lines again. Point to the third line and ask youngsters to tell whom Jane means when she says *you* and *me*. Repeat with pages 23 and 24.

Children's responses to this exercise will indicate the amount of guidance needed with page 8 of the *Think-and-Do Book*.

Visual imagery: This exercise is designed to strengthen ability in creative visual imagery. (See the italic insert on page 79 of this *Guidebook*.) Turn to page 21 and establish the setting as an upstairs bedroom in Jane and Sally's house. Note that the girls are ready but that Mother is just putting on her hat. Pretend with youngsters that this is the first picture in a movie and ask, "Do the characters stand still in a movie? What do they do? What do you suppose Jane and Sally are doing as they watch Mother? What do you think they are saying? Can you think of something Mother might need to keep her hat in place? Do you suppose she had to look for the right hatpin?" Children will quickly get the idea of how to fill in a picture to make it a part of a movie. Guide them continually with encouragement and a warm acceptance of all logical ideas.

Turn the page and consider whether the first picture gave a hint that Jane and Sally were going outside. "What do you suppose happened between the time Jane and Sally were watching Mother and the time we saw them outside? Close your eyes and tell us what you see them doing." When pupils have contributed imagined actions and conversations, join this scene with the others in the movie by asking, "What are Jane and Sally doing in this picture?"

Guide the visualizations of the remainder of the story in the same manner. If pupils seem reluctant or limited in ability to visualize, ask guiding questions: "Close your eyes again. Can you see Jane picking flowers? What colors are they? When Jane picked all the flowers she wanted, what do you suppose she did with them? Do you think Sally put the flowers on her hat all by herself? How do you think they made the flowers stay on the hats? What might Jane and Sally have said as they decorated their hats?" As the story is reread, note the inclusion of details discussed in this exercise.

Structural analysis: To strengthen the ability to recognize words formed by adding *s* to the root forms of words, write the word *look* and have it pronounced. Then comment, "I am going to add something to this word. [Add *s* to *look* to make *looks*.] Now what is the word?" Repeat with the words *help, helps; want, wants; cookie, cookies.*

Through the type of group work suggested here and on pages 89 and 93 of this Guidebook, *children gradually begin to develop the basic language understanding that root words retain their meaning in inflected and compounded forms and that inflectional endings are meaning units in words.*

Children who had difficulty with the "Structural Analysis" section of the new Basic Reading Test *for the Pre-Primers may need additional practice of the kind suggested in this exercise.*

Think-and-Do Book: Use page 8.

EXTENDING INTERESTS

Enjoying literature: Select poems from Milne's *When We Were Very Young* and *Now We Are Six* to read to the children just for fun. Then reread any of the stories the children have enjoyed. Rereading *Hide and Seek Day* should inspire more hiding stories from the children—baby birds hide in their nests, children hide under warm covers until morning, and so on.

We Three PAGES 25-27

New Words: *cannot* *ride*
Word Card: 109
Phrase Cards: 11, 33, 34, 82, 83

PREPARING FOR READING

Establishing background: Center conversation around improvised toys by mentioning that Dick, Jane, and Sally liked to play "pretend" games. Ask, for example, "Have you ever pretended that a chair was an airplane or a boat? that a broomstick was your pony? What games did you play?"

the second grade. Although pupils write more as they progress from the 2–1 reader through the 3–2 reader, there are fewer activities involving writing than oral language activities.

A Newer Series Beginning with Phonics

How has the recent interest in increased phonics for beginning readers affected the basal series?

To investigate this question I looked at the first-grade program of *Basic Reading*, the series coauthored by Charles C. Walcutt and Glenn McCracken and published by Lippincott in 1963. This series begins with a phonic emphasis and selects words on a phonic-regularity principle. Admittedly, the analysis did not tell me everything I might want to know about how intensifying the dose of phonics affects first-grade basal-reading instruction. Yet it did indicate some ways in which introducing a phonic approach right from the start can change other aspects of a basal program.

In brief, I found that the Lippincott (1963) series differs from the other two series most markedly in its approach to teaching and practicing new words: more new words are introduced, and they are presented differently. In other aspects—e.g., methods of guiding the pupil's reading and type of follow-up activities—this program does not differ greatly from the conventional basals, and perhaps not as much as we might expect.

LESSONS BUILT AROUND PHONIC ELEMENTS

Unlike the beginning lessons in Scott, Foresman (1956) and Ginn (1961), those in Lippincott (1963) are not organized around stories. Instead, they center around the presentation of phonic elements and lists of words employing those phonic elements. This material is sometimes followed by a few sentences, a short poem, or a little story.

To make comparison possible I divided the Lippincott (1963) first-grade readers into lessons by stories and poems with introductory phonics and lists of words attached to them. This gave 102 first-grade lessons, as compared with 116 in Scott, Foresman (1956) and 122 in Ginn (1961).

The Lippincott stories in the first-grade readers are considerably shorter (averaging 131 words) than those in Scott, Foresman (1956) and in Ginn (1961) (which average 178 and 182 words, respectively). The most dramatic difference is in the number of new words per 100 words

Vocabulary List

This First Reader, *On Cherry Street*, follows ***The Little White House***, the Primer of the GINN BASIC READING SERIES. This First Reader introduces 171 new words. The 155 words previously taught in the series are repeated and maintained in this book. All variants of a word, except the *s* forms of nouns and verbs, are counted as new words.

The lines in the list indicate the ending of one story or unit and the beginning of another.

New Words in This Book

UNIT I
5. school

---

6. . . .
7. cannot
8. mitten
9. . . .
10. Miss
Hill

---

11. sing
12. sat
13. . . .
14. . . .

---

15. bag
book
16. into
17. . . .
18. . . .

---

19. dress
20. pocket
21. Pat
22. just

---

23. button
found
24. let's
25. lost
26. his

---

27. all
Dick
28. bus

---

29. wonderful
30. balloon
man
31. one
so
32. over
33. pop
34. was

UNIT II
35. . . .

---

36. snowman
snow
37. . . .
38. old
back
39. had
time
40. be
there

---

41. sled
42. again
as
43. Cherry
street
44. . . .

---

45. going
46. win
boys
47. faster
48. . . .

---

49. . . .
50. story
51. wanted
52. find

---

53. scat
cat
54. woman
55. . . .
56. . . .
57. hear
58. may
her

UNIT III
59. Mac's

---

60. bring
61. soon
62. am
63. . . .
64. nothing
that
65. . . .

---

66. hurry
67. money
eggs
68. how
drop

---

69. jingle
70. good-by
71. could
bump
72. were
think

---

73. must
74. took
monkey
75. . . .
76. Ben
give
77. . . .

---

78. ice cream
groceries
79. shall
Mrs.
80. call
telephone
81. stay
82. worked

UNIT IV
83. . . .

---

84. Rooster
ate

85. brook
pan
86. by
87. met
88. . . .

---

89. lamb
fox
90. . . .
91. drum
rolled
92. foot
day

---

93. feather
94. goat
gone
95. cold
96. sleep

---

97. pancake
98. from
99. catch
after
100. sang
101. bear
102. . . .
103. . . .

---

104. night
rain
105. build
tomorrow
106. sun
about
107. next
108. never

---

109. rabbit
cabbage
110. hoppity-
hop
111. . . .
112. . . .
113. bee
114. . . .
115. buzzed
116. nose

UNIT V
117. . . .

---

118. hide
us
119. around
120. noise
tink-tinkle
121. organ
122. . . .

---

123. dance
basket
124. fire
125. . . .
126. . . .
127. . . .

---

128. ring
129. . . .
130. . . .
131. . . .
132. . . .
133. . . .

---

134. sprinkler
splash
135. . . .
136. . . .

---

137. window
138. better
than
139. other
140. . . .

---

141. letter
postman
142. two
143. step
144. Billy

UNIT VI
145. . . .

---

146. him
147. . . .
148. . . .

---

149. fish
150. pole
151. . . .
152. . . .
153. . . .
154. . . .

---

155. . . .
156. . . .
157. three
four
158. . . .
159. . . .
160. turtle

---

161. . . .
162. tractor
163. clinkety-
clank
164. . . .
165. . . .
166. . . .

---

167. . . .
168. corn
garden
169. chicks
170. . . .

---

171. fence
172. seesaw
173. . . .
174. . . .

UNIT VII
175. . . .

---

176. side
177. across
178. frogs
179. ears
180. . . .

---

181. squirrel
182. . . .
183. . . .
184. flower
185. honey
186. picnic
187. . . .

---

188. . . .
189. . . .
190. . . .
191. . . .
192. . . .

---

193. learns
194. . . .
195. . . .
196. . . .
197. . . .
198. . . .

---

199. bicycle
200. . . .
201. . . .
202. . . .
203. . . .
204. . . .

---

205. muffs
206. . . .
207. . . .
208. . . .

---

209. puddle
crying
210. . . .
211. . . .
212. . . .
213. baby
214. . . .

---

215. . . .
216. . . .
217. . . .
218. . . .
219. . . .

---

220. *Poem*
221. *Poem*

Pages 222 and 223 from Odille Ousley and David H. Russell, On Cherry Street, *Primer of the* Ginn Basic Readers, *Ginn and Company, Boston, 1961.*

Sound-spelling Sequence in Grade 1

Pre-Primer

SOUND	PAGE	SOUND	PAGE	SOUND	PAGE
short a	1	r	8	p	20
short e	2	s	10	dr,gr	22
short i	3	d	11	sp,mp	24
short o	4	nd	12	hard c	26
short u	5	t	14	h	28
m	6	st,nt	16	f	30
n	7	hard g	18		

Primer

SOUND	PAGE	SOUND	PAGE	SOUND	PAGE
ar	1	le	22	ai	44
er	5	k	24	long i,ie	50
ed	6	ck	26	ir	51
w	7	magic e	31	long o	57
ow(cow)	12	a(care)	31	ore,or	58
l	14	long a	32	oa,oe	64
ll	15	long e,ee	36	j	68
b	21	ea	40	v	73

Reader 1-1

SOUND	PAGE	SOUND	PAGE	SOUND	PAGE
sh	1	-ing	33–38	dg,dge	89
ch,tch	5	-ed	44–47	-tion,-sion	97
th	8	er as er	52	oo(cook)	101
wh	14	ar as er	53	oo(food)	102
qu	17	ir,or,ur as er	54	ow(snow)	115
x	18	-y,-ay	64	ow(cow)	118
y	19	-ey	64	ou	119
z	20	soft c	75	oi,oy	130
ng	26	soft g	88		

Reader 1-2

SOUND	PAGE	SOUND	PAGE	SOUND	PAGE
long u	1	wr,kn	26	ea as long a	62
long ue	1	silent b	36	ear	62
long ui	1	silent l	36	ie as long e	72
ew,eau	8	silent g	48	ei as long e	72
aw,au	14	silent h	48	ei as long a	78
ph as f	18	silent gh	48	eigh as long a	78
hard ch	18	gh as f	48	ey as long a	78
ch as sh	18	ea as short e	62	ough	101

Next-to-last page of Basic Reading, *Teachers' Edition, 1–1 and 1–2, J. B. Lippincott Co., Philadelphia, 1963.*

of text—from about two for Scott, Foresman (1956) and Ginn (1961) to about 37 for Lippincott (1963). [Presumably the child using the Lippincott (1963) readers is expected to read so many new words because he has been pretaught the phonic elements found in them and exposed to lists of words containing these phonic elements.]

Lippincott (1963) does not follow the usual basal pattern of indicating the new words in the back of the reader or in the teachers' manuals. It does follow the conventional pattern of including profuse illustrations: at least one picture per page, covering from one-fourth to one-half of the page.

GREATER VARIETY IN TEACHING NEW WORDS

The Lippincott (1963) first-grade teachers' manuals are roughly as long as those in the other two series, but the approaches to teaching suggested in them differ somewhat (Table 8–11).

Since many Lippincott (1963) lessons start with phonics, the conventional method of introducing a lesson by establishing background and interest is not used as often. Where it is used, it receives less elaborate treatment. As we see from Table 8–11, the Lippincott manuals suggest only about two questions or statements for each lesson, while the conventional series suggest five or six. Questions and statements are not given word for word as often; here, and in other sections of the Lippincott (1963) manual, the instructions are more general, and the teacher is expected to state the idea or question in her own words.

Of the three series, only the Lippincott (1963) first-grade program prepares the child for learning new words according to instructions pertaining to phonics (see Table 8–12). In contrast to the conventional basals, the teacher is not told to introduce new words by presenting them in sentences or phrases or by writing them on the blackboard and telling a story. Instead, she is to present the words as illustrations of the sound values of the letters that she has already taught. Children are to receive

Table 8–11 Comparison of Contents of First-grade Teachers' Guidebook in Three Basal Series

Guidance material per average lesson	*Scott, Foresman (1956)*	*Ginn (1961)*	*Lippincott (1963)*
Pages of instruction	4.7	6.6	4.1
Questions and statements to introduce the story	5.5	4.6	2.4
Words teacher speaks	65	47	15

Table 8–12 Preparing for a First-grade Lesson and Practicing New Words in Three Basal Series

Average lesson	*Scott, Foresman (1956)*	*Ginn (1961)*	*Lippincott (1963)*
Preparation for new words:			
Questions and statements pertaining to phonics	0	0	11
Presentation of new words:			
How presented	Sentence, isolated, phrase	Sentence, isolated, phrase	Isolated
Oral buildup	Yes	Yes	No
Times word is practiced	4.3	3.2	3.2
Pupil's response mode	Silent to oral reading	Silent to oral reading	Oral reading, writing, listening to sound
Practice of new words:			
Questions and directions to practice new words	10	9	134
Percentage of material devoted to:			
Just reading	60	50	34
Meaning	20	15	24
Visual aspects	15	19	5
Structural analysis	2	1	4
Phonic analysis	2	10	11
Context	1	5	0
Writing	0	0	22
Total	100	100	100

considerable practice in writing the new letters; they listen for and say words beginning with new sounds, write from dictation new words containing the new elements learned, and read the words out loud.

The three series suggest about the same amount of practice for each new word. However, since the Lippincott (1963) first-grade lessons contain about ten times as many new words as those in Scott, Foresman (1956) and Ginn (1961), the Lippincott (1963) program must devote considerably more time to practice in recognizing words.

The *kind* of practice suggested does differ, as Table 8–12 shows. Compared with Scott, Foresman (1956) and Ginn (1961), Lippincott (1963) calls for more oral reading. A look-say type of practice (my just-read category) still predominates, but is less important than in the other series; instructions to "just read" in the first-grade program represent only about one-third of all suggested directions in Lippincott (1963), but 60 percent in Scott, Foresman (1956) and 50 percent in Ginn (1961).

Strange as it may seem for a series that emphasizes phonics, questions about what words mean represent 24 percent of all questions and directions in Lippincott (1963)—a greater proportion than in the two conventional series that emphasize reading for meaning.

A unique feature of the Lippincott (1963) first-grade program is the use of writing in practicing new words; writing is involved in over one-fifth of all suggestions for practice. Attacking words through phonic analysis is about as important as in Ginn (1961), but more important than in Scott, Foresman (1956). The child is asked to notice visual aspects of the word (configuration, length, etc.) much less often than in the other two programs.

Overall, the teacher who follows the Lippincott (1963) first-grade program encourages children to use a greater variety of approaches to recognizing and practicing new words. Scott, Foresman (1956) and Ginn (1961) tend to stress word recognition (the look-say approach) primarily, giving secondary emphasis to word meaning and analysis of visual aspects of the words. Lippincott (1963) also expects the child to "just read" by recognizing whole words, but puts almost as much stress on having him write the word and give its meaning.

A SIMILAR EMPHASIS ON COMPREHENSION

Lippincott (1963) differs very little from the more conventional series in its suggestions to the teacher for guiding reading (see Table 8–13). She is to do just as careful and precise a job—covering one line at a time in the preprimer and advancing to from two to nine lines in the first-grade reader. The Lippincott (1963) first-grade manual also suggests that the children read silently, although some oral reading is called for in answering questions. It gives the teacher even more questions to ask per story than the two conventional series' manuals if we take into account that stories in Lippincott (1963) are shorter.

To what aspects of the story does the teacher direct attention during the guided reading? As in the conventional series, about one-third of the time is devoted to nontextual aspects—pictures, pictures and print, and evaluations and judgments that can be made independently of pictures and print. Questions about the pictures, however, are not quite as frequent.

A teacher using the Lippincott (1963) series is to direct about the same percentage of questions to comprehension of the text as a teacher following Scott, Foresman (1956) and Ginn (1961), but the Lippincott manual suggests fewer questions that require the child's interpretation.

The manual instructs the teacher to draw the child's attention to phonic and other "decoding" aspects of the text during the guided-

Table 8–13 Comparison of Guided-reading Sections in the Teachers' Guidebooks of Three Basal Series: The First-grade Program

Average lesson	Scott, Foresman (1956)	Ginn (1961)	Lippincott (1963)
Mean no. of questions, statements, directions per story	47	22	48
Percentage of total questions, statements, directions devoted to:			
Nontextual aspects:			
Pictures	22	19	13
Pictures and print	4	5	1
Previous stories	2	1	0
Personal experience	17	14	17
Total nontextual	45	39	31
Textual aspects:			
Just read	22	10	28
Meaning:			
Literal	21	38	29
Interpretation	10	13	4
Total meaning	31	51	33
Print as "code":			
Word form	1	0	½
Structural analysis	1	0	½
Phonetic analysis	0	0	7
Context clues	0	0	0
Picture clues	0	0	0
Total "code"	2	0	8
Total textual	55	61	69
Grand total	100	100	100

reading period more often than the other series do, although not as much as would be expected in a program emphasizing phonics.

Judging from the guided-reading section of the manuals, Lippincott (1963) not only stresses the importance of meaning but also interprets meaning in a vague sense, since, like the conventional basals, as many questions can be answered from the pictures and from the child's past experience as from the text itself. The manual also maintains the conventional practice of calling the child's attention to the pictures before the text.[9]

[9] That the Lippincott (1963) program suggests this type of close questioning is odd in view of the fact that one of its authors, Charles Walcutt, has sharply criticized the prevailing emphasis on meaning in beginning reading as a worthless practice with no proved benefits. Surely his own program, too, is subject to this criticism. Perhaps in creating a new program the authors, and more likely the publisher, who has to sell the books, discover that it is more politic to maintain a pattern to which teachers are accustomed than to make radical reforms.

SIMILAR FOLLOW-UP ACTIVITIES

The Lippincott (1963) first-grade program contains about the same number of follow-up activities as the two conventional series, and these activities are distributed similarly (see Table 8–14). In fact, an almost equal percentage of nonlanguage activities (art, music, etc.) is found in each. As in the conventional series, reading-comprehension exercises dominate. If we add word-meaning exercises to those on reading comprehension, the Lippincott (1963) follow-up activities contain even more meaning activities than the conventional series.

Phonic and structural analysis follow-up exercises account for only a slightly higher proportion of the total in Lippincott (1963) than in the two conventional series. The placement of these exercises, however, is less consistent: the phonics exercises in Lippincott (1963) may be the first, second, third, or even sixth in a long series, preceded by literary-appreciation, art, reading-comprehension, or word-meaning activities.

One marked difference in the Lippincott (1963) follow-up activities is that they contain practically no oral language activities—only 1 percent, as compared with 13 percent in Scott, Foresman (1956) and 19 percent in Ginn (1961).

Table 8–14 Comparison of First-grade Follow-up Activities in Three Basal Series

Average lesson	*Scott, Foresman (1956)*	*Ginn (1961)*	*Lippincott (1963)*
Total follow-up activities	8	13	9
Percentage of total follow-up activities involving:			
Reading comprehension	25	28	31
Word meaning	4	6	10
Whole-word recognition	9	6	9
Phonic & structural analysis	15	16	20
Independent silent reading	7	0	0
Oral language	13	19	1
Literary appreciation	13	8	12
Art	6	5	9
Music	5	6	1
Social studies	0	1	3
Science	0	0	0
Films & filmstrips	0	3	0
Creative writing	0	0	1
Miscellaneous	3	2	3
Total	100	100	100

Table 8–15 How First-grade Follow-up Activities Are Directed in Three Basal Series

Average lesson	*Scott, Foresman (1956)*	*Ginn (1961)*	*Lippincott (1963)*
Total follow-up activities	8	13	9
Percentage of total follow-up activities:			
Teacher directs completely	66	66	26
Teacher directs partly	29	33	74
Pupil does independently	5	1	0
Total	100	100	100

The follow-up activities in Lippincott (1963) require considerably less teacher direction and guidance than those in the other two series (see Table 8–15). While in the latter, two-thirds of the activities need the complete guidance and direction of the teacher, in Lippincott (1963) only about one-quarter do. However, all Lippincott (1963) activities require *some* guidance from the teacher.

In Lippincott (1963) a greater proportion of the follow-up activities call for a silent reading response than in Scott, Foresman (1956) or Ginn (1961) (see Table 8–16). (Silent reading, of course, requires less teacher guidance.) Overall, though, when we combine the different kinds of reading called for, we see that Lippincott (1963), like Scott, Foresman (1956) and Ginn (1961), provides reading practice (whether oral or silent) in only about one-half of the follow-up activities.

Table 8–16 Comparison of First-grade Follow-up Activities by Mode of Response in Three Basal Series

Average lesson	*Scott, Foresman (1956)*	*Ginn (1961)*	*Lippincott (1963)*
Total follow-up activities	8	13	9
Percentage of total follow-up activities responded to by:			
Reading:			
Silent	31	28	48
Silent and oral	6	14	0
Oral	15	9	5
Total reading	52	51	53
Listening and discussing	39	43	37
Construction and other nonlanguage activities	9	6	10
Total	100	100	100
Writing (in addition to other modes of response)	0	4	25

oo—as in cook

foot soot good hood book stood

wood cook hook shook took look

brook crook wool

The Rook

A rook
Sat hooked
To a crooked
Tree.
He shook
As he looked,
—Took an owl
For me!

—Adele H. Seronde

101

To illustrate some of the points made above about phonics-oriented basal readers, we reproduce several pages (101–106) from the pupil's edition of the 1–1 book of Basic Reading together with the teaching suggestions (pages 81 to 88) in the Teachers' Edition for the 1–1 book. J. B. Lippincott Co., Philadelphia, 1963. The story, "The Oogle-Google Goblin" continues through page 114 of the pupil's edition but was not reproduced in its entirety here.

oo—as in food

food moon boot hoot loot root toot
mood too proof cool pool tool stool
spool room bloom boom gloom spoon
soon loop droop stoop hoop goose
loose broom shoot coop scoop boost
groove smooth troop tooth choose
coo poor

102

The Bat

A bat
  in an attic
Kept still,
  so still;
Still until
  the red moon
Went up
  by the hill.
"When the red moon is up,
I will not sit still!
  But I will flit
Up by the red moon
  on the hill."

—Adele H. Seronde

103

The Oogle-Google Goblin

Hoot Tooter was a small goblin who lived in a drain pipe. The pipe was in front of Ronny Hooper's home. It was for rain water. It ran from a pipe in the yard to the big drain under the street. It was very dark and dingy there.

Hoot was an oogle-google goblin. Hoot made a google-oogle-glup-glup, when the water ran down into the pipe. Then away it goes to the street.

Hoot, the goblin, lived in Ronny's water drain for a strange reason. The oo's in his name were the same as those in Ronny Hooper's last name. This was the first reason.

He also had a second reason for living in the pipe, as you will soon see.

104

One day Ronny was playing in his yard after a rainstorm. The water was gurgling down off the roof to the drain pipe. It made a last google and glug before it went to the street. Ronny was playing with a string rolled up on a spool. He made a loop at one end of the string. Then he dropped it loosely into the cool gloom inside the drain pipe.

105

All of a sudden, there was a big "glug," and the string jerked and shook.

Then there was a tiny cry, "O-O-O-O . . . googly-oogly-glug! Let go of my neck!"

Ronny was surprised. He paid attention to the tiny cry. He pulled up his loop of string very gently and

I went to Paris and brought home an *apple* and a *box*.

apple *box* *cat,* etc.

2. Put short sentences on the board in mixed sequence. Direct the children to number them in correct sequence.

☐ Tim sat in a chair marked VISITORS.
☐ After the program Tim operated one of the cameras.
☐ Tim went to visit a TV station.
☐ Tim liked the program he saw.

3. Have the children name the TV programs they like best. List them according to days in the week and approximate hour. Build a TV station in the room, using an old piano crate or oversized box. The children may wall-paper or paint this and name the station. Each day a poem or a story, either original or from a library book, may be read over this TV station. Spelling meets or songs sung by individuals or groups may be televised.

Pages 101 and 102 — Short and long sounds of oo

Introduction

Explain to the children that they have already learned a great deal about the letter **o.** They know its name, how to write it, its long and short sounds, and that it can sound like short **u**, as in **some.** Now they are going to study **oo** when it is short, as in **look,** and when it is long, as in **too.**

Procedure for the Short Sound of *oo*

1. As you talk, put the word **look** on the board and underline **oo;** then put **too** on the board and underline **oo.**

2. Ask what medial sound is heard in the words **foot, soot, good,** and **hood.** Refer to the word **look** and ask if it has the same medial sound. Put on the board, beside the numbers 1 to 10, the letters **oo.**

1. __ oo __ (*foot*) 6. ____ oo __ (*stood*)
2. __ oo __ (*soot*) 7. __ oo __ (*wood*)
3. __ oo __ (*good*) 8. __ oo __ (*cook*)
4. __ oo __ (*hood*) 9. __ oo __ (*hook*)
5. __ oo __ (*book*) 10. ____ oo __ (*shook*)

Then dictate the ten short **oo** words given above, and have the children complete the words on the board.

3. As you give a clue to the meaning, ask the children to identify the word by underlining it in the list on the board. This clarifies all meanings, as words are useless if meanings are not explained. After all individual words are in the child's reading, writing, and meaning vocabulary, the children can write phrases, sentences, and stories.

4. Have the children put the correct word in the following sentences:

The skirt was made of ______.
The ______ made a nice cake.
She ______ her lunch to the beach.
He likes to read a ______ each day.
She ______ first in the line.

cook wool took book stood

5. Further vocabulary experience may be given by multiple choice questions such as the following:

A stream of water is a ______.

look took brook

Hang your coat on that ______.

hook look cook

The child has a sore ______.

hood food foot

6. Put a list of words on the board with their definitions in random order beside them. Have children match the words with their definitions by connecting them with a line.

brook	cloth
wool	stare
foot	bake
look	part of the body
cook	stream of water

7. Write the following sentences on the board:

I will ______ at her story book.
He ______ at it yesterday.
It ______ easy to read.
We will be ______ at the illustrations.

Direct the children to put the correct words on the lines. Have them select the words from a group of words written on the board: *looks, looked, looking, look*.

8. To promote the ability to make inferences, mimeograph sheets of riddles which have two possible answers. The pupils may read and circle the correct phrase at the right.

82

Suggested riddles:

I am used to give heat.	some wood
I am used to make houses.	some wool
I move in the summer.	a brook
I am hard in the winter.	a book
I am black and white.	a book
I teach all by myself.	a crook

9. List the following topics on the board: *Water, Worker, Parts of the Body.* Have the children classify the words listed below under these topics.

leg	carpenter	cleaner
sea	hand	farmer
teacher	river	foot
arm	face	pond
cook	brook	finger
fireman	toe	driver
puddle	creek	lake
ear	sailor	stream

Procedure for Long *oo*

1. Proceed with the nine steps outlined for short **oo.** The list of words having long **oo** is more extensive.
2. Have the children turn to page 101 in the text and say the short **oo** words. Then refer to **too** on the board and guide the children in reading the long **oo** words.
3. As you give a clue to the meaning, have a pupil write the word on the board. Put these words under the key words *look* (short **oo**) and *too* (long **oo**).
4. With the two complete lists on the board, have a pupil give a clue to the meaning and have another child read the word and erase it.
5. Have the children find the four missing rhymes in verses similar to the following:

Said Gerald, "Good,
Go chop the ______.
And then keep cool
Beside the ______."

Said Ann, "Come, look
At this good ______.
Forget your mood
For eating ______."

pool *wood* *book* *food*

Suggestions for Further Activities

1. Put two separate lists of words on the board as suggested in this sample lesson. Have the children complete the fifteen short **oo** words:

beginnings			*endings*		
f	st	t	oot	ood	ook
s	b	l	oot	ook	ook
g	c	br	ood	ook	ook
h	h	cr	ood	ook	ook
w	sh	w	ood	ook	ool

2. The children should read the completed list of words. Do a similar exercise with the long **oo** words in the text.

Enrichment

Stories: Seuss, Dr., *The 500 Hats of Bartholomew Cubbins,* Vanguard.

Collections: Gruenberg, Sidonie, *Favorite Stories Old and New,* Doubleday.

Recordings: "500 Hats of Bartholomew Cubbins," Wing, Paul.

Page 101 — The Rook

This little poem will use the sound the children have been studying in a stimulating, humorous situation. Have the children read the poem silently. Ask what they think a rook is. If no one can explain, tell them that it is a bird of the crow family. Ask what mistake the rook made. Read the poem to the group, helping them to understand the sentence structure through the inflection of your voice. Have the children read the poem in unison.

Page 103 — The Bat

Again we have a humorous situation in which to review the long sound of **oo.** Read the poem with much expression, having the children close their eyes as you create a picture with these words. Reread it, if necessary, to stimulate the imaginations of the listeners.

Now have the children find the words with the long **oo** sound, then read the poem aloud either individually or as a group.

Page 104 — The Oogle-Google Goblin

Note: This is the story for the long and short sounds of **oo.**

Introduction

Put the title of the story on the board. Have the children identify the story in the Table of Contents. The child who finds it first may put the page number on the board.

Guided Reading

Let several children say the title, then have them find the goblin's name. Have them read to find the sentence that tells where the drain pipe was. Ask for the first reason the goblin gave for living in Ronny's water drain.

Have the entire page read aloud for enjoyment of the delightful detail. After the children have finished, ask if there is a second reason. Is it given? They will have to read further into the story for this reason.

Page 105

Guided Reading

Have the children read silently and try to see how quickly they can find the sentence that best fits the picture. Select a child to read the complete paragraph aloud. Ask, "When did this story take place?" (*after a rainstorm*) Then ask *what* happened to the string before turning the page.

The interest level should be high to see what happened to the string.

Pages 106 and 107

Guided Reading

Have the children read to find out what jerked the string. Continue the silent reading to the bottom of page 107. After they have read these pages, ask them to find the words that mean *suddenly,* and the sentences that describe what kind of boy Ronny is. Ask the children how the goblin was holding the string.

Pages 108 and 109

Guided Reading

After the children have read silently from the last paragraph on page 107 through page 109, have one child read the conversation of Ronny and another child the conversation of the goblin. Ask why the goblin cannot be pulled any farther from the pipe. Discuss the reason why he cannot be pulled farther, and ask why he is being punished. For how long is he being punished, and by whom?

Pages 110 and 111

Guided Reading

Have the children read pages 110 and 111 silently. Ask them now to tell the two reasons why the goblin was in the drain pipe. How did Ronny feel about this? What did he plan to do? What very important question did Ronny ask the goblin?

Ask the children to find some of the more difficult words: *expression, question, breathe,* and *lonesome*. As they find each one, call on a child to read the complete sentence containing the word.

At this time it is suggested that the children turn back to page 104 and read the story aloud up to this point. A discussion should follow about the descriptive words and how both Ronny and the goblin feel.

Page 112

Guided Reading

Start with the last paragraph on page 111 and have the children read silently Ronny's conversation with the gardener, which continues to the top of page 113. Ask whom Ronny is calling in the picture on page 111. (*the gardener*)

After they have read this section, ask when the gardener came to assist Ronny. Call upon someone to describe what the gardener did.

Pages 113 and 114

Guided Reading

Have the children read silently to find out how Ronny felt as the gardener worked. Get the answer and continue on to page 114 to complete the story.

Ask the children to find the complete sentence that best describes the picture on page 114. Have them read what the green goblin told Ronny about his escape. Discuss what the green goblin must promise the Queen.

After the children have finished the silent reading of the story, turn to page 111, the last paragraph, and read this final section of the story aloud.

Conclusion

After discussing the story and the lesson learned by the little goblin, have the children list titles of their favorite stories under the headings:

Fanciful or Fairy Tales *Real Stories*

Suggestions for Further Activities

1. Have the children make a list of the short and long **oo** words in the story, grouping them under these headings on the board, for example:

Long	*Short*
oogle	good
google	took
Hoot	stood
Hooper	looked

2. Taking words from the story, have the children match them with related words, rhyming words, and words of different meanings:

Related Words

Queen	goblin
Ronny	boy
Hoot	dark
gloomy	lady

Rhyming Words

oogle	proof
spool	google
roof	hoop
loop	stool

Words of Different Meanings

stood	bad
cool	gave
took	hot
good	sat

3. Write down some of the imaginary experiences the children dictate. Have the children illustrate the stories and share the stories and pictures with the members of the class.

Enrichment

Stories: Gramatky, Hardie, *Little Toot,* Putnam.
Seuss, Dr., *And To Think That I Saw It On Mulberry Street,* Vanguard; *The Cat in the Hat, The Cat in the Hat Comes Back,* Random.

Poem: Stevenson, Robert Louis, "The Unseen Playmate," in *A Child's Garden of Verses,* Scribner.

Pages 115 and 118 — The Sound of ow as long o sound and ou sound

Introduction

Use either magazine pictures, outlines, or sketches on the board to illustrate words such as *snow, yellow, pillow, bowl, throw.* Have the word printed under the picture. Ask the children what they hear in each word as you say it; then ask what they see that is the same in each word. (*ow*) Emphasize that **ow** sounds like long **o.**

Procedure for *ow* as Long *o*

1. Have the children use the text and take turns saying the first group of **ow** words. Ask the children to say only the one-syllable words. Put them in a list on the board under the number *1.* Under the number *2,* make another list including the two-syllable words. Number the words on the board. Have a race, with the children reading the words as the numbers are called.

2. In the list of one-syllable words, call on children to erase the digraph that says long **o.** In the list of two-syllable words, have the children erase *only* the second syllable. Have them pronounce the word first and then erase the second part. The children may then complete the words using a different colored chalk to emphasize what they have written.

The greatest difference in mode of response is in the amount of writing called for. Scott, Foresman (1956) and Ginn (1961) require hardly any writing; one-quarter of the Lippincott (1963) exercises call for the child to write.

Trends in the Conventional Basal Series: 1920 to 1962

In 1962 Scott, Foresman, publisher of the most widely used basal-reading series, issued a new edition. Not so innovative as the basal series coauthored by Walcutt, the 1962 edition nevertheless departs from the 1956 edition in some important respects. I found it interesting to compare the first-grade (1–2) reader and accompanying material in the 1962 edition with the reader and accompanying material in the immediately preceding, 1956 edition. For greater perspective I also briefly compared the first-grade readers of the five Scott, Foresman editions produced since 1920.

SCOTT, FORESMAN 1962 EDITION[10]

The new Scott, Foresman first-grade reader seems designed to answer in part two major criticisms of basal-reading series now current. Control over vocabulary is looser, and there is more phonics instruction. Also, pupils are put on their own faster. The basic approach to beginning reading, however, remains the same: the 1962 Scott, Foresman first-grade program still emphasizes reading for meaning from the start and the acquisition of a sight vocabulary.

The 1962 edition introduces more new words per 100 running words —1.9, as compared with 1.4 in the 1956 edition (see Table 8–17). Pictures, however, have the same importance in both editions.

The Scott, Foresman 1962 guidebook gives the teacher more instructions on how to arouse interest and establish background for each story (see Table 8–18). Four statements and directions are given, as compared with three in the 1956 edition. Although new words are still pretaught, the suggested teaching method is different. The 1962 edition recommends focusing the child's attention less on straight look-say. Much more emphasis is given to meaning. Instructions to "just read" are nowhere to be found in the 1962 edition, whereas they represent half of all preparation instructions in the 1956 edition.

[10] Findings presented here are the result of an analysis of every eighth lesson of the 1962 first-grade (1–2) reader and accompanying teachers' guidebooks and pupils' workbook.

Table 8–17 Comparison of First-grade Story Content (1–2 Reader) in Two Scott, Foresman Editions

	1956	1962
Stories analyzed	4	5
Average story characteristics:		
Running words	305	230
New words	4.3	4.2
New words per 100 running words	1.4	1.9
Pages	5.0	4.0
Pictures	4.8	3.8

Teachers are told in the 1962 edition to call attention to the structural and phonic aspects of the word more often. The new edition has completely dropped all references to straight visual aspects of the word (length, configuration, etc.). Fourteen percent of the suggestions and questions in the 1956 edition are involved with these.

In guiding the pupil's reading of each story, teachers following the 1962 manual are no less verbose: both editions instruct the teacher to ask about one question for every seven words the pupil reads (see Table 8–19). Questions about nontextual aspects of the story are just as impor-

Table 8–18 Preparing for a First-grade Lesson (1–2 Reader) in Two Scott, Foresman Editions

Average lesson	*1956*	*1962*
Pages of instruction to teacher	5.0	5.0
Questions and statements to arouse interest and establish background	3.5	4.4
Words teacher speaks to prepare pupils for story	45	55
How new words are introduced	Sentences, isolated, phrases	Isolated, phrases, sentences
Oral buildup?	Yes	Yes
How pupils read	Silent to oral	Silent to oral
Percentage of word practice devoted to:		
Just reading	50	0
Meaning	25	71
Visual form	14	0
Structural analysis	5	19
Phonetic analysis	4	10
Context	2	0
Total	100	100

Table 8–19 Comparison of Guided-reading Sections in the Teachers' Guidebooks of Two Scott, Foresman Editions: The First-grade Program

Average story	*1956*	*1962*
Words in story	305	230
Questions, statements, directions suggested in guidebook	46	35
Percentage of total questions, statements, directions devoted to:		
Nontextual aspects:		
Pictures	10	13
Pictures and Print	6	6
Previous Stories	2	2
Personal experiences	10	14
Total nontextual	28	35
Textual Aspects:		
Just read	23	10
Meaning:		
Literal	30	31
Interpretation	16	24
Total meaning	46	55
Print as "code":		
Word form	1	0
Structural analysis	1	0
Phonetic analysis	1	0
Context clues	0	0
Picture clues	0	0
Total "code"	3	0
Total textual	72	65
Grand total	100	100

tant. The manual does, however, suggest a smaller percentage of instructions to "just read" and a higher percentage of questions requiring interpretation of the printed matter. Like the 1956 edition, it pays no attention during the guided reading to the print as code.

Fewer follow-up activities are given in the 1962 edition (see Table 8–20). Even more important, those given are distributed differently. Gone are activities involving art, music, and construction. In fact, all non-language activities have disappeared. In the 1962 edition the heaviest emphasis is still on activities concerning reading comprehension, however; in fact, reading-comprehension activities increase from 19 percent of the total in the 1956 edition to 32 percent in the 1962 edition. Phonic and structural analysis exercises have doubled in the 1962 edition—they

Table 8–20 Comparison of First-grade Follow-up Activities in Two Scott, Foresman Editions

Average lesson	*1956*	*1962*
Total follow-up activities	8.0	5.6
Percentage of total follow-up activities involving:		
Reading comprehension	19	32
Word meaning	0	4
Whole-word recognition	13	14
Phonetic and structural analysis	13	25
Independent silent reading	9	4
Oral language	13	7
Literary appreciation	13	14
Art	6	0
Music	6	0
Other	8	0
Total	100	100
Mode of response:		
Reading:		
Silent	28	43
Silent and oral	6	7
Oral	18	29
Total reading	52	79
Listening and discussing	39	21
Nonlanguage	9	0
Total mode of response	100	100
Writing (in addition to others)	0	4
Teacher direction:		
Teacher directs completely	72	57
Teacher directs partly	19	43
Pupil does independently	9	0
Total	100	100

constitute one-quarter of all exercises, as opposed to 13 percent in the 1956 edition.

More follow-up activities require reading; fewer require just listening and discussing. Writing, never suggested in the 1956 edition for first graders, is to be used in 4 percent of the 1962 activities.

The teacher is somewhat less important in the 1962 edition follow-up activities; she is indispensable for 57 percent of the activities, as opposed to 72 percent in the previous edition.

THE SCOTT, FORESMAN READING PROGRAM SINCE 1920

By combining my analysis of the Scott, Foresman first-grade (1–2) readers of 1956 and 1962 with a similar analysis by Marion Klein (1964) of the 1920, 1930, and 1940 editions, I was able to make a limited study of changes during this forty-two-year period (see Table 8–21).

A major change is the steady decrease in vocabulary load—from 2.4 new words per 100 running words in 1920 to 1.4 in 1956. This trend is reversed in the 1962 edition, as we have seen.

From 1920 to 1962, more and more space is devoted to illustrations. Until 1962 the picture load (number of pictures per 100 running words) increases steadily, becoming heavier than the vocabulary load (number of new words per 100 running words) in the 1956 edition. This trend appears to have stopped with the 1962 edition, in which the child meets more new words than new pictures per 100 words read.

The teachers' manuals have changed even more than the readers (see Table 8–22). From 1920 to 1962 they have grown steadily. By the 1956 edition, the introductory sections of the teachers' manuals became a veritable textbook on the teaching of reading. There appears to be a stabilization of "weightiness" in the 1962 edition.

From 1920 to 1962 the teacher is given more and more suggestions and directions for each lesson, i.e., for teaching new words, guiding the story, and directing a variety of follow-up activities. In the 1920 edition about 561 words of instruction to the teacher accompany the average lesson. Lesson plans in the 1956 edition are so elaborate and detailed that the teacher using this edition has to wade through five pages of tightly packed print—about twenty-three hundred words. Remember that during the 1940s teachers began the current practice of dividing classes into three reading groups and preparing a different lesson for each group.

Table 8–21 Comparison of Various Characteristics of First-grade (1–2) Readers in Five Scott, Foresman Editions

	1920	*1930*	*1940*	*1956*	*1962*
Pages per average story	4	6	5	5	4
Words per average page	83	64	59	61	58
Running words per average story	333	385	295	305	230
New words per average story	8.0	8.0	5.0	4.3	4.2
New words per 100 running words	2.4	2.1	1.7	1.4	1.9
New (different) words in entire book	425	282	178	177	153
Pictures per average story	3.0	5.0	4.0	4.8	3.8
Pictures per 100 running words	0.9	1.3	1.4	1.6	1.7

Table 8–22 Comparison of Aids to the First-grade Teacher in Five Scott, Foresman Editions

	1920	1930	1940	1956	1962
Total pages in manual	157	192	192	244	256
Pages devoted to general philosophy	None	32	25	46	15 (plus 25 pp. of special articles)
Words of instruction to teacher per average lesson (story and follow-up)	561	814	1,266	2,300	2,000

Thus, not only has the amount of instructional material for each lesson been increasing, but the teacher's task has been tripled.

Why have the manuals grown and grown? Partly, as Klein notes, because the 1920 and 1930 manuals simply list the words or phonic elements to be taught, while the 1940 and later manuals embed these in both general and specific suggestions. Also, beginning with the 1940 edition some suggestions—particularly for establishing background and guiding the reading—are given in the exact words that the teacher is to speak. And from 1920 on, the guided-reading section has become increasingly more elaborate: while the 1920 edition contains one comprehension question for the teacher to ask for every forty-seven words read by the child, the 1962 edition suggests one question for every twelve words read (see Table 8–23).

Table 8–23 Comparison of Guided-reading Sections in the Teachers' Guidebooks of Five Scott, Foresman Editions: The First-grade Program

	1920	1930	1940	1956	1962
Words per average story	333	385	295	305	230
Questions on text per average story	7	15	12	22	19
Words child reads per question asked by teacher	47	26	25	14	12

Although the analysis of basal series and the philosophy behind them presented in the last two chapters has been primarily descriptive, at various points I raised questions on content, emphasis, sequencing, and pacing. Here I want to highlight some of these questions.

I do not do so merely to criticize the basal series. Indeed, these programs have become too easy a target for faultfinding. In contrast with many critics, I believe that most children need readers or some kind of structured materials, especially at the beginning, to gain the mastery that will enable them ultimately to enjoy the marvels of Alice in Wonderland *and* Gulliver's Travels. *And most teachers need them even more to impart this mastery. Since the conventional basal series already have the confidence of administrators and teachers, their authors and publishers are in a unique position to translate what we know about teaching reading into classroom practice. It is in the hopes of helping them realize this opportunity that I raise my questions.*

First, is the heavy reliance on a word method—so basic to these series—justified? Should the basals start with and continually stress throughout the first three grades the whole-word, or configuration, approach to learning words, giving only minor attention to the alphabetic-phonic aspects of these words? As we have seen, the experimental, correlational, and clinical evidence indicates that a code emphasis is the better way to start.

Second, should reading for meaning, appreciation, and application be stressed so much, especially in the first grade? What we know about language development, the reading process, and factors related to reading success and failure all lead us to question this emphasis in beginning reading.

But we question it most on commonsense grounds. Why spend so much time on explication de texte *when there is no text to explicate? Since the content of first-grade readers is necessarily limited by the pupils' decoding skills, meaning and appreciation questions must naturally feed on the pictures. It would seem that first graders already know how to "read" pictures and that the task of beginning reading instruction is to teach them to read* words. *No one has yet demonstrated that pictures help the child either to recognize words or comprehend the text. In fact, recent experimental evidence indicates that pictures may even hinder the child's attempts at building comprehension.*[1] *At any rate, if his attention is constantly directed to pictures, the beginner may be distracted from the words and get a completely erroneous idea of what reading is all about.*

Moreover, we have a very practical reason for examining the worth of so many pictures in a reading series. The full-color illustrations are probably the most expensive feature of these series. If they are not essential, this expense could be cut down. The money saved could be used by the schools to purchase additional library books or by the publishers to increase research and development efforts.

Third, is such constant and detailed guidance from the teacher necessary to the learning process? The first-grade teacher following the teachers' manual talks more than the pupils read. Her questions and directions tend to take the child's attention

[1] Weintraub (1960).

away from the text, rather than help him focus and concentrate on it. Why can't the teacher write some of her questions on the board for pupils to answer themselves from their own reading? Indeed, many teachers make such adjustments in order to survive, but this requires experience or help.

Fourth, does the teacher herself need so much guidance in teaching? Why must teachers' manuals be so weighty? No doubt the manuals are as expensive to publish as the readers are. Not only is it unrealistic to expect a teacher to wade through all the detailed suggestions in the manuals, but with such detail both teachers and pupils are likely to get bogged down, losing sight of the overall structure and purpose of the lessons. For example, providing so many different kinds of follow-up activities for each lesson may serve to slow down the children of an overconscientious and inexperienced teacher who hasn't yet learned to distinguish essentials from nonessentials. Instead, the manuals could provide some useful information not now presented thoroughly enough—for example, information on the kinds of errors children may be expected to make and suggestions on how to correct them.

Also, couldn't the manuals say what they have to say more plainly? It is difficult enough for a first-grade teacher to cope with the problems of teaching thirty-five energetic youngsters without having to wade through material that makes a mystique of teaching. I hope that future editions can avoid explanations like this one:

The last story, for example, is told almost entirely through language, but the mood that invests the conversation with special meaning must be read from the action and attitudes of the individual characters. Sally's frustrated exertions for a share in the game are a clue to the feeling and tone with which she repeats "I want to see." To get the complete meaning of what Sally said, the young reader must again understand these words in a total context of feeling and action. In interpreting the story, boys and girls must rely on their powers of visual imagery and create mental pictures of such details as the little house and three little dogs mentioned in the conversation of the characters but not shown in the illustrations. More important, perhaps, young readers must call up an auditory imagery that goes beyond the sound of the individual words to the sound of these words as they are spoken by the character at a specific time in a particular set of circumstances. (*Teachers' Guidebook for the Pre-primers*, Scott, Foresman, 1962 edition, p. 13)

Fifth, do the basal series teach enough of the code? Is it taught well enough? In an attempt to integrate code learning with the total reading program, the authors have worked the phonics they do present so thoroughly into the follow-up activities that it can easily be lost. Further, is the best use made of what is taught, when the child is given little opportunity to apply the specific phonics skills he has acquired to his reading?

Sixth, why are so few words taught, and why are they repeated so often? In analyzing the research basis for the basals' vocabulary control in 1958, I found that by the late 1940s this control was much stricter than any research evidence justified. Indeed, more recent research by Gates (1961) indicates that children in the middle of grade 2 and at the end of grade 3 already know most of the words in the readers of the grades beyond their own. Yet until the early 1960s, each succeeding edition of a series had a lower vocabulary load.

There is no question that some form of vocabulary control is essential for beginning instructional materials. But must the control be based only on the commonest, most irregularly spelled words? Couldn't some of the control result from a consideration of the phonic elements previously taught?

Seventh, is the child who is learning to read really best served by a very early stress on mature, silent reading? There is evidence to refute the assumption that oral reading is "harder" than silent reading and that oral (and other articulatory) responses produce word callers and therefore must be inhibited if the child is to engage in meaningful reading. In fact, evidence from the clinic indicates that inhibiting oral and articulatory responses and other secondary aids such as finger pointing and whispering retards rather than fosters the development of meaningful reading.

My comparison of the 1956 and 1962 editions of the most popular conventional basal series indicates that changes have already taken place in line with some of these questions. The 1962 edition of Scott, Foresman does show some loosening of vocabulary control, an earlier and heavier emphasis on the code, and a reduction in the quantity of nonreading follow-up activities. These changes are all in the right direction.

4

CHILDREN LEARNING TO READ

WE listen to the proponents of the various methods of teaching children how to read. We examine the research on beginning reading and find that there is evidence that programs providing an initial code emphasis achieve better results than those providing a meaning emphasis at the beginning. We take a close look at the basal-reading series and find them somewhat lacking, but not as hopeless as their critics would have us believe. As a result, we know a great deal about beginning reading methods.

But some important subjects remain unexplored: How are children actually taught to read? Why are they taught one way and not another?

To gather the information in these areas that I felt I needed to complete my picture of the controversy over beginning reading, I spent several months during 1962–63 visiting schools, sitting in classrooms, and talking with teachers, supervisors, and principals who were using the teaching methods I have been discussing. Altogether I visited more than three hundred classrooms (kindergarten and grades 1, 2, and 3) in the United States, England, and Scotland. The visits were arranged for me by either the proponent of the reading program in use or the school's principal or superintendent. In some schools the person who made the arrangements accompanied me; in others I was free to roam around the school, observing and talking with anyone I wished. I tried to observe the use of each approach in schools representing three sociocultural levels—upper, middle, and low.

These visits, I hoped, would provide evidence on many questions, among which were the following:

1. Are some programs more interesting to the children than others? Is each method as interesting as its proponents say? As dull as its critics claim?

2. Are differences between the new programs and the conventional ones evident in the classroom? Do the new programs differ from one another? How closely do the teachers adhere in practice to the method they are supposed to be following?
3. What else being done in the classroom or in the school might account for the results claimed for the various methods? (In clinical and medical research, for example, it is known that what the therapist thinks is having the effect may not be responsible for the difference at all. Teachers, too, may be unaware of "other things" they are doing to produce good results.)
4. Who are the innovators? Do certain kinds of schools, administrators, and teachers tend to innovate in certain directions?
5. What conditions lead to innovation? What forces resist it?
6. How do teachers, supervisors, and principals feel about the reading controversy? How satisfied are they with the state of affairs in reading instruction?

My visits left me with more than ten shorthand notebooks, each tightly packed with observations, verbatim conversations, hypotheses, and generalizations. Alas, I can present here only the highlights from this mass of material, selected particularly for their relevance to the present controversy over beginning reading methods and the theory, research, and practice in beginning reading.

In discussing what I saw, I do not name schools, teachers, or administrators (even though I am tempted to identify the courageous, conscientious, and fine teachers and administrators who were doing a superb job, often under great handicaps). It was never my intention to praise or criticize specific school systems; indeed I would not be qualified to do so after a short visit.

Chapter 9 describes what I learned in the classrooms I visited that bears on differences between methods, differences between theory and practice, factors other than method that affect results, and so on. Chapter 10 is concerned with the phenomenon of change itself.

NINE

In the Classroom

AMERICAN CHILDREN LEARN to read in almost any kind of building you can picture: wooden compounds on stilts; decaying four-story brick buildings; modern, low-slung, glass-walled buildings with a terrace for each classroom. First graders in this country are still taught in rooms with sixty nailed-down desks and seats in neat rows in which they are expected to sit with a decorum that we associate with the 1890s. A ten-minute walk away from such a setting you might find a more typical group: about twenty-five first graders in a spacious room fully equipped with sinks, bathrooms, and easels, planning the morning's activities. Upon a word from their teacher they move chairs and tables quickly: make way for the workers, painters, and players.

Most revealing to an observer is the children's art work. In some classrooms I was dazzled by displays of expressive, boldly painted productions on oversized paper. In others, I found a series of small, controlled crayon drawings, all on the same subject, neatly arranged above new green chalkboards.

Each school's general character can be read in the smallest signs. Take, for example, the way the children reacted to a visitor. In some classes they went about their work as if I were not there. In others, I was formally introduced, and the children rose in a body to recite in unison their "good mornings" in a fashion reminiscent of my own school days.

Classroom atmosphere ran the full gamut from formality to informality. In one school I stood in awe of a masterful sister's consummate skill; with the slightest click of her cricket to signify that the next child should read, she kept a class of fifty-five second graders alert, working, and proud in the dignity of their achievement. I was equally impressed with the fine work of a second-grade teacher and her assistant in a private school. Here fifteen children were busy doing independent advanced work in modern mathematics and reading. They were dressed with the casualness of the well-to-do—the boys in blue jeans and well-worn tennis shoes, the girls in casual shifts—and they called the teachers and headmaster by their first names.

The variation by social levels was a textbook come to life. Children of the more fortunate parents were tall, sleek, and independent. Children of the poorer, less-well-educated parents (now called by various euphemisms, e.g., "culturally deprived," "culturally disadvantaged," or "culturally different") found it difficult to sit quietly in their seats. A low noise was ever present in their rooms.

I was also struck by regional differences. The West appeared to be innovating more than the East. California, in particular, seemed in a feverish state of experimentation. Some schools were experimenting with the free, self-expressive, individualized programs; others were trying the *most formal* phonics programs.

The differences in achievement of different groups of five- and six-year-olds were breathtaking. Two six-year-olds in Omar K. Moore's laboratory in an independent suburban school read for me from the *Annals of Political and Social Sciences.* In January of the first grade, a group of youngsters in a slum school were still struggling with reading-readiness workbooks.

Contrasts and variations were great, but the similarities were even greater. Whether the classes were highly structured or loosely organized, and whether the teachers were competent or incompetent, kindliness and concern for the children prevailed. Of course, most of the teachers I saw had probably been selected, but I did manage to make unscheduled visits to a sufficient number of classes and to talk with other teachers, whom I did not observe in the classroom, during lunch and coffee breaks. The great majority of the teachers I met—in the United States, in England, and in Scotland—exhibited decency, sincerity, and genuine love of their pupils.

My main concern, of course, was not to determine how teachers in America teach generally, but to discover what differences I could find between various methods of teaching reading as they are actually applied. I was able to formulate definite differences, some of them based on impressions and some based on more quantifiable observations. However,

I discovered that most of these differences were not clear-cut—that success with a given reading program depends on many things besides the characteristics of the program as it is presented in instructional materials.

PUPIL INTEREST

An observer senses definite changes in moving from a classroom where one method is taught to one where another is taught, and yet many of these changes cannot be measured; they can only be described. Take pupil interest, for example. Interest is a subtle thing to measure—indeed, even to observe. Every method ever proposed has claimed pupil interest as one of its strengths. Ironically, it is the one effect that experimental classroom tryouts have not measured in any objective way.

How interesting various methods are for children has also been a key issue in the current debate on methods. Each proponent claims pupil interest for *his* program—and stultifying dullness for all the others.

Obviously, this could not possibly be the case. After observing procedures in more than three hundred classrooms and talking with as many teachers and administrators, I formed the distinct impression that pupil interest, like beauty, is to a great extent in the eyes of the beholder. A judgment that a method is interesting or dull for the children is as much a statement about the observer as about the observed. Several times when I thought I had detected extreme apathy and listlessness in a group of bored children, the author of the reading program or an enthusiastic supervisor sitting beside me exclaimed: "Isn't it wonderful how the children are enjoying it!" Personal investment in a particular reading program can destroy perspective and make one see what one wants to see, rather than what is actually there. The need for more disinterested observers and researchers became obvious to me after only a few visits.

Often, too, a proponent of a particular method, in stressing the "interest" and "love of reading and learning" generated by his method, spoke derogatorily of the fidgeting and anxiety in classrooms where another method, sometimes very similar to his, was being used. While these people were all anxious that I not come to a hasty conclusion about their programs, each was quick to do so about competing ones. These conclusions differed according to the commentator. Thus, teachers and administrators commented very often on Omar K. Moore's work and particularly on his film on preschool children learning to read with an electric typewriter; those sympathetic to the Moore experiments spoke only of the interest and enthusiasm of the children shown in the film, while those critical of an early start could see only the children's anxiety and tension.

Fully realizing that the observer cannot keep himself out of the observations and that I, too, have my own biases and preconceptions, I present the following impressions about interest. They are based on observations of more than ten different classes and teachers using each reading program discussed.

How interested pupils are in learning to read, I concluded, is not determined by what method or set of materials they are using. I saw excitement, enthusiasm, and general interest exhibited in classes using every reading program. I also saw children respond to each with listlessness, apathy, boredom, and restlessness.

Generally, it was *what the teacher did* with the method, the materials, and the children rather than the method itself that seemed to make the difference. More specifically, I would say that interest is highly related to pacing—how instruction is geared to that tenuous balance between ease and difficulty for the child. In classes where pupils seemed to enjoy the reading period, the children knew what was expected of them, and the pace was neither too slow nor too fast. Instead, where classwork belabored the obvious or when only one or two pupils were working while others watched, interest seemed to wane.

Most reading specialists have long held that it is the story—the content of what is read—that makes for interest and enjoyment. This is, of course, the philosophy behind the most widely used conventional basal-reading series and the self-selection programs: that the child's interest in reading the story is the key to his desire to develop reading skills.

I did not find this assertion valid. The little children I watched were as excited and keenly interested in words, sounds, spellings, and rules as they were in stories. They did not seem to find studying letters and sounds and rules dull or abstract. On the other hand, I did not see the boredom with the conventional basal primers and readers that their critics claim they produce. Children seem to be just as eager to learn about the spelling and sound of words as they are to read stories that adults think are silly. They seem to be just as interested in working together on the same task as in pursuing individual goals.

In one kindergarten where the *Phonovisual Method* was being used, children were matching sounds with letters. The only complaint came from a little girl who informed her teacher that her friends had had *two* turns at matching, while she had had only *one*.

In a first-grade class using Donald Rasmussen and Lynn Goldberg's experimental linguistic program (*Basic Reading Series*), pupils were circling one letter out of four as the teacher said "Circle *B*, circle *C*," etc. One boy called out eagerly: "I knew it. I knew it. I knew you would ask for *C*."

My conclusion was that children can become interested in anything. Mostly they seem to react to an atmosphere created by the teacher and the program. Each method evolves its own in-group language and customs. In some classes using supplemental phonics programs, first and second graders were able to rattle off the whys of sounding and spelling words in a way that left me breathless. In some of the conventional basal-reader classes, first and second graders were able to make judgments and evaluations about simple stories and pictures that escaped my adult sophistication.

Does this mean that the teacher is all, that methods and materials do not count? Not completely. Certain hazards are characteristic of different methods.

The criticism that systematic phonics leads to dull drill is not completely unfounded. While most of the classes I observed did not confirm the general claim that phonics is dull, I did find that certain systematic-phonics programs used words for "sounding" that were so beyond the child's interest and comprehension that he was left quite uninvolved. It was rough going for a first-grade teacher and her class to sound out and define words like *traitor, slender, pewter,* and *county.* Let me make clear that it was not the process of sounding and defining that the children found dull, but the *words* they were asked to work with. When they came to words like *basket* and *basement,* the eager hands went up again.

A hazard of the conventional basal-reading programs, shared by *Phonetic Keys to Reading,* one of the supplemental phonics programs, was the persistent questioning to which the children were subjected on all aspects of meaning and interpretation of rather simple stories. Even for children of average intelligence, such detailed questioning to ensure that they were reading for meaning appeared unnecessary and tiring. True, not all the stories were interesting. But the main reason for the yawns and listlessness was the "wringing of the story dry" through questioning. The teachers who asked questions excessively were following the suggestions in the manuals.

Even the organization and size of classes did not alone seem to make for interest or dullness. Classes of twenty children encouraged to select their own materials and to express themselves freely ran the gamut from interested, engaged pupils to listless and bored ones. Classes of fifty-five children working on spelling and sounding and oral reading, all from the *same* book, also exhibited reactions ranging from interest to boredom.

This does not, of course, mean that the children were not learning differently in these classes. In fact, I came away with the distinct impression that the important issue is not interest or dullness, but rather what a particular method and classroom organization does to the child as a learner. It is perhaps false to compare the amount of interest produced by an approach that depends upon strong teacher control with that produced by one that relies on the pupil's taking the initiative in his own learning. What is more important is how these affect the young learner. Similarly, it is not of primary importance to know whether a phonic approach that depends upon rules and explanations of all possible soundings and spellings is more interesting than a linguistic approach that depends on self-discovery of sound-to-spelling correspondences. It is more important to know how each type of program affects the learner—in terms of *learning how to read* and *learning how to learn.*

In reading programs of all types, I often observed apathy among the children who were not working with the teacher. In most classrooms, such children were assigned tasks in workbooks or teacher-made worksheets. Generally, pupils working on these materials were listless and bored. Walking around the room, I observed much copying and numerous errors that went undetected. Many teachers and principals I talked with noted this problem and expressed a need for more imaginative self-teaching, immediately reinforcing materials. Of course, probably the best way to keep children who have already mastered some of the fundamental skills, and who are not working with the teacher, constructively occupied and interested is to provide a good classroom library. But a good classroom library takes a considerable budget, a larger one than most of the schools I visited had.

"NEW" VERSUS "OLD" PROGRAMS

Some of the other characteristics I noticed in the classrooms I visited are attributable to method. However, the controlling factor seems to be not which method is used but whether the method is "new" or "old." This can cause great differences in, for example, spirit and morale.

The innovators I observed, no matter what their new approach, had the spirit of pioneers. While programs differed considerably in timing and activities, this spirit was universal among them. It was especially noticeable in the "new" innovators as compared with the "older" innovators—those who had adopted new programs as long as ten years before. The older innovators showed less zeal and more readily admitted that they had not solved, and could never solve, all reading-instruction problems with the new method. It was hard to get the new innovators to admit that some children were failing under the new approach. They were all convinced that they had attained better results since initiating the new program. They failed to consider that record keeping was usually quite haphazard and contaminated by other simultaneous changes.

I found other differences, not necessarily inherent in the new reading method, between schools that were innovating and those which were not. The innovators often lifted the "difficulty ceiling" on instructional materials, using readers and textbooks above the children's grade placement. More often, they tended to organize classes homogeneously on the basis of reading ability; a smaller range of ability in her class gives the teacher more time for instruction. Innovating teachers seemed to be better supervised, to attend more teacher meetings and workshops, and to engage in more discussion with other teachers about how to get the most out of the program.

All the innovators seemed to draw in the parents more than those who held to the prevailing view. This comes partly from a desire to prove that what they are doing is right, that they are using the "one best method." Thus, in a school using *The Writing Road to Reading*, books were sent home in the first grade, and parents had to sign a note that the child had read the material out loud to them.

An important, though not easily quantified, factor in producing this atmosphere of innovation is the self-selection of people who innovate. When there is consensus that the present way of doing something is the best way possible and then a minority group decides to dissent from this view and try another approach, it is usually the more ambitious and independent teachers and administrators—those dissatisfied with established procedures—who volunteer.[1] Generally, they are courageous, intelligent, industrious, and full of hope for improvement.

Supported by a program of change, these people feel free to innovate in other, sometimes unrelated, areas as well. Thus, the "phonic innovators" are those experimenting with an early start in reading. They also question the content and methodology of existing basal readers. The Individualized Reading innovators also experiment with whole-class teaching of skills.

An innovating teacher is likely to find herself changing her approach to teaching. She may be reexamining what it is she is doing when she teaches beginning reading. The workshops become a time for reconsidering the reading process, probably not questioned for a long time by the experienced teachers and perhaps never before questioned by the inexperienced ones. I have already mentioned the two-day workshops that teachers using Pitman's Initial Teaching Alphabet in England attended

[1] Few published classroom experimental comparisons report evidence about teacher characteristics. An exception is the study by Tensuan and Davis (1963) cited in Chap. 4, which suggests that the teachers in their experimental classes were more able and experienced than the control teachers.

(see Chapter 4). After such a workshop one teacher commented: "ITA has given me a completely different view about teaching reading. I have rethought all my ideas about what it is that children do when they are first learning to read and what I should do to teach them."

Of course, innovation can bring new restrictions and new shibboleths as well as benefits. In a school that was experimenting with a Bloomfield type of linguistic program, a supervisor cautioned a first-grade teacher *not* to illustrate any of the words on the board. The year before, when she was teaching from conventional basal readers, this teacher would have been praised for "enriching meaning" by doing exactly this. In an English infant school using *The Royal Road Readers*, the children, when they hesitated on a word during oral reading, were warned: "Don't guess! Sound it!" On the other hand, the first graders using the Bloomfield materials in America were stopped from sounding and were told, instead, to spell it.

Fortunately, children are quite resilient, and in spite of differing cautions and restrictions they often choose the course most helpful to them. When I observed Omar K. Moore's youngsters, one who had been chosen to demonstrate his skill kept sounding the words not immediately recognized, although Moore kept reminding him to spell it. In England, in an infant school where, the teacher informed me, the children do mostly sight reading the first year and do not start word-building (phonics) until the second year, one five-year-old boy in the first-year class proceeded to sound out difficult words in a book he read to me. When I asked who taught him to do this, he answered, "My father."

OBSERVABLE DIFFERENCES AMONG PROGRAMS

On the basis of what I saw in the classroom, I believe I can formulate some generalizations about differences between programs regardless of whether the method used was an established one or an innovation.

For one, teachers using one of the separate, supplemental phonics programs definitely spent more time on direct teaching of phonics, especially in the first and second grades, than those using the basal-reading programs. Some started as early as kindergarten; most continued some work in phonics through the third grade. Some of the supplemental phonics programs prescribe a half hour daily for phonics instruction, and then another half hour per day for connected reading, usually from conventional basal readers. The phonics taught, and how it is taught, in the supplemental phonics programs differed from program to program and also differed considerably from the phonics taught by the teachers using the complete basal-reader package. These differences were clear in the analysis of currently used reading programs (see Appendix A and Chapter 8), but classroom observation revealed them in practice as well.

Where supplemental phonics programs were used, even the connected reading lessons tended to have a different flavor and emphasis, although usually the children were reading from the same basal readers. Teachers using only the basal-reading program tended to follow more closely the suggestions in the basal-reader teachers' manual. They spent more time motivating the children, discussing the pictures, preteaching the new words (in phrases and sentences), guiding the silent and oral reading, etc. Teachers using separate systematic-phonics programs engaged in the same activities, but not as extensively. They asked their children fewer questions on content; with less questioning, the pupils read more pages, and things seemed to go at a faster pace. They also had the children read stories orally more often.

Let me emphasize that teachers using separate phonics programs did not ignore comprehension. They wanted their pupils to react to the meanings of words and phrases and to the story as a whole. But the stress on comprehension was not as thorough as suggested in the teachers' manuals of the basal readers and observed in classrooms where the prevailing view was followed. In these special phonics classes, during the lessons devoted to sounding out words, teachers asked what the words meant if there was any doubt about the children's knowledge.

Blackboards revealed a good deal about the methods in use. In classrooms where systematic phonics was taught, lists of words, sometimes with diacritical markings or other markings characteristic of the particular phonics system, were written on the blackboard. Parts of words were underlined, syllables separated. In classrooms where the basal-reading word-study programs were being followed, I saw mainly phrases or sentences with whole new words underlined.

Children in classes using separate phonics programs were more apt to be reading from basal readers above their grade placement than children using only the total basal-reading programs. I found many second-grade classes reading third- and fourth-grade readers and literature books —and not because the children in these classes were more advanced.

I observed one guided-reading lesson from a third-grade basal reader in the most advanced of four third-grade classes in a school following a conventional basal-reader program. After the lesson the teacher proudly showed me recent standardized reading test scores indicating that the average reading attainment of her class was equivalent to that of typical fifth graders. When I asked why she was using a third-grade reader, she explained that if she went beyond this level the pupils might miss some important skills. But, she said, they could read harder books during their library period and would be put into an Individualized Reading program the next year because they were so advanced.

Upon further inquiry, I discovered that administrative rulings within some schools, school systems, and state departments of education prohibit giving a child instruction from a book above his grade placement. This largely explains the popularity of the Individualized Reading and Language Experience approaches, which do not limit teachers or pupils to books of particular grade levels.

Another difference I noted was in how errors were corrected. In most classes using separate phonics programs, ITA, or the Language Experience approach, when teachers corrected their pupils' word-recognition errors they directed them to the phonic elements or "rules" they had learned. This was true even when the pupils were reading from conventional basal readers. In general the teachers tried to help the pupils transfer what they had learned during the separate phonics lessons to the reading of stories from the basal reader.

In classrooms using the total basal-reader program, on the other hand, the teachers usually dealt with errors in word recognition by giving the child the correct word, saying "look again," or calling on another child to supply the word. If the teacher cued the child to correct his own error, it was usually by reminding him to read the rest of the sentence to see what made sense or by providing a synonym. Thus, she concentrated primarily on the word's meaning. When she used phonics, she called attention to the first sound only. The most common phonic cue was: "What is the first sound? Look at the first sound and get the meaning from the rest of the sentence."

Thus, these teachers gave little help to the child during the connected reading lesson in applying what he learned in the phonics (word-analysis) part of the lesson. In fact, they did not seem to expect that phonics would be used in connected reading. This is somewhat ironic, since proponents of the basal-reading series repeatedly emphasize that one of their great advantages is the integration of "word perception" with the total reading program. They strongly criticize separate, systematic phonics programs, which, they feel, give "isolated" practice (or "drill," if the critic is less gentle) that does not carry over into the true goal of reading—reading for meaning. Yet in practice it is the supplemental phonics programs that seem to give the greater emphasis to transfer of phonics knowledge.

Some of the phonics manuals actually suggest this emphasis. However, it probably springs even more from the conception of reading that, judging from their teaching, most teachers using the supplemental phonics programs seem to have. These teachers conceive of reading as having two aspects: word recognition and meaning. They take accuracy in word recognition more seriously than the typical basal-reader-program teacher. It is the core of their beginning reading program; furthermore, since their programs are newer, the impact of the method is fresher. Thus, teachers using supplemental phonics programs see to it that children apply the phonics they learn in the morning to reading in the afternoon.

The correction of errors was a very noticeable feature in the Language Experience approach. The child learns a great deal when his teacher shows him how a word he has misspelled should be written because of the conventions of our language, whether sensible or otherwise. But only a very skillful teacher can do this successfully. I saw just a few who could realize the full potential of this method. One teacher, in fact, asked *me* when she should begin to correct the spelling errors of her second graders. Although it was May, nearly the end of the school year, she had not yet done so for fear that any corrections might inhibit self-expression and the desire to write.

In classrooms where ITA was being used, the correction of errors was usually delightful to observe. The teachers were less critical of errors and praised the children for "intelligent" ones—those which made sense. The newness of the ITA symbols to the teachers themselves gave them an insight into misspellings.

DIFFERENCES IN EXPECTATION

At the beginning of this chapter, I mentioned having seen two children in Omar K. Moore's laboratory read from the *Annals of Political and Social Sciences,* while in a slum school other children of the same age were still struggling with reading-readiness workbooks. What accounts for such differences in achievement?

According to their teacher, the slum-school children were of at least average intelligence. "But," she added, "they do not have the concepts for beginning reading. That is why they are still on the readiness books." The day I visited their classroom these children were "reading" a set of pictures of household objects and deciding whether they belonged in a living room (which many of them did not have), a kitchen, or a bathroom. One object, a stack of magazines, gave them particular difficulty, and the teacher took quite a bit of time to explain it. According to the teachers' manual, magazines belong in the living room. My assistant and I agreed that we, too, would have had difficulty with that "concept."

In several schools I visited, the motto was "the sky's the limit." In some, first graders were reading from second- and third-grade readers in

May. In other schools, committed to the prevailing view, the teachers used subject-matter books (science and social studies) of a higher level for some of the reading instruction. (As we have seen, however, in most schools using the basal-reading series, the pace was slower because of administrative policy or because teachers feared children would not understand or would miss skills.) The purists of the Language Experience and Individualized Reading approaches used no basal readers at all, but let the children read whatever they wanted to.

Some of this variety in achievement levels no doubt springs from differences in native intelligence. But much more important determinants of achievement, I believe, are socially, culturally, and educationally established expectations.

In England, five-year-olds are expected to read. In this country they are not. When I happened to mention to an English infant-school head-teacher (principal) that in America many people are upset about the growing trend to start formal reading instruction in kindergarten, she could not quite understand our concern. "Five-year-olds enjoy a little work," she said. "We would not know what to do with them the entire school day if they could not do a little reading. They get tired of playing. They want to work and do a little reading." American reading experts, principals, and teachers, however, usually feel that reading instruction at age five will strain the child. Many are concerned about what it will do to the whole child. Some say, "Yes, many five-year-olds are 'ready.' But most are not."

Oddly enough, English teachers and principals, as well as their American counterparts, often repeated to me the long-refuted belief: "Well, as you know, *research says* that a mental age of six or six-and-a-half is best for starting." In practice, however, if not in theory, very different levels of achievement are expected of children of the same inherent ability.

SORTING OUT THE EVIDENCE

One reason I visited so many schools was to obtain evidence to test the various claims made for some of the new methods and materials. Were the schools using the newer methods getting the promising results that the popular books and articles were claiming? Had they really eliminated the problem of reading failures?

All the schools using new methods claimed they were achieving better results than before the innovation. But when I asked for comparative test results, few were able to produce them. For those which did, I found that although on the record they did have higher test scores, it would not be valid to attribute the improvement to the change in method of reading instruction alone. Usually other innovations had been made at the same time or resulted from the change in method.

Thus, many of the schools that Flesch and Terman and Walcutt had praised for obtaining such a high level of reading achievement by introducing an earlier and heavier phonics diet had also made other changes: they had cut down class size, initiated split schedules, provided more library books, increased supervision of teaching, and lifted administrative restrictions on the level of reader from which a child received his other reading instruction. Others had made organizational changes by introducing nongraded classes, team teaching, or homogeneous grouping of classes based on reading ability. Still others had adopted a new spelling program. Thus, although many of these schools could truthfully say their pupils were doing better in reading than before, it would be difficult to tell what was responsible for the improvement—a change in method, changes in other procedures, or both.

Even achievement above the national norm, which some of the innovating schools reported, is not sufficient evidence. In many of the schools using prevailing approaches, children achieve above the national norms. We know from past studies that the more able the children and the better educated their parents, the better they tend to do with *any* reading method.[2] Therefore, whenever a school reported that its pupils had been above the national norm in reading since they had begun using the new method, I asked about the children's overall ability, to determine whether better-than-average achievement would *normally* be expected in reading. I found this information hard to obtain. The most common answer was, "Our children are not unusual. They are just average." Yet by probing further and actually checking the records, I found that most of these "just average" children were in fact superior, often with IQs averaging as high as 120. After many years, bright children seem just average to those who teach them.

The schools using the prevailing methods were not as enthusiastic about the reading achievement of their children, although large proportions of their pupils, too, were achieving above the national norms. Where classes were grouped homogeneously, it was not unusual to find a second-grade class averaging third- to fourth-grade reading ability, but these schools did not make as big a point of it as the innovating schools.

Schools using the prevailing methods were also more open about the existence of reading problems, especially among the culturally disadvantaged. The schools that had adopted newer methods were generally loath

[2] See Barton and Wilder (1964) and Morris (1959).

to admit problems—although it appeared to me that they, too, had them (and published reports confirm this). Perhaps these schools do have fewer problems; this could not be determined. But that they have some "failures" is undeniable. In every class I visited—whether the method used was a prevailing one or a new one—I saw several children who were having extreme difficulty and were trailing behind the others. The explanations for this differed. Those using prevailing methods gave the usual reasons for the difficulties—lack of general intelligence, lack of motivation, emotional problems, brain injury, immaturity, etc. When the innovating schools did admit to "some" problems, their explanations were usually the same—except for one difference. Seldom did they say the child was deficient in concepts—although in England, Sir James Pitman is giving this "cause" first priority for failure with ITA.[3]

A typical answer to my question about failures under the new methods was that given by a supervisor in one of the innovating schools: "We have no nonreaders, although not all of them progress at the same rate." However, in discussing the composition of one school, this principal made a special point of saying that some of the children had illiterate parents; in fact, one child whose parents were illiterate and who still could not read was discovered in the sixth grade. Once detected, he was sent to the first grade for help with the "method." When I pointed out to the principal that there was, then, a nonreader in the sixth grade, although the method had been used for six years, he countered with, "Oh, but the child is reading now."

Not all the innovating schools presented this optimistic a picture. Several principals and teachers in schools that had made innovations as much as ten years before spoke freely about their reading problems. One principal said, "Method will never solve the reading problem. There are many good methods of teaching reading, but we have to put many ingredients in to get good results—good teachers and preparation for the teachers, smaller classes, supervision, libraries." One superintendent informed me that he had to remind the school board about the limitations of method when they refused to pay for a reading consultant on the grounds that his school used the new method and therefore should have no problems. (This method had received wide publicity in newspapers and national magazines.)

The best evidence that a new, even a better, method will not solve all reading problems came from an outstanding private school that had been experimenting with Bloomfield-type linguistic materials. Although the classes were small (approximately fifteen children per class) and the

[3] See Pitman (1963).

teaching excellent (the teachers were far more qualified than most I had met and were, in addition, aided by a teaching assistant), some children were receiving remedial instruction. The new method had been in use for at least three years, but the remedial teacher was still performing her function, and she was as busy as ever. My talk with her revealed that the pupils were having the same kinds of difficulties they had had with other methods: they could not recognize the printed words easily.

In general, the new innovators tend to be so convinced that their method will, "if used properly," eliminate the mass of reading problems that they keep this view in spite of evidence to the contrary. This phenomenon, no doubt, is due to the spirit of "novelty" or "pioneering," which keeps cropping up in connection with all new methods, whether in mathematics, science, or reading.[4] Although administrators and teachers admit verbally that there are no panaceas, inwardly they tend to hold fast to the hope that they are wrong—that at last, this is the way!

I do not wish to give the impression that the claims of improved achievement with the newer approaches are not valid. (As I have noted, there is sufficient evidence to indicate that reading programs emphasizing a more systematic teaching of sound-symbol relationships *do* get better results.) I wish to say only that many of the extravagant claims are influenced by the wish to believe that things are better and by a novelty effect that may, with time, diminish.

I felt it best not to use school records as proof of the superiority of one method over another. Not all schools kept records; many of those which had kept records either could not make them available to me or had used tests that were not comparable. Furthermore, I had no way of checking on any other changes that might have been instituted at the same time that the newer methods were adopted.

The search for evidence—test evidence—did at least make me very aware of the lack of consistent record keeping in our schools and the haphazard way in which test results are generally used. When we realize that almost every school system gives standardized tests periodically, it seems strange that no national, or even statewide, system has been instituted whereby these tests can become a means of self-evaluation and self-study. Given the claims and counterclaims that children are reading or spelling less well than they used to, one would think that school systems, as well as state and national agencies, would attempt to keep adequate records that could provide evidence on these questions.

This suggestion, of course, is not so easy to implement. For historical comparisons, grade-level scores from standardized tests would not be

[4] See Miles (1964).

sufficient because the "absolute" amount and kind of reading ability indicated by a score differ according to the test and the time it was standardized. Perhaps someday we will have standard measures of achievement spelled out, as suggested by John Carroll (1960) and more recently by Francis Keppel, recent United States Commissioner of Education. This would make it possible to determine, say, that seven-year-olds in a particular school in 1972 are reading as well as eight-year-olds did in 1962.

SOMETHING OLD, SOMETHING NEW

Even with a perfect testing system and a strict rule that a change in method not be accompanied by any other innovations, we still could not be sure that a given method alone accounted for improved results. This is because a new method is rarely completely innovative.

As I went from school to school observing the use of different approaches, it became quite evident to me that every school that introduces a new method still retains a good deal of the old one. Who is to say that retention of some of the old way of doing things is not a crucial factor in improved results?

One thing that struck me was the similarity of the basic text materials used. Almost all classes were using the conventional basal readers—perhaps not all the exercises suggested in the teachers' manuals, but certainly the readers. The supplemental phonics programs—Hay-Wingo, the *Phonovisual Method, Phonetic Keys to Reading, Breaking the Sound Barrier, The Writing Road to Reading,* and some of the linguistic programs—actually suggest at what point the child is to use the basal readers and library books. Some, in fact, start their special programs at the same time as the regular basal program. Even the Individualized Reading and Language Experience programs, whose proponents are quite critical of basal readers, often make use of them.

No matter what the new program, when the conventional basal readers are used the teacher tends to follow a procedure associated with these materials. The children read in small groups (called by various euphemisms, although when asked any child in the class can tell a visitor which is the "best" group, which the "middle," and which the "low"). The group working with the teacher sits around her on little chairs. Guided by oral questions from her (as suggested by the teachers' manual), the pupils read silently and then read some portions of the text orally to answer her questions.

Usually in classes trying new programs, fewer questions are asked when the basal readers are being used than in classes patterned after the prevailing view. Straight oral reading is more common.[5] But one can still detect the basal-reading-program format. In other words, although the innovators may be critical of the prevailing methods and materials, they incorporate much of the old into the new.

Because of this, it is quite difficult to make valid comparisons between methods. Were we to consider all aspects of the reading programs to be compared, we might find that there is little difference between them, except perhaps in the label. Thus, although the schools using *Phonetic Keys to Reading* do start the first graders on phonics first, the general pattern of motivating the story and quizzing the children on content and meaning in this program is quite similar to that in the Scott, Foresman Reading Program and the other basal series. In a school priding itself on the superior results achieved with the *Phonovisual Method*, I saw the familiar scene: little groups seated around a teacher, reading from the regular basal readers, answering questions about the pictures and the text, and discussing their reactions to it. There was no way to tell that these children were not following a total basal-reading program.

In fact, in many of the classes I visited where phonics and linguistic programs were in use, the teachers were calling the pupils' attention to meanings of words, phrases, sentences, and stories to a much greater extent than the instructional manuals or the "philosophy" behind the new method prescribed. Why did the teachers do it? My hypothesis is that teachers tend to bring to new methods the same procedures they have used previously in other methods or that were in use when they received their training in teaching children to read. Most of the teachers I observed had had their training and experience with reading programs that emphasized child interest and silent reading for meaning, and they tended to retain some of this approach in their current teaching. I believe they were acting unconsciously, as they seemed to persist in using some procedures even when instructed not to.

Perhaps this is another reason why new methods and materials often produce better results at the beginning and in time tend to lose some of their strength. Thus, in all probability when the pure sight approach was proposed as the "true" and "natural" way to start, teachers persisted in teaching the children something about the letters and sounds, although this was not part of the sight method. Some teachers no doubt did it

[5] Straight oral reading (also known as "barbershop" or "round-robin" reading) has been very much criticized by most reading experts since the early 1920s. It "violated" several assumptions, probably the most important being that oral reading, without previous silent reading, results in "mere word calling," i.e., reading without meaning. See Austin and Morrison (1963), who use "barbershop" reading as one of the criteria for evaluating reading programs.

more consciously than others. Guy Buswell, for example, in his study comparing a nonoral method with an oral method of beginning reading (1945), reports that his results were probably contaminated somewhat because many of the nonoral method teachers did not follow through completely, but instead gave their children some oral reading for fear that they would not learn to read without it. The same was reported to me many times by teachers who, during the period when some school systems discouraged the teaching of phonics, could not keep from teaching it. They got out their old phonics charts, *closed the doors,* and hoped the supervisor or principal would not enter unannounced. Several times during my visits, the proponents who accompanied me were quite embarrassed to find that the teachers were doing many things that were "not permitted" by the method.

I can go so far as to say that for each method, I observed teachers doing certain things that directly violated the theoretical position of the program's author. I do not make this point here to indicate that such teachers were not sufficiently trained in the method or that they could not follow the authors' written instructions, although these may very well have been reasons for breaking the rules. I would say that a more fundamental reason is that the teachers were pulled in another direction by their previous training and, perhaps, by their own good sense. I have often heard ultraenthusiasts of a special approach say that some schools are not getting good results because the teachers do a bit of this and a bit of that and do not give the approach its full chance. This may well be the case. But generally speaking, when the teachers using a new approach are well trained, the carryover of some of the old into the new may be very beneficial. Since teachers are the ones who work with the children, they can be more pragmatic, realistically adjusting the often extreme, even fanatical theories of the authors and proponents. Thus, I venture to guess that the extreme nonoral method of McDade survived as long as it did just because most teachers using it were sensible enough not to inhibit the children from saying or whispering the words. They refused to throw out the baby with the bath water.

Probably it is the next generation of teachers, trained in only one of the new methods, who feel the full weight of the method's limitations. Perhaps this is what occurred when the old phonics programs were dropped in the 1920s. The teachers of the 1920s and 1930s had themselves learned to read by a systematic phonic method and were therefore instilled with enough of a sense of word structure so that they may have obtained better results by letting up a bit on drilling their pupils. On the other hand, for the teachers of the 1940s, 1950s, and 1960s, who had learned neither to read by phonics nor to teach it in their education courses, moderate, integrated phonics may not have been enough.

If this is the case, then today, when a greater emphasis on decoding (linguistic approaches, phonics, ITA) characterizes the new methods, these programs will produce better results because those teaching them now have not forgotten that reading for meaning cannot be sacrificed. Should the stronger decoding programs, the Individualized Reading programs, or the Language Experience method begin to be used widely by teachers who have not had the benefit of experience with a different approach, results may be inferior because these teachers will lack the background necessary to temper the method's excesses.

The mingling of old and new teaching approaches raises fundamental issues for the reporting of research. By putting a label on a method, we do not define its scope. We must also describe in as much detail as possible what the program actually covers. The scheme presented in Appendix A is an attempt to indicate what aspects should be described. In addition, it would seem necessary to have impartial observers in the classrooms to discover what the teachers are *actually doing* with the method. (And since children are also taught at home by their parents, knowing what goes on after school would also be helpful.) I suggest that impartial observers be used not because I think they are needed to check on the investigators who carry on research but, rather, because I believe they could help in understanding what actually goes on during the teaching and, in the end, come closer to the research goal of knowing *what leads to what.*

AMERICAN AND BRITISH CLASSROOMS

During my travels I noticed some interesting differences between teachers in the United States and those in England and Scotland. I would like to note some of these, although they have very little to do with method.

The American teachers seemed more knowledgeable about child psychology. They were also more anxious about whether they were using the right approach to teaching reading. This was reflected in how they explained why certain children were not doing well. The American teachers usually gave rather elaborate explanations, such as broken homes, immaturity, or emotional problems. The British teachers gave a simpler explanation ("Well, he is just that way. He cuts up, but some children are like that.")

Another indication of these differences was the fact that most of the British teachers went about their business in the usual manner when I visited their classes, while many American teachers seemed to put on a demonstration for me. It may be that the American teachers felt more involved in the outcome of the study I was making and believed that they, or the method they were using, were being evaluated. The Britains, not knowing about the study (which was concerned primarily with the controversy in America), viewed me as a routine American visitor. Although I concede that this is a factor, I do not think it is the most significant one.

The American teachers seemed to believe that there is a *right* and a *wrong* way to teach reading. The British teachers seemed to be more amenable to variation in methods. Perhaps the attitude of American teachers reflects the almost universal consensus on methods in this country, as evidenced by the similarity between basal readers, with their detailed teachers' manuals. "The English and Scottish teachers would be insulted," said the editor of one of the most popular English reading schemes (basal series), "were they to get the wordy, detailed manuals that are the standard equipment of American primary school teachers." The English manuals are brief, general guides. It is characteristic for them to present separate general instructions for "sight" teachers and "phonics" teachers. No major American basal series gives teachers that kind of leeway.

Another difference is the greater involvement of parents in the schools in America. In almost every school system I visited, especially in those trying a new approach, some mention was made of parents—that the new approach was one endorsed by parents or that confirmation for trying it came from parents who had complained that their children were not learning to read well enough. In one California first-grade classroom, when I inquired about a schedule on the blackboard that listed separate time for phonics and reading, the principal said, "We do it for the parents' sake."

Perhaps the same editor who smiled bemusedly about our teachers' guides—with their ponderous, detailed instructions *on what to say and what to do*—had a point when he added:

> You in America can afford such tomes. We can't. Paper is too expensive. And besides, you are more subject to pressures from parents. In England, parents in general trust that the teacher knows best, and the teacher, when she completes her professional training, feels that she knows how to do it herself. In America, should a parent come in to complain about Johnny's reading, the teacher and the school need some protection. And their protection is that they followed a reading program developed by experts. If the child did not learn, it was not the teacher's or school's fault.

Generally, I found a strong desire for consensus in the schools I visited in the United States. The innovators were attempting to go against the old consensus, but they wanted to replace it by a new one. This was especially noticeable in larger school systems.

Most of the English and Scottish schools I visited were in small towns and villages and thus did not seem to show this need for consensus. The larger school systems in London and Glasgow, however, did. For example, the schools I saw in London had an overall teaching plan, using specific basal readers geared, in order of difficulty, by the head teacher. And the teachers, too, although they showed an independence of style, asked for my advice and approval in a manner reminiscent of that of American teachers. Thus, the "drive" toward consensus is probably more a function of size than of national differences.

In London, the children also seemed to be grouped according to ability, as they are in most American schools. In the smaller towns in England, however, there was generally a considerable amount of independent effort, with each child working on a different task. I learned then why there was no controversy over Individualized Reading in England. They had been practicing it for a long time.

TEN

Forces For and Against Change

WHY DOES A school decide to abandon one method of teaching children to read and adopt a different one? Why does another school, despite the existence of some convincing evidence that a new method is more effective than the one currently in use, persist in retaining its present method? As I traveled from school to school, observing and interviewing in an attempt to gather information on results with various methods, I also sought answers to these questions.

It soon became clear that the findings of research in beginning reading, which we have discussed here in such detail, are not an important factor in practical decisions about beginning reading instruction. Of the many teachers and administrators I talked with, not one ever said that he or she had been influenced to make a change by an article that reported an experiment or that described a finding about the reading process. It seems that research findings, carefully selected for the purpose, serve primarily to back up decisions and commitments already made.

Those in a position to decide how our children are taught to read are under constant pressure from various groups, each with its own beliefs on this question. Some want to innovate, and others defend the prevailing view. In this chapter I examine some of these groups and how they affect the dynamics of change. For the most part, I will be concerned with the phenomenon of innovation itself and will not usually consider which of the many new methods those in favor of change are proposing.

WHO ARE THE INNOVATORS?

In schools abandoning prevailing methods for new reading programs, I usually found that the change had resulted mainly from the dissatisfaction of one person in the school who insisted that teaching could be improved. In most instances this person was strongly enough convinced to proceed in spite of much resistance. Sometimes it was the remedial-reading teacher, sometimes a supervisor, and sometimes a classroom teacher who happened to take a workshop or hear about a new reading program from a friend. Thus, the impetus for change seems to arise primarily out of everyday practical needs and pressures. What I heard from teachers and administrators who had recently made changes in beginning reading methods would tend to confirm Fries's observation that most method changes have been instituted by school people searching for ways to improve on existing programs that they find faulty.[1]

Innovating schools are generally found at the two ends of the socioeconomic scale. The early innovators in reading instruction were mainly schools with a large proportion of children of professional parents—private, parochial, and suburban schools—and schools with many culturally disadvantaged children.

The independent and suburban schools adopted these new reading programs in a search for new ways of accelerating their pupils. These schools, particularly those with a large upper-middle-class population, were also experimenting early with other innovative programs—for example, in mathematics and science. Their main motivation for innovating has been to help their pupils achieve "earlier, faster, and better." Parental pressure for change in such schools is considerable; it was

[1] Charles C. Fries, *Linguistics and Reading*. Fries comments: ". . . The educational research of the last forty years seems to have had comparatively little effect in originating new approaches to the teaching of reading. That research studies from 1916 to 1960 (or what some people believed these research studies had 'proved') may have, from time to time, supported particular practices of certain teachers, or may have contributed to practical decisions concerning materials and methods cannot be denied; but the important changes in approach that characterize the history of the teaching of reading in the schools have grown out of the earnest struggle of the teachers and administrators themselves to find better ways—ways to achieve specific types of ability that the approach then in use neglected, ways to make their teaching measure up to their ideals of all that must be accomplished. . . . The chief methods and combinations of methods now discussed so vigorously were actually in use long before the time of modern educational research." (pp. 5–6)

mentioned often by teachers and administrators. Quite typical is the statement of the superintendent of a small suburban school system in California, which had adopted a supplemental phonics program about ten years before:

> The parents keep us on our toes. They are doctors, businessmen, professionals. They don't ask; they demand. They like the phonic approach. Now they are clamoring for the new arithmetic programs. They don't realize that it takes time to get a new program started. We have to educate the teachers in its use; otherwise, it goes all wrong.

Why should phonics and linguistic programs appeal to the more educated parents? Since its publication in 1955, the persuasive and pervasive Flesch book has no doubt been one factor.[2] The readers of the book were mostly college-educated parents, and they were impressed by it, judging from the favorable reviews it received in the general and literary magazines (Riedler, 1962).

Phonic and linguistic approaches probably also interest educated parents because they seem to be based more on logic and reason and to promise a more orderly and complete teaching of basic reading skills than the prevailing approaches of the 1950s. Still another reason is the direct appeal that some of the authors of supplemental phonics programs make to upper-middle-class parents by promising to achieve not only better results in reading but also more accurate speech and writing. Two of these authors give workshops to parents, at a cost of about $40 or $50 per person. These attract young professionals or corporation executives who are worried that their children might be left behind in the ever more hectic scramble for admission to college. Some of the supplemental phonics programs also have a "snob" appeal. As one author put it, "My method is a quality method. I want quality education. The method must be good when so many people of quality are behind it. The finest private and parochial schools have adopted it."

Many aspects of the early call for a "return to phonics" can be associated with the general reaction against progressive education. Since the prevailing approach to teaching beginning reading came into being at a time when progressive education was in favor, and since much of its ideology derives from this educational philosophy (see Chapters 1 and 2), it has shared with progressive education the wrath of a community increasingly interested in "high standards" and convinced that these standards have not been upheld by the schools. I found some of these young parents to be deeply concerned about providing a proper educa-

[2] See Wilder (1965). From a survey of the public, Wilder found that communities with higher socioeconomic standing are more exposed to reading controversies and thus are more critical of prevailing practices in reading instruction.

tion for their children, many of whom were still in kindergarten. They were worried that the public schools were not giving pupils a good foundation in the early grades and that as a result these children would not be able to enter a college of their choice.

Moore's computerized typewriters were first adopted by suburban and private schools. Indeed, he carried on his early experimental work in a small, independent school with high standards of academic achievement. The membership of the Reading Reform Foundation[3] also reflects "class" influence and concern; most of the institutional members listed on its stationery are headmasters of well-known independent schools. The anti-progressive-education aspect of this foundation is reflected in its close association (through memberships and speakers) with the Council for Basic Education. The Montessori schools, which were started in Italy for retarded preschool children of the very poor and stressed early reading (with phonics), have had their main popularity in the United States among the very rich!

The fact that a heavy phonic emphasis has appealed so markedly to the "elite" has actually prevented many of the people associated with public school education from making an objective examination of the claims of the code-emphasis proponents. These people have feared being in "bad company." Until recently, some public school people considered frank adoption and avowal of, say, a stronger phonics program a sign of joining up with the enemy—those who advocated cutting taxes, doing away with frills, and teaching only the three R's.

The other main group of schools that adopted phonic and linguistic approaches early were those with a large population of culturally disadvantaged children. But it seems to me that the push for innovation in these schools was not as great as in the first group, probably because they are predominantly in urban centers. Large urban school systems find it administratively and financially difficult to innovate. If a change is to take place, the person first proposing and undertaking it must have considerable freedom. Also, it is expensive to try out new programs, to give them the full support they require if they are to have a fair chance. Teachers must be retrained, new materials purchased, parents informed, and other concomitant changes in curriculum made. A richer and smaller school system can make changes more easily than a large one with many administrative rulings and more formal procedures.

Parents, it seems to me, do not play as strong a role in innovation in

[3] An association formed in 1962 by a group of "interested" laymen, teachers, principals, and headmasters of independent schools to support all phonic and alphabet methods against configuration or sight methods.

urban schools. In talking with the superintendent of a school system in an industrial area outside of Chicago, for example, I got the impression that parental pressure was not as important a factor there as in the suburban schools. Here, instead, the impetus for change appeared to have come from one devoted teacher who, on her own, had tried out a new system with her class nearly twenty years before and found that it produced good results. The superintendent became interested in the results she was getting, and through his interest the new system was adopted by all the other teachers.

Recently, owing to the national concern for the culturally disadvantaged child, the large urban school systems have been experimenting more with new procedures. The innovations they are making, however, seem to be minor modifications of the prevailing methods of teaching reading rather than radical departures. Thus, the emphasis in these schools is on motivating children by giving them books with more realistic content (see Chapter 1). In principle, this has been accepted since at least 1920.

Why are most of the innovations in the larger school systems essentially within the prevailing methods? My guess is that responsibility for change rests mostly with people in the school system who are sensitive to the pressures for conformity. In a word, the people making the decisions are conservative.

While there is agitation for change in schools serving both the culturally and the economically advantaged and disadvantaged, the middle socioeconomic group seems to remain quite satisfied with the *status quo*. Perhaps this is because this group is precisely the one for whom the existing basal-reading programs were devised and are most appropriate. The suburban middle-class child—not too affluent, and doing the ordinary things that all ordinary children in America do—can identify with Ted and Sally, Dick and Jane, Alice and Jerry, and the other heroes and heroines of the conventional basal readers. These readers are probably most suitable for this middle group; the pacing is not too taxing, and the questions they ask can be answered from the children's previous home experience.

HOW DO THEY INNOVATE?

As most school people described it, their adoption of new programs is rather haphazard. The superintendent of a small suburban school district put it this way:

> When I first came to the district nine years ago, one of the teachers used Hay-Wingo successfully with the poor readers. I didn't pay too much attention to it because nine

> years ago phonics was a dirty word. I visited her class and saw she was getting tremendous results. I was very enthusiastic about it. It was then given to a few other teachers to try. It was not forced on teachers, if they didn't think it had merit. We first started using it for remedial purposes. Then we used it for regular classes. After that, it worked out quite satisfactorily. If the teacher objected, she used another system. But it's like the mathematics program. Unless the teachers are trained and given a good in-service program, it is not very good. We have a big teacher turnover now, and will have to reactivate the program.

Another principal recounted:

> One of the teachers in my school used the *Phonovisual Method* with her poor readers. I reviewed the *Phonovisual* material one summer and thought it very rigid. I went to see the author, who showed me the fine results they had been getting in one school over the past five years, and I decided to let more teachers try it.

From the teachers, I got an even greater sense that chance circumstances lead to change. For example, the teacher of a second-grade class in a public school told me:

> I heard about Sister Mary Caroline's method being tried in the laboratory school during the summer session at the University of ———. They were getting results. I then sent for the manual and received the student edition. I could not make sense out of it. I asked the superintendent if I could try it. He said all right, but with only one copy, my own. He would not buy the pupil editions. I took a workshop on the method and still could not understand it. I took the workshop a second time and then tried it. My one criticism is that it requires the teacher to unlearn all her previous concepts. I was quite confused about phonics. I myself was a product of a progressive school and knew little about phonics. I was looking for something, and then found, after using this method for ten weeks with the children, that it was working.

Most schools or school systems I visited referred to their trial use of some new approach as "experimental." Usually, however, no definite procedures for evaluating the program were being used. If it worked and teachers liked it, that was enough to prove success.

In only one school system I visited did the course of innovation at all resemble research and development by involving some kind of systematic self-study and evaluation before, during, and after the introduction of the new program to determine whether it was indeed compensating for the lacks revealed by the original evaluation. But this process, like innovation itself, could come about only through the courage and determination of one person. This was a curriculum supervisor, who found after the new program got under way that she had a "hot potato" on her hands:

> Here I was, a little supervisor, doing my job. Suddenly, I became the object of much criticism—from people in the field of reading and from the big publishers who accused me of bringing psychological damage to the children by using and advocating this new phonics program.

How did it start?

> Back in 1951, when the basal series we were using was to be revised, our teachers' committee charged with selecting textbooks decided to look at the reading test results to see what the strengths and weaknesses were. The results showed that we were doing a better-than-average job of teaching reading, but a weak spot was in word perception (recognition and analysis). Since we also had complaints from the fourth-, fifth-, and sixth-grade teachers that the children could not sound out new words when they left the highly controlled vocabularies of the basal readers, we decided that a stronger phonics program was in order.

This hypothesis was further confirmed by the difficulties the remedial pupils were experiencing—these were consistently in word perception. The committee then undertook a search for phonics programs, but found none acceptable, since they wished to conform to the recommendations made by reading specialists on the basis of the "research" in phonics—namely, that the phonics program should not be taught in isolation from the regular reading period. (In Section 2, I reached an opposite conclusion from that indicated by the "research.") They did not find such a program until the salesman of a new company called at the supervisor's office with one that fulfilled their criteria: (1) The phonics was not taught in isolation; (2) it was not mechanical; and (3) what was learned was used.

The supervisor showed the materials to her teachers' committee, but they were hesitant. "After all," she explained, "they had all been trained that they must develop sight words first, and then use that vocabulary as a base for word analysis."

The supervisor then decided to use the new program experimentally, in a three-year study. It was not instituted widely: "If it was going to damage the children, we didn't want to damage too many." Three teachers volunteered, and two others were recruited. They all learned it together:

> I was in the classes a good deal. They were all quite scared because the children did little reading until January. But after January, things began to happen. The children had gotten through a primer and then other primers, and they began to read everything they could get their hands on. At the end of the first year, we tested the children and were dumbfounded by the results. Soon other teachers wanted to join the experiment, and parents were clamoring to have their children in the experimental rather than the control classes.
>
> The news got out, and people began to inquire about the results, which were surprisingly superior to the results from the old program. But I held them off until the end of the third year. At that point we called in college people as consultants.

Quite a different course to effect innovation was taken by the author of another new method, a course that almost committed the education department of one state to a series of experiments that would have cost about ½ million dollars. This author insisted at a public hearing of the school board that his new method was far superior to the one used in the public schools and that the public schools should adopt it immediately, since they were getting very poor results with the method then in use. If the public schools would not admit that they were "robbing" the children of their "true potential," he proposed, *let them prove* that their reading method was better than his. Community pressure led to a tentative commitment by the state department of education to undertake a series of long-term, experimental comparisons. This idea was later dropped, but the school board did insist that a separate, supplemental phonics program be adopted, and the state education department complied. But it was not the insistent author's program! Here was an example of "reverse science": an innovator challenging those unwilling to innovate as he saw fit to conduct tests, at their expense, to prove that the old is as good as the new.

Perhaps this is the pattern of all significant pioneering. The consensus on beginning reading instruction in the 1950s and early 1960s was so strong that only a variety of attacks together could challenge it. Except for a few dissenters here and there—looked upon by most people in the field as the lunatic fringe—everyone implicitly assumed that most of what was important to know about teaching the young child to read had already been discovered and that any improvements would consist in doing better what was already being done. It takes individuals with a great deal of courage, enthusiasm, and dedication to take a stand against so strong a consensus.

The first time a teacher uses a new program, she too needs determination and faith to carry it through. The enthusiastic phonics teachers were especially vocal about the frustrations they suffered the first year. One first-grade teacher told me:

> It's real hard. I was a frustrated teacher. With a sight vocabulary, the children started reading by the end of six weeks. But with this program, I worried about when they would start reading. This program gives the children a slower start, but it is rewarding by March.

This remark points to a crucial factor in the interpretation of the results of experimental comparisons. As reported in Chapter 4, many of the early investigators started with the assumption that reading achievement after five or six months in the first grade would give them a fairly good basis for judging the value of a method. Since many of the newer methods—both the supplemental phonics programs and the linguistic programs—imply different conceptions of how the beginner reads (and, therefore, different definitions of what is adequate achievement at the beginning), results with these programs in the early stages can be quite frightening to unprepared teachers. As a result, the sincere, hard-working teacher may become terribly concerned that her pupils are losing out. Parents, too, can have the same reaction, asking, as one teacher quoted, "Why isn't Jane reading at the end of six weeks, when her brother read?" Unless she has been told what to expect by others who have tried the same method and found it successful, the teacher who is going to cope with this kind of change in expectation must be a very convinced and determined person—or have a confident supervisor.

THE SCHOOLS OF EDUCATION

Many administrators and supervisors I spoke with expressed great dissatisfaction with the courses on the teaching of reading given in colleges and universities. Over and over again they complained that the young teachers came to them unprepared to teach reading. As one put it, "The beginners are filled with all good intentions, often with high ideals for developing concepts, appreciations, and interests, but with little specific knowledge about how to proceed."

The beginning reading teachers themselves felt that they had not been properly prepared to cope with the realities of teaching children how to read. They considered in-service courses and reading conferences equally worthless. The public school people commented that college teachers are often condescending to the classroom teachers, repeating what is "in the books" and failing to deal with the problems that the teachers were experiencing from day to day.

Those who discussed the effect of their education on their later attitudes commented that what they had learned in their own college courses had worked to prevent them from considering new ideas freely. One school principal—a man who thought of himself as a latecomer to a code-emphasis method—attributed his reluctance to investigate the merits of a phonic emphasis to the prejudice that had been instilled in him during his course work at the local university. Here, as in most colleges of education, he recounted, the instructors held that the research was against it. They explained that there were two main approaches—synthetic and analytic—and that "research says" the analytic is better. When he asked *what* research, the principal said, no one was able to tell him.

Judging from what they told me, the education in the teaching of reading received by teachers, principals, and supervisors generally acts as a force against experimentation and change.

PUBLISHERS' INVOLVEMENT IN CHOICE OF METHODS

Methods of teaching beginners how to read reach the classroom in the form of teaching materials. With rare exceptions, these materials are published commercially. It is not surprising, therefore, that publishers feel they have a stake in the outcomes of debates, research, and other means whereby the use of one method can be justified over the use of another.

In my visits to schools I found evidence over and over again that the companies that publish beginning reading materials play an important role in determining how children are taught to read. The representatives (salesmen) of these companies are very able and persuasive, and many school administrators listen to them carefully. One administrator told me, "The publishers' representatives are often more informed than the principals and teachers, who don't have the time to be informed." Another specifically noted that it was the representative of a publisher, calling with a new program, who convinced the people in his school what reading program to adopt.

Once they have sold a set of materials to a school system, the publishers continue to influence the teaching of reading in that system. We have seen how important the teaching manuals that accompany the reading materials are to most teachers. In addition, the publishers distribute newsletters, promotional materials, and reprints of articles by authorities. They also contribute significantly to in-service and teacher education through demonstration and training programs.

The larger companies, of course, can offer more of these services than the smaller ones. They have reading consultants on their staffs who run workshops, put on demonstration lessons, and in other ways help train teachers in the use of their materials and in the teaching of reading generally. These consultants are usually former teachers or principals. They are especially important in school systems that do not have a reading consultant or specialist of their own.

Not all school administrators put so much trust in the publishers as the one quoted above. Some are more shocked by the aggressiveness of these companies than impressed by the services they offer. One administrator, for example, told me that as soon as he began to write about a method he had developed that does not use basal readers, several authors from the major companies approached him to join their basal-reader teams. They wished to incorporate his "innovation" in their published programs. This same administrator said that a representative selling one of the new phonics programs threatened to sue him when he refused to let him in his school.

Other administrators who used new programs often mentioned how publishers' representatives put pressure on them by spreading rumors about reading-program adoptions. The representatives often cite the fact that one school system has adopted a new program as an argument for persuading another system to do so. One superintendent told me this story: He had been using one of the supplemental phonics programs for ten years to supplement the basal readers of one of the larger companies. When he reordered the basal readers, the publisher's representative spread the rumor throughout his region that this school system was finally abandoning the supplemental phonics program in favor of his company's materials. The truth was that the superintendent had always used, and planned to continue using, these basal readers for connected reading only, while relying on the separate phonics program for teaching word-perception skills.

As might be expected, publishers' representatives are very critical of competing beginning reading programs. The publishers, however, are also just as critical of the research that backs up these programs. Comparing what two competing publishers have to say about the same research findings can have ludicrous results. I was in a position to get the reactions of the publishers of both sets of materials involved in two recent comparative studies. Quite consistent with previous comparisons, one report concluded that the addition of a separate, systematic phonics program to the regular basal-reading program produced better results. The other found that it produced results that were not significantly better. One could have predicted the publishers' reactions to these studies from a knowledge of their products. The representative of the special phonics program spoke highly of the scientific validity of the study that concluded to the advantage of his program, and he freely proclaimed that investigator bias, Hawthorne effect, and veritable falsification of evidence characterized the other study. The representative of the basal-series publisher, of course, said exactly the same thing—but about the first study. The study that concluded for his company's program was, he assured me, highly scientific.

This behavior on the part of publishers' representatives may seem petty and childish, but there is, in fact, a good reason for it. Producing a reading series, as we have seen, involves a very large financial commit ment on the part of the publisher. The decision of a single school system especially a large one, to adopt a given set of materials automatically ensures a large number of sales. Further, the sale of materials, even on a small scale, is often used by the publishing house as evidence that a school system has given these materials its approval. If it is a particularly large school system, this information carries a great deal of weight. Convincing school systems to adopt a new program is a difficult job, requiring all the persuasion a publisher's representative can come up with. Large school systems, especially, develop various criteria for the selection of teaching materials that become a fixed part of general policy, even though they may be based on questionable research evidence and may, in fact, be wrong. Often this policy may keep a school system from trying out something new unless it is presented with the most convincing arguments for doing so.

We could, perhaps, dismiss any questionable actions on the part of publishers as natural to the competitive publishing game. But isn't teaching children to read too serious a "game" to be left to publishers?

Many have thought so. Beginning with Rudolf Flesch, the publishers (and the authors) of the basal-reader programs have been accused of a conspiratorial plot. Terman and Walcutt took up this cry, and so did most (but not all) of the proponents of minority views.

Unfortunately, however, critics have a way of falling silent when their own materials are accepted for commercial publication and distribution. Once today's innovations are institutionalized into published reading programs, will their proponents remain critical of the way publishers produce and promote materials, or will they become the "new establishment" to replace the "old establishment" they found so deplorable? My guess is that they will follow the usual patterns of political change. Today's radicals become tomorrow's conservatives.

And yet this is inevitable, since any method or plan must ultimately be put into some form of materials for the children and manuals for the teachers if it is to be used. Once published, these materials must be adequately distributed, explained, tried out, and adopted. Beginning reading instruction is an area where objectivity has not prevailed in the past, and there is little reason to believe that those concerned with it—from parents to teachers to administrators to experts—will suddenly become less emotional and more rational overnight. Where uncertainties abound, people tend to take strong stands: some resist change and overdefine their positions; others, convinced that change is necessary, tend to oversell and overdemonstrate.

Innovation with new methods involves the reputation of users as well as proponents. When school administrators finally decide to adopt a new reading system, even if only experimentally, they invest a great deal of money, time, and effort in it. Sometimes their trial receives publicity; "little supervisors" can even gain national fame by experimenting with, and reporting on, a new program. Should later evaluation indicate that results are not as glorious as had been hoped, can these people be expected to admit this freely—after, say, a five-year trial period that receives much publicity?

The publishers alone cannot be blamed for the rigid viewpoints, the tenacious grasp on the *status quo*, or the fanatical espousal of new methods that characterizes those concerned with beginning reading methods. Although the publishing houses are more vulnerable in that they can always be accused of basing their actions on the hope of financial gain, it should be remembered that they are speaking to people who for the most part do not use objective research evidence as a criterion for selection. As we have seen, 77 percent of 900 reading experts surveyed by Barton and Wilder in 1964 agreed that, for all practical purposes, the basal series are essentially alike. What, then, makes a school system select one and not another? On the basis of what criteria do those states which still have state adoption policies "adopt" one series over the others? Could it be the reputation of the author, the extra services that a company makes available to the school through consultants, the fact that many teachers prefer the series because they studied with the author, or the skill of the company's representatives in promoting its materials? And if these are the reasons, can we expect that the publishers will not put a great deal of effort into providing the desired services, obtaining noted authors, and hiring persuasive salesmen?

This situation is not different from that which surrounds textbook adoption and selection in general. But in the field of beginning reading, more money is at stake, and the impression is given to teachers and administrators (who want such reassurance) that the reading programs are based on research and incorporate the best of what is known. In the same study, Barton and Wilder found that most teachers and principals surveyed believed that the basal programs are based on "definite scientific proof." Compare this assertion with the fact that in talking to administrators and other school people I never heard one mention of research evidence as a determinant of choice of method. Doubtless these people have been oversold by the publishers. However, if they never actually look at the research evidence, the job of overselling them cannot have been too difficult.

In this section I briefly observed that teachers using a new method in the classroom can sometimes create new myths and new shibboleths to replace the old. This tendency to rigidify a reform to the point where it becomes as inflexible as the practices it replaced is not restricted to teachers. Principals and supervisors, once they give their approval to experimentation with a new method, are almost automatically forced to become its defenders. Proponents of innovations, who are usually also our sharpest critics of the status quo, *will certainly modify, if not forget, their criticism once they are no longer treated as threats but as the new establishment.*

The truth is that with time, the innovators themselves become a force against change.

As I pointed out in discussing differences between British and American teachers, Americans seem to have a great need for consensus. Most of the teachers I talked to, whether they advocated an old or a new method, believed that there is a right and a wrong way to teach. Those still loyal to the prevailing view felt that the innovators had been taken in by fanatical proponents, overambitious parents, and aggressive book salesmen. The innovators, instead, firmly believed that they had finally seen the light, after a period—perhaps lasting many years—of grievous error. These latter were often made very unhappy by the thought that in the past they had done less than their best for their pupils; they blamed this failure on the reading experts and their professors in teachers' colleges, who, they thought, had grossly misled them.

So Americans became crusaders for consensus. I cannot simply say here that consensus is bad. Some agreement within a school and within a school system—even throughout the country—is necessary, Americans being as mobile as they are. Indeed, as Gates (1922) and Agnew (1935 and 1939) have noted, consistency is one important aspect of early progress. Thus, there are advantages to having children learn from similar readers and having teachers follow similar manuals. The English can afford more freedom partly because as a nation they are still less mobile than we.

Further, we have seen that not all teachers rely on others to tell them what to do. There will always be some who listen to an inner voice speaking from experience and good sense. Such teachers are fortunate if they have supervisors and administrators who permit them to go their own way.

And yet, we should acknowledge this drive toward uniformity, this intolerance of other viewpoints, for what it is. Among those concerned with beginning reading, there is a kind of schizophrenic attitude toward consensus. On the one hand, every reading specialist, no matter what his allegiance, assures us that no reading method can ever be a panacea. All talk a good deal about how important it is to recognize that different children must be allowed to learn in different ways.

On the other hand, only two kinds of individualization have gained any acceptance. The first of these is differentiation in pacing: the same materials are used, the approach to teaching is unchanged, but one child moves through the material faster than another. (Differential pacing, as we have seen, is often hampered by administrative rulings and the fear that children will miss something important if accelerated.) The second kind is differentiation in content and subject matter: the child is allowed to read whatever he wants, at whatever rate he wants. But usually, only a very good teacher can make this work. Generally, only those who have already failed to learn how to read are exposed to a "no holds barred" approach as far as method is concerned.

As long as this drive for consensus so strongly colors our attitude toward experimentation and change, we can expect that new methods will turn into old ones, especially after the first generation of teachers, who still remember other approaches, are replaced by a second generation schooled exclusively in the accepted approach. Then those fixed in their views will again be shaken only by others equally convinced that a radical change will solve all problems.

Can this trend be broken? To do so will take a great effort on the part of all those concerned with teaching beginners to read—researchers, publishers, administrators and teachers, and parents. The quest for simple answers to questions of what is "right" and what is "wrong" will need to involve a more dispassionate—in a word, a more scientific—*view of the problem.*

Hopefully, the currently increasing government support for educational research and for the training of educational researchers will contribute to a change. Another encouraging sign is the government's investment in various regional laboratories to help school systems effect change. Still another is the trend toward new publishing-industrial combines. The recent mergers of General Electric and Time, International Business Machines and Science Research Associates, and Xerox and Systems Development have brought new companies into the educational business. Perhaps these companies will apply a research and development style to the publication of instructional materials. Industry is accustomed to spending a fixed proportion of its budget on research and development. Ideally the large companies now entering the field will carry this policy into educational publishing. The investments they will have to make in reading programs, for example, will be so great that they will have to look to the evidence, and produce evidence of their own, to ensure the development of materials of true educational value.

But the research sophistication of the consumers (the teachers, administrators, curriculum directors, and their *teachers in colleges of education) will have to keep pace with that of the producers of the materials. For why should the principle that operates in other fields not operate in the field of instructional materials as well—that what one gets is as good as what one demands? If schools do not ask for better published programs, and for hard evidence that they are better, they will not get them.*

Where Do We Go from Here?

Conclusions and Recommendations

WE HAVE traveled a long way in our search for the facts in the reading debate. As we examined the evidence, we tried to get at the underlying issues and assumptions—not only to sift out the facts, but also to understand why they have been so difficult to come by and how intelligent, serious scholars could have interpreted them so differently.

The existence of a controversy is in itself a phenomenon deserving serious study. We can no longer afford the luxury of anger and indiscriminate blaming. When a body of "truths" has been accepted in theory and practice for nearly fifty years, we must closely examine the foundation upon which it was built before replacing it with a new set of truths. The foundation for the new truths must be studied carefully as well. Otherwise we build on sand.

The evidence, together with my interpretations, hypotheses, and conclusions, was presented in the preceding chapters. I also outlined some recommendations for practice and research in some of the chapter summaries. These I shall not repeat. I include here only the major conclusions drawn from my inquiry, along with recommendations for change—for, indeed, many changes in theory, research, and practice are indicated.

In presenting the conclusions of this study, and especially the recommendations growing out of these conclusions, I am keenly aware that I, too, can never hope to escape from the influence of my time. I write in a period when excellence in academic work is highly valued, when intellectual precociousness is viewed as a promise of later accomplishment, when "normal" achievement is not enough. I write at a time when automation is making obsolete abilities that once were indispensable, and when there is a desperate push to "up" the standards of literacy. Indeed, what was once good is no longer good enough—not only for holding a job, but for making use of one's leisure time, as well. This is an ambitious age for knowing and for doing. The first graders now learning to read will be exploring the moon and Mars. They will be called upon to search for a cure for cancer and for ways of alleviating mental illness. And they will be trying to live with one another and the rest of the world without blowing themselves up.

I am mindful, too, that this is a "structural" age. I have lived through a period when semantics, with its concern for the nuance in representational meaning, influenced the thought of behavioral scientists. This influence has now been replaced by the linguist's concern for meaning through structure.

I write at a time when psychologists are attempting to program the learning of the most complex skills and disciplines by means of a minute analysis of the steps involved. Only yesterday, psychologists were putting more of their faith in the learner's ability to "program" his own learning; if the student wanted to learn and was ready to learn, they thought, the teacher's job was to expose him to the material in as natural a setting as possible. This view has changed.

I preface my conclusions and recommendations with the above because several times in this book I have noted that scholars and researchers in reading have been influenced by the philosophical commitments and assumptions of their time. It would be foolish to think that I do not share in this human condition. On the other hand, I am hopeful that, like the investigators of the past, I have not covered up my tracks—and that this inquiry may provide data for a new synthesis, as new research evidence accumulates. Also, I hope I have adequately stressed that the conclusions and recommendations I present here hold for *now*—for the present available evidence, for existing school conditions (as I see them), and for the goals we seek now. As these change, I fully realize, so the theory, research, and practice in beginning reading instruction must change.

Another fact to give us pause in attacking present problems is that we still have much to learn about the process of learning to read. Some of the most fundamental questions have yet to be asked. But research is never ending. It will always uncover more questions than it answers. And, in an area as crucial as beginning reading instruction, we cannot wait for all the answers to be in before we try to improve the present situation.

What, then, have we learned from our inquiry into how the quality of beginning reading instruction can be improved? In the remainder of this section, I discuss five major recommendations.

MAKE A NECESSARY CHANGE IN METHOD

My review of the research from the laboratory, the classroom, and the clinic points to the need for a correction in beginning reading instructional methods. Most schoolchildren in the United States are taught to read by what I have termed a meaning-emphasis method.[1] Yet the research from 1912 to 1965 indicates that a code-emphasis method—i.e., one that views beginning reading as essentially different from mature reading and emphasizes learning of the printed code for the spoken language—produces better results, at least up to the point where sufficient evidence seems to be available, the end of the third grade.

The results are better, not only in terms of the mechanical aspects of literacy alone, as was once supposed, but also in terms of the ultimate goals of reading instruction—comprehension and possibly even speed of reading. The long-existing fear that an initial code emphasis produces readers who do not read for meaning or with enjoyment is unfounded. On the contrary, the evidence indicates that better results in terms of reading for meaning are achieved with the programs that emphasize code at the start than with the programs that stress meaning at the beginning.

I cannot emphasize too strongly that the evidence *does not endorse any one code-emphasis method over another*. There is no evidence to date that ITA is better than a linguistic approach, that a linguistic approach is better than a systematic-phonics approach, or that a systematic-phonics approach is better than ITA or a linguistic approach. Neither do we have any evidence to date that one published code-emphasis program is superior to another, although some undoubtedly are.

Nor can I emphasize too strongly that I recommend a code emphasis only as a *beginning* reading method—a method to *start* the child on—and that I do *not* recommend ignoring reading-for-meaning practice. Once the pupil has learned to recognize in print the words he knows (because they are part of his speaking and listening vocabulary), any additional work on decoding is a sheer waste of time. It saddens me to report that some authors and publishers of reading materials are already misinterpreting the evidence. They are developing decoding exercises for upper elementary and high school pupils, erroneously assuming that if this approach is good at the beginning, it is also good later on. (The same

[1] There are definite signs, however, that more children are now learning by a code-emphasis method than in the early 1960s.

kind of error was made in the 1920s, when, because silent reading was found to be good for older pupils, it was assumed that it must be desirable at the beginning of first grade, too.) Any students at these higher levels who need such work are still deficient in the first step of reading—translating written into spoken language. But if pupils can already do this, the teachers and the authors and publishers who give them decoding exercises are building another kind of superstructure that is bound to produce another reaction. If they continue, we will be confronted in ten or twenty years with another best seller: *Why Robert Can't Read.* The culprit in this angry book will be the "prevailing" linguistic, systematic-phonics, or modified alphabet approach—whichever happens to "win out" now. The suggested cure will be a "natural" approach—one that teaches whole words and emphasizes reading for meaning and appreciation at the very beginning.

In calling for a change in beginning reading methods, I am not recommending a complete housecleaning—an across-the-board abandonment of existing practices for new ones. Many teachers have developed methods of their own that are far superior to any that have been investigated and commercially published. In their quiet, unassuming way, these teachers are getting results that would be the envy of any of the authors of "scientifically" developed and tested methods.

However, just because some teachers can create their own methods and achieve excellent results with them, we cannot assume that all teachers can do so. One of the main lines of defense for the meaning-emphasis method has been the assumption that since no one method works with all children, and since all good teachers adapt any method to the needs of their pupils, a methods change is unnecessary. I do not agree with this position. The majority of teachers rely on published reading programs and on the manuals that have a built-in method. Further, a new generation of teachers is constantly being prepared. How should they view beginning reading? What methods should they be taught to use? Of course, they should be instructed to be flexible, but flexible with what? One has to have a method, even if it serves only as a point of departure.

My belief that the choice of beginning reading method is important does not lessen in any way my conviction about the importance of good teaching. Indeed, as we learn more about the teaching of beginning reading, we may find that a poor method in the hands of a good teacher produces better results than a good method in the hands of a poor teacher. But this is not the point. This inquiry did not find that good teaching is obsolete. Good teaching is always needed. But a good method in the hands of a good teacher—that is the ideal. In fact, if my visits to classrooms during the present study and my contacts with thousands of teachers over the past twenty years have taught me anything, it is that the good teachers are constantly searching for the good methods.

My recommendation for a methods change does not apply to all pupils. Some pupils may have a unique or uncommon way of learning. Insisting on one method for all may complicate things further.

My recommendation for a change in beginning reading methods does not apply to school systems that have been getting excellent results with their present methods and materials that the teachers use with confidence. Many factors may make existing methods and materials better suited to these schools than new ones. What is effective for a class of thirty-five may be too slow-moving for a class of ten or fifteen. The functional type of learning that leaves the programming pretty much up to the individual pupil may work perfectly for a small class of able children with a creative teacher who already knows what to teach and when. Imposing a set, systematic program on a teacher who is knowledgeable about reading and keenly attuned to the strengths and weaknesses of her pupils may very well destroy the beauty of what she has already achieved.

A beginning code-emphasis program will *not* cure all reading ills. It cannot guarantee that *all* children will learn to read easily. Nor have the results of meaning-emphasis programs been so disastrous that all academic and emotional failures can be blamed on them, as some proponents and publishers of new code-emphasis programs claim. But the evidence does show that a changeover to code-emphasis programs for the beginner can improve the situation somewhat, and in this all too imperfect world even a small improvement is worth working for. I believe that method changes, if made in the right spirit, will lead to improved reading standards.

Since most children in the United States are currently learning to read by a meaning-emphasis method, how is a changeover to a code-emphasis method to be effected?

Perhaps the smoothest way to initiate change is to modify the prevailing instructional materials for children and the accompanying manuals (guidebooks) for teachers. The conventional basal-reading series are the most widely used instructional programs, and they have the almost unquestioned acceptance of elementary school teachers and principals. The authors and publishers of these series can, I believe, play a major role in effecting the needed change in method by adjusting their programs in line with the available research evidence. Our analysis of the

1962 edition of one basal series indicates that they have already begun to do so. (Suggestions for specific changes in the conventional basal readers are given in Section 3 and will not be repeated here.)

School systems can improve reading standards by using one of the "complete" code-emphasis programs (some are described in Appendix A) or one of the separate supplemental phonics programs as a replacement for the word-perception program in the conventional basal-reader series. Indeed, some of the basal-reader publishers are already producing their own supplementary decoding programs and in other ways are strengthening the decoding component of their series (see Glossary of Names for Reading Programs in the Bibliography).

When a new program is adopted, the teachers should receive in-service training in how to use it. In-service training is a necessity because the previous training of most teachers has been opposed to the theory and practice underlying code-emphasis methods. If the code-emphasis methods are imposed on these teachers unaccompanied by adequate reorientation and training, they will not receive a fair chance, and results with them may be disappointing. In many schools I visited I heard that teachers had threatened to resign when told that their school system had changed over to a code-emphasis beginning reading program. If they do not understand the new program, some teachers may merely "close their doors" and continue to do what they did before, while others will use it grudgingly.

When new reading programs are adopted, they should be cast in a research and development framework. The school need not conduct a series of controlled experiments to prove that the new is better than the old. I should like to suggest, instead, that new programs be tried out in a spirit of discovering *what they can do* and *what they cannot do* for certain kinds of children and for certain kinds of teachers. What are the new program's strengths? What are its weaknesses? Who are the high achievers under the new program? Who are the failures? Which teachers succeed with the new? No program can do all things for all children, and no program can be all things for all teachers.

REEXAMINE CURRENT IDEAS ABOUT CONTENT

What about the content of beginning reading materials?

I have not studied content as thoroughly as method, and therefore I cannot make specific recommendations on this aspect of reading instruction. However, I should like to comment that too many people are making too many recommendations about content without any proof whatsoever. I came across no evidence that a certain kind of content in beginning reading programs influences reading achievement favorably or unfavorably. There is some limited evidence on what *some* children like or do not like to read about. But even this evidence is inconclusive because the choices offered the children were limited.

The producers of some beginning reading programs (especially the conventional basal-reading series) are in a dilemma about content, above all for the first grade. These programs emphasize meaning and appreciation, while their rigid vocabulary control makes possible only content that contains little to be understood or appreciated. If meaning is pursued, then a meatier content is needed.

What should this content be like? Should the emphasis be, as now, on familiar experiences? And should these familiar experiences be broadened to include all kinds of children—nonwhite as well as white, urban as well as suburban, poor as well as middle class?

If the stories are to be built around familiar experiences, the only possible answer to the second question is "yes." Whether such broadening of content will help urban, poor children learn to read better, however, I do not know. The children's attitudes may be improved. This is desirable. But a reading program that improves attitudes only and does not improve the teaching of reading is just not enough.

At the moment, many people are pinning their hopes for helping culturally disadvantaged children to read better on a change in content rather than in method. They are assuming that these children do poorly in reading because they lack the necessary concepts and cannot identify with the suburban, white, well-to-do children in their readers.

This assumption has gone untested. Raising the reading attainment of culturally disadvantaged children is too important a problem for us to concentrate all our efforts on one solution—namely, a change in content—whose effectiveness is as yet unsubstantiated. On the other hand, our inquiry indicates that the reading standards of culturally disadvantaged children can be improved by a change in method. The evidence points to a code-emphasis start for them. A change in method, I believe, should accompany any modifications in content for these children.

My own personal content preference for first and second graders is folktales and fairy tales. They have universal appeal. In my work with children, I never found one who could not identify with "Cinderella," "The Gingerbread Boy," or "The Three Little Pigs." These tales contain struggle and triumph, right and wrong, laughter and tears—themes that have disappeared from modern stories based on familiar experiences. Most authors who select and adapt stories for first- and second-grade readers seem to have forgotten that children, like adults, enjoy a good cry once in awhile. To make all stories come out happily at the end is not only unrealistic but also dulling.

REEVALUATE GRADE LEVELS

Another needed change indicated by my inquiry is a reevaluation of grade levels. If the grade levels of readers remain the same, the number of different words they contain will need to be reconsidered. The research evidence to date hardly justifies the restricted vocabularies of most present-day basal readers, particularly those at the primary levels. Indeed, the use of a heavier vocabulary load will make it possible to write stories of greater substance and literary merit. If vocabularies are increased, the readability formulas used to estimate the difficulty of primary-level materials will need revision. Most of the formulas and vocabulary specifications now used for grading primary-level books are based on the standards of the basal readers published in the late 1940s and early 1950s. If we do not develop new standards, we will be overestimating difficulty and underchallenging the children.

Even before these changes in published materials are made, schools should take the ceilings off the levels of readers from which children now receive instruction. The "skill-building" exercises suggested in the manuals and in the workbooks are not all needed. In fact, as we learned from the basal-reader analysis, many of the exercises are of questionable value. If a child can read library books on a level two or three grades above his grade placement with profit and enjoyment, is there any reason why he should not be instructed from a reader of similar difficulty?

DEVELOP NEW TESTS

Generally, I believe that teachers should be given more freedom in the use of methods and materials, providing they are achieving good results. Whether this is the case can be determined by testing.

I found, however, that most teachers and principals have little faith in the standardized tests now given periodically in every school. The results of these tests are not used, as they might be, as a basis for instruction and for decisions on methods and materials. Further, the standardized reading tests often mask some of the important outcomes of reading instruction because they measure a conglomerate of skills and abilities at the same time.

Thus, there is a need for single-component tests—tests of word recognition, tests of mastery of the alphabetic principle (ability to apply knowledge of letter-sound correspondences), as well as tests of reading comprehension, critical reading, and appreciation. For the primary grades, tests of code mastery are most essential. The teacher needs simple diagnostic tests, while the researcher needs more complex ones. The present standardized group tests seem to be a poor compromise between the two.

We also need tests that provide absolute measurements—that can tell us how much of each component of reading a child has mastered at a given time. Such tests can also tell us how well eight-year-old children, say, are doing in 1965 as compared with eight-year-olds in 1975, thus avoiding the periodic accusations that too many Johnnies can't read.

IMPROVE READING RESEARCH

Now for the improvements necessary in research.

First, the reading field must find a way to avoid a situation like the one that produced a *Why Johnny Can't Read.* It prides itself on its wealth of research—indeed, in examining the *Handbook of Research on Teaching* (Gage, 1963) every researcher in mathematics, sciences, and other school subjects looked with envy at the voluminous research in reading—but it seems not to have paid sufficient attention to its own research findings.

With more than one thousand reading research studies completed each year, it is understandable that no one person can keep up with the evidence. The summaries of research are quite useful, but they are not sufficient. The field, it seems to me, is prolific and important enough to warrant a computerized storage and retrieval service. Such a service can help pull together the relevant research for a periodic synthesis of findings on crucial issues; it can also produce a monthly or bimonthly journal of reading abstracts to serve researchers and college teachers of reading.[2]

But school people—administrators, supervisors, and teachers—need to have the research put into a form that they can use more directly. Periodic summaries on important issues, translated into practical terms, can help. Of greater value to them, however, would be a commitment on the part of authors and publishers of instructional materials to "keep up" with the research and to put it to use in developing their reading programs. Further, publishers of reading programs have an obligation, similar to that of pharmaceutical companies manufacturing drugs, to test

[2] Indeed, we will have one soon. The USOE has supported such a service to be housed at Indiana University.

out their materials, not only for anticipated effects but also for unanticipated consequences.

The research in beginning reading itself needs improvement. As I have indicated throughout this book, too much of the research was undertaken to prove that one ill-defined method was better than another ill-defined method. We need, instead, series of coordinated laboratory as well as extensive longitudinal studies—studies that can give us some definitive answers so that we don't keep researching the same issues over and over again. I do not believe that the kind of research now needed can be left to the schools—to teachers and administrators, who necessarily become emotionally involved with a given approach. Nor can it be left to the part-time interests of a few reading specialists. The conflict between the enthusiasm and involvement that the practitioner must have and the cool, dispassionate observation and analysis that mark the true educational experimenter will not be solved if the experimentation is left to those concerned more with helping than with knowing.

Likewise, the authors of reading programs are not the best researchers to test their own programs. While they should be involved in the early pilot studies of their programs, comparing one's own product with the products of others requires a kind of objectivity that is difficult for any author to develop toward his own work.

My final recommendation is that experiments in beginning reading not be undertaken as if they were the first studies of their kind. Research in reading should follow the norms of science. Each researcher must try to learn from the work of those who preceded him and to add to a unified body of knowledge—knowing that neither he nor anyone following him will ever have the final word.

Bibliography

BOOKS, ARTICLES, DISSERTATIONS, AND OTHER STUDIES

AGNEW, DONALD C.: "The Effect of Varied Amounts of Phonetic Training on Primary Reading," unpublished doctoral dissertation, Duke University, Durham, N.C., 1935.

———: *The Effect of Varied Amounts of Phonetic Training on Primary Reading,* Duke University Research Studies in Education, no. 5, The Duke University Press, Durham, N.C., 1939.

ALMY, MILLIE C.: *Children's Experiences Prior to First Grade and Success in Beginning Reading,* Bureau of Publications, Teachers College, Columbia University, New York, 1949.

ATKINSON, RICHARD C., and DUNCAN H. HANSEN: *Computer-assisted Instruction in Initial Reading: The Stanford Project,* Institute for Mathematical Studies in the Social Sciences, Technical Report 93, Stanford University, Stanford, Calif., March 17, 1966.

AUSTIN, MARY, and COLEMAN MORRISON: *The First R: The Harvard Report on Reading in Elementary Schools,* The Macmillan Company, New York, 1963.

———, ———, et al.: *The Torch Lighters: Tomorrow's Teachers of Reading,* Harvard University Press, Cambridge, Mass., 1961.

BARTON, ALLEN H., and DAVID E. WILDER: "Research and Practice in the Teaching of Reading: A Progress Report," in M. B. Miles (ed.), *Innovation in Education,* Bureau of Publications, Teachers College, Columbia University, New York, 1964, pp. 361–398.

BEAR, DAVID E.: "Phonics for First Grade: A Comparison of Two Methods," *Elementary School Journal,* vol. 59, pp. 394–402, 1959.

———: "Two Methods of Teaching Phonics: A Longitudinal Study," *Elementary School Journal,* vol. 64, pp. 273–279, 1964.

BELL, H. M.: "The Comparative Legibility of Typewriting, Manuscript, and Cursive Script," *Journal of Psychology,* vol. 8, pp. 311–320, 1939.

BENDER, LAURETTA: "Research Studies from Bellevue Hospital on Scientific Reading Disabilities" (résumé), *Bulletin of the Orton Society,* vol. 1, pp. 3–5, 1951. (Reprinted in *Bulletin of the Orton Society,* vol. 6, pp. 1–2, 1956.)

———: "Problems in Conceptualization and Communication in Children with Developmental Alexia," in F. H. Hoch and J. Zubin (eds.), *Psychopathology of Communication,* Grune & Stratton, Inc., New York, 1958, chap. 11.

BETTS, E. A. "Phonics: Practical Considerations Based on Research," *Elementary English,* vol. 33, pp. 357–371, 1956.

BISHOP, CAROL: "Transfer of Word and Letter Training in Reading," unpublished master's thesis, Cornell University, Ithaca, N.Y., 1962. (Cited in Eleanor J. Gibson, "Analysis of the Reading Process as Perceptual Learning," paper presented at the Conference on Perceptual and Linguistic Aspects of Reading, Center for Advanced Study in the Behavioral Sciences, Stanford, Calif., Oct. 31–Nov. 2, 1963.)

BLIESMER, EMERY P., and BETTY H. YARBOROUGH: "A Comparison of Ten Different Beginning Reading Programs in First Grade," *Phi Delta Kappan,* vol. 56, pp. 500–504, 1965.

BLOOMER, RICHARD H.: "An Investigation of an Experimental First Grade Phonics Program," *Journal of Educational Research,* vol. 53, pp. 188–193, 1960.

———: "Reading Methodology: Some Alternative Organizational Principles," *The Reading Teacher,* vol. 14, pp. 167–171, 1961.

BLOOMFIELD, LEONARD: *Language,* Holt, Rinehart and Winston, Inc., New York, 1933.

———: "Linguistics and Reading," *Elementary English Review,* vol. 19, pp. 125–130, 183–186, 1942.

BLOOMFIELD, MILDRED: "Phonics: Specialized Systems Compared to a Basal Reading System," unpublished graduate research seminar paper, The City College, The City University of New York, December, 1962.

BOND, GUY L.: *The Coordinated Phases of the Reading Study,* progress report presented at the Annual Conference of the International Reading Association, Dallas, Tex., May, 1966.

——— and MILES A. TINKER: *Reading Difficulties: Their Diagnosis and Correction,* Appleton-Century-Crofts, Inc., New York, 1957.

BREWER, WILLIAM F., JR.: "Specific Language Disability: Review of the Literature and Family Study," social relations honors thesis, Harvard College, Cambridge, Mass., 1963.

BURT, C., and R. B. LEWIS: "Teaching Backward Readers," *British Journal of Educational Psychology,* vol. 16 pp. 116–132, 1946.

BUSWELL, GUY T.: *Fundamental Reading Habits: A Study of Their Develop-*

ment, Supplementary Educational Monographs, no. 21, The University of Chicago Press, Chicago, 1922.

———: *Non-oral Reading: A Study of Its Use in the Chicago Public Schools,* Supplementary Educational Monographs, no. 6, The University of Chicago Press, Chicago, 1945.

CARROLL, JOHN B.: "Research in Education: Where Do We Stand?" *Graduate School of Education Association Bulletin,* vol. 5, pp. 3–7, Winter, 1960.

———: "Research on Reading and Its Teaching," *Educational Psychology and Educational Research,* study prepared for James B. Conant, Harvard University, Cambridge, Mass., September, 1961. (Mimeographed.)

———: "The Analysis of Reading Instruction: Perspectives from Psychology and Linguistics," in *Theories of Learning and Instruction,* Sixty-third Yearbook of the National Society for the Study of Education, The University of Chicago Press, Chicago, pp. 336–353, 1964.

CATTELL, J. MCK.: "The Time It Takes to See and Name Objects," *Mind,* vol. 11, pp. 63–65, 1886.

CHALL, JEANNE: "The History of Controlled Vocabulary," in J. Allen Fugurel (ed.), *Reading for Effective Living: International Reading Association Proceedings,* vol. 3, pp. 177–180, 1958a.

———: *Readability: An Appraisal of Research and Application,* Bureau of Educational Research, Ohio State University, Columbus, Ohio, 1958b.

———:"The Roswell-Chall Diagnostic Reading Test of Word Analysis Skills: Evidence of Reliability and Validity," *The Reading Teacher,* vol. 11, pp. 179–183, 1958c.

——— and SHIRLEY FELDMANN: "First Grade Reading: An Analysis of the Interactions of Professed Methods, Teacher Implementation and Child Background," *The Reading Teacher,* vol. 19, pp. 569–575, 1966.

———, FLORENCE ROSWELL, LEONARD ALSHAN, and MILDRED BLOOMFIELD: "Language, Visual, Auditory, and Visual-motor Factors in Beginning Reading: A Preliminary Analysis," paper presented to the American Educational Research Association, Chicago, Feb. 11, 1965.

———, ———, and SUSAN H. BLUMENTHAL: "Auditory Blending Ability: A Factor in Success in Beginning Reading," *The Reading Teacher,* vol. 17, pp. 113–118, 1963.

CLYMER, THEODORE: "The Utility of Phonic Generalizations in the Primary Grades," *The Reading Teacher,* vol. 16, pp. 252–258, 1963.

COMMITTEE ON RESEARCH AND GUIDANCE OF THE DEPARTMENT OF PUBLIC INSTRUCTION, QUEENSLAND, AUSTRALIA: *An Investigation of Methods of Teaching Reading in Infant Schools,* Bulletin 9, 1955.

COOK, DESMOND L.: *The Relation of Possible Hawthorne Effect Components to Stages of Experimental Investigation,* Bureau of Educational Research and Service, Ohio State University, Columbus, Ohio, 1963. (Mimeographed.)

COTTRELL, ALICE, and GRACE BROWN: *Stanford Diagnostic Phonic Survey Manual* (research edition), Consulting Psychologists Press, Palo Alto, Calif., 1958.

CROSSLEY, BEATRICE A.: "An Evaluation of the Effect of Lantern Slides on

Auditory and Visual Discrimination of Word Elements," unpublished doctoral dissertation, Boston University, Boston, Mass., 1948.

CURRIER, LILLIAN B.: "Phonics and No Phonics," *Elementary School Journal,* vol. 23, pp. 448–452, 1923.

——— and OLIVE C. DUGUID: "Phonics or No Phonics?" *Elementary School Journal,* vol. 17, pp. 286–287, 1916.

DANIELS, J. C., and HUNTER DIACK: *Progress in Reading,* Institute of Education, University of Nottingham, Nottingham, England, 1956.

——— and ———: *Progress in Reading in the Infant School,* Institute of Education, University of Nottingham, Nottingham, England, pp. 1–99, 1960.

DAVIDSON, HELEN P.: "An Experimental Study of Bright, Average, and Dull Children at the Four-year Mental Level," *Genetic Psychology Monographs,* vol. 9, pp. 119–225, 1931.

DECHARMS, RICHARD, and GERALD H. MOELLER: "Values Expressed in American Children's Readers: 1800–1950," *Journal of Abnormal and Social Psychology,* vol. 64, pp. 136–142, 1962.

DE HIRSCH KATRINA: "Gestalt Psychology as Applied to Language Disturbance," *Journal of Nervous and Mental Disorders,* vol. 120, pp. 257–261, 1954.

———: "Tests Designed to Discover Potential Reading Difficulties at the Six-year-old Level," *American Journal of Orthopsychiatry,* vol. 27, pp. 566–576, 1957.

———, JEANNETTE J. JANSKY, and WILLIAM S. LANGFORD: *Predicting the Failing Reader,* Harper & Row, Publishers, Incorporated, New York, 1966.

DEWEY, GODFREY: *Experimental Investigation of Use of a Phonemic Notation for the First Teaching of Reading and Writing,* Lake Placid Club, New York, 1960, 7 pp. (Mimeographed.)

DOLCH, EDWARD W., and MAURINE BLOOMSTER: "Phonic Readiness," *Elementary School Journal,* vol. 38, pp. 201–205, 1937.

DOMAN, GLENN: *How to Teach Your Baby to Read,* Random House, Inc., New York, 1964.

DOWNING, JOHN A.: "Experiments with an Augmented Alphabet for Beginning Readers in British Schools," paper presented at the Educational Records Bureau Conference, New York City, November, 1962.

———: "The i.t.a. (Initial Teaching Alphabet) Reading Experiment," *The Reading Teacher,* vol. 18, pp. 105–109, 1964a.

———: *The i.t.a. Reading Experiment: Three Lectures on the Research in Infant Schools with Sir James Pitman's Initial Teaching Alphabet,* Evans Brothers, Ltd., London (Published for the Institute of Education, University of London), 1964b.

———: "Current Misconceptions about i.t.a.," *Elementary English,* vol. 42, pp. 492–501, 1965.

———: "i.t.a. Research Studies," paper prepared for the Third International ita Conference, Cambridge, England, 1966a.

———: "Research Report on the British Experiment with ITA," in J. A. Downing, et al., *The ITA Symposium,* National Foundation for Educational Research in England and Wales, Slough, Buckinghamshire, 1966b.

DUNCAN, ROGER L.: "What's the Best Way to Teach Reading?" *School Management,* pp. 46–47, December, 1964a.

———: "Two Methods of Teaching Reading," *Tulsa School Review,* vol. 21, no. 1, pp. 4–5, September, 1964b.

DURKIN, DOLORES: "Early Readers—Reflections after Six Years of Research," *The Reading Teacher,* vol. 18, pp. 3–7, 1964.

DURRELL, DONALD D.: "First-grade Reading Success Study: A Summary," *Journal of Education,* vol. 140, pp. 2–6, 1958.

——— and HELEN A. MURPHY: "The Auditory Discrimination Factor in Reading Readiness and Reading Disability," *Education,* vol. 73, pp. 556–560, 1953.

EDFELDT, AKE W.: *Silent Speech and Silent Reading,* The University of Chicago Press, Chicago, 1960.

FERNALD, GRACE: *Remedial Techniques in Basic School Subjects,* McGraw-Hill Book Company, New York, 1943.

FEUERS, STELLE: "The Relationship between Knowledge of Letter Names and Sounds and Word Recognition in First Grade," unpublished master's thesis, The City College, The City University of New York, 1961.

FLEMING, JAMES T.: "The Measurement of Children's Perception of Difficulty in Reading Materials," unpublished doctoral dissertation, Harvard University, Cambridge, Mass., 1966.

FLESCH, RUDOLF: *Why Johnny Can't Read and What You Can Do about It,* Harper & Brothers, New York, 1955.

FLINTON, DORIS H.: *A Three-year Research Project in Beginning Reading and Language Teaching,* Bethlehem Central Schools, Delmar, N.Y., 1962. (Mimeographed.)

FORMAN, NAOMI: "The Relationship of Phonic Ability to Reading Performance and Intelligence of Elementary School Students," unpublished graduate research seminar paper, The City College, The City University of New York, June, 1962.

FOWLER, WILLIAM: "Cognitive Learning in Infancy and Early Childhood," *Psychological Bulletin,* vol. 59, pp. 116–152, 1962.

FRIES, CHARLES C.: *Linguistics and Reading,* Holt, Rinehart and Winston, Inc., New York, 1962.

——— et al.: *To Teach Reading: The Transfer Stage, a Manual and Guide for Basic Reading Series Developed upon Linguistic Principles* (revised experimental edition), Ann Arbor, Michigan, 1965.

FRY, EDWARD: "A Diacritical Marking System for Beginning Reading Instruction," paper presented at the Conference on Perceptual and Linguistic Aspects of Reading, Center for Advanced Study in the Behavioral Sciences, Stanford, Calif., Oct. 31–Nov. 2, 1963.

GAGE, N. L. (ed.): *Handbook of Research on Teaching,* Rand McNally & Company, Chicago, 1963.

GARDNER, D. E. M.: *Testing Results in the Infant School,* Methuen & Co., Ltd., London, 1942.

GARRISON, S. C., and M. T. HEARD: "An Experimental Study of the Value of Phonetics," *Peabody Journal of Education*, vol. 9, pp. 9–14, 1931.

GATES, ARTHUR I.: *Psychology of Reading and Spelling with Special Reference to Disability*, Contributions to Education, no. 129, Bureau of Publications, Teachers College, Columbia University, New York, 1922.

———: "Studies of Phonetic Training in Beginning Reading," *Journal of Educational Psychology*, vol. 18, pp. 217–226, 1927.

———: *New Methods in Primary Reading*, Bureau of Publications, Teachers College, Columbia University, New York, 1928.

———: *Interest and Ability in Reading*, The Macmillan Company, New York, 1930.

———: "The Necessary Mental Age for Beginning Reading," *Elementary School Journal*, vol. 37, pp. 497–508, 1937.

———: *A Review of Rudolf Flesch's Why Johnny Can't Read*, The Macmillan Company, New York, 1955.

———: "Results of Teaching a System of Phonics," *The Reading Teacher*, vol. 14, pp. 248–252, 1961a.

———: "Vocabulary Control in Basal Reading Material," *The Reading Teacher*, vol. 15, pp. 81–85, 1961b.

———, MILDRED I. BATCHELDER, and JEAN BETZNER: "A Modern Systematic versus an Opportunistic Method of Teaching: An Experimental Study," *Teachers College Record*, vol. 27, pp. 679–700, 1926.

——— and ELOISE BOEKER: "A Study in Initial Stages in Reading," *Teachers College Record*, vol. 24, pp. 469–90, 1923.

———, GUY L. BOND, and DAVID H. RUSSELL: *Methods of Determining Reading Readiness*, Bureau of Publications, Teachers College, Columbia University, New York, 1939.

——— and DAVID H. RUSSELL: "Types of Materials, Vocabulary Burden, Word Analysis, and Other Factors in Beginning Reading," *Elementary School Journal*, vol. 39, pp. 27–35, 119–128, 1938.

GAVEL, SYLVIA R.: "June Reading Achievements of First-grade Children," *Journal of Education*, Boston University, vol. 140, pp. 37–43, 1958.

GIBSON, ELEANOR J.: "A Developmental Comparison of the Perception of Words, Pronounceable Trigrams and Unpronounceable Trigrams," unpublished research memorandum, Cornell University, Ithaca, N.Y., 1962.

———: "Analysis of the Reading Process as Perceptual Learning," paper presented at the Conference on Perceptual and Linguistic Aspects of Reading, Center for Advanced Study in the Behavioral Sciences, Stanford, Calif., Oct. 31–Nov. 2, 1963.

———, J. J. GIBSON, ANNE DANIELSON, H. OSSER, and MARCIA HAMMOND: "The Role of Grapheme-phoneme Correspondence in Word Perception," *American Journal of Psychology*, vol. 75, pp. 554–570, 1962.

GILL, EDMUND J.: "Methods of Teaching Reading: A Comparison of Results," *Journal of Experimental Pedagogy*, vol. 1, pp. 243–248, 1912.

GOLD, HYMAN: *A Comparison of Two First-grade Reading Programs*, doctoral dissertation, University of Southern California, Los Angeles, 1964. (Cited in *Dissertation Abstracts*, vol. 25, no. 6, December, 1964.)

GRAY, WILLIAM S.: *Remedial Cases in Reading: Their Diagnosis and Treatment,* Supplementary Educational Monographs, no. 22, The University of Chicago Press, Chicago, 1922.

———: *Summary of Investigations Relating to Reading,* Supplementary Educational Monographs, no. 28, The University of Chicago Press, Chicago, 1925.

———: "Summary of Reading Investigations" [1925–1932], *Journal of Educational Research,* vol. 26, pp. 401–424, 1933. (Similar summaries published yearly in the February issue of the same journal, 1934–1960.)

———: *On Their Own in Reading,* Scott, Foresman and Company, Chicago, 1948; 2d ed., 1960.

———: *The Teaching of Reading and Writing: An International Survey,* Scott, Foresman and Company, Chicago, 1956.

GRIMES, J. W., and WESLEY ALLINSMITH: "Compulsivity, Anxiety, and School Achievement," *Merrill-Palmer Quarterly of Behavior and Development,* vol. 7, pp. 247–269, 1961.

HALL, ROBERT A., JR.: *Sound and Spelling in English,* Chilton Company—Book Division, Philadelphia, 1961.

HANSEN, CARL F.: *The Amidon Elementary School,* Prentice-Hall, Inc., Englewood Cliffs, N.J., 1962.

HARRIS, ALBERT J.: *Effective Teaching of Reading,* David McKay Co., Inc., New York, 1962.

HARRIS, THEODORE L.: "Some Issues in Beginning Reading Instruction," *Journal of Educational Research,* vol. 56, pp. 5–20, 1962.

———: "Summary of Investigations Relating to Reading," *Journal of Educational Research,* vols. 55, 56, 57, 58, 59, February 1962, 1963, 1964, 1965, 1966.

HENDERSON, MARGARET G.: *Progress Report of Reading Study 1952–1955,* Board of Education, Community Unit School District no. 4, Champaign County, Ill.

HILGARD, ERNEST R.: *Theories of Learning,* Appleton-Century-Crofts, Inc., New York, 1948.

HOLMES, JACK A.: "When Should and Could Johnny Learn to Read?" *Challenge and Experiment in Reading: Proceedings of the Seventh Annual Conference of the International Reading Association, Scholastic Magazines,* vol. 7, pp. 237–241, 1962.

——— and HARRY SINGER: *The Substrata-Factor Theory: Substrata-Factor Differences Underlying Reading Ability in Known Groups,* University of California Press, Berkeley, Calif., 1961.

HUEY, EDMUND B.: *The Psychology and Pedagogy of Reading,* The Macmillan Company, New York, 1908.

HUNT, J. MCV.: "Introduction: Revisiting Montessori," in *The Montessori Method,* Schocken Books, Inc., New York, 1964.

HUSET, MARTHA: "Relationship between Difficulty in Auditory Blending and Some Diagnostic Indicators of Organicity in Children of Average or Superior Intelligence with Reading Disability," unpublished master's thesis, The City College, The City University of New York, 1961.

HYATT, ADA V.: *The Place of Oral Reading in the School Program: Its History and Development from 1880–1941,* Contributions to Education, no. 872, Bureau of Publications, Teachers College, Columbia University, New York, 1943.

i/t/a bulletin, Initial Teaching Alphabet Publications, Inc., 20 E. 46th St., New York, N.Y.

KELLY, BARBARA: "The Economy Method versus the Scott, Foresman Method in Teaching Second-grade Reading in the Murphysboro Public Schools," *Journal of Educational Research,* vol. 51, pp. 465–469, February, 1958.

KLEIN, MARION: "Three Decades of Beginning Reading: A Comparison of the Scott, Foresman Series," unpublished master's thesis, The City College, The City University of New York, May, 1964.

KUHN, THOMAS S.: *The Structure of Scientific Revolutions,* The University of Chicago Press, Chicago, 1962.

Learning to Read, A Report of a Conference of Reading Experts, Educational Testing Service, Princeton, N.J., 1962.

LEE, DORIS M., and R. V. ALLEN: *Learning to Read through Experience,* Appleton-Century-Crofts, Inc., New York, 1963.

LEFEVRE, CARL A.: *Linguistics and the Teaching of Reading,* McGraw-Hill Book Company, New York, 1964.

LENNON, ROGER: "The Relation between Intelligence and Achievement Test Results for a Group of Communities," *Journal of Educational Psychology,* vol. 41, pp. 301–308, 1950.

LEVIN, HARRY: "Reading and the Learning of Variable Grapheme-to-phoneme Correspondences," paper presented at the Conference on Perceptual and Linguistic Aspects of Reading, Center for Advanced Study in the Behavioral Sciences, Stanford, Calif., Oct. 31–Nov. 2, 1963.

———: "Reading Research: What, Why, and for Whom?" *Elementary English,* vol. 43, pp. 138–147, 1966.

——— and J. WATSON: *The Learning of Variable Grapheme-to-phoneme Correspondences,* final report of the Basic Research Program on Reading, USOE, Cornell University Press, Ithaca, N.Y., 1963.

———, ———, and MARGARET FELDMAN: "Writing as Pre-training for Association Learning," *Journal of Educational Psychology,* vol. 55, pp. 181–184, 1964.

LINEHAN, ELEANOR B.: "Early Instruction in Letter Names and Sounds as Related to Success in Beginning Reading," *Journal of Education,* Boston University, vol. 140, pp. 44–48, 1958.

LOBAN, WALTER: *The Language of Elementary School Children,* National Council of Teachers of English, Research Report no. 1, 1963.

LORGE, IRVING, and JEANNE CHALL: "Estimating the Size of Vocabularies of Children and Adults: An Analysis of Methodological Issues," *Journal of Experimental Education,* vol. 32, pp. 147–157, 1963.

MCDOWELL, REV. JOHN B.: "A Report on the Phonetic Method of Teaching Children to Read," *Catholic Education Review,* vol. 51, pp. 506–519, 1953.

MACKINNON, A. R.: *How Do Children Learn to Read? An Experimental Investigation of Children's Early Growth in Awareness of the Meanings of Printed Symbols,* The Copp Clark Publishing Co., Ltd., Toronto, Canada, 1959.

MCNEIL, JOHN D., and EVAN R. KEISLAR: "Value of the Oral Response in Beginning Reading: An Experimental Study Using Programmed Instruction," *British Journal of Educational Psychology,* vol. 33, pp. 162–168, 1963.

MALONE, JOHN R.: "Single-sound UNIFON: Does It Fill the Need for a Compatible and Consistent Auxiliary Orthography for Teaching English and Other European Languages?" paper presented at the Conference on Perceptual and Linguistic Aspects of Reading, Center for Advanced Study in the Behavioral Sciences, Stanford, Calif., Oct. 31–Nov. 2, 1963.

MARCHBANKS, GABRIELLE, and LEVIN, HARRY: "Cues by Which Children Recognize Words," *Journal of Educational Psychology,* vol. 56, pp. 57–61, 1965.

MAYER, MARTIN: "The Trouble with Textbooks," *Harper's Magazine,* pp. 65–71, July, 1962.

MAZURKIEWICZ, ALBERT J.: "Teaching Reading in America Using the Initial Teaching Alphabet," *Elementary English,* vol. 41, pp. 766–772, 1964.

MILES, M. B. (ed.): *Innovation in Education,* Bureau of Publications, Teachers College, Columbia University Press, New York, 1964.

MILLS, ROBERT E.: "An Evaluation of Techniques for Teaching Word Recognition," *Elementary School Journal,* vol. 56, pp. 221–225, 1956.

MONEY, JOHN (ed.): *Reading Disability: Progress and Research Needs in Dyslexia,* The Johns Hopkins Press, Baltimore, 1962.

MONROE, MARION: *Children Who Cannot Read,* The University of Chicago Press, Chicago, 1932.

MONTESSORI, MARIA: *The Montessori Method,* Schocken Books, Inc., New York, 1964.

MOORE, OMAR K.: *Autotelic Responsive Environments and Exceptional Children,* Responsive Environments Foundation, Inc., 20 Augur St., Hamden, Conn., Sept. 1, 1963.

——— and ROSS A. ANDERSON: "Early Reading and Writing," a film report, Basic Education, Inc., Washington Plaza, Apt. 2004, 1420 Centre Ave., Pittsburgh, Pa. 15219.

MORGAN, ELMER, JR., and MORTON LIGHT: "A Statistical Evaluation of Two Programs of Reading Instruction," *Journal of Educational Research,* vol. 57, pp. 99–101, 1963.

MORGAN, W. P.: "A Case of Word Blindness," *British Medical Journal,* vol. 2, p. 1378, 1896.

MORPHETT, MABEL V., and C. WASHBURNE: "When Should Children Begin to Read?" *Elementary School Journal,* vol. 31, pp. 496–503, 1931.

MORRIS, JOYCE: *Reading in the Primary School: An Investigation into Standards of Reading and Their Association with Primary School Characteristics* (National Foundation for Educational Research in England and Scotland), London: Newnes Educational Publishing Company, Ltd., 1959.

MOSHER, RAYMOND M.: "Some Results of Teaching Beginners by the Look-and-say Method," *Journal of Educational Psychology,* vol. 19, pp. 185–193, 1928.

——— and SIDNEY M. NEWHALL: "Phonic versus Look-and-say Training in Beginning Reading," *Journal of Educational Psychology,* vol. 21, pp. 500–506, 1930.

MURPHY, HELEN A.: "An Evaluation of the Effects of Specific Training in Auditory and Visual Discrimination on Reading Readiness," unpublished doctoral dissertation, Boston University, Boston, Mass., 1943.

NICHOLSON, ALICE: "Background Abilities Related to Reading Success in First Grade," *Journal of Education,* vol. 140, pp. 7–24, 1958.

OLSON, ARTHUR V.: "Growth in Word Perception Abilities as It Relates to Success in Beginning Reading," *Journal of Education,* vol. 140, pp. 25–36, 1958.

ORTON, SAMUEL T.: *Reading, Writing and Speech Problems in Children,* W. W. Norton & Company, Inc., New York, 1937.

PETERS, M. L.: "The Influence of Certain Reading Methods in the Spelling Ability of Junior School Children" (abstract), *Bulletin of the British Psychological Society,* vol. 19, 1966.

PEYTON, EDITH M., and JAMES P. PORTER: "Old and New Methods of Teaching Primary Reading," *Journal of Applied Psychology,* vol. 10, pp. 264–276, 1926.

PITMAN, I. J.: "Learning to Read: An Experiment," *Journal of the Royal Society of Arts,* vol. 109, pp. 149–180, 1961.

PITMAN, SIR JAMES: "The Future of the Teaching of Reading," paper presented at the Educational Conference of the Educational Records Bureau, New York City, Oct. 30–Nov. 1, 1963.

POPPY, JOHN: "Sullivan's Crusade: Schools without Pain," *Look,* June 18, 1966, p. 39.

PORTER, DOUGLAS, HELEN POPP, and JOANNE ROBINSON: *Development and Validation of Wide-range, Flexible, Self-instructional Reading Programs,* proposal to the Ford Foundation, Harvard University, Cambridge, Mass., 1965. (Mimeographed.)

Project Literacy Reports, Cornell University, Ithaca, N.Y. (Mimeographed.)

Project Literacy: Summary of First Grade Study, 1965–1966, Cornell University, Ithaca, N.Y., 1966. (Mimeographed.)

RABINOVITCH, R. D., A. L. DREW, R. M. DEJONG, W. INGRAM, and L. WITNEY: "A Research Approach to Reading Retardation," in R. McIntosh and C. C. Hare (eds.), *Neurology and Psychiatry in Childhood,* The Williams & Wilkins Co., Baltimore, 1956, Chap. 15.

The Reading Teacher, vol. 19, no. 8, May, 1966. (Contains summaries of most of the twenty-seven USOE First-grade Studies.)

RIEDLER, CAROLE R.: "A Content Analysis of Reviews of Rudolf Flesch's Book: Why Johnny Can't Read," unpublished graduate research seminar paper, The School of Education, The City College, The City University of New York, 1962.

ROBINSON, HELEN M.: *Why Pupils Fail in Reading,* The University of Chicago Press, Chicago, 1946.

———: "News and Comment: Methods of Teaching Beginning Readers," *Elementary School Journal,* vol. 59, pp. 419–426, 1959.

———: "Summary of Investigations Relating to Reading," *Journal of Educational Research,* February, 1961.

———: *The Reading Teacher,* February, 1963, 1964, 1965.

ROGERS, MAURINE: "Phonic Ability as Related to Certain Aspects of Reading at the College Level," *Journal of Experimental Education,* vol. 6, pp. 381–395, 1938.

ROSWELL, FLORENCE, and GLADYS NATCHEZ: *Reading Disability: Diagnosis and Treatment,* Basic Books, Inc., Publishers, New York, 1964.

RUDISILL, MABEL: "The Interrelations of Functional Phonic Knowledge, Reading, Spelling, and Mental Age," *Elementary School Journal,* vol. 42, pp. 264–267, 1957.

RUSSELL, DAVID H.: "A Diagnostic Study of Spelling Readiness," *Journal of Educational Research,* vol. 37, pp. 276–283, 1943.

SAN DIEGO COUNTY, CALIF., SUPERINTENDENT OF SCHOOLS: "Description of Three Approaches to the Teaching of Reading," *Improving Reading Instruction,* Monograph no. 2, pp. 10–13, 20–25, May, 1961.

SANTEUSIANO, NANCY C.: "Evaluation of a Planned Program for Teaching Homophones in Beginning Reading," unpublished doctoral dissertation, Boston University, Boston, Mass., 1962.

SCHONELL, FRED J.: *Backwardness in the Basic Subjects,* Oliver & Boyd, Ltd., Edinburgh and London, 1938; 4th ed., 1948.

SEXTON E., and J. HERRON: "The Newark Phonics Experiment," *Elementary School Journal,* vol. 28, pp. 690–701, 1928.

SHOLTY, MYRTLE: "A Study of the Reading Vocabulary of Children," *Elementary School Teacher,* vol. 12, pp. 272–297, 1912.

SILBERMAN, HARRY F.: *Reading and Related Verbal Learning,* Systems Development Corporation, Santa Monica, Calif., Aug. 9, 1963.

SILVER, ARCHIE A., and ROSA HAGIN: "Specific Reading Disability: Delineation of the Syndrome and Relationship to Cerebral Dominance," *Comprehensive Psychiatry,* vol. 1, pp. 126–134, 1960.

SINGER, HARRY: "Substrata-factor Theory of Reading: Theoretical Design for Teaching Reading," in J. Allen Fugurel (ed.), *Challenge and Experiment in Reading: International Reading Association Proceedings,* vol. 7, pp. 226–232, 1962.

SISTER MARY EDWARD, P.B.V.M.: "A Modified Linguistic versus a Composite Basal Reading Program," *The Reading Teacher,* vol. 17, pp. 511–515, 1964.

SISTER MARY FIDELIA: "The Relative Effectiveness of Bloomfield's Linguistic Approach to Word-attack as Compared with Phonics We Use," unpublished doctoral dissertation, School of Psychology and Education, University of Ottawa, Ottawa, Canada, 1959.

SLEDD, JAMES: *A Short Introduction to English Grammar,* Scott, Foresman and Company, Chicago, 1959.

SMITH, HENRY L.: *Linguistics and the Teaching of English,* Harvard University Press, Cambridge, Mass., 1956.

SMITH, NILA B.: "The Construction of First-grade Reading Material," *Journal of Educational Research*, vol. 17, pp. 79–89, 1928.
———: *American Reading Instruction*, Silver Burdett Company, Morristown, N. J., 1934.
———: "What Research Tells Us about Word Recognition," *Elementary School Journal*, vol. 55, pp. 440–446, 1955.
———: *Historical Research on Phonics and Word Method in America*, New York University, New York, 1963. (Mimeographed.)
———: *American Reading Instruction*, The International Reading Association, Newark, Del., 1965.
SOFFIETTI, JAMES: "Why Children Fail to Read: A Linguistic Analysis," *Harvard Educational Review*, vol. 25, pp. 63–84, 1955.
SPARKS, PAUL: "An Evaluation of Two Methods of Teaching Reading," unpublished doctoral dissertation, School of Education, Indiana University, Bloomington, Ind., August, 1956.
——— and LEO C. FAY: "An Evaluation of Two Methods of Teaching Reading," *Elementary School Journal*, vol. 42, pp. 386–390, 1957.
STRICKLAND, RUTH G.: "The Language of Elementary School Children: Its Relationship to the Language of Reading Textbooks and the Quality of Reading of Selected Materials," *Bulletin of the School of Education, Indiana University*, vol. 38, no. 4, July, 1962.
TANYZER, HAROLD J., and HARVEY ALPERT: "Three Different Basal Reading Systems and First Grade Achievement," *The Reading Teacher*, vol. 19, pp. 636–642, 1966.
TATE, HARRY L.: "The Influence of Phonics on Silent Reading in Grade I," *Elementary School Journal*, vol. 37, pp. 752–63, 1937.
———, THERESA M. HERBERT, and JOSEPHINE K. ZEMAN: "Nonphonic Primary Reading," *Elementary School Journal*, vol. 40, pp. 529–37, 1940.
TAUBER, ABRAHAM: *Spelling Reform in the United States*, unpublished doctoral dissertation, Columbia University, New York, 1958.
TEMPLIN, MILDRED C.: "Phonic Knowledge and Its Relation to the Spelling and Reading Achievement of Fourth Grade Pupils," *Journal of Educational Research*, vol. 47, pp. 441–454, 1954.
TENSUAN, EMPERATRIZ S., and FREDERICK B. DAVIS: "The Phonic Method versus the Combination Method in Teaching Beginning Reading," *Educational Developmental Laboratories Reading Newsletter*, vol. 28, pp. 1–6, January, 1963. See also "The Psychology of Beginning Reading: An Experiment with Two Methods." Paper Presented at Conference on Perceptual and Linguistic Aspects of Reading, Oct. 31–Nov. 2, 1963, Center for Advanced Study in the Behavioral Sciences, Stanford, California.
TERMAN, SIBYL, and CHARLES C. WALCUTT: *Reading: Chaos and Cure*, McGraw-Hill Book Company, New York, 1958.
THORNDIKE, EDWARD L.: "Reading as Reasoning: A Study of Mistakes in Paragraph Reading," *Journal of Educational Psychology*, vol. 8, pp. 323–332, 1917.
TIERNEY, CATHLEEN: "The Relation of Phonic Ability to Reading and Intelli-

gence of High School Students," unpublished graduate research seminar paper, The City College, The City University of New York, June, 1961.

TIFFIN, JOSEPH, and MARY MCKINNIS: "Phonic Ability: Its Measurement and Relation to Reading Ability," *School and Society,* vol. 41, pp. 190–92, 1940.

TINKER, MILES, and D. PATTERSON: "Eye Movements in Reading a Modern Face and Old English," *American Journal of Psychology,* vol. 54, pp. 113–115, 1940.

TISCHER, ESTELLE: *A Critical Review of Research and Opinion on Phonics,* The University of the State of New York, The State Education Department, Division of Research, Albany, N.Y., 1963.

TRACE, ARTHUR, JR.: *What Ivan Knows That Johnny Doesn't,* McGraw-Hill Book Company, New York, 1962.

TRAXLER, ARTHUR, with the assistance of the staff of the Educational Records Bureau: *Research in Reading,* Educational Records Bureau, New York, 1941, 1946, 1955, 1960.

VALENTINE, C. W.: "Experiments on the Methods of Teaching Reading," *Journal of Experimental Pedagogy,* vol. 2, pp. 99–112, 1913.

VERNON, M. D.: *Backwardness in Reading: A Study of Its Nature and Origin,* Cambridge University Press, New York, 1957.

WALCUTT, CHARLES C. (ed.): *Tomorrow's Illiterates,* Little, Brown and Company, Boston, 1961.

WEINER, MAX, and SHIRLEY FELDMANN: "Validation Studies of a Reading Prognosis Test for Children of Lower and Middle Socio-economic Status," *Educational and Psychological Measurement,* vol. 23, pp. 807–814, 1963.

WEINTRAUB, SAM: "The Effect of Pictures on the Comprehension of a Second-grade Basal Reader, doctoral dissertation, University of Illinois, Urbana, Ill., 1960. (Available from University Microfilms Inc., Ann Arbor, Mich.)

WILDER, DAVID E.: "Social Factors Related to the Public Awareness, Perception, and Evaluation of the Teaching of Reading," paper presented at the Annual Meeting of the American Educational Research Association, Chicago, Feb. 8, 1965.

———: "The Reading Experts: A Case Study of the Failure to Institutionalize an Applied Science of Education," unpublished doctoral dissertation, Columbia University, New York, 1966.

WILEY, E. G.: "Difficult Words and the Beginner," *Journal of Educational Research,* vol. 17, pp. 278–89, 1928.

WILSON, FRANK T., and C. W. FLEMMING: "Correlations of Reading Progress with Other Abilities and Traits in Grade 1," *Journal of Genetic Psychology,* vol. 53, pp. 33–52, 1938.

———, ———, AGNES BURKE, and C. G. GARRISON: "Reading Progress in Kindergarten and Primary Grades," *Elementary School Journal,* vol. 38, pp. 442–449, 1938.

WINCH, W. H.: *Teaching Beginners to Read in England: Its Methods, Results, and Psychological Bases, Journal of Educational Research* Monographs, no. 8, Public School Publishing Company, Bloomington, Ill., 1925.

WITMER, L.: "A Case of Chronic Bad Spelling: Amnesia Visualis Verbalis Due to Arrest of Post-natal Development," *Journal of Clinical Psychology,* vol. 1, pp. 53–64, 1907.

WOHLEBER, SISTER MARY: *A Study of the Effects of a Systematic Program of Phonetic Training on Primary Reading,* unpublished doctoral dissertation, University of Pittsburgh, Pittsburgh, Pa., June, 1953.

WOLLAM, WALTER A.: *A Comparison of Two Methods of Teaching Reading,* unpublished doctoral dissertation, Western Reserve University, Cleveland, Ohio, 1961.

WOODWARD, ETTA K.: "Perception of Artificial Words by Beginning Readers," unpublished master's thesis, Cornell University, Ithaca, N.Y., 1962.

WYCKOFF, A. E.: "Constitutional Bad Spellers," *Pedagogical Seminary,* vol. 2, pp. 448–451, 1893.

READING PROGRAMS

ALLEN, ROBERT A., and VIRGINIA F. ALLEN: *Read Along with Me,* Bureau of Publications, Teachers College, Columbia University, New York, 1964.

BANK STREET COLLEGE OF EDUCATION: *The Bank Street Basal Reading Program,* The Macmillan Company, New York, 1965 and 1966.

BLOOMFIELD, LEONARD, and CLARENCE L. BARNHART: *Let's Read: A Linguistic Approach,* Wayne State University Press, Detroit, Mich., 1961.

——— and ———: *Let's Read* (experimental ed.), Clarence L. Barnhart, Inc., Bronxville, N.Y., 1963.

BUCHANAN, CYNTHIA D., and SULLIVAN ASSOCIATES: *Programmed Reading,* McGraw-Hill Book Company, New York, 1963.

CARDEN, MAE: *The Carden Method,* Mae Carden, Inc., Glen Rock, N.J., 1953.

CARILLO, LAWRENCE W. (ed.): *Chandler Language-Experience Readers,* Chandler Publishing Company, San Francisco, Calif., 1964.

DANIELS, J. C., and HUNTER DIACK: *The Royal Road Readers,* Chatto & Windus, Ltd., London, 1960.

ELSON, WILLIAM H., and WILLIAM S. GRAY: *The Elson Basic Readers, Book One,* Scott, Foresman and Company, Chicago, 1931.

——— and LAURA E. RUNKEL: *The Elson Readers, Book One,* Scott, Foresman and Company, Chicago, 1920.

——— and ———: *Manual for the Elson Readers, Book One,* Scott, Foresman and Company, Chicago, 1920.

FRIES, CHARLES C., AGNES C. FRIES, ROSEMARY G. WILSON, and MILDRED K. RUDOLF: *A Basic Reading Series Developed upon Linguistic Principles,* (preliminary and experimental edition), Ann Arbor, Michigan, 1963. (1966 edition entitled *Merrill Linguistic Readers,* Charles E. Merrill Books, Inc., Columbus, Ohio.)

GATTEGNO, CALEB: *Words in Color,* Encyclopaedia Britannica, Inc., Chicago, 1964.

GIBSON, CHRISTINE M., and IVOR A. RICHARDS: *Language through Pictures Series,* Washington Square Press, Pocket Books, Inc., New York, 1963.

GILLINGHAM, ANNA, and BESSIE STILLMAN: *Remedial Training for Children with Specific Difficulty in Reading, Spelling and Penmanship,* Sackett and Williams Lithographing Corp., New York, 1940.

GRAY, WILLIAM S., and MAY ARBUTHNOT: *Our New Friends,* Book 1–2, Scott, Foresman and Company, Chicago, 1946.

——— and LILLIAN GRAY: *Guidebook for Our New Friends,* Scott, Foresman and Company, Chicago, 1946.

———, MARION MONROE, A. STERL ARTLEY, et al.: *The New Basic Reading Program,* Curriculum Foundation Series, Scott, Foresman and Company, Chicago, 1956.

——— and EDNA B. LICK: *Manual for the Elson Basic Readers, Book One,* Scott, Foresman and Company, Chicago, 1931.

GROLIER, TMI, Teaching Machine Course TM-002: *First Steps in Reading for Meaning,* 1964.

HALL, FRANCES A.: *Sounds and Letters,* Linguistica, Box 723, Ithaca, N.Y., 1964.

HAY, JULIE, and CHARLES E. WINGO: *Reading with Phonics,* J. B. Lippincott Company, Philadelphia, 1948 and 1954.

MCCRACKEN, GLENN, and CHARLES C. WALCUTT: *Basic Reading,* J. B. Lippincott Company, Philadelphia, 1963.

MCKEE, PAUL, et al.: *The Reading for Meaning Series,* Houghton Mifflin Company, Boston, 1963.

MAZURKIEWICZ, ALBERT J., and HAROLD J. TANYZER: *Early-to-Read: i/t/a Program,* Initial Teaching Alphabet Publications, Inc., New York, 1963.

PARKER, DON: *Reading Laboratory Ia,* Science Research Associates, Inc., Chicago, 1961a.

———: *Reading Laboratory I: Word Games,* Science Research Associates, Inc., Chicago, 1961b.

RASMUSSEN, DONALD, and LYNN GOLDBERG: *Basic Reading Series,* experimental ed., Science Research Associates, Inc., Chicago, 1964.

ROBINSON, HELEN M., MARION MONROE, and A. STERL ARTLEY: *The New Basic Reading Program,* Curriculum Foundation Series, Scott, Foresman and Company, Chicago, 1962.

RUSSELL, DAVID H., et al.: *The Ginn Basic Readers,* Ginn and Company, Boston, 1961.

SCHOOLFIELD, LUCILLE D., and JOSEPHINE B. TIMBERLAKE: *Phonovisual Method,* Phonovisual Products, Box 5625, Friendship Station, Washington, D.C., 1944, 1945, 1953, 1960, and 1961.

SISTER MARY CAROLINE, I.H.M.: *Breaking the Sound Barrier,* The Macmillan Company, New York, 1960.

SLOOP, CORNELIA B., et. al.: *Phonetic Keys to Reading, and Keys to Independence in Reading,* The Economy Company, Oklahoma City, Okla., 1952, 1953, and 1958.

SPALDING, ROMALDA B., and WALTER T. SPALDING: *The Writing Road to Reading,* William Morrow and Company, Inc., New York, 1962.

STERN, CATHERINE: *The Structural Reading Series,* The L. W. Singer Company, Inc., Syracuse, N.Y., 1963.

STRATEMEYER, CLARA G., and HENRY L. SMITH, JR.: *The Linguistic Science Readers,* Harper & Row, Publishers, Incorporated, New York, 1963.

VEATCH, JEANETTE: *Individualizing Your Reading Program,* G. P. Putnam's Sons, New York, 1959.

WOOLMAN, MYRON: *Reading in High Gear,* Science Research Associates, Inc., Chicago, 1964.

———: *Lift Off to Reading,* Science Research Associates, Inc., Chicago, 1966.

WRITERS' COMMITTEE OF THE GREAT CITIES SCHOOL IMPROVEMENT PROGRAM OF THE DETROIT PUBLIC SCHOOLS: *City Schools Reading Program,* Follett Publishing Company, Chicago, 1962.

GLOSSARY OF NAMES FOR READING PROGRAMS

This section is intended to help the reader identify beginning reading programs frequently referred to in this book and elsewhere either by their full titles or by the popular shortened versions that teachers, school administrators, and researchers generally use. These and other, less frequently mentioned programs are listed in the second section of the bibliography under their authors' names.

This section also contains up-to-date information on the programs gathered from a questionnaire that I sent to the various publishers in late Spring, 1966. At that time I asked the publishers to indicate the major emphasis of their programs; note that their answers do not always agree with my classifications.

Multiple publication dates for a program indicate either several copyrights or single copyrights for individual books in a series.

ALLEN READING MATERIALS

Full title: Read Along with Me (stories, manual, rhyming words, alphabet cards, and films

Author(s): Robert A. Allen and Virginia F. Allen

Publisher: Teachers College Press, Teachers College, Columbia University, New York

Copyright date(s): 1964

Edition analyzed: 1964

Major emphasis (according to publisher): Spelling patterns

Recent changes and/or plans for revision: No revisions planned, although there will be some adaptation of the films

BANK STREET READERS

Full title: The Bank Street Readers

Author(s): The Bank Street College of Education

Publisher: The Macmillan Company, New York

Copyright date(s): 1965, 1966

Edition analyzed: 1965

Major emphasis (according to publisher): Language Experience

Recent changes and/or plans for revision: None specified

BLOOMFIELD SYSTEM

Full title: Let's Read

Author(s): Leonard Bloomfield and Clarence L. Barnhart

Publisher: Clarence L. Barnhart, Inc., Box 359, Bronxville, N.Y.

Copyright date(s): 1963, 1964, 1965, 1966

Edition analyzed: 1963

Major emphasis (according to publisher): Association of sound and spelling

Recent changes and/or plans for revision:

None specified. The authors are still gathering data.

BREAKING THE SOUND BARRIER

Full title: *Breaking the Sound Barrier*
Author(s): Sister Mary Caroline, I.H.M.
Publisher: The Macmillan Company, New York
Copyright date(s): 1960
Edition analyzed: 1960
Major emphasis (according to publisher): Phonics
Recent changes and/or plans for revision: None specified

BRS

Full title: *SRA Basic Reading Series*
Author(s): Donald Rasmussen and Lynn Goldberg
Publisher: Science Research Associates, Inc., Chicago
Copyright date(s): 1964, 1965, 1966
Edition analyzed: 1964 (experimental)
Major emphasis (according to publisher): Linguistic
Recent changes and/or plans for revision: None specified

THE CARDEN METHOD

Full title: *The Carden Method*
Author(s): Mae Carden
Publisher: Mae Carden, Inc., Glen Rock, N.J.
Copyright date(s): 1946–1948,* 1950–1955, 1959, 1964–1966
Edition analyzed: 1953
Major emphasis (according to publisher): Language-arts approach
Recent changes and/or plans for revision: None specified

CHANDLER READERS

Full title: *The Chandler Reading Program* (books, films, etc.); *Chandler Language-Experience Readers* (pupils' readers)
Author(s): Lawrence W. Carillo (ed.)
Publisher: Chandler Publishing Company, San Francisco
Copyright date(s): 1964 (readiness materials); all other materials: 1965, 1966
Edition analyzed: 1964
Major emphasis (according to publisher): Eclectic ("every established method of teaching reading")
Recent changes and/or plans for revision: Books will be continued through grade 6. The author of the second-grade book will be Dr. Marjorie Westcott Barrows.

CITY SCHOOLS

Full title: *City Schools Reading Program*
Author(s): Writers' Committee of the Great Cities School Improvement Program of the Detroit Public Schools
Publisher: Follett Publishing Company, Chicago
Copyright date(s): 1962, 1964, 1965, 1966
Edition analyzed: 1962
Major emphasis (according to publisher): Phonics ("although, as you say, you understand that no single approach is used in any series")
Recent changes and/or plans for revision: None specified

GIBSON-RICHARDS,† *or* FIRST STEPS IN READING ENGLISH SERIES

Full title: *Language through Pictures Series*
Author(s): Christine M. Gibson and Ivor A. Richards
Publisher: Washington Square Press, Pocket Books, Inc., New York
Copyright date(s): 1957–1959, 1959 (Books 1 to 4 revised)
Edition analyzed: 1963

* Hyphenated dates indicate that various parts of the series were written or revised in different years and that the development or revision of the complete series took place between the years specified.

† I refer to this program as Gibson-Richards.

Major emphasis (according to publisher): Reading for meaning with attention to alphabetic identification and word intake
Recent changes and/or plans for revision: None specified

GINN BASIC READERS
Full title: The Ginn Basic Readers
Author(s): David H. Russell et al.
Publisher: Ginn and Company, Boston
Copyright date(s): 1948, 1949, 1952, 1953, 1963–1966
Edition analyzed: 1961
Major emphasis (according to publisher): Developmental
Recent changes and/or plans for revision: In the 1966 (Ginn 100) edition Theodore Clymer is associated with grades 3 to 6. To provide materials for teachers who favor earlier introduction of phonics skills and a faster pace of instruction, Ginn and Company has in preparation the *Ginn Word Enrichment,* by Theodore Clymer and Thomas C. Barrett. These materials may be used either with the 1966 edition or with earlier ones.

HAY-WINGO
Full title: Reading with Phonics
Author(s): Julie Hay and Charles E. Wingo
Publisher: J. B. Lippincott Company, Philadelphia
Copyright date(s): 1948, 1954, 1960 (revised), 1967 (in process of being revised)
Editions analyzed: 1948, 1954
Major emphasis (according to publisher): Phonics
Recent changes and/or plans for revision: The 1967 edition will include multicultural or multiethnic art. The basic philosophy will remain the same.

i/t/a SERIES
Full title: Early-to-Read: i/t/a Program
Author(s): Albert J. Mazurkiewicz and Harold J. Tanyzer
Publisher: Initial Teaching Alphabet Publications, Inc., New York
Copyright date(s): 1963–1964 (preliminary edition), 1965, 1966 (revised)
Edition analyzed: 1963
Major emphasis (according to publisher): Eclectic
Recent changes and/or plans for revision: In the latest (1966) revision, the authors have added material to beginning readers to strengthen a child's developing skills when he is just starting to gain fluency; they have included a series of library books coordinated with text levels to extend the i/t/a pupil's reading practice into supplementary books he can read independently; and they have reduced the number of stories at the upper-reader level when the pupil is in the fluency-transition stage and reads books in our regular alphabet as easily as he reads i/t/a.

LINGUISTIC READERS *or* FRIES LINGUISTIC READERS
Full title: A Basic Reading Series Developed upon Linguistic Principles
Author(s): Charles C. Fries, Agnes C. Fries, Rosemary G. Wilson, and Mildred K. Rudolf
Publisher: Fries Publications, Ann Arbor, Mich. *Also published by:* Charles E. Merrill Books, Inc., Columbus, Ohio
Copyright date(s): 1963, 1964 (preliminary and experimental edition), 1965 (revised), 1966 (revised)
Edition analyzed: 1963
Major emphasis (according to publisher): Teaching the child to *read* for the meanings involved. ["Definitely not a decoding program" (the authors)]
Recent changes and/or plans for revision: The new 1966 edition, published by Charles E. Merrill, will have no basic changes.

LIPPINCOTT BASIC READING PROGRAM
Full title: Basic Reading
Author(s): Glenn McCracken and Charles C. Walcutt

Publisher: J. B. Lippincott Company, Philadelphia
Copyright date(s): 1963, 1965, 1966 (grades 1 to 3: revised)
Edition analyzed: 1963
Major emphasis (according to publisher): "Phonological Linguistic"
Recent changes and/or plans for revision: Recent revisions were made to reflect the multicultural, multiracial composition of American society. No future plans have been specified.

PHONETIC KEYS TO READING (Grades 1–6)

Full title: *Phonetic Keys to Reading* and *Keys to Independence in Reading*
Author(s): Theodore L. Harris, Mildred Creekmore, and Margaret Greenman
Publisher: The Economy Company, Oklahoma City, Okla.
Copyright date(s): *Phonetic Keys to Reading:* 1952, 1964; *Keys to Independence in Reading:* 1960, 1965
Editions analyzed: 1952, 1953, 1958
Major emphasis (according to publisher): "Dual approach" (timing and emphasis on phonics and the relationship of phonics to the development of the reading vocabulary, along with the skills for teaching reading).
Recent changes and/or plans for revision: None specified

PHONOVISUAL METHOD

Full title: *Phonovisual Method*
Author(s): Lucille D. Schoolfield and Josephine B. Timberlake
Publisher: Phonovisual Products, Box 5625, Friendship Station, Washington, D.C.
Copyright date(s): 1944, 1960
Editions analyzed: 1944, 1945, 1953, 1960
Major emphasis (according to publisher): Phonic ("phonics" is "another tool"—a "supplement" not a "substitute" for sight reading or the various other means of word recognition)
Recent changes and/or plans for revision: More detailed instructions and refinements for use at kindergarten, primary, and remedial levels are to be included.

PROGRAMMED READING SERIES

Full title: *Programmed Reading*
Author(s): Cynthia D. Buchanan and Sullivan Associates
Publisher: McGraw-Hill Book Company, New York
Copyright date(s): 1963–1966
Edition analyzed: 1963
Major emphasis (according to publisher): Linguistic approach
Recent changes and/or plans for revision: The first three levels will be revised; but the authors, the content, and the methods emphasis are not likely to change. Books will be extended through grade 6.

THE READING FOR MEANING SERIES

Full title: *The Reading for Meaning Series*
Author(s): Paul McKee, Annie McCowen, Lucile Harrison, Elizabeth Lehr, and William Durr
Publisher: Houghton Mifflin Company, Boston
Copyright date(s): 1949, 1957, 1963, 1966 (revised)
Edition analyzed: 1963
Major emphasis (according to publisher): Consonant-sound plus context approach
Recent changes and/or plans for revision: The most recent revision (1966) included a new author, William K. Durr; new multicolor art; story revisions and replacements; and greater emphasis on the use of consonant-sound associations together with context in unlocking strange words. "No change in the methodology or philosophy."

THE ROYAL ROAD SERIES

Full title: *The Royal Road Readers*
Author(s): J. C. Daniels, and Hunter Diack
Publisher: Chatto & Windus, Ltd., London
Copyright date(s): 1954, 1959 (revised edition)
Edition analyzed: 1960
Major emphasis (according to publisher): Phonic-word method
Recent changes and/or plans for revision: No immediate plans specified

SCOTT, FORESMAN READING PROGRAM

Full title: *The New Basic Readers Curriculum Foundation Series*
Author(s): Helen M. Robinson, Marion Monroe, and A. Sterl Artley
Publisher: Scott, Foresman and Company, Chicago
Copyright date(s): From 1912 to 1965
Editions analyzed: 1956, 1962
Major emphasis (according to publisher): Meaning approach
Recent changes and/or plans for revision: Another edition will appear in the 1970s, but the changes have not yet been specified.

SOUNDS AND LETTERS

Full title: *Sounds and Letters*
Author(s): Frances A. Hall
Publisher: Linguistica, Box 723, Ithaca, N.Y. *Distributed by:* Chronicle Guidance Publications, Moravia, N.Y.
Copyright date(s): 1956, 1964
Edition analyzed: 1964
Major emphasis (according to publisher): Phonemically based ("I definitely do *not* consider it a *phonic* approach")
Recent changes and/or plans for revision: The series is to be completed, and editorial improvements are to be made.

THE STRUCTURAL READING SERIES

Full title: *The Structural Reading Series*
Author(s): Catherine Stern
Publisher: The L. W. Singer Company, Inc., Syracuse, N.Y.
Copyright date(s): 1963, 1966 (revised)
Edition analyzed: 1963
Major emphasis (according to publisher): Synthetic approach to phonics also called a "modified linguistic approach"
Recent changes and/or plans for revision: In the 1966 edition the author remains the same, as does the method. "The content has changed to reflect the philosophy which acknowledges that we are a nation of many peoples. The synthetic phonic approach has been tightened considerably, and the content reflects the philosophy that words in groups must have significant meaning."

WOOLMAN PROGRAM

Full title: *The Basal Progressive Choice Reading Program* (mimeographed)
Author(s): Myron Woolman
Publisher: The Institute for Educational Research, Inc., Washington, D.C.
Copyright date(s): 1963
Edition analyzed: 1963
Major emphasis (according to publisher): "The most fundamental concern is meaning, and therefore a meaning approach" (the author).
Recent changes and/or plans for revision: Basically the same Woolman program is now published as *Lift off to Reading,* Science Research Associates, Inc., Chicago, 1966. Another program, written by Woolman expressly for adolescents and adults reading at zero to ninth-grade literacy level and using a similar structure, is *Reading in High Gear: The Accelerated Progressive Choice Reading Program,* Science Research Associates, Inc., Chicago, 1964.

THE WRITING ROAD TO READING

Full title: *The Writing Road to Reading: A Modern Method of Phonics for Teaching Children to Read*

Author(s): Romalda B. Spalding and Walter T. Spalding
Publisher: William Morrow and Company, Inc., New York
Copyright date(s): 1957, 1962 (revised)
Edition analyzed: 1962
Major emphasis (according to publisher): Phonics
Recent changes and/or plans for revision: An adaptation of the book, called *The Self-teaching Edition of the Writing Road to Reading: A Modern Method of Phonics for Learning the Language Arts,* was published by Whiteside and Morrow in 1966.

APPENDIX A

Classification of Twenty-Two Beginning Reading Programs

PURPOSE

As we have seen, most researchers investigating approaches to beginning reading instruction have settled for an insufficiently rigorous definition of the methods and programs under study. Too often, the emphasis has been on "*Which* works better?" and seldom on "*What aspect* of an approach (or given reading program) leads to what, and why?"

I hope the classification scheme offered here will help prevent future experimental comparisons from being made of approaches or programs which are essentially similar or in which so many significant variables are not comparable that any differences in results can be attributed only to the unique combination of variables found in each. I also hope it will clarify some of the current controversy by pointing up what questions are really at issue. In addition, it may help authors and publishers planning new programs or contemplating revisions of existing ones by highlighting the internal consistencies and inconsistencies in their present programs.

General Explanation

SCOPE

The classification presented here represents only a limited scheme. Finer distinctions can be made, especially with regard to the content of the materials read by the child. I thought that by providing a somewhat limited scheme rather than attempting an all-inclusive one, I might encourage others to devise more thorough or perhaps different kinds of classifications.

To analyze an approach to beginning reading instruction or a beginning reading program completely, of course, we would need to study not only its components but also how the teacher implements the instructions it embodies and the learners' readiness and ability to respond—crucial factors in its effectiveness. Here, however, I must limit myself to analyzing what can be found in, or inferred from, published programs, including the teachers' manuals.

PROGRAMS CHOSEN

The twenty-two programs classified are a sample of the beginning reading programs that were being widely discussed or experimented with during 1962–1963. My objective was not to classify all existing programs, but to find a workable scheme for analyzing programs; to this end, I made sure to include at least one representative of each important approach. Since 1962–1963 other programs have been published, and some published earlier have come to my attention. These, I believe, may be fitted into the classification scheme.

Each program is identified by the familiar name that best applies (see the bibliography on the preceding pages for a glossary of familiar names of published programs).

THE COMMON LABELS

The nine common labels under which programs are classified serve to identify them in terms of the current, generally accepted discourse in the field. As Table A indicates, programs with the same common label differ in many respects, while programs with different labels are on the same end of a continuum on various points. For a description of the approaches designated by the common labels, see Chapter 1.

RATINGS

It is important to note that comparative ratings such as high, moderate, and low are valid only within the confines of the twenty-two programs. They, of course, have no connotations whatsoever of "good" or "bad."

Table A Classification of Twenty-two Reading Programs according to Common Label and Variables

	Common Label						
	Conventional basal		Phonics programs: partial (supplemental)				
Variables	Ginn Basic Readers (1961)	Scott, Foresman Reading Program (1956, 1962)	*Breaking the Sound Barrier* (1960)	Hay-Wingo (1954)	*Phonetic Keys to Reading* (1958)	*Phono-visual Method* (1960)	*The Writing Road to Reading* (1962)
Completeness:							
Complete (Total Package or Guide Only)	TP	TP					
Partial (Total Package or Guide Only)			TP	TP	TP	TP	GO
Structure: (High, Moderate, Low)	H	H	M	H	H	H	H
Goals: (Meaning, appreciation, application; or learning Code)							
Ultimate	Me	Me	Me	Me	Me	Me	Me
Beginning	Me	Me	Me	Co	Co	Co	Co
Motivational appeal at beginning: (Primarily on Content or on Process of learning to read)	Cont	Cont	Proc	Proc	Proc + Cont	Proc	Proc
Stimulus controls:							
Units to control difficulty (Words, Phonic Elements, Spelling Patterns, Letters, Language Patterns)	W	W	W	PE	PE	PE	PE
Major Criterion for Selecting Words (Meaning Frequency or Spelling Regularity)	MF	MF	MF	SR	MF	SR	MF
Vocabulary Load: First Year (High, Moderate, Low)	L	L			L		
Picture Load: First Year (High, Moderate, Low, None)	H	H	L	L	H	H	N
Content, first year: Stories—familiar experiences, Stories—imaginative, Miscellaneous content, Little or No connected reading material	SF	SF	No	No	SF	No	No
Learning of grapheme-phoneme correspondences (phonics):							
How? (Analytic or Synthetic)	A	A	A	S	A	S	S
Number of verbalized rules (High, Moderate, Low, None)	M	M	H	M	H	L	H
Teacher guidance (High, Moderate, Low)	M	M	H	H	H	H	H
Phonic load, first year (High, Moderate, Low)	L	L	H	H	H	H	H
Concentrated practice on individual correspondences (High, Moderate, Low)	L	L	L	M	L	L	L
Opportunity for transfer (High, Moderate, Low)	L	L	L	L	M	L	L
"Set" (For Regularity or Diversity)	D	D	D	R	D	R	D
Cues to use (Structural or Meaning)	Me	Me	St-Me	St	St-Me	St	St
Structural clues employed (Sounding and Blending; Visual Analysis and Substitutions; or Spelling)	VAS	VAS	VAS	SB	SB	SB	SB
Response modes:							
Preferred reading at beginning (Silent or Oral)	Si-O	Si-O	?	?	O-Si	?	?
Use of writing (High, Moderate, Low)	L	L	L	L	L	M	H
Programming of meaning, appreciation, and application responses (High, Moderate, Low)	H	H			H		
Whole Words or Letters first?	WW	WW	WW	Let	Let in WW	Let	Let
Readiness for reading: (Defined in Global or Specific terms)	Glo	Glo	Glo	Spec	Spec	Spec	Spec
Need for teacher: (High, Moderate, Low)	H	H	H	H	H	H	H

Common Label							
Phonics-first programs complete			Linguistic Approach				
The Carden Method (1956)	Lippincott Basic Reading Program (1963)	*The Royal Road Readers* (1960)	Bloomfield System (1963)	Fries Linguistic Readers (1963)	Gibson-Richards (1963)	*Basic Reading Series* (1964)	*The Structural Reading Series* (1963)
TP	TP	TP	TP	TP	TP	TP	TP
H	H	H	H	H	H	H	H
Me Co	Me Co	Me Co	Me Co	Me Co	Me Me	Me Co	Me Co
Proc	Proc + Cont	Proc	Proc	Proc	Cont + Proc	Proc	Proc
PE	PE	PE	SP	SP, LP	LP, L, W	SP	PE
SR	SR	SR	SR	SR	Mixed	SR	SR
H	H	H	H	H	M	H	H
L	H	M	N	N	M	M	H
Misc	SI	Misc	Misc	Misc	Misc	Misc	Misc
S	S	A	A	A	A	A	S
M	M	L	N	N	N	N	M
H	H	M	L	L	L	L	H
H	H	H	H	H	L	H	H
H	H	M	H	H	L	H	H
H	H	M	H	H	L	H	H
R	R	R	R	R	D	R	R
St	St	Me-St	St	St	Me	St	St
SB	SB	VAS	Sp	Sp	?	Sp	SB
O-Si	O-Si	O-Si	O-Si	O-Si	?	O-Si	O-Si
M	M	L	L	L	M	L	H
H Let	H Let	L WW	L Let	M Let	H WW	M Let	M Let
Spec	Spec	Spec	Spec	Spec	?	Spec	Spec
H	H	H	H	H	H	H	H

(Continued on next page)

Variables	i/t/a Series (America) (1963)	ITA Series (England) (1961)	Omar K. Moore	IR	LE	Programmed Reading Series (1963)	Woolman Program (1963)
	Common Label: Initial Teaching Alphabet		Responsive environment	Individualized Reading	Language Experience	Programmed Learning	
Completeness:							
Complete (Total Package or Guide Only)	TP	TP	GO	GO	GO	TP	TP
Partial (Total Package or Guide Only)							
Structure: (High, Moderate, Low)	H	H	M	L	L	H	H
Goals: (Meaning, appreciation, application; or learning Code)							
Ultimate	Me	Me	Me	Me	Me	Me	Me
Beginning	Me	Me	Co	Me	Me	Co	Co
Motivational appeal at beginning: (Primarily on Content or on Process of learning to read)	Cont + Proc	Cont	Proc	Cont	Cont	Proc	Proc
Stimulus controls:							
Units to control difficulty (Words, Phonic Elements, Spelling Patterns, Letters, Language Patterns)	W	W	?	W	W	PE	PE
Major Criterion for Selecting Words (Meaning Frequency or Spelling Regularity)	MF	MF	Mixed	MF	MF	SR	SR
Vocabulary Load: First Year (High, Moderate, Low)	H	L	H	H	H	H	H
Picture Load: First Year (High, Moderate, Low, None)	H	H	L	Varies	Varies	H	H
Content, first year: Stories—familiar experiences; Stories—imaginative; Miscellaneous content; Little or No connected reading material	SF–SI	SF	Mixed	Mixed	Mixed	Misc	Misc
Learning of grapheme-phoneme correspondences (phonics):							
How? (Analytic or Synthetic)	A	A	S	A	A	S	S
Number of verbalized rules (High, Moderate, Low, None)	L	L	N	Varies	Varies	L	L
Teacher guidance (High, Moderate, Low)	H	M	L	Varies	Varies	H	H
Phonic load, first year (High, Moderate, Low)	H	Varies	H	Varies	Varies	H	H
Concentrated practice on individual correspondences (High, Moderate, Low)	H	M	?	?	?	H	H
Opportunity for transfer (High, Moderate, Low)	H	M	M	L	L	H	H
"Set" (For Regularity or Diversity)	R	R	D	D	D	R	R
Cues to use (Structural or Meaning)	St-Me	Varies	St	Me	Me	St	St
Structural clues employed (Sounding and Blending; Visual Analysis and Substitutions; or Spelling)	VAS	Varies	Sp	Varies	Varies	SB	SB
Response modes:							
Preferred reading at beginning (Silent or Oral)	Si-O	?	O-Si	Si-O	Si-O	O-Si	O-Si
Use of writing (High, Moderate, Low)	H	H	H	M	H	M	H
Programming of meaning, appreciation, and application responses (High, Moderate, Low)	H	?	L	Varies	Varies	M	M
Whole Words or Letters first?	Let	?	Let	Varies	Varies	Let	Let
Readiness for reading: (Defined in Global or Specific terms)	Spec	?	Spec	Glo	Glo	Spec	Spec
Need for teacher: (High, Moderate, Low)	H	H	M	M	M	L	L

Variables Used in the Scheme

COMPLETENESS

This variable is important since one would expect that results of a partial program—i.e., one containing only general instructions for the teacher—would vary more than results of a program containing reading and exercise materials for the children as well as an instructional guide for the teacher.

Complete programs. A complete program contains both textbooks and exercise materials for the pupils and guidebooks for the teachers.

Although no author of a complete program claims that his program provides everything the child needs, the programs classified as "complete" are full enough to allow the child to achieve real reading, which has been defined as "the perception and comprehension of written messages in a manner paralleling that of the corresponding spoken messages." (Carroll, 1964, p. 3)

Three programs classified as "complete" contain no definite set of published materials for the children. Instead, they provide only a set of instructions for the teacher or a basic philosophy or approach. Thus, there is *no one way* to carry out an Individualized Reading program; different writers may stress different aspects of it. However, all tend to follow a general set of principles. As we have seen, variations in recommendations and in teacher implementation also characterize the Language Experience approach and Moore's responsive environment.[1]

Partial programs. About one-fourth of the programs analyzed are partial programs designed solely for teaching letter-sound correspondences.[2] (*Phonetic Keys to Reading*, however, approaches a complete program since the workbooks contain conventional reading matter as well as phonics exercises.) Except for *The Writing Road to Reading*, all the partial phonics programs have a set of exercise materials for the pupils and a guide for the teacher. Most authors of these partial programs suggest using conventional basal readers at certain points in their programs to provide necessary practice in connected sight or "meaningful" reading.

STRUCTURE

Program structure has to do with the extent to which the reading materials and the teaching steps are worked out in a definite sequence.

[1] Other teaching plans have been devised that use automated typewriters like those used by Omar K. Moore. Lasser Gotkin, of the Institute for Developmental Studies, New York City, has developed a more structured series of steps than Moore in his experimental work with culturally disadvantaged preschool children.

[2] Separate phonics programs are not the only kind of partial programs available. Several partial programs are designed to give additional practice in reading for meaning. The SRA Reading Lab, a graded set of reading selections with a variety of exercises, was a frequent addition to the regular basal-reading program in many schools in 1962–1963.

Generally, I classified as "high" all programs containing a set of graded reading materials for the pupils and a guide for the teacher. The programs classified as "low" depend on a variety of published reading materials or on materials produced by the pupils themselves. *Breaking the Sound Barrier* was classified as "moderate" because the order in which phonic generalizations are taught in this program is based on the words the children meet in their basal readers and is generally left to the individual teacher's discretion.

Moore's program is classified as "moderate" because the child does much of his own programming; however, the Moore program is generally not as unstructured as the Individualized Reading or Language Experience approach.

GOALS

I identified two possible goals of reading instruction: (1) apprehension of meaning, appreciation, and application, or "mature reading," and (2) reconstruction of speech.

Ultimate goal of reading instruction. This variable was included to emphasize that the ultimate goal of all programs, whether partial or complete, is mature reading, defined as the ability to "get meaning from the printed page" efficiently and critically and in such a way that any information so obtained can be put to use and a love and appreciation of literature can be developed. Unfortunately, in the heat of debate this basic unity of purpose has often been overlooked.

Stated goal of beginning instruction. Here I made a simple division between programs that pursue, right from the start, the achievements of mature reading and those which put the initial emphasis on mastery of the code (reconstruction of speech).

I based my judgment on the author's introductory material and also on an analysis of the program itself. It was not always simple to classify programs according to stated goals of beginning instruction, and it was especially difficult to classify some programs published at the high point of the controversy. I had the impression that the authors of these programs, in seeking acceptance by administrators and teachers who held to the prevailing meaning-emphasis view, tried to mask any code emphasis by discussing at length the importance of meaning and appreciation at the beginning.

Generally, though, most of the programs labeled "phonic" or "linguistic" frankly stated that the first task of reading is learning to master the printed code. An exception was *Breaking the Sound Barrier,* whose author holds fast to the prevailing basal-reader philosophy of delaying the teaching of sound-letter correspondences until the child has learned some sight words and has engaged in meaningful reading in basal readers.

As we have already seen, the phonic and linguistic approaches vary in their emphasis on the code. They can be put on a continuum with "pure code" emphasis at one end and "code plus meaning" emphasis at the other. The Bloomfield System is the closest to a pure code emphasis. The Fries Linguistic Readers fall more on the decoding plus meaning end, since they stress reading for meaning. Fries's program, however, is not concerned with application, appreciation, and use at the beginning, and was therefore classified, in relation to the other twenty-one programs, as "code emphasis."[3]

MOTIVATIONAL APPEAL

I classified as "process" programs those which appeal primarily to the child's desire to master the process of learning to read. Programs that appeal primarily to the child's interest in content were classified as "content" programs.

It was often difficult to classify programs according to motivational appeal. All programs try to be as appealing as possible in as many ways as possible. Even those classified as "process" show some concern for content appeal. Four of the code-emphasis programs do this so much that I had to classify them as both "process" and "content" programs.

[3] I present here excerpts from a letter received from C. C. Fries:

"Our approach is certainly *not* a phonic approach. It is *not* an approach that gives primary emphasis to decoding. . . . we would have to insist that our type of approach gives primary emphasis to *reading* for *meanings*.

"Notice also that we have said 'reading for meanings' for we are concerned from the very beginning with not only situation meanings but with the lexical meanings of the words, the structural meanings of the sentences, and the cumulative meanings of the succession of sentences as connected by sequence signals into a unit. . . .

"We do teach them to read the alphabet first. In teaching the alphabet there is no connection of the letter symbols with any sound. This is the 'readiness program' in which we are teaching the child to recognize the letter shapes as they are distinct from one another . . . not only the single letters but letters in groups that differ in their items as well as in the sequence of their items.

"If you have to classify it, put it first with 'reading for meanings,' with special emphasis on the word *reading* and on the plural of *meanings*." (letter from C. C. Fries dated July 8, 1966)

Although I fully appreciate Fries's views, I believe, after having analyzed his program in relation to the twenty-one others considered in detail in Appendix A, that it falls within my "decoding" classification. It is important to realize that this decoding or code-emphasis classification does not in any sense mean that the program does not teach children to read for the meanings involved nor that it is necessarily a phonic method. In fact, I could find no program either among the published ones that came to my attention or among those which I observed (see Chap. 9) that did not have the children read for meaning.

It is a cliché that phonic approaches pay no attention to meaning. Indeed, my classroom visits indicated that some of these emphasized lexical meanings and sentence meanings even more than the conventional basal programs that purport to stress reading for meaning. (See especially *The Carden Method,* a phonic approach that programs "linguistic meanings" similarly to the Fries program.)

It is also a cliché that reading-for-meaning programs pay no attention to decoding (see Chap. 9). They must. Even if the decoding phase is poorly programmed, the child no doubt absorbs the sound-to-spelling correspondences in some way. If he did not it is questionable whether he would learn to read.

With these cautions in mind, I believe a decoding-meaning dichotomy has merit. Although *all beginning reading programs* are concerned with both components of reading—decoding and meaning—some may be said to emphasize one more than the other, when they are studied in relation to one another. Thus, in its relative position to other beginning reading programs, I still think the Fries program fits better into the "decoding" classification than into the "meaning" classification.

STIMULUS CONTROLS

Every reading program follows a plan for presenting material in order of difficulty, a plan for sequencing and integrating component parts, and a plan for pacing. Thus the current preprimer classic, "Look, look, look; see, see, see," a previous generation's "The fat cat sat on a mat," and the more recent linguistic-type gem, "Nan can fan," all reflect the application of a plan. These plans impose a control that is necessary, whether we find the results sensible or ridiculous. I classified programs according to several types of such controls.

Basic units to control difficulty. Most programs control difficulty on one or more of the following: words, phonic elements, spelling patterns, language patterns, and letters.

I classified as "word" programs those which control difficulty on the number of different words in the child's textbook. The conventional basal readers, which carefully control the number of words taught in each book and in each lesson, fall neatly into this classification. The Individualized Reading and Language Experience approaches exercise the same *kind* of control, although control of word *quantity* is not as strict.

I classified as "phonic-element" programs those which teach and control difficulty primarily on letter-sound correspondences. In such programs, when all the consonants and the short *a* have been taught, various permutations such as *cab, lag,* and *fan* are considered of equal difficulty.

Somewhat different from the above programs are those which control difficulty on spelling patterns (the Bloomfield System, the Fries Linguistic Readers, and Moore's program). In the Bloomfield program, for example, although the child can read *fad, dad, lad,* and *sad,* he will not be expected to know *fan, dan,* and *ran,* which are practiced separately. This type of control tends to make for a slower pace in teaching than phonic-element control. The slower pace is also due, I believe, to the basic assumption that in beginning reading the child has to build up conditioned responses to letter groups or, as Fries puts it, to make "high-speed recognition responses." In fact, these three programs do not have the child verbalize the rules, as do most of the programs that control on phonic elements. Instead, the child is expected to discover the relationship between sounds and spelling patterns by practicing on groups of words containing these patterns.

I classified as "language-pattern" programs those which use grammatical or syntactical factors as controls. Only two programs (Gibson-Richards and the Fries Linguistic Readers) appear to do this, although the conventional basal readers (and in fact all beginning programs) control language patterns to some extent by controlling sentence length.[4]

Programs that incorporate "letter" control use words composed only of the letters that have already been introduced—irrespective of the sound values of the letters. Only the Gibson-Richards program controls on the letters in the

[4] Considerable criticism of the rigid language control found in basal readers has come from various sources. See especially Strickland (1962) and *Learning to Read* (1962).

beginning reading book, although no attempt is made to control the sound values of these letters.

Major criterion for word selection. I classified as "meaning-frequency" programs those which select words primarily because they are the commonest in the English language and are probably part of the child's meaning and speaking vocabulary.

I classified as "spelling-regularity" programs those which select words primarily on the basis of the regularity of their letter-sound correspondences. Most phonic and linguistic approaches control difficulty on spelling regularity. However, some of the special phonics programs do not. *Breaking the Sound Barrier,* for example, does not list words that are to be practiced. Instead, it suggests that the teacher select words from the basal reader. Thus, there is a strong probability that words are selected on a meaning-frequency criterion. *The Writing Road to Reading* was classified as a "meaning-frequency" program because the words selected for practice are the commonest words used in spelling. These include a high load of irregularly spelled words, although by the time the child practices sounding and writing these words, he has been exposed to the most essential letter-sound correspondences (with rules). Generally, the Spalding system is difficult because the words are not selected on a spelling-regularity principle to ease the transfer of the various elements learned.

Of course, programs that select words on the basis of spelling frequency also take meaning frequency into account to some extent—some take it into consideration more than others. Thus, the spelling-regularity programs may be further ranked on a continuum from little concern for meaning frequency to great concern.

Vocabulary load: first year. This refers to the total number of different words used in the first-grade materials only. It includes both the practice words (lexical units) in lists and the words in sentences and stories.

Since the conventional basal readers contained the lowest number of different lexical units per total number of running words, I rated them "low."

The less structured programs—Individualized Reading and Language Experience—were classified as "high" because the great variety of materials tends to give the child a high exposure to different words. Even if the child reads only a variety of basal readers in his first year, we can assume that he is exposed to thousands of different words.

Picture load: first year. This refers to the number of illustrations included in the first-grade program or the total number of pictures per 100 running words of text.

I classified as "high" basal readers in which the space devoted to illustrations is either equal to, or greater than, the space devoted to text. The picture load of these readers is in some instances higher than the vocabulary load.

There are variations within classifications, not only in terms of quantity of pictures but also in terms of the way they are used in relation to the text. In the Gibson-Richards program, the black-and-white stick figures appear to serve as useful clues to reading the sentences (MacKinnon, 1959). In the Programmed Reading Series and the Woolman Program (see Glossary) basal readers, the illustrations serve to cue the learner to a specific word or sentence and act as checks on word recognition and comprehension. In the SRA Basic Reading Series, the illustrations seem to do nothing more than add some color to the page. They neither illustrate the text nor are selected to help the child recognize or learn the words.

Content of connected reading materials: first year. I used a very simplified four-part classification scheme here: stories with a concentration on familiar experiences, stories primarily of an imaginative nature (e.g., folk tales and fairy tales), a miscellaneous collection of sentences and short passages, and little or no connected reading material. Currently, stories based on familiar experiences are being broadened to include characters living in large urban centers who have different racial and ethnic backgrounds.

LEARNING OF LETTER-SOUND CORRESPONDENCES

Analytic or synthetic. This classification refers both to the way children learn letter-sound relationships and to the way they are taught to use them in identifying words not immediately recognized. An analytic approach (from wholes to parts) teaches these relationships through analysis of known sight words. A synthetic approach (from parts to wholes) teaches letter-sound relationships first and then teaches the child to combine these to form words.

It was easy to classify most of the programs on this point. The Bloomfield System and the Fries Linguistic Readers, however, presented difficulties. Since they teach the letters before words are read, and since they teach words by having the child say the letters, they might be considered synthetic. I decided, however, to classify these programs as analytic because, after awhile, the words are read as wholes and letter-sound correspondences are not specifically taught, but are to be induced by the child. According to both, words that are not immediately recognized are not to be sounded by parts and blended, but are to be spelled.

Omar K. Moore also teaches letters before words. However, I classified his program as primarily synthetic because the child types or writes the words and thus necessarily works from parts to wholes.

Note that in beginning reading, the distinction between analysis and synthesis is one of teaching method, not necessarily of learning process. In actual reading, the child probably engages in both processes, regardless of how he was taught.

Number of verbalized rules (generalizations) taught. Here I had in mind such generalizations as "the final *e* in a one-syllable word makes the preceding vowel long." All three linguistic programs were easily classified as having "none," since they teach no rules or generalizations. The others were classified on the basis of *relative* emphasis because I had no absolute yardstick by which to make these judgments.

Amount of teacher guidance. This category refers to the relative amount of direct instruction given pupils in learning letter-sound correspondences. Programs rated "high" provide a considerable amount of direct teaching—generally daily practice drill on association of sounds with letters. Programs rated "moderate" present a series of words from which pupils are to generalize specific letter-sound relationships or rules. They may call for some direct teaching, but first pupils are allowed to discover for themselves, from known sight words, that certain letters have given sound values or that all the spoken words in a given list begin or end with the same sound. Then they are encouraged by the teacher to verbalize the generalization.

Programs that rely completely on the pupil's discovery of letter-sound relationships were classified as "low." In these the teacher makes no effort to help pupils deduce the relationships, but expects the children to acquire an awareness of them through practice. The Bloomfield System and the Fries Linguistic Readers provide practice words with common or contrasting patterns to make this discovery easier. The Gibson-Richards program, which also relies on pupil discovery of letter-sound relationships, does not select practice words for spelling regularity or common phonic elements, and hence "self-discovery" is probably more difficult with this program.

Load of correspondences learned the first year (phonic load). Programs may be said to have a phonic load as well as a vocabulary load. Irrespective of how letter-sound correspondences are taught—whether primarily through direct teaching, teacher-aided induction, or self-discovery—we can determine the actual number of correspondences the pupil is expected to learn with each program. These ratings are again relative.

Specific (concentrated) practice on individual correspondences. Programs were rated on the three factors discussed below on the basis of the published materials only. Teachers, of course, may give more concentrated practice on their own.

Opportunity to transfer newly learned correspondences to sentence and story reading. This variable concerns the deliberate and concentrated use in connected reading matter of examples of a taught letter-sound correspondence to give the pupils an opportunity to transfer their knowledge to a meaningful reading situation.

A high degree of opportunity for transfer can be best achieved by a complete program. However, fewer than half of the complete programs, even those with a heavy phonic emphasis, afford a high degree of opportunity for transfer of letter-sound correspondences to the connected reading material they provide.

I rated the special phonics programs "low" in transfer opportunity because most do not contain any connected reading materials of their own, or else they contain so little (e.g., Hay-Wingo) that it is not significant. They tend to rely on the conventional basal readers for connected reading. Since the conventional basals select their words on a meaning-frequency principle, with no attention paid to spelling regularity, the child has little opportunity to transfer his knowledge to connected reading. The one partial phonics program that does contain connected reading matter, *Phonetic Keys to Reading,* I rated "moderate" because few of the words in the stories follow the particular correspondence taught.

Set for regularity or set for diversity. This category concerns such questions as whether both sounds of *c* (/*s*/ and /*k*/) are taught together or whether one value is taught and mastered first, before a second is introduced. Programs that teach more than one sound value for a letter or set of letters, or more than one spelling for the same sound, *at the same time,* were classified as having a "set for diversity." Those programmed to teach one sound for one spelling pattern (or letter) were classified as having a "set for regularity." (See Chapter 4.)

Clues to identify new words and to correct errors. This particular aspect of letter-sound correspondence learning (suggested by John Carroll, 1964) refers to how the pupil is *generally* trained to approach new words (words he cannot recognize immediately) or how he is told to correct his errors of recognition. Is he encouraged primarily to use *structural* clues (letter or phonic), or is he encouraged to use mainly *meaning* clues (context, i.e., surrounding words or pictures), from which he is to make an "educated guess"?

Most programs could be classified easily into one of these two categories. Those which could not were designated "S & M" or "M & S," depending on which method seemed to receive the greater weight.

Structural (letter or phonic) clues employed. Here I distinguished between programs teaching *sounding* and *blending,* those teaching *analysis* and *substitution,* and those teaching the child to *spell* (say the letters). An example of the first is the *Phonovisual Method,* which teaches blending of sounds through a simple technique that uses the concept of a moving train. The conventional basal series, instead, suggest that the teacher help the child "attack" the unknown word (e.g., *mop*) by having him recall words he has learned previously as sight words (e.g., *man* and *top*). What the basal teacher is actually saying is that *mop* begins like *man* and ends like *top.* The Bloomfield System, the Fries Linguistic Readers, and the Moore program encourage the children to spell the word.

RESPONSE MODES

Oral or silent reading at the beginning. Not all programs explicitly prefer one over the other. Those which do state that the one preferred is the *primary* mode of response for beginning reading instruction; they do not, however, exclude use of the other as a secondary mode.

Use of writing with reading. Writing is interpreted broadly here to encompass copying words and letters; writing words, letters, or sentences dictated by the teacher; writing words or letters to fill in blanks in a workbook; and also the writing of original stories.

Only four programs were rated "high" in the use of writing as a form of practice. There is considerable variation among these four in terms of both quantity and kind. *The Writing Road to Reading* has a highly structured system that integrates reading, sounding, writing, and spelling. The American ITA program of Mazurkiewicz and Tanyzer uses writing both in a structured way (writing practiced in workbooks as a means of learning the letter-sound correspondences) and in a creative way (writing of original stories).

In the Language Experience approach, writing is primarily creative. The major stress is not, as in *The Writing Road to Reading,* on writing as a means of reinforcing the learning of letter-sound relationships, but as a means of creative expression. Whether it is used as a way of learning letter-sound correspondences depends a good deal on the individual teacher who edits the child's productions and assigns exercises to help him overcome his weaknesses. Omar K. Moore, of course, uses typing as a major mode of response, but he uses a good deal of writing as well.

Stress on meaning, appreciation, and applicational responses. This category refers to how much attention a program gives to encouraging and checking on the pupil's understanding and appreciation of the content of the reading matter and his ability to apply the ideas gained from his reading.

Most of the complete programs, except perhaps for the Bloomfield System, seem to program some reading for meaning and appreciation.

There are differences in kind among the programs rated "high" on this variable. The Programmed Reading Series implies meaning responses when it has the child write in a correct letter to complete a word. For example, one frame in this program shows a picture of a tan doormat. Next to it the child finds this phrase: "A t_n mat." He has to fill in the letter *a.* By filling it in correctly, he responds not only to the sound value for the letter *a* but also to the meaning of the sentence and the picture.

The basal-reader format is quite different. Most of the meaning responses are called forth by verbal questioning from the teacher during the guided reading of the story. These are supplemented by follow-up workbook activities in which the child reads short selections and underlines words and phrases to show that he understands them. In *The Carden Method,* the Gibson-Richards program, and the Fries Linguistic Readers, the teacher also asks questions on the selections, but her questions are more specifically related to the content. These programs tend to cue the child to where in the sentence answers to questions such as Who? When? What? and Where? may be found. The teachers using basal programs are directed to ask questions that are more diffuse. They skip from literal and interpretative questions on the pictures, to literal and interpretative questions on the text, to requests for comments by the pupils about their own experiences.

Whole words or letters first? Is the child instructed to respond to the whole word first or to the letters (word parts)?

DEFINITION OF READINESS FOR THE READING PROGRAM

Most programs either include a readiness (preparedness) book for the children and an accompanying guide for the teachers or say something about preparing the child for the particular program. Usually the general introductory material describes what a child needs to know in order to be ready to benefit from the particular reading program. Using these statements and the kind of readiness exercises provided, I classified the programs as either "global" or "specific" in their approach to reading readiness.

Programs classified as "global" tend to define readiness in terms of such characteristics as language ability, experience, general intelligence, interest, and emotional and social development. The activities they suggest or provide in the published package to prepare the children for reading generally reflect this definition. They put heavy stress on picture reading, listening, and discussion. Some of the exercises call for the child to note similarities and differences between pictures or geometric forms, but seldom is any practice given in letter or word discrimination. They do not teach the names of the letters.

Programs classified as "specific," on the other hand, tend to suggest or provide exercises in letter and word discrimination. They usually suggest that the child learn to identify the letters by name or sound before formal reading instruction is begun.

DEPENDENCE ON THE TEACHER

How important is the teacher's role in each program in presenting material, guiding practice, checking progress, etc.? I classified programs on this point on the basis of a study of each program's materials for teachers and children. Most of the programs fall into the "high" category. Individualized Reading, Language Experience, and Omar K. Moore's program were rated "moderate." Only the two programmed learning plans were rated "low." Thus, the great majority depend highly on the teacher.

Other Possible Variables

I cannot emphasize too strongly that reading programs may be usefully classified on many other points not indicated here. For example:

1. *The use of either all uppercase or all lowercase letters at the beginning:* Some of the newer programs (the Woolman Program and the Fries Linguistic Readers) use all capital letters first and then gradually ease the child into lowercase letters. ITA uses lowercase letters exclusively.

2. *The order in which letter-sound correspondences are taught:* Most programs teach all the common single consonants first, then the short vowels, and then the long. However, some teach the vowels first and then the consonants. Some intermix them.

3. *The linguistic validity of the phonic distinctions and rules taught:* John Carroll (1961),* in a linguistic analysis of *The Carden Method,* notes that it teaches more distinctions than would probably be considered valid by linguistic scholars. In fact, some linguists claim that many widely used phonics programs give the child "wrong" information on letter-sound correspondences.

4. *The application value of the phonic distinctions and rules taught:* A

* John B. Carroll, *A Linguistic Evaluation of a Phonic Method for Teaching Elementary Reading.* Mimeographed report to the public schools of Berkeley, California.

study by Clymer (1963) concludes that most of the phonic generalizations taught in conventional basal readers have limited value for recognizing the words in the basal readers. If we knew more about sound-spelling correspondences, we could probably rate programs on the value of the generalizations they teach. Programs teaching, and teaching well, the most valuable generalizations—that is, those with the greatest application to words of certain frequency levels—would probably be more effective than those teaching less useful generalizations.

5. *The extent to which sound-discrimination training alone precedes the teaching of letter-sound correspondences:* Many of the programs, particularly the conventional basal-reader programs, teach auditory discrimination (the perception of like sounds in words such as *mother, mild, monkey; sight, fight, right*) before the child learns to associate the letters with their sound values.

6. *Training in auditory blending: The Carden Method* and *The Writing Road to Reading* teach the child to blend auditorily and then visually. Most other systems tend to skirt blending. In fact, they discourage it for fear that extraneous sounds will be introduced or, as Fries and Bloomfield contend, that the sounds corresponding to the individual letters are not consistent and serve only to confuse the child.

7. *The use of pictures to concretize the learning of sounds and letter-sound correspondences: Phonovisual Method* and Hay-Wingo use standard pictures to teach letter-sound associations. *The Carden Method, The Writing Road to Reading,* and *Breaking the Sound Barrier* do not.

8. *The use of color and other cues for teaching letter-sound correspondences:* In some of the newer phonic and linguistic type of programs (e.g., *The Structural Reading Series* and Hay-Wingo), color cues are used to sharpen the child's learning of letter-sound correspondences. It appears to be the unique feature of *Words in Color.*

9. *Emphasis on reading words from left to right:* In emphasizing visual analysis and substitution, some systems (particularly the conventional basals) encourage the child to look at the end, middle, or beginning of a word. The Bloomfield System appears to encourage a left-to-right scanning.

Summary of Major Differences between Code-emphasis and Meaning-emphasis Programs

Here, on the basis of the information uncovered by the classification, I summarize significant differences between what I have called the code-emphasis and meaning-emphasis programs. (See Table A for a classification of the twenty-two programs according to these categories.)

MOTIVATION

Meaning-emphasis programs rely for motivational appeal mainly on the child's interest in content. The stories and pictures—and, consequently, the discussion of these—are of primary importance.

The code-emphasis programs, on the other hand, tend to rely more on the child's interest in the process of learning to read. However, they vary on this point. The linguistic code-emphasis programs generally put low emphasis on story content and pictures, while the new phonic-emphasis basals follow the conventional basal pattern of putting high emphasis on them.

STIMULUS CONTROLS

In controlling difficulty, the meaning-emphasis programs use words rather than phonic elements or spelling patterns. The criterion used for selecting the words is commonness in the language and high frequency in other beginning reading materials. The vocabulary load tends to be low, and the picture load high.

The code-emphasis programs use common phonic elements or spelling patterns to control difficulty, not words, regardless of how much story content is stressed. They tend to have a higher vocabulary load. This, of course, is made possible by the many permutations that can be made of a single spelling pattern (e.g., *Dan, can, ran, fan, man*) or of a single letter-sound correspondence (e.g., *cab, cat, lag, mad*).

CONTENT

The reading matter in almost all the meaning-emphasis programs places first stress on childlike, familiar experiences, although many also include some imaginative content.

The code-emphasis programs are again divided. A large group (Hay-Wingo, *Breaking the Sound Barrier, Phonovisual Method,* and *The Writing Road to Reading*) have no connected reading matter of their own. Of programs that do have their own reading selections, the great majority use short sentences, paragraphs, and "stories" of a general nature. Only one of the programs analyzed had a strong literary emphasis—The Lippincott Basic Reading Program.

PROGRAMMING OF LETTER-SOUND CORRESPONDENCES

All the meaning-emphasis programs teach letter-sound correspondences through a process of analysis—going from whole words to parts. In fact, they tend to avoid teaching the letter names before word reading is started lest they distract the child from the word form (configuration) and its meaning.

Some of the code-emphasis programs share this preference for analysis. Three of the phonics programs also prefer analysis to synthesis—*The Royal Road Readers, Phonetic Keys to Reading,* and *Breaking the Sound Barrier.*

Generally, the meaning-emphasis programs tend to have a low phonic load—i.e., they teach relatively few letter-sound correspondences—in the first year. Generally, too, the teacher is instructed to help the child generate his own correspondence rules. They tend to give less concentrated practice in phonics and less opportunity to transfer to connected reading material, compared with other programs.

The code-emphasis programs are divided on these points. While all have a high phonic load the first year, some teach the correspondences directly, and others allow the child to discover them for himself. They also provide varying amounts of concentrated practice for learning and applying correspondence rules and encourage varying amounts of transfer to connected reading materials.

The linguistic programs and the Moore program share a preference for self-discovery, but offer different amounts of concentrated practice and opportunity for transfer.

The phonics programs tend, as a group, to teach correspondence rules directly, although the number of rules taught varies. Generally, a high phonic load goes with a heavy concentration of practice and a high opportunity for transfer. However, the partial phonics systems do not seem to be consistent in this respect. All program a heavy load of phonics during the first year, but most of them provide, in their published programs, only a limited amount of concentrated practice on these correspondences. It is no doubt up to the teacher to supply the needed practice. These supplemental phonics programs also afford a low opportunity for transfer to connected reading materials, since they rely on the conventional basals, which select words on a meaning-frequency principle.

All the meaning-emphasis approaches—with the exception, of course, of ITA, which builds in regular letter-sound correspondences—are programmed to produce a set for diversity (see the discussion of variables above).

On this point code-emphasis programs again vary. About half of them seem to be programmed in a manner that produces a set for regularity, and the other half, in a manner that produces diversity. Theoretically, all supplemental phonics programs relying on other published connected reading materials that select words according to meaning frequency have a built-in set for diversity.

In training the child to identify a word not immediately recognized, the meaning-emphasis programs, as would be expected, put first priority on meaning aspects—that is, context clues and picture clues. The last to be called on are phonic or structural clues—assigning sound values to individual letters or groups of letters. Furthermore, all the meaning-emphasis programs that have published materials encourage the child to use a system of visual analysis and substitution, rather than sounding and blending, as an approach to new words.

The code-emphasis programs are not so consistent on this question. Most, of course, give first priority in word recognition to structural or "phonetic" (phonic) aspects of a word, rather than to its meaning (context and picture clues). But they differ on how they teach the child to use the structural (or phonic) clues. More than half teach sounding and blending. The others are divided into those which use spelling (saying the letters)—e.g., the Bloomfield

System, the Fries Linguistic Readers, BRS, and the Moore program—and those which use visual analysis and substitution: *The Royal Road Readers*, the American ITA program, and *Breaking the Sound Barrier*.

PREFERRED RESPONSE MODES

Generally, the meaning-emphasis programs prefer silent to oral reading, make little use of writing, program a great many meaning and appreciation responses, and have the child respond to whole words first, rather than to letters or sounds.

The code-emphasis programs tend to prefer oral reading and generally have the child respond first to letters or sounds, rather than to words. However, on the other two response modes—meaning and writing—there is considerable variation. About half of the code-emphasis programs make moderate or high use of writing. And nearly half program a high load of meaning responses right from the start.

READING READINESS

The meaning-emphasis programs tend to define and develop reading readiness in a broad sense, while the code-emphasis programs tend to define and develop readiness in the more specific terms of testing and teaching letter names (or sounds).

Where the line between readiness activities and formal reading instruction is drawn is not always clear. Many of the code-emphasis programs recommend teaching the letter-sound correspondences in kindergarten as a readiness activity, while others consider learning letter names the first step of formal reading instruction.

RELIANCE ON THE TEACHER

Almost all the programs in both groups rely heavily on the teacher. The two that rely least on the teacher are the Programmed Reading Series and the Woolman Program—the only two programmed type of materials. Both are code-emphasis programs. But even with these, the teacher is needed a great deal at the very beginning.

Three programs that depend to a moderate extent on the teacher are the Language Experience and the Individualized Reading approaches and Moore's. All these are "individualized" programs in the sense that the major portion of the teaching is done with one child at a time. The Individualized Reading and the Language Experience approaches are, of course, carried out in a classroom; because the teacher may have as many as thirty or more pupils in her class, the amount of individual attention given each is considerably less than in the Moore laboratories. However, the pupils work on their own to a much greater extent in these programs than in the conventional basal-reader and most of the code-emphasis programs.

As explained above, Omar K. Moore's program uses no teacher only in the first stage, when the child learns the letter names with the computerized typewriter. The learning of some words is also computerized, but in certain later steps a teacher is required to present words and sentences, order them, and check the correctness of the child's responses. She is part of the "responsive environment" that permits the child to discover the "rules" on his own. This type of relationship between the teacher and pupil gives some observers the impression that Moore's program provides no teaching—that the child learns by himself. This is not true if we define teaching as ordering material, supervising practice, and responding to the learner's productions.

It may well be possible to computerize an entire beginning reading program so that no teacher is needed. To the best of my knowledge, this has not yet been done. Even the experimental Stanford computer-assisted program referred to briefly in Chapter 1 is not completely "teacher-free."

APPENDIX B

Schedules Used in Study

I. SCHEDULE FOR ANALYZING CLASSROOM EXPERIMENTAL STUDIES

AUTHOR:	TITLE:
POSITION:	AFFILIATION:
JOURNAL:	VOL. NO. DATE Pp.

DESCRIPTIVE MATERIAL (use judicious quotes)	ANALYST'S COMMENTS AND INFERENCES

Reason for Study

Theoretical orientation:

Questions raised (why the study):

Definition of reading (if included):

Methods or Procedures Compared

Hypotheses:

The methods to be compared (names & brief descriptions):

Experimental Design

Name given by author:

Dates of study: from:________ to:________

Description of groups:

Experimental:

Control:

Other:

Place:

Urban:____________Rural:____________

Suburban:____________Other:____________

Atmosphere of School:

Description of population:

Total number:	Experimental		Control		Other	
Grades:	Boys	Girls	Boys	Girls	Boys	Girls
Chronological age:						
IQ (Mean)						
(Standard deviation)						
(Range)						

DESCRIPTIVE MATERIAL
(use judicious quotes)

ANALYST'S COMMENTS
AND INFERENCES

Basis for selection of population:
Experimental:
Control:
Other:
What variables controlled (or how groups were equated):
Description of method:
Experimental group
Specific published and unpublished materials used:
Time spent on special method:
Total time spent in reading:
Silent: ____________________
Oral: ____________________
Total: ____________________
Amount and kind of supervision of teachers:
Description of method:
Control group
Specific published and unpublished materials used:
Time spent in lieu of special treatment —what additional activities, if any:
Total time spent in reading:
Silent: ____________________
Oral: ____________________
Total: ____________________
Amount and kind of supervision of teachers:

Instruments Used to Measure Success

Tests: (dates, names, forms, etc.)
Number of books read:
Attitudes of children:
Attitudes of teachers and administrators:
Attitudes of parents:
Other:

DESCRIPTIVE MATERIAL
(use judicious quotes)

ANALYST'S COMMENTS
AND INFERENCES

Results—Statistical Analyses (copy tables or duplicate pages):
For total groups:
For any breakdowns by IQ, sex, teachers, etc.:

Author's Conclusions (use quotes):

Author's Suggestions and Recommendations:

Author's Bibliographic References:

ANALYST'S REACTIONS TO STUDY
Probable degree of involvement of the author in the outcome of his experiment (quotes):
Analyst's overall reaction to the experiment:

ADDENDA TO SCHEDULE I

DESCRIPTIVE MATERIAL	ANALYST'S COMMENTS AND INFERENCES
Other data culled from study (not included as part of experimental design):	
Readiness (any objective data regarding prereading skills of experimental and control populations):	
Socioeconomic-status information:	
Ethnic background:	
Language background:	

DESCRIPTIVE MATERIAL	ANALYST'S COMMENTS AND INFERENCES		
How teachers were selected for the experiment:			
	Experimental	**Control**	**Other**
Attitude:			
Age:			
Experience:			
Other:			
Data on classroom environments:			
	Experimental	**Control**	**Other**
Size of classes:			
Organization for reading (e.g., whole class, group, individualized, departmentalized, nongraded):			
IQ range in classes:			
"Psychological" atmosphere in the classrooms:			
Other relevant information:			

II. SCHEDULE FOR ANALYZING A BASAL-READER LESSON AND ITS FOLLOW-UP ACTIVITIES

Publisher__________ Copyright date__________ Basal-reader title__________
Story title__________ Pages in story__________
Level of book__________ Number of running words in story__________
Number of pictures__________ Size of pictures__________
TEACHERS' MANUAL: Number of **pages** devoted to instructions on teaching the "code" of the reading lesson __________ on follow-up __________ total __________
number of **words** devoted to instructions on teaching the "code" of the reading lesson __________ on follow-up __________ total__________
WORKBOOK COORDINATED WITH BASAL READER: title__________
pages (exercises coordinated with story)__________

I. How is lesson begun? (brief description)__________

II. Preparation or introduction
What called in this manual?__________
Subgroupings (titles)

If discussion is takeoff:
Number of questions or statements to be asked or made by teacher to lead children into story__________
Number of words teacher speaks (actually directed by manual)__________
Number of additional words teacher speaks (can be inferred)__________
Total__________
Estimated time for this discussion__________

III. Presenting the new words and checking them (if combined with preparation or introduction, record here)
Number of new words__________ List the words__________
What is this section called in the manual__________
Subgroupings if any (titles)
How are the new words to be presented?
Teacher gives oral buildup (in spoken story form), then places new words on board__________; on chart__________; either board or chart __________; while saying the words.
Other __________
Relationship between pupil practice and teacher presentation of new words:
Each word practiced as presented__________
Some words practiced as presented, but major part after presentation__________
Practice immediately after presentation__________
Mode of practice: Silent reading first, then oral__________; oral first, then silent__________; other__________
Mode of practice not suggested here__________
Are suggestions given for the number of times that words, phrases, or sentences are to be read? Yes__________; no__________.
If yes, about how many times?__________ Any other suggestions on amount? __________

To What Aspects of Printed Words Is Child's Attention Directed?

Number of questions or directions to "just read" word, sentence, or phrase ____________

Number of questions or directions to "find" or say word or words that answer comprehension questions (who, what, etc.) ____________

Number of questions or directions to scrutinize the word visually (e.g., its length; ways in which it is similar to, or different from, other words; its characteristic features) ____________

Number of questions or directions to look at or practice structural units (roots, prefixes, suffixes, spelling patterns) ____________

Number of questions or directions concerning phonic aspects of words (sound-letter relations) ____________

Number of questions or directions concerning getting the word from context (makes sense) ____________

Other ____________

"Teacher Talk": Number of words teacher speaks to present the new words and to direct the practice. **Actually** directed by

Manual ____________

Additional words that may be inferred ____________

Total ____________

Are any suggestions given on how errors are to be corrected?

Yes____________; No____________. **If yes, describe briefly:**

____

Estimated time for "teaching" the new words (including presentation and practice) ____________

IV. Guided reading of the story

What is this section in the manual called? (major title) ____________

____

Subcategories (if any):

Introductory remarks (brief description)____________

____

Where does manual say to draw child's attention first? To pictures?____________

To print? ____________ Other____________

Nontextual Directives

Number of questions or statements by teacher directed to **pictures** (that may be answered from pictures alone) ____________

Number of questions that may be answered by pictures and print ____________

Number of questions or statements devoted to recall of information in previous stories ____________

Number of questions and statements to evoke evaluations, judgments, feelings, anticipations (Child can gather data for responses from neither the pictures nor the print in the story.) ____________

Number of statements or directions to "just read" next line, page, etc. ____________

Directives to

Print as conveyor of meaning:

Number of questions or statements directing the child to read in order to answer specific "literal" questions (who, what, when, etc.) __________

Number of questions or statements directing the child to interpret the print (draw conclusions; make judgments, evaluations, inferences, etc.) __________

Directives to

Print as code:

Number of questions or statements directing child to scrutinize word form (e.g., length; ways in which it is similar to, or different from, other words; its characteristic features; etc.) __________

Number of questions or statements directing child to structural units (roots, prefixes, suffixes, spelling patterns) __________

Number of questions or statements directed to phonic aspects of word __________

Number of questions or statements directed to context clues (verbal) __________

Number of questions or statements directed to picture clues __________

In general, how much is the child instructed to read in order to answer each teacher question or series of questions?

1 line__________; 2 lines__________; ⅓ page__________;
½ page__________; 1 page__________; other__________

In general, what is the mode of reading suggested for the child?

Silent first, then oral__________; silent only__________
Oral first, then silent__________; oral only__________
other __________

In general, does the manual supply "typical" answers to be expected from the child with the questions suggested for the teacher?

Yes__________; no__________
If some answers are supplied, which? (give some idea)__________
____

Does the manual give the teacher any suggestions on how pupil errors are to be corrected during the general reading lesson?

Yes__________; no__________
If yes, give some idea of kinds of suggestions__________
____

Estimated **time** for teaching the guided reading__________

V. Rereading: Is rereading of the story suggested? Yes__________; no __________.
If yes, what should the purpose of rereading be, according to the manual?__________
____

Mode of rereading: Silent__________; oral__________; other__________
Number of words teacher speaks to direct the rereading__________
Cite anything particularly interesting about the rereading (use quotes)__________
____

III. SCHEDULE FOR ANALYZING EACH FOLLOW-UP ACTIVITY SUGGESTED IN MANUAL TO FOLLOW THE GUIDED-READING PORTION OF THE LESSON (one schedule to be used for each activity)

1. Title of follow-up activity:
   Subtitles (if any):
2. Marginal titles:
3. Stated purpose or purposes:
4. Brief description of the activity:
5. Is activity primarily teacher-directed?__________
   Teacher-initiated, then pupil-directed?__________
   Pupil- (self-) directed?__________
6. Mode of reading by pupil (when reading is called for):
   Oral__________; silent__________
   Oral followed by silent__________
   Silent followed by oral__________
   Which emphasized (if combination)__________
7. Writing—how much and what kind?
8. Relationship of this follow-up activity to the major portion of the reading lesson (i.e., lesson covered by major schedule):
9. Does manual give suggestions on how to deal with errors?__________
10. Estimated time for this exercise?__________
11. Classification:
    Activity is primarily concerned with giving pupils additional practice in **(check):**

    Reading:
    Reading comprehension (reading to answer questions):__________
    Word meaning:__________
    Whole-word recognition (no analysis of word parts):__________
    Phonic analysis relation between letters and sounds, or sounds alone):__________
    ____
    Structural analysis:__________
    Independent silent reading (no questions to be answered):__________

    Nonreading Activities:
    Oral language (pupil-teacher discussion):__________
    Literary appreciation (e.g., teacher reads stories or poems to children):__________
    Art (pupils draw, paint, construct, etc.):__________
    Music (pupils listen to records, are taught a song, etc.):__________
    Social studies (e.g., drawing a map):__________
    Science (e.g., doing an experiment):__________
    Films and filmstrips (e.g., the teacher is instructed to show a particular film or filmstrip): __________

    Creative Writing:
    (e.g., children are directed to write a story):__________

    Miscellaneous:
    (activities that do not fit above categories):__________
12. Comments and interesting quotes:

Index

Credits

Adkins, Frances. Excerpt from *Sounds and Letters: A Nan and Dan Reader* by Frances Adkins Hall. Copyright © 1964 by Frances Adkins Hall. Reprinted by permission.

Excerpt from *The Bank Street Readers,* by The Bank Street College of Education. Copyright © 1965, 1966 by The Bank Street College of Education. Reprinted by permission of Macmillan/McGraw-Hill School Publishers.

Bloomfield, Leonard, and Clarence J. Barnhart. Excerpt from *Let's Read: A Linguistic Approach* by Leonard Bloomfield and Clarence L. Barnhart. Copyright © 1963 by Leonard Bloomfield and Clarence J. Barnhart. Reprinted by permission of Barnhart Books.

Bond, Guy L. Excerpted from "Coordinated Phases of the Reading Study," from *The Reading Teacher.* May 1966, pages 2, 8–9. Reprinted by permission.

Buchanan, Cynthia Dee. Excerpt from *The Programmed Reading Series,* Book 1 by Cynthia Dee Buchanan. Copyright © 1963 by Sullivan Associates. Reprinted by permission of Macmillan/McGraw-Hill School Publishers.

Carrillo, Lawrence W. Excerpt from *Slides,* of the Chandler Readers Series. Copyright © 1965 by Lawrence W. Carrillo. Reprinted by permission of the author.

Daniels, J. C., and Hunter Diack. Excerpt from *The Royal Readers* by J. C. Daniels and Hunter Diack. Copyright © 1960 by J. C. Daniels and Hunter Diack. Reprinted by permission.

Durrell, Donald D. Excerpts from "First Grade Reading Success Study: A Summary," from *Journal of Education,* February 1958, Volume 140, Number 3.

Fernald, Grace. Excerpt from *Remedial Techniques in Basic School Subjects,* by Grace Fernald. Copyright © 1966 by Grace Fernald. Reprinted by permission of Macmillan/McGraw-Hill School Publishers.

Fries, Charles C. Excerpts from Personal Letter, dated July 1966.

Fries, Charles C., et al., From *Laugh with Larry,* by Charles C. Fries, et al. Copyright © 1963 by the Follett Publishing Company. Reprinted by permission of Silver Burdett Ginn.

Fries, Charles C., Agnes C. Fries, Rosemary G. Wilson, and Mildred K. Rudolph. From *Reader 1 of The Merrill Linguistic Readers,* by Charles C. Fries, et al. Copyright © 1966. Reprinted by permission.

Gates, Arthur. Excerpt from "Contributions to Education, No. 129," *Psychology of Reading and Spelling with Special Reference to Disability.* Copyright © 1922 by Teachers College Press. Reprinted by permission.

Gates, Arthur I., Guy L. Bond, and David H. Russell. Excerpt from *Methods of Reading Readiness.* Copyright © 1939 by Teachers College. Reprinted by permission.

Gibson, C. M., and I. A. Richards. Excerpt from Language Through Picture Series, by C. M. Gibson and I. A. Richards. Copyright © 1959 by Washington Square Press, Inc. Reprint by permission of Language Research, Inc.

Gray, William S., et al. Excerpt from *The New Fun With Dick and Jane,* Primer of The New Basic Readers by William S. Gray, et al. Teaching notes from *The Guidebook for the New Fun With Dick and Jane* by William S. Gray, et al. Copyright © 1956 by Scott, Foresman and Company, Inc. Reprinted by permission of Macmillan/McGraw-Hill School Publishers.

Gray, William. Exerpt from *Remedial Cases in Reading: Their Diagnosis and Treatment,* Supplemental Educational Monographs, No. 22 by William S. Gray. Copyright © 1922 by the University of Chicago Press. Reprinted by permission of the publisher.

Harris, T. L., M. Creekmore, and M. Greenman. Exerpt from *Tag of Phonetic Keys to Reading,* by T. L. Harris, M. Creekmore, and M. Greenman. Copyright © 1952 by T. L. Harris, M. Creekmore, and M. Greenman. Reprinted by permission of Macmillan/McGraw-Hill School Publishers.

Hay, Julie, and Charles E. Wingo. Excerpt from *Reading with Phonics* by Julie Hay and Charles E. Wingo. Copyright © 1954 by Julie Hay and Charles E. Wingo. Reprinted by permission of Macmillan/McGraw-Hill School Publishers.

Levin, Harry. From "Reading Research: What, Why, and for Whom?," from *Elementary English,* Volume 43, February 1966, pages 139–140. Copyright © 1966 by the National Council of Teachers of English. Reprinted with permission.

Mazurkiewicz, Albert J., and Harold J. Tanyzer. Excerpt from *Early to Read: i/t/a Program,* Revised Book 2 by Albert J. Mazurkiewicz and Harold J. Tanyzer. Copyright © 1966 by Albert J. Mazurkiewicz and Harold J. Tanyzer. Reprinted by permission.

McCracken, Glen, and Charles C. Walnut. Excerpts from *Basic Reading, Pre-Primer,* and Teaching Suggestion from *Basic Reading, Pre-Primer,* Lippincott Basic Reading Series, by Glen McCracken and Charles C. Walnut. Copyright © 1963, 1965, 1966 by Glen McCracken and Charles C. Walnut. Reprinted by permission of Macmillan/McGraw-Hill School Publishers.

McKee, Paul A., Annie McCowan, Lucile Harrison, Elizabeth Lehr, and William K. Durr, *The Reading for Meaning Series,* by Paul A. McKee et al. Copyright © 1949, 1957, 1963 revised 1966 by Paul A. McKee et al. Reprinted by permission of Macmillan/McGraw-Hill Publishers.

Monroe, Marion. Excerpt from *Children Who Cannot Read* by Marion Monroe. Copyright © 1932 by the University of Chicago Press. Reprinted by permission of the publisher.

Montgomery, Ruth Bolen, and Selma Coughlan. Excerpt from *The PhonoVisual Vowel Book* by Ruth Bolen Montgomery and Selma Coughlan. Copyright © 1955 by Phonovisual Products. Reprinted by permission of Phonovisual Products.

Orton, Samuel T. Excerpt from *Reading, Writing, and Speech Problems in Children,* by Samuel T. Orton. Copyright © 1937, renewed © 1964 by Samuel T. Orton. Reprinted by permission of W. W. Norton & Company, Inc.

Rasmussen, Donald E., and Lenina Goldberg. Excerpt from *SRA Basic Reading Series Workbook for Level B* by Donald E. Rasmussen and Lenina Goldberg. Copyright © 1964, 1965 by Donald E. Rasmussen and Lenina Goldberg. Reprinted by permission of Educational Publication Corporation.

Robinson, Helen M. Excerpt from *Why Pupils Fail in Reading,* by Helen M. Robinson. Copyright © 1946 by the University of Chicago Press. Reprinted by permission of the publisher.

Russell, David, and Odille Ousley. Excerpt from *On Cherry Street,* Primer of the Ginn Basic Readers. Copyright © 1961 by David Russell and Odille Ousley. Reprinted by permission of Silver Burdett Ginn.

Sister Mary Caroline. Excerpt from *Breaking the Sound Barrier,* by Sister Mary Caroline. Copyright © 1960. Reprinted by permission of Macmillan/McGraw-Hill School Publishers.

Spalding, Romalda Bishop, and Walter T. Spalding. Excerpt from *The Writing Road to Reading* by Romalda Bishop Spalding and Walter T. Spalding. Copyright © 1957, 1962 by Romalda Bishop Spalding. Reprinted by permission of Macmillan/McGraw-Hill School Publishers.

Stern, Catherine, et al. From *We Read and Write,* Book C (1–2 Level) of The Structured Reading Series by Catherine Stern et al. Copyright © 1963 by L. W. Singer Company, Inc. Reprinted by permission of Macmillan/McGraw-Hill School Publishers.

Teachers Guidebook to the Pre-Primers. Copyright © 1962 by Scott Foresman and Company. Reprinted by permission of Macmillan/McGraw-Hill School Publishers.

Wilson, F. T., et al. Excerpt from "Reading Progress in Kindergarten and Primary Grades," from *Elementary School Journal.* Volume 38, (1939), pages 442–449. Reprinted by permission of Teachers College Press.

Woolman, Myron. Excerpt from *Reading in High Gear: The Accelerated Progressive Choice Reading Program.* Learner's Workbook, Cycle 1 by Myron Woolman. Copyright © 1964, 1966 by Myron Woolman. Reprinted by permission of Educational Publishing Corporation.